Finance Capital Today

# Historical Materialism Book Series

The Historical Materialism Book Series is a major publishing initiative of the radical left. The capitalist crisis of the twenty-first century has been met by a resurgence of interest in critical Marxist theory. At the same time, the publishing institutions committed to Marxism have contracted markedly since the high point of the 1970s. The Historical Materialism Book Series is dedicated to addressing this situation by making available important works of Marxist theory. The aim of the series is to publish important theoretical contributions as the basis for vigorous intellectual debate and exchange on the left.

The peer-reviewed series publishes original monographs, translated texts, and reprints of classics across the bounds of academic disciplinary agendas and across the divisions of the left. The series is particularly concerned to encourage the internationalization of Marxist debate and aims to translate significant studies from beyond the English-speaking world.

*For a full list of titles in the Historical Materialism Book Series available in paperback from Haymarket Books, visit:*
https://www.haymarketbooks.org/series_collections/1-historical-materialism

# Finance Capital Today

*Corporations and Banks
in the Lasting Global Slump*

François Chesnais

Haymarket Books
Chicago, IL

First published in 2016 by Brill Academic Publishers, The Netherlands
© 2016 Koninklijke Brill NV, Leiden, The Netherlands

Published in paperback in 2017 by
Haymarket Books
P.O. Box 180165
Chicago, IL 60618
773-583-7884
www.haymarketbooks.org

ISBN: 978-1-60846-827-0

Trade distribution:
In the US, Consortium Book Sales, www.cbsd.com
In Canada, Publishers Group Canada, www.pgcbooks.ca
In the UK, Turnaround Publisher Services, www.turnaround-uk.com
All other countries, Ingram Publisher Services International, ips_intlsales@ingramcontent.com

Cover design by Jamie Kerry of Belle Étoile Studios and Ragina Johnson.

This book was published with the generous support of Lannan Foundation and the Wallace Action Fund.

Printed in Canada by union labor.

10 9 8 7 6 5 4 3 2 1

Library of Congress Cataloging-in-Publication data is available.

# Contents

Acknowledgements  IX
List of Figures, Tables, and Boxes  X

Introduction  1
    No End to Crisis in View  2
    Finance Capital and Financial Capital  5
    The World Economy as an Analytical Aim  10
    From the Theory of the Internationalisation of Industrial Capital to the Theory of Financial Globalisation  12
    Financialisation as Discussed in this Book  14
    No 'Diversion of Profits' but the Accumulation of Fictitious Capital  17
    The 'Crisis in the Sphere of Credit and Money' in 2008  19

1  The Historical Setting of the Crisis and Its Original Traits  22
    1  The Crisis in a Long-Term Trajectory  24
    2  A Crisis Which Has Not Been Allowed to Run Its Course  35

2  Financial Liberalisation and Globalisation from the 1960s onwards and the Return of Financial Crises  44
    1  Industrial Profits and the Eurodollar Market in the Resurgence of Concentrated Interest-bearing Capital  45
    2  The End of the Bretton Woods Monetary System and the Advent of Floating Exchange Rates  47
    3  The Recycling of Petrodollars and the Third World Debt Trap  51
    4  The Growth of Government Debt at the Heart of the System  56
    5  The Political Implications of Market-based Retirement Schemes  56
    6  World Money Since the Demise of Bretton Woods  58
    7  The 'Semi-completion' of Financial Globalisation and the Financial Crises of the 1990s  62
    Appendix: The 'Club of Paris' and Brady Bonds  64

3  The Notion of Interest-Bearing Capital in the Setting of Present Centralisation and Concentration of Capital  67
    1  Steps in Approaching the Analysis of Financial Profits  68
    2  Interest-bearing Capital: Exteriority to Production and the Blurring of Lines between Profit and Interest  78
    3  The Theory of Fictitious Capital  81

Appendix 1: The Centralisation and Concentration of Capital in Marxist Theory   88

4   **The Organisational Embodiments of Finance Capital and the Intra-Corporate Division of Surplus Value**   93
   1   A Brief Historical Perspective on the Bank-Industry Relationship   93
   2   Contemporary Issues Regarding Corporate Governance and Interlocking Boards of Directors   102
   3   Banks as Merchants and TNCs as Money Capitalists   109
   4   Concentrated Commodity or Merchant Capital and the Sharing Out of Total Surplus Value   113
   5   Natural Resource-based Monopoly Profit and Oil Rent   121
   Appendix 1: Control in the ETH Zurich Studies   125
   Appendix 2: The Three Major New York Investment Banks' Activities in Commodities   128
   Appendix 3: Three Examples of Industrial Corporation Ownership of Financial Corporations   130

5   **The Internationalisation of Productive Capital and the Formation of Global Oligopolies**   133
   1   The Internationalisation of Productive Capital: Theory and History   133
   2   The Collective Global Monopoly Power of Transnational Corporations   142
   3   The Place of Emerging Countries' Corporations in the Global Oligopoly   148
   Appendix: Recent Developments Affecting the Statistical Data on FDI   154

6   **The Operational Modes of TNCs in the 2000s**   158
   1   Industrial Capital: From Internationalisation to Globalisation   158
   2   Value Chains in Business Management Theory   159
   3   Buyer-Driven Global Commodity Chains   161
   4   Outsourcing and Offshoring and Global Value Chains in Manufacturing   163
   5   'Non-equity Modes of International Production'   165
   6   TNCs and the Present Configuration of World Trade   167
   7   Overexploitation and the 'Global Law of Value'   169

7   **The Further Globalisation of Financial Assets and Markets and the Expansion of New Forms of Fictitious Capital**   173
   1   Factors Underlying the Growth of Global Financial Transactions   173

## CONTENTS

    2    The Growth of Global Transactions in Derivatives   181
    3    Financial Globalisation and Developing Countries in the 2000s   188

8    **Financialisation and the Transformation of Banking and Credit**   198
    1    The Transformation of Banking in the United States   199
    2    Financial Liberalisation in Europe and European 'Universal Banks'   204
    3    Securitisation, the Originate-to-distribute Model and the Shadow Banking System   209

9    **Global Financial Contagion and Systemic Crisis in 2008**   220
    1    Investment Banks and Hedge Funds   220
    2    The Channels of International Financial Contagion   232
    3    Specific Systemic Vulnerability in the European Banking System   235

10    **Global Endemic Financial Instability**   245
    1    The Effects and Potential Backlashes of Quantitative Easing   246
    2    The Very Long Continuous Fall in Interest Rates and the Growth of Debt   247
    3    Non-bank Financial Corporations and Systemic Contagion Risks Today   249
    4    The Potential for Financial Turmoil in Emerging Countries   252

    **Conclusion**   256
        The Institutional Difficulties of Doing Marxist Economic Research   256
        Persistent Very Low Global Growth Coupled with Endemic Financial Instability   258
        How Could Slow Growth be Brought to an End and a New Long Upswing Start?   260
        Non-ecological Approaches to Capitalism's Possible 'Intrinsic Absolute Limits'   264
        The Advent of a New More Formidable Immanent Barrier and Its Implications   267

    **References**   273
    **Glossary of Financial Terms**   297
    **Topic Index**   302
    **Index of Names**   307

# Acknowledgements

Throughout the production of this book I enjoyed the encouragement of Sebastian Budgen. Tom Norfield, Laurent Baronian and Claude Serfati kindly read and commented on certain chapters at different moments of its writing, while Michael Roberts was always ready to answer questions or objections concerning some of his website postings. My thanks also go to Simon Mussell and Danny Hayward who were particularly helpful in their editing.

This lone endeavour would never have been finished without the loving care and constant support of Catherine, to whom the book is dedicated.

# List of Figures, Tables, and Boxes

### Figures

1.1   US profit curve   31
1.2   Growth of Global Financial Assets and World GDP (1990–2010)   37
2.1   Changes in the relative weight of global financial assets 1980–90/91 (US$ Billions)   62
8.1   ROE for the main product segments in European banks in 2003   208
8.2   The securitisation process   212
9.1   Interplay of credit and liquidity risk   232
9.2   European Banks within the Global Shadow Banking System   234

### Tables

2.1   Capital flight from developing countries (in billions of 1987 $US)   55
2.2   United federal and developing countries debt 1982–95 (millions $US)   57
4.1   Top 10 global retailers, net sales (2010)   118
4.2   Top 5 TNCs in the retail industry, ranked by foreign assets, 2012   118
6.1   Wage levels in apparel in selected countries   162
6.2   Share of exports accounted for by the largest exporters in selected countries   168
7.1   Estimated global foreign ownership of financial assets (1998–2007)   173
7.2   Capital inflows into the United States, 1997–2012 (in billion US$)   176
7.3   Overall composition of global financial transactions: 2002–8   178
7.4   External debt of developing countries 2005–10   189
8.1   United States: Indebtedness by sector, 1980–2008   198
9.1   Top ten US and European hedge funds (2007)   227

### Boxes

2.1   International loans in Rosa Luxemburg's *The Accumulation of Capital*   51
3.1   The accumulation of loanable capital as a separate form   70
3.2   Fictitious capital in the form of government bonds and stock   82

| | | |
|---|---|---|
| 3.3 | The fetish form of capital | 86 |
| 5.1 | World Concentration in Agribusiness | 146 |
| 6.1 | Motives for Offshoring and Moving Corporate Boundaries | 163 |
| 7.1 | A counter-example to Ecuador: The non-cancellation of apartheid debt by South Africa | 192 |
| 8.1 | Securitisation | 210 |
| 9.1 | Key Hedge Fund Characteristics | 225 |

# Introduction

This book focuses on two interconnected yet distinct dimensions of the contemporary world capitalist economy. The first has to do with the forms and the consequences of the intermeshing of highly concentrated and internationalised global banks, large transnational industrial and service corporations and giant retailers, which constitutes finance capital in its contemporary form. The second concerns *finance qua finance*, namely the processes associated with and resulting from the spectacular growth over the last 40 years of assets (bonds, stocks, derivatives) held by financial corporations (large banks and funds), but also by the financial departments of TNCs and of the particular markets on which they operate.

In the Bank of International Settlements' (BIS) 2014 Annual Report, one reads that 'it is hard, for its authors, to avoid the sense of a puzzling disconnect between the financial markets' buoyancy and underlying economic developments globally'.[1] In its March 2016 Quarterly Review it warns again of the dangers this carries. The sluggishness of world GDP growth (global growth for 2015 is estimated by the IMF as having been at 3.1 percent, 0.3 percentage points lower than in 2014; for 2016 3.4 percent is projected)[2] contrasts both with the intensity of labour exploitation in the setting of factories and offices in industrialised countries, or of those like Bangladesh, and with the amount of what is deemed to be money, incessantly moving around the world financial system and passing from one form of asset or one financial centre to another. Going back to the late 1980s, one can only be struck by the extremely sharp contrast between the downward trend in the rates of GDP growth and of investment, the rise in the rate of exploitation as the political and social power relationships between capital and labour tip increasingly in favour of capital, and the increasingly rapid increase in the nominal value of assets traded in financial markets only briefly halted by the financial crisis of 2008. One of the aims of the present book is to account for this divergence.

The economic and political context of the analysis is that of the ongoing world economic and financial crisis. As argued in Chapter 1, it is a crisis of over-accumulation and overproduction compounded by a falling rate of profit. It was in the making since the second half of the 1990s and delayed by massive credit creation and the full incorporation of China into the world economy. Some scholars have named it a 'crisis of financialisation' or a crisis of

---

1  BIS 2014, p. 1.
2  http://www.imf.org/external/pubs/ft/weo/2016/update/01/.

'financialised capitalism'.[3] This is misleading. It is a crisis of capitalism *tout court* at a given moment of its history, of which the completion of the world market (globalisation) and financialisation (as defined later in this introduction) are major traits. Given that the US, both as state and capital, was absolutely central in the making of global capitalism,[4] not unsurprisingly it was there that the genie of finance escaped from the bottle. All the more so since in the US more than anywhere in the world system, the credit system had been pushed, starting at least in 1998, to its 'extreme limits'.[5] But the ongoing crisis is that of 'capital as a whole'. Even in its financial dimensions it was, from the outset in August 2007, a world crisis. The slump which began in late 2008 was global in nature[6] and not just a North American 'Great Recession'. Initially it hit mainly the industrialised economies. Emerging countries, which first thought that they would remain largely immune to its effects, were from 2010 onwards to lose this illusion. The situation at world level has been and continues to be one of endemic over-accumulation and overproduction. Calculations of the rate of profit from data in national accounts have documented its fall. Key pieces of the world capitalist system are broken or in a very bad state. The US is the most powerful economy and state in the world but no longer a hegemon in the way it once was. No single economy alone can lift global capitalism out of the crisis, as the US economy could in the 1940s in the context of the Second World War and its aftermath. In this respect, as in some others, 'American Empire', as analysed by Leo Panitch and Sam Gindin, belongs to the past.[7] The making of global capitalism was indeed the result of US state and capital, but globalisation has had its price for the US economy as for all others and originated huge novel domestic political tensions.[8]

### No End to Crisis in View

If an 'end to crisis' is defined as the moment when sustained overall accumulation of productive capital gathers steam again in the world system as

---

3   Lapavitsas 2012.
4   Panitch and Gindon 2012.
5   Marx 1991, p. 572.
6   McNally 2011.
7   Panitch and Gindin 2012.
8   One is reminded of the words of Trotsky in 1932: 'the inevitable growth of the world hegemony of the United States will entail further deep contradictions both in the economy and in the politics of the great American republic. In asserting the dictatorship of the dollar over the whole world, the ruling class of the United States will introduce the contradictions of the whole world into the very basis of its own dominance' (Trotsky 1973).

a whole, then nine years after the start of the world economic and financial crisis in July 2007 there is no end in sight. Each in their own field, the major international organisations all make this clear. With respect to investment and trade, UNCTAD characterises public policies, almost without exception, as 'not addressing the rise of income inequality, the steady erosion of policy space along with the diminishing economic role of governments and the primacy of the financial sector of the economy, which are the root causes of the crisis of 2008'.[9] WTO reports that without precedent since the end of the Second World War, trade has ceased to boost growth.[10] World merchandise trade grew just 2.2 percent on average during 2012–13, roughly equal to the rate of growth of world GDP. WTO forecasts a 2.8 percent growth rate in 2015, down from the previous estimate of 3 percent.[11] In its annual Financial Stability Reports of 2014 and 2015, the IMF is concerned about the continued dependence of industrialised countries on the injection of liquidity by central banks and the forms of financial instability this produces. All these assessments preceded the marked slowdown in the Chinese rate of growth and the collapse of its stock markets. The expression 'from global slump to long depression'[12] can be used to express the transition that has taken place as the crisis has lasted. The measures taken in 2008–9 in the G20 to preserve the status quo internationally, combined with the fact that China was in a high growth phase and received government support funding, have meant that the classical purgative effects of capitalist crises have been weak. Too little productive capacity has been destroyed to clear the decks for new accumulation. The concomitant rescue of the banks and the scale of the assets bought by the Fed strongly limited the destruction of fictitious capital from the start, even before 'unconventional policies' became current central banking practice.

Large oligopolistic corporations are thriving, but as exemplified by the US data for the corporate sector as a whole, the 2010–11 recovery in the rate of profit was short-lived. Furthermore, the world market is one where macroeconomic conditions shaping the capital-labour relations of power prevent the whole of the surplus value produced globally from being realised. Capital is faced by a roadblock at C′ of the complete accumulation process (M-C ... P ... C′-M′).[13] Nonetheless the expression 'excess of surplus value' as used by Bhir[14] is

---

9   UNCTAD 2014b.
10  WTO 2014.
11  WTO 2015.
12  Roberts 2013.
13  The fact that a 'realisation problem' exists alongside the insufficient rate of profit is now recognised somewhat reluctantly by Michael Roberts (2016).
14  Bhir 2010.

misleading. What can be seen analytically in those terms, in a reading of Marx which puts emphasis on the realisation of surplus value, is experienced by capital as a limit that it must break through at all costs. Capital's thirst for profit is unquenchable. Its dangerousness lies there. This is also why the term 'stagnation' is misleading. Accentuated overall difficulties of realisation are answered in the universe of firms by increased competition with its consequences both in terms of intensified worker exploitation, aggravated exploitation of natural resources and an accentuation of what the Hungarian philosopher Istvan Mészaros referred to as 'generalised waste-production'.[15] In parallel, a growing fraction of M′ has not been re-injected as M into the accumulation process and instead has fuelled a process of a plethora of capital seeking valorisation in financial markets.

In different combinations with the effects of territorial expansion, and as in the twentieth century of major wars, previous long phases of accumulation were built on the emergence of a whole new set of technologies involving large industrial investments and calling on larger numbers of workers. The growth effects of the technological revolution bear no resemblance to those of the ones that preceded it.[16] The spectacular developments in Big Data, in state and corporate political and social control, and in personal IT devices are trees hiding the forest. The notion of 'secular stagnation' has re-emerged and is now discussed by US Keynesian economists.[17] It is inappropriate from a Marxian perspective. In the setting of the twenty-first century, the absence of the conditions permitting the launching of a new phase of long-term, sustained, overall accumulation of productive capital means that human society is confronted with the consequences of capitalism's 'historical limits'. This has ceased to be simply an intuitive concept. Today, the degree to which, in Marx's words, 'production is production only for *capital*, and not the reverse, i.e. the means of production are not simply means for a steadily expanding pattern of life for the *society* of the producers', and the extent to 'which the maintenance and valorization of the capital-value... depends on the dispossession and impoverishment of the great mass of the producers',[18] is something to which figures can now be put. Today, inequalities in wealth are once again as high as they were in the 1920s.[19] Even in the industrialised countries, high work insecurity and low wages is the daily lot of the great majority of workers. The world is reeking with

---

15   In *Beyond Capital*, he already analyses its 'triumph' (Mészaros 1995).
16   Gordon 2012.
17   Eichengreen 2015.
18   Marx 1981, Vol. III, p. 358.
19   Picketty 2013.

money and yet, with the exception of military budgets, any socially needed public investment is always 'too expensive'. Despite their evident failure to lift their economies out of the crisis, governments seem to be committed ever more to economic and monetary policies shaped by the interests of the richest with increasingly serious consequences for the most dominated layers of the working classes. However, the climatic and environmental crisis is, of course, the gravest dimension of the historical impasse of capitalism. Given the latter's hold over contemporary society, it is one that endangers civilised human society as such.[20] I will return to this in the concluding chapter.

## Finance Capital and Financial Capital

I keep the term finance capital as used by Hilferding and Lenin not for reasons of 'orthodoxy' but of *analytical clarity*. In a necessarily different configuration from that of Hilferding, I use the term to designate the simultaneous and intertwined concentration and centralisation[21] of money capital, industrial capital and merchant or commercial capital as an outcome of domestic and transnational concentration through mergers and acquisitions (M&As).[22] This is different from what is today generally called financial capital, namely concentrated money capital operating in financial markets. In this book the term financial capital designates what national accounts call 'financial corporations', namely banks and investment funds of all types, broadened to include the financial departments of large industrial 'non-financial corporations'.[23]

---

[20] See Moore 2014 and his notion of the Capitalocene.
[21] Industrial economics and anti-trust legislation retains the sole term of concentration. So I may have to do so but the proper term, not always respected by Hilferding and Lenin, is centralisation: 'Capital grows to a huge mass in a single hand in one place, because it has been lost by many in another place. This is centralization proper, as distinct from accumulation and concentration' (Marx 1976, Vol. I, pp. 776–777). Sweezy 1944 was very careful in making the distinction.
[22] At the time of revising the final manuscript of this book, my attention was brought to the definition proposed by Overbeek in 1982, which comes closer to mine than any other: 'By finance capital we mean the integration of the circuits of money capital, productive capital and commodity capital under the conditions of monopolization and internationalisation of capital by means of a series of links and relationships between individual capitals' (Overbeek 1982, p. 102).
[23] In an interesting article, the Turkish economist Hoca 2012 has attempted to overcome the difficulty by defining finance capital as 'capital as commodity': 'Finance capital is commodified capital, which circulates in financial markets and is controlled by the class

In distinguishing 'finance capital' and 'financial capital' I am departing from the position taken for instance by the editors of *Monthly Review*.[24] In French financial capital is designated by the term 'finance'.[25] In English the latter word is fairly indeterminate. The organisations just mentioned centralise surplus value in the form of dividends, interest from government and corporate debt, and retained profits, as well as current income flows and savings of households. They seek to valorise the money they manage through loans and through speculation in financial markets. Financial profits presuppose the centralisation of already created surplus value. The largest part of financial activity, notably trading operations in financial markets, concerns essentially its distribution and endless redistribution among financial corporations through speculation. As put by Hilferding, 'one trader's gains are another's losses'.[26] The mass of money capital pursuing the same goal in a context of low investment and insufficient creation of surplus value necessarily leads to repeated episodes of more or less serious financial crisis. Much more importantly still, however, is the political and organisational strength of financial capital's pretension

---

of finance capitalists mainly through financial institutions, and monopolises industrial capital by constituting a large and increasing part of it, especially after crises' (Hoca 2012, p. 428). Hoca's suggestion is debatable and I have not followed it, but his careful reading of Marx, Hilferding and Lenin has been very helpful.

24   John Bellamy Foster writes 'in using the term "finance capital" I am not doing so in the specific sense ... introduced by Hilferding's great work where it was defined at one point as "capital controlled by the banks and utilized by the industrialists". Rather the term is meant in this case to refer to the employment of money capital in financial markets and speculation more generally' (Foster 2006, p. 12). Where I use the term finance capital, the editors of *Monthly Review* use broadly that of 'monopoly capital'.

25   The term finance is used by Lapavitsas in his latest book. He differentiates it from credit and defines it as 'a broad economic category that refers to the various methods through which capitalist enterprises obtain and deploy funds to support profit-making activities' (Lapavitsas 2013, p. 109). Duménil and Lévy's very special theory of classes and of periodisation under capitalism leads them to 'denote as "Finance" the upper fractions of capitalist classes and their financial institutions. (Finance, directly or indirectly, owns the entire large economy, not only financial corporations.) Two other features must be added to this broad characterization. First, the control of financial institutions – now supposed to work to the strict benefit of capitalist classes – is a prominent component of the new social order. Second, the transition, under capitalist leadership, to this new power configuration would have been impossible if it had not been conducted in alliance with managerial classes, notably their upper segments' (Duménil and Lévy 2012). I do not accept this definition, let alone their account of the 'transition'.

26   'One's loss is the other's gain. *"Les affaires, c'est l'argent des autres"*' (Hilferding 1910, Chapter 8).

to autonomy. What Marx names 'the autonomisation of the form of surplus-value, the ossification of its form as against its substance, its essence' which stems from 'the division of profit into profit of enterprise and interest'[27] have reached a degree arguably without precedent in the history of capitalism and enjoy the unfailing support of central banks and governments.

The study of financial capital begins with the notion of interest-bearing capital. It entails paying close attention (as is done below in Chapter 3) to Part Five of Volume III of *Capital* on 'The division of profit into interest and profit of enterprise'. The point of departure is twofold. First 'money as capital becomes a commodity... [T]he owner of money who wants to valorise this as interest-bearing capital parts with it to someone else, puts it into circulation, makes it into a commodity as capital; as capital not only for himself but also for others'.[28] Second, 'interest... originally appears, originally is, and remains in reality nothing but a part of the profit, i.e. the surplus-value, which the functioning capitalist, whether industrialist or merchant, must pay to the owner and lender of capital in so far as the capital he uses is not his own but borrowed'.[29] In capitalism, production is the 'predominant moment'.[30] As discussed in later chapters, interest in its varying numerous forms (commissions and fees of many kinds) and commercial profits both have their ultimate source in a single stock of previously produced and successfully realised surplus value, in the terrain – a very uneven playing field – of the world economy. But again the historical context is that of the global power relations very unfavourable to labour and so the institutional support backing financial capital's pretention to autonomy.

David Harvey classically opposed 'the process view' of finance, e.g. the movement of interest-bearing loan capital, developed by Marx in Volume III of *Capital*, and 'the power bloc view' which emerged in Hilferding and Lenin. Harvey's 1982 reading of Marx remains an indispensable introduction to the complexities of the movement of interest-bearing capital. He was sceptical about the power bloc view and argued in 1982 that 'countervailing forces simultaneously create and undermine the formation of coherent power blocs within

---

27    Marx 1981, Vol. III, p. 966. Making the link with Chapter 4 of Volume I (Marx 1976, Vol. I, p. 255), he adds that: 'If capital originally appeared on the surface of circulation as the capital fetish, value-creating value, so it now presents itself once again in the figure of interest-bearing capital as its most estranged and peculiar form'.

28    Marx 1981, Vol. III, pp. 463–4.

29    Marx 1981, Vol. III, p. 493.

30    See Musto 2008 for an unambiguous commentary of this point in the famous Introduction to the *Critique of Political Economy* in the *Grundrisse*.

the bourgeoisie'.[31] Here it is argued that since then, in the context of the liberalisation and the globalisation of capital, a merging of finance capital as 'process' *and* as 'power' has progressively taken place, leading effectively to the formation within states of a single power bloc. This bloc did not break up in 2008–9, as might have been expected, but on the contrary, it consolidated. Highly centralised financial capital, particularly in the form of banking conglomerates (or diversified financial services corporations as they are named), has been in the limelight, but these entities are in no way in sole command over capital as a whole. The power bloc of finance capital is not, as in Hilferding's generalisation of the nineteenth-century German case or in the US's early twentieth-century money trusts,[32] under the hegemony of banks. In the US, the executives of Exxon, General Motors or Wal-Mart are on an equal footing with those of Goldman Sachs and JP Morgan for instance, along with key shareholders (typically Warren Buffet). Contemporary capitalism confronts us with the *simultaneous and combined* centralisation/concentration of money capital, industrial capital, and merchant or commercial capital. Harvey's 1982 position that 'no matter what the circumstances, the state can never be viewed as the unproblematic partner of industrial and banking capital within a dominant power bloc'[33] must be reassessed in light of the September 2008 crisis and the behaviour then and since of central banks and governments.

Large industrial corporations are heedful of shareholder activism led by hedge funds, but they are not under the control of banks and are deeply engaged themselves in financial market operations including the most speculative ones. The parasitical traits of interest-bearing capital intuited by Marx and later emphasised by Lenin permeate the operations of all money, commercial, and industrial capital alike. As one leaves the inner circle of finance capital, the pre-eminence of banks and funds over firms begins to assert itself. Smaller corporations are more likely than larger ones to be the object of leveraged buy-outs (LBOs) by equity capital funds – the most common form of predatory capital. When one moves to the periphery of the world system analysed in its dimension of financial globalisation, notably to the US's 'backyard' in Latin America, the weight of financial capital is striking, as inflowing financial investment interfaces and merges with domestic capital accumulation, consolidating oligopolies based on the predation of natural resource endowments in agribusiness and mining.[34]

---

31   Harvey 1982/1999, p. 283.
32   See Chapter 4 below.
33   Harvey 1982/1999, p. 323.
34   This has influenced Latin American work. Thus the Mexican economist Arturo Guillen who follows Sweezy 1994 in replacing 'finance capital' by 'financial capital' argues that

Some authors have placed emphasis on the importance of the functions carried out by finance as outweighing the problems it creates for the management of global capitalism.[35] Similarly the term 'rentier capital' is considered by many to be politically loaded and so to be avoided. Yet, in a Marxian, classical ('non-vulgar economic') and Kaleckian theoretical perspective, no analysis of the foundations of capital's social and political domination, domestically or internationally, can simply put the term aside. The notion is central to the economic, political, and social dimensions specific to the Hobsonian and Marxist theory of imperialism. Market-based retirement systems have strongly contributed to 'financial accumulation' as defined below and discussed throughout the book, and so to the full resurgence of the rentier,[36] whose euthanasia Keynes considered necessary. Market-based retirement systems have also given a new dimension to Lenin's analysis of the economic roots of the 'labour aristocracy'. This is an unpleasant fact with huge social and political consequences domestically and at an international level. As a result of the growth of government debt and its place in financial portfolios in the wake of the 2008 economic turmoil and the Eurozone banking crisis of 2011, in the European Union in particular economic policy *in toto* has become pro-cyclical. It is so because it is pro-rentier. The holders of government debt, a part of which consists of workers with savings in banks and insurance companies, must be paid, whatever the economic and social consequences. The dissemination throughout society of the 'fetishism of money', through well-studied mechanisms of the 'financialisation of everyday life',[37] explain to a large extent why governments have not met more resistance as yet in their support to debt-holders.

---

'the finance-dominated accumulation regime subordinates the entire logic of capital accumulation to the valorization of financial capital. At the peak of the financial pyramid are the transnational corporations, the large banks, the investment banks, the insurance companies, the operators of investment and pension funds, and the cream of the crop of large financial capital funds, which manage the resources of the richest men on the planet: hedge funds and private equity funds' (Guillen 2013, p. 12).

35  This is the case in one of the essays by Panitch and Gindin 2011.
36  See Joan Robinson: 'We use the term *rentier* in an extended sense, to represent capitalists in their aspect as owners of wealth, as opposed to their aspect as entrepreneurs. We include in the incomes of rentiers dividends as well as payments of interest and we include the sums handed over to their households by entrepreneurs who own their own businesses' (Robinson 1956, p. 247).
37  Konings (ed.) 2010 contains a number of chapters on this issue.

## The World Economy as an Analytical Aim

The analysis in this book will be placed as far as possible in the setting of the completion of the 'world market',[38] which Marx, in the *Grundrisse*, argued to be contained in the very concept of capital. However imperfect the figures and calculations may be, we must attempt, following Trotsky, to take the world economy not as a sum of national parts but as 'a mighty and independent reality',[39] or again, as recalled by McNally, a totality.[40] With the entry of China into the WTO, 'the establishment of the world market' contained 'in the very concept of capital' as put by Marx, is achieved. Early in my work, I defined the 'world economy' as a 'hierarchically differentiated totality'.[41] In the late nineteenth century, the 'first globalisation', as historians name it, was driven by trade, by big targeted international trade-creating loans (in mining, agriculture and harbours in particular), and to a lesser degree by foreign direct investment proper, which Hilferding was the first to identify specifically. From the 1960s onwards, when the process leading to the 'second globalisation' took off again, foreign direct investment was the driving force. As one moves into the 1980s, the insertion of countries into the international trading system is increasingly shaped by the FDI and sub-contracting strategies of TNC. As discussed in Chapters 5 and 6, these strategies evolved as liberalisation went forward. 'Production as the predominant moment' means that investment by TNCs plays the central

---

[38]   Marx 1981, Vol. III, p. 375.
[39]   'Preface to The Permanent Revolution', Trotsky 1931: Marxist analysis must take 'its point of departure from the world economy seen not as a sum of national parts but as a mighty and independent reality which has been created by the international division of labour and the world market, and which in our epoch imperiously dominates the national markets'.
[40]   McNally 2009, p. 43: 'We need to treat the world-economy as a totality that is more than the sum of its parts. This may seem a mundane protocol but it is one that is regularly breached. Much discussion of the neoliberal period has focused on a number of capitalistically developed nations – the US, Germany and Japan – and treated the world-economy as largely an aggregate of these parts. This is both methodologically flawed and empirically misleading'.
[41]   Chesnais 1994/1997. The notion of the 'hierarchically differentiated totality' as a way of approaching the analysis of world economy takes its cue from remarks by Marx in a passage of the *Grundrisse* on the method of political economy: 'The conclusion we reach is not that production, distribution, exchange and consumption are identical, but that they all form moments of a totality, distinctions within a unity.... Mutual interaction takes place between the different moments. This is the case with every organic whole'. On the key importance of the notion of totality, one should again consult Musto 2008.

INTRODUCTION

role in shaping the pattern of international trade and configuring the channels along which surplus value is centralised in financial centres.[42]

Taking the world economy as the point of departure is of course easier said than done. All that this book has been able to do, partially in Chapters 1 and 2 and a few sections of later chapters, is to bring in protagonists other than the US state and capital in the process of financial accumulation and globalisation. Some discussions ignore the leading role played by the City and British governments in recreating the institutional foundations of financial globalisation and in allowing banks and financial markets to get back on the horse.[43] As argued by Norfield,[44] the City's place in the global financial system is wrongly minimised in relation to that of Wall Street. In work that has received insufficient attention to date, Minqi has attempted to approach the world economy by putting China squarely at the centre of the scene.[45] In this book, China is brought into the picture in a number of ways: as a mainstay of world capitalism during the first phase of the world crisis; as a major locus of overaccumulation and overproduction; and, along with India, as a core part of the global industrial reserve army placed at the disposal of domestic and foreign capital alike. Japan has been left out only for lack of time to do the required reading. Of course, this would have been unthinkable 20 years ago and reflects the fact that Japanese growth suffered a very severe blow from the 1991 stock market and housing bubble collapse. Again, everything that concerns banking is unfortunately almost exclusively centred on the US and Europe and, in the case of financial markets, on New York and London. South Africa and the Gulf States, for which first-class Marxist studies exist,[46] and Latin American countries, have been brought into the picture a little.

The 'world market', as fully established in the 1990s through the action of capital and state led by the United States, is the space in which TNCs deploy their operations as well as being that of inter-capitalist, inter-imperialist rivalry. There will be much, in particular in Chapter 6, on the new globalised forms of appropriation and centralisation of surplus value. As argued by John Smith, the working of the law of value must now be analysed in the setting

---

42  Respecting the methodological principle of starting from production made the work of Charles-Albert Michalet (1985) important.

43  This is the case for Peter Gowan 1999 and for Panitch and Gindin 2011. It is also one of the weaknesses of the account of financial liberalisation and globalisation given by John Bellamy Foster and Fred Magdoff (Foster and Magdoff 2009).

44  Norfield 2016.

45  See his Chapter 4, 'Can the capitalist world economy survive the rise of China?' (Li 2008).

46  Ashman, Fine and Newman 2011, and Hanieh 2012.

of contemporary globalised capitalism.[47] However, the approach to the world economy through the notion of the world market chosen in this book differs from Smith's 'concept of the whole', which privileges one dimension of Lenin's theory of imperialism, namely the division between oppressor and oppressed nations, and takes it as the starting point.[48] Here the emphasis is rather on the first three features summarised in the final chapter of *Imperialism, the Highest Stage of Capitalism*: 'monopoly arising out of the concentration of production at a very high stage; the seizure (by monopolies) of the most important sources of raw materials, especially for the basic and most highly cartelised industries in capitalist society; development of banks from modest middleman into the monopolists of finance capital'. Furthermore, it is imperative that the dividing line between oppressor and oppressed nations be recognised as having changed. China has become both a pillar of world capitalism and economically an oppressor nation, the seat of very large oil and mining oligopolies.

## From the Theory of the Internationalisation of Industrial Capital to the Theory of Financial Globalisation

I wrote above that the crisis is not a 'crisis of financialisation', but of capitalism *tout court* at a given moment of its history. This does not mean that the notion of financialisation can be sidestepped, let alone ignored. It has been given different meanings by different authors. Many approaches have been proposed.[49]

---

47   Smith 2011. This issue as well as differences in the rate of exploitation between countries are discussed in Chapter 5.

48   Smith 2011, p. 3. The principal quote from Lenin is 'the division of nations into oppressor and oppressed forms the essence of imperialism' and the second are taken as a bloc. Certainly there are many truly oppressed nations, but China, India and Brazil's place in the hierarchical structure and working of world capitalism cannot be encompassed by the notion of 'oppressed nations'. The Chinese Communist Party and the bureaucratic-capitalist class can hardly be termed a 'comprador' bourgeoisie.

49   In the mid-2000s, Epstein 2005 quotes Krippner's summary of the discussion at the time: 'some writers use the term "financialization" to mean the ascendancy of "shareholder value" as a mode of corporate governance; some use it to refer to the growing dominance of capital market financial systems over bank-based financial systems; some follow Hilferding's lead and use the term "financialization" to refer to the increasing political and economic power of a particular class grouping: the rentier class; for some financialization represents the explosion of financial trading with a myriad of new financial instruments; finally, for Krippner herself, the term refers to a "pattern of accumulation in which profit making occurs increasingly through financial channels rather than through trade

INTRODUCTION                                                                                    13

Personal theoretical frameworks and/or fields of research have led each author to give the term financialisation a specific content. My own analysis is the result of more than twenty years of work, during which my assessment and definitions evolved quite significantly. The initial impetus of the first edition of *La mondialisation du capital* came from my work on multinational enterprises (MNEs) at OECD and my participation in the group led by Charles-Albert Michalet at Nanterre University. Its intellectual setting was the research and debate on the internationalisation of industrial capital among French Marxist and 'heterodox' economists.[50] The theory of the 'mondialisation du capital', as named by French and more generally by Latin language authors, which emerges in France in the late 1980s, has a distinctively Marxian colourisation, contrary to the Anglophone world where, with the exception of Stephen Hymer, the theory of productive globalisation developed first under the impetus of John Dunning and then in business management schools. The theory of the internationalisation of productive capital and the differentiated relationships of countries to the world market, as also analysed by Regulationists,[51] permitted a broad interface with the question of economic development and so with Third World economists, notably Samir Amin, Celso Furtado and André Gunter Frank. The larger part of the 1994 edition of my book on globalisation concerned industrial capital, but a long chapter was already devoted to financial globalisation.[52] The book owed a lot to the characterisation of industrial corporations by French heterodox economists as 'financial corporations principally engaged in industrial activity' (*groupes financiers à dominante industrielle*), as analysed and defined notably by François Morin.[53] This is why the 1994 book discusses the internalisation of finance by large corporations in the form of the intra-group financial markets managed by the holding company. In the revised and expanded 1997 edition,[54] the analysis of financial globalisation was broken up into two chapters: one on the financial operations of

---

and commodity production"'. Epstein goes on to say that all these definitions capture some aspect of the phenomenon. So he proposes to 'cast the net widely and define financialization [as] the increasing role of financial motives, financial markets, financial actors and financial institutions in the operation of the domestic and international economies'.

50   Leading participants in the debate included Charles-Albert Michalet, Christian Palloix and later Vladimir Andreff.
51   Shorthand for members of the Ecole de la régulation.
52   In Chesnais 1994, p. 207, I even call it 'the most advanced field of globalisation'.
53   Morin 1974. A broad range of articles can be found in the Revue d'Economie industrielle 1989.
54   Chesnais 1997.

MNEs which owed a lot to the detailed analysis on the internal management of corporate liquidities and foreign exchange hedging just carried out by Claude Serfati,[55] and another entitled 'A global accumulation regime, dominated by finance'. In the latter chapter, financialisation and the internationalisation of industrial corporations were analysed jointly, in a Marxian framework which bore proximity to Regulationist theory.[56]

In France, the first fully-fledged research project on financial globalisation was led by Michel Aglietta and its results published in 1990.[57] The French debate then developed around different definitions of the 'finance-dominated accumulation regime'[58] and the 'power of finance'.[59] The disregard of this discussion by most French Marxists at the time was founded, for some, on their rejection of Regulationist theory and, for others, on their neglect of the importance of finance in Marx.[60] This started changing with the setting up, at Gerard Duménil and Dominique Lévy's initiative, of the Séminaire d'Etudes Marxistes which, in 2006, produced a book squarely centred on finance.[61] It spurred me personally to read Part V of Volume III of *Capital* attentively and so to break completely with the Regulationist approach. The word 'financialisation' appears in English in the very late 1990s. In the 2000s, work by Anglophone Marxists takes off and attains a critical mass with the acceleration of work after 2008.

### Financialisation as Discussed in this Book

Financialisation concerns both finance and production, making it indissociable from contemporary 'actually existing' capitalism. The last 40 years has seen a strong continuous growth of financial assets in the form of bonds, dividends

---

[55] Serfati 1996.
[56] Paulani 2010b gives a good account in English of Regulationist theory and its use by some Marxists. I wrote a number of articles or book chapters using this notion to which Lapavitsas refers (Lapavitsas 2013). The last time was in my chapter in Coriat et al. 2006. See, in Portuguese, the evolution of my positions in Sabadini and Lupatini 2014.
[57] Aglietta et al. 1990.
[58] Lapavitsas 2013 gives one of the only accounts in English of this French debate.
[59] Orléan 1999.
[60] Some may have felt justified in this because of the scant treatment of Part V by Mandel in his Introduction to the Penguin edition of Volume III of *Capital* (just some three pages) (Mandel 1981).
[61] Séminaire d'Etudes Marxistes 2006, with chapters by de Brunhof, Chesnais, Duménil, Lévy and Hussson.

and currencies and in the mid-2000s an explosion of derivatives. Chapters 2 and 6 seek to recall the successive phases of the process of 'financial accumulation' as distinct from real accumulation[62] and of the process of financial liberalisation and globalisation which constitutes one of its pillars. Following its partial destruction in the 1930s and 40s, financial accumulation starts again in the late 1950s and 60s with the hoarding of a part of profit and its investment in London as loan capital, followed by the servicing of government debt, first in the Third World and then in the core capitalist countries. The end of the Bretton Woods international monetary system opens up a huge new field for the particular form of financial profit pertaining to foreign exchange speculation. 'First World' government debt explodes with the military outlays under the Reagan Administration ('Star Wars' programme), but it rises quickly in other industrialised countries as governments resort to debt rather than to taxes.[63] Additional mechanisms endogenous to financial markets then developed in the 1990s leading to the very rapid growth of financial assets in the form of bonds, stock, currencies and their derivatives and later in the 2000s, increasingly in that of asset and mortgage-backed securities. The way the progression of financial accumulation took place hand in hand with that of financial globalisation is discussed in Chapters 2 and 7, while Chapters 5 and 6 show its anchorage in the global production and appropriation of surplus value. Chapter 2 also discusses the way the progression of financial liberalisation and globalisation saw the reappearance of international financial crises with strong domestic and international repercussions, increasingly triggered off by the entry and sudden withdrawal of foreign portfolio investment.

Behind broad indicators such as the high growth rate of financial assets and their level in terms of domestic and world GDP, the exponential growth curb of derivatives and the scale of international financial trading,[64] financialisation refers to the pervasiveness of features of interest-bearing capital identified

---

62   What Marx calls 'the accumulation of money capital as such' (Marx 1981, Vol. III, p. 606), or again 'financial accumulation' as distinct from 'actual accumulation'. Lapavitsas 2013, pp. 201–202. See Chapter 3 below for a full discussion of the term.

63   In Chesnais 2012 I have documented the start of the process in France through government policies made under the first Mitterrand presidency.

64   The Forbes 400 list of the wealthiest Americans is a specific US indicator (Foster and Hollemen 2010). It shows that those deriving their wealth from financial assets grew from 9 percent in 1982 to 17 percent in 1992 and 18 percent in 1992 before jumping to 27.3 percent in 2007 with over a third of the richest 400 Americans deriving their wealth principally from finance, insurance and real estate (FIRE). The process is not over. The cap to the 2015 Forbes list reads: 'Making The Forbes 400 is harder than ever. Admission to the list starts at a record $1.7 billion, up $150 million from a year ago. It's a high bar that

by Marx in Part Five of Volume III of *Capital*.[65] They must be taken in combination with the implications of today's very high degree of centralisation/concentration[66] of capital in its three forms. Thus notably with the advent of financialisation, (1) the worldview of 'capital as property' has permeated 'capital as function';[67] (2) the operations of highly concentrated industrial capital in a position of oligopoly and monopsony are directed to a very high degree to the 'appropriation of surplus-value, or surplus-product, as distinct from its creation'; (3) the 'financialisation' of industrial corporations concerns not just the scale of their financial operations and revenue from interest and speculation,[68] but also the most recent forms of corporate organisation, which now focuses less on the exploitation of labour *intra-muros* than on the predatory appropriation of surplus value from weaker firms, allowed through their monopolistic and monopsony positioning along value-chains; (4) the credit system has undergone a process of deep degeneration culminating in the development and the taking root of 'shadow banking'; (5) financial markets have pushed the process of the autonomisation of capital understood as 'the inherent tendency of capital to "autonomise" itself from its own material support'[69] ever further; (6) the mass of money capital bent on valorisation in financial markets resorts to the holding and trading of fictitious capital taking the form of assets more and more distant from the processes of surplus value production and appropriation and leads to endemic permanent financial instability; (7) money fetishism is rife in financial markets and it pervades contemporary society well beyond them on account of a wide set of social relations shaped by finance 'organically embedded in the fabric of social life';[70] (8) capitalism has achieved, to an extent still varying from country to country, forms of domination amounting to 'the "real subsumption of labour to finance"'.[71]

---

145 U.S. billionaires failed to clear. Still, 25 newcomers debut thanks to hot stocks, big deals and rising property values'.

65   I am aware of the controversies around the status of Volume III and of this part in particular. But this does not affect the extreme importance of the theoretical avenues Marx opens up.

66   The distinction made by Marx between the two notions and the way it was lost is discussed in Appendix to Chapter 3. Today industrial capital has achieved what Riccardo Bellofiore calls 'centralisation without concentration (Bellofiore 2014, p. 11).

67   This notion and several others used here are discussed in Chapter 3.

68   In a Marxist analytical framework, there is a *non sequitur* between the valuable data produced by Gerta Krippner and the notion of 'profits without production' she draws from it (Krippner 2005).

69   This is well developed by the two Brazilian economists Teixeira and Rotta (2012, p. 450).

70   Konings 2010, p. 5.

71   Bellofiore 2014, p. 11.

## No 'Diversion of Profits' but the Accumulation of Fictitious Capital

Williams and Kliman have vigorously challenged the position held by several heterodox and some Marxist economists that the cause of the fall in the rate of capital accumulation is due to the diversion of profits from productive investment towards financial uses.[72] Paul Sweezy defended this position quite early, relating the reemergence of finance to the return of 'stagnation'.[73] In heterodox industrial economics, this diversion was first argued as the outcome of corporate governance.[74] The thesis was then developed within a Post-Keynesian framework by Stockhammer,[75] and defended again by Krippner.[76] But the notion of the diversion of profits from productive investment is also quite central to Duménil and Lévy's critique of 'neoliberalism'.[77] Williams and Kliman argue, on the basis of sophisticated statistical data, that the fall in the rate of accumulation (i.e. the growth rate of accumulated productive investment) over the postwar period as a whole was, on the contrary, due entirely to the fall in corporations' rate of profit. Firms did not slow down their investments for lack of funds, which were available on the financial markets, nor because of the shift in the distribution of profits between retained profits and dividends, but because the rate of profit fell and so profitable investments declined. The fall in the rate of profit leads necessarily to 'forced hoarding'. Albeit at a slower rate, profits continue to accumulate. As the profit rate and the overall

---

72  Williams and Kliman 2014.
73  'Financial activity, mostly of a traditional kind, had been stimulated by the postwar boom of the 1950s and 1960s, suffering something of a letdown with the return of stagnation. Financiers were therefore looking for new business. Capital migrating out of the real economy was happily received in the financial sector. Thus began the process which during the next two decades resulted in the triumph of financial capital' (Sweezy 1994).
74  Lazonick 2000.
75  Stockhammer 2004. Because of his use of the term 'finance-led accumulation' (Stockhammer 2008), Stockhammer is sometimes thought to be a Regulationist. In a discussion with Boyer and Clévenot (Boyer and Clévenot 2011), he explains how he moved away from Regulationism on account of the impossibility of testing 'empirically', e.g. statistically and using econometrics, the School's hypotheses about the capitalist economy and its changing institutional setting. According to him, a range of approaches within Marxian and certainly Post-Keynesian economics can be tested statistically.
76  Krippner 2011.
77  Duménil and Lévy 2011, p. 153, argue that the rate of accumulation is closely related to the 'level of retained profits', what is left to managers once interest and dividends are paid. Later in the book, when they offer their expertise to US policymakers, one point concerns the need to 'invert neo-liberal trends towards dis-accumulation' (Duménil and Lévy 2011, p. 301).

economic climate that this breeds make productive investment more and more unattractive, these profits must go somewhere. They will be entrusted to corporate financial departments and seek, in competition with banks and pension, mutual and hedge funds, valorisation through loans and successful asset trading in the markets. As accumulation falters and the amount of surplus value appropriated slows down despite increases in the rate of exploitation, a cumulative process sets in. The insatiability of investors (the financial form of capital's unquenchable thirst for surplus value) accentuates financialisation in the form of financial innovations and the development of fictitious capital in its new contemporary forms.

In recent Marxist writing, the notion of fictitious capital has been given somewhat more attention than was previously the case. Fictitious capital has several interrelated dimensions, discussed in Chapter 3, and has developed in new forms, which are examined in Chapter 7. After setting out the notion over 30 years ago in his 1982 book, Harvey has recently revisited it.[78] It is used by Ashman, Fine and Newman in their analysis of South Africa's specific accumulation regime.[79] Loren Goldner pays considerable attention to fictitious capital,[80] as do Smith and Butovsky[81] and Maria Ivanova.[82] Tony Norfield[83] and David McNally[84] in their analysis of derivatives are now regularly using the term. Other English-speaking researchers are also beginning to discuss it seriously on blogs and even exploring ways to assess it statistically.[85] Costas Lapavitsas saw it, in an earlier publication, as a 'widow's cruse of extraordinary arguments regarding financial activities'.[86] He treats it more carefully in his latest book but remains very cautious if not reserved.[87] In France, Cedric Durand has published a book with the term in the title.[88] In the sections devoted to the notion, I hope to successfully argue for the need to retain and develop it. The same applies to the notion of money fetishism.

---

[78] Harvey 2012.
[79] Ashley, Fine and Newman 2011.
[80] Goldner 2013.
[81] Smith and Butovsky 2013.
[82] Ivanova 2011 and 2013.
[83] Norfield 2012.
[84] McNally 2011, p. 103.
[85] See Michael Roberts, http://thenextrecession.wordpress.com/2013/12/19/the-us-rate-of-profit-extending-the-debate/.
[86] Lapavitsas 2011, p. 614.
[87] Lapavitsas 2013, p. 161.
[88] Durand 2014.

## The 'Crisis in the Sphere of Credit and Money' in 2008

The run up to this crucial moment in the world crisis and its unfolding are analysed in Chapters 7 and 8. For Marx, crises in the sphere of credit and money are an 'integral part' of crises of overproduction and over-accumulation. This applies to the current world crisis; the task remains to explain how and why this is the case. Marx noted that 'In a system of production, where the entire interconnection of the reproduction process rests upon credit, a crisis must evidently break out if credit is suddenly withdrawn and only cash payment is accepted in the form of a violent scramble for means of payment. At first glance therefore the entire crisis presents itself as a credit and monetary crisis'.[89] In the context of mid-nineteenth-century capitalism, it involved 'simply the convertibility of bills of exchange into money. The majority of these bills represent actual sales and purchases, the basis of the entire crisis being the expansion of these far beyond the social need'.[90] He goes on to say something which sounds very familiar in the wake of the settlements paid to Wall Street banks for fraudulent behaviour in 2008: 'On top of this, however, a tremendous number of these bills represent purely fraudulent deals, which now come to light and explode; as well as unsuccessful speculations conducted with borrowed capital, and finally commodity capitals that are either devalued or unsaleable, or returns that are never going to come in'. In the context of early twenty-first-century capitalism, with a credit system based on securitisation, the withdrawal of credit took place in the mutual money fund (MMF) market and involved the rush to replace worthless securities by even slightly safer ones. In 2008, the collapse of one very specific form of credit, US mortgage-backed securities (MBS),[91] linked to one industrial sector (the construction sector) and one commodity (houses) possessing the property of also being a financial asset but one with very low liquidity, had the potential to endanger 'the entire interconnection of the reproduction process' not only in the US, but also, on account of the depth of financial globalisation, right across the transatlantic financial system with further repercussions in other parts.

Chapter 8 focuses on the transformations of the credit system, its 'financialisation'. It begins by recalling the organisation of 'classical' bank credit, before examining the way in which it began to change on account of liberalisation and deregulation driven in the US by the emergence of pension and mutual funds as loaners. Credit disintermediation constrained banks to find new sources of

---

89   Marx 1981, Vol. III, p. 621.
90   Ibid.
91   See the Glossary of financial terms for all these acronyms.

profit. The large commercial banks and the Wall Street investment banks alike campaigned for the repeal of the 1933 Glass-Steagall Act. Banking systems in Europe went through their own processes of liberalisation and concentration leading to the full restoration of 'universal banks'. The period saw a qualitative expansion in the securitisation of loans, the range of assets traded and the scale of levering by financial corporations in the form of debt internal to the banking sector. A new 'originate-to-distribute' banking model was devised along with the development of a 'shadow banking system', unrecognised until 2008, outside the regular banking system but in close symbiosis with it. By the mid-2000s, 'interest-bearing paper' came to mean asset and mortgage-backed securities (ABS and MBS) pooled in further types of securities, notably CDOs, what I have named fictitious capital to the *nth* degree.[92] Leda Paulani speaks of social processes which 'naturalise the fictitious processes of formation and valorisation of capital' and in which 'the most degenerated forms of financial assets seem to be the source of their own increase'.[93] The recourse to credit creation after the 1998 Asian and Russian crisis and yet more after the 2001–2 Nasdaq crisis, on a scale that one could speak of a US 'debt-led growth regime', took place at a time when this new banking model was becoming increasingly well established. During the same period, European banks adhered to the shadow banking system and made it transatlantic, while the Eurozone worked essentially as a mechanism for the profitable recycling of savings from Northern countries. It served to finance overproduction in housing and overaccumulation in construction and industries to fuel the associated domestic expansion of credit in countries such as Spain, Ireland and Portugal which was to precipitate them into crisis in 2009.

In Chapter 9, I come to the course taken by the financial crisis from July 2007 to September 2008. Here the main French author actively engaged from the start in the theory of financialisation to have helped me is Aglietta.[94] The chapter presents the *dramatis personae* of the financial crisis, notably the New York investment banks, the US hedge funds and the large European banks engaged in the diffusion of the opaque structured assets. It analyses the nodal position of the very short-term, even overnight, interbank loan market, the London ICE LIBOR in late August and then in April and especially September 2008 of the New York MMF market. The rapidity of international financial contagion had as its foundation and terrain the transatlantic shadow banking system.[95] The

---

92  Chesnais 2007.
93  Paulani 2010a.
94  Aglietta, Khanniche and Rigot 2010.
95  For an analysis by French academics working on finance, see Jeffers and Plihon 2013.

chapter ends with the Eurozone banking crisis of 2011 and the mechanism of crisis contagion at work in the specific institutional context of the EU and the Eurozone.

The rescue of the US and European financial system in September–October 2008 and the emergence of quasi-permanent financial policy instruments – quantitative easing and non-conventional forms of support of fictitious capital – express in the field of finance the impasse of capitalist production. In Chapter 10, I take readers through the last IMF and BIS reports to be published before I bring the manuscript to a close. The problems being tackled by the authorities in charge of the financial system are those of the effects and potential backlashes of quantitative easing, the very long continuous fall in interest rates independent of those set by central banks and the consequence of this for the growth of debt, the amount of money held by mutual and hedge fund managers and the level of systemic contagion risk this entails today, and finally the potential for financial turmoil, in emerging countries in particular, resulting from all this. My concluding chapter returns to a pace of accumulation commanded by presently unsolved economic and political factors and the endless shocks resulting from financial speculation. It ends with reflections on the topicality of the notion of capitalist production's historical limits.

CHAPTER 1

# The Historical Setting of the Crisis and Its Original Traits

Although in a very different historical setting, the ongoing world economic and financial crisis belongs to the same category as the Great Depression that followed the 1929 crash on Wall Street. In the specific context of contemporary globalisation, the financial events of 2007–8 were typically an integral part of a crisis 'in the sphere of money and credit',[1] the underlying causes of which are overproduction and over-accumulation at a world level along with an effective play of the tendency of the rate of profit to fall, despite the recourse by capital to the offsetting factors. The crisis was in gestation since 1998 and had been postponed essentially by the surge of accumulation in China and the massive recourse to debt in the US and some other countries. In 2008, the brutality of financial crisis was accounted for by the amount of fictitious capital accumulated and the degree of vulnerability of the credit system following securitisation. It had an immediate impact in the US on production and employment in the sectors (real estate) and industries (construction and automobile) that most depended on credit, triggering the US Great Recession with effects on world trade and production, in particular in Europe. Its resemblance in terms of length and scope to the great crisis of the twentieth century[2] has progressively increased as Brazil and other South American and South East Asian commodity producing countries ceased to be decoupled from the crisis. Since 2014, this resemblance has been accentuated by the marked slowdown of growth in China. A major difference with the 1930s is that world trade has receded but not collapsed and that the crisis has not led to outright frontal confrontation between major powers.[3]

The crisis has naturally led to a major debate among Marxists, as among remaining Keynesians, about the causes of capitalist crises in general and the present one in particular.[4] Much of the theoretical Marxist debate has

---

1  The full discussion is in Chapter 8.
2  The term 'Lesser Depression' used by Paul Krugman is a recognition of this.
3  This point is stressed by Panitch and Gindin 2012.
4  See the long chapter in Callinicos 2014.

concerned the law of the tendency of the rate of profit to fall (LTRPF).[5] Harvey is right in saying that it has attracted the most attention and given rise to the greatest number of articles, both in academic journals and on websites,[6] which all use, albeit in different ways, the same statistical data produced by national accounting systems, that of the US in particular. Roberts claims that the priority given to the behaviour of the rate of profit still represents a minority position, subject to 'the weight of rejection',[7] but there is clearly no Marxist of the authority of Sweezy to expound the theory of crises stemming from underconsumption.[8] Heinrich has been the object of strong attacks and has only really been defended by the *Monthly Review* and by Harvey.[9]

On account of my interest in the processes leading up to but also delaying the outbreak of the crisis, I pay considerable attention to the factors counteracting the fall in the rate of profit discussed by Marx in Chapter 14 of Volume III of *Capital*. I have also taken a strong lead from the observation in Chapter 15 of Volume III that 'capitalist production seeks continually to overcome its immanent barriers, but overcomes them only by means that set up the barriers afresh and on a more powerful scale'.[10] In that chapter, Marx discusses a range of issues, not simply the LTRPF but also the over-accumulation of capital and the accompanying overproduction of commodities, as well as raising the hypothesis of the 'absolute over-production of capital'[11] which is hardly ever mentioned in today's debates. So I agree with Harvey that there is no single causal theory of crisis formation and I single out, as he does, the same statement by Marx: 'The contradictions existing in bourgeois production [not only the LTRPF – F.C.] are reconciled by a process of adjustment, which, at the same time, however, manifests itself as crises, violent fusion of disconnected factors operating independently of one another yet correlated'.[12] If I have a query it concerns the notion of 'reconciliation by a process of

---

5   Some particularly radical authors, notably Carchedi and Roberts, claim that all crises, major and minor, are preceded by a fall in the rate of profit and that exit from crisis requires a rise in the rate of exploitation and a fall in the organic composition of capital. Even if he goes on to temper the statement, Roberts 2014 writes: 'We need to identify the underlying or ultimate cause of crises in the same way that Newton identified the underlying cause of motion of earthly bodies in gravity and in force and counter-force'.

6   Harvey 2014.
7   Roberts 2014.
8   Sweezy 1944, Chapters X and XII.
9   Heinrich 2013.
10  Marx 1981, Vol. III, p. 358.
11  Marx 1981, Vol. III, pp. 359–360.
12  Marx 1981, Vol. III, p. 357.

adjustment' today. Does the mode of production still have the scope and space for expansion and renewed long-term accumulation that it did when Marx used the expression?

## 1    The Crisis in a Long-Term Trajectory

An economic and financial crisis which embraces in a differentiated manner the whole of the world economy must be set in its historical context. Taking his lead from Engels's assessment of the 1873–96 first worldwide great depression, Paul Mattick observed:

> the periodicity of crisis... is affected by historical circumstances. If the ultimate reason for every crisis is capitalism itself, each particular crisis differs from its predecessors just because of the continuous transformation of world market relations and of the structure of global capital. Under these conditions neither the crises themselves nor their duration and gravity can be determined in advance.[13]

He adds that the crisis cannot be reduced to

> purely economic events, although it arises 'purely economically', that is, from the social relations of production clothed in economic forms. The international competitive struggle, fought also by political and military means, influences economic development, just as this in turn gives rise to the various forms of competition. Thus every real crisis can only be understood in connection with social development as a whole.[14]

The two most important 'social developments' of the last 50 years have been, first, the 'globalisation of capital' in its three forms, and second, an acceleration of the transformations by humankind, living under capitalist production and capitalist property relationships, of the ecosystems that permitted the development of civilisation to an extent that potentially jeopardises social reproduction. The setting of the ongoing crisis is the full 'establishment of the

---

13    As a great crisis stretches out in time this becomes progressively less true. The perspective of a new world war grew from 1933 onwards. Today an increasing convergence between the world economic crisis and the economic, social and political effects of climate change can be predicted.

14    Mattick 1981.

world market'[15] in the specific configuration of the late twentieth century. The globalisation of financial flows, foreign direct investment and trade; the full re-conquest of the USSR and its satellite states by capital; the incorporation of China into the WTO in 2001; and the rapid advance of liberalisation in India; all these make the crisis a 'global one' to a degree unknown to previous crises. It is on this account that the crisis is truly a global crisis of over-accumulation of capital in the double form of productive capacity leading to overproduction and of a 'plethora of capital' in the form of aspiring interest-bearing and fictitious capital.

## 1.1   In the Advanced Capitalist Countries, Slowing Accumulation before the Deep Break in 2008

The ongoing crisis ended the longest – gradually slower but nonetheless unbroken – phase of accumulation in the history of capitalism. Over 60 years, if the end of the Second World War is taken as the starting point; a little over 40 years even if 1976, which saw the end of the first postwar world recession, is chosen. Taking the growth rate of GDP as a proxy, the pace of accumulation in the advanced capitalist economies slowed continually but only broke in 2009.

In understanding the length of this phase, the 'way out of crisis' that marked the end of the Great Depression is very important. In Europe, in a context of unsettled imperialist hegemony between Germany, Britain and France, the Great Depression led straight into the war. In the United States, return to full employment only came with its entry into the war in 1942.[16] During the postwar Golden Age, the impetus of long-term accumulation came from the large-scale opportunities for profitable investment stemming from the combined result of low investment over part of the Great Depression, the massive destruction of plant, infrastructure and housing during the Second World War, and technologies with massive employment effects whose introduction had been curbed with the Great Depression. In Continental Europe, accumulation restarted around 1950, once the most basic industries and communication systems had been made to work again. It took off vigorously in Japan with the help the US gave to Japanese capital in rebuilding its industry to serve as a second productive base for the war in Korea. The US experienced a very short crisis in 1952 before launching this war and, in doing so, made the arms industry one of its major motors of accumulation over a long period, as well as the principal basis of its innovation system to this day. Due to the outcome of the Second World War,

---

15   Marx 1981, Vol. III, p. 375.
16   Dating the end of the Great Depression has been and remains a point of debate between US historians. See recently *inter alia* Romer 1992 and Steindl 2007.

the working class and its unions and political parties were in a position to limit the power of corporations and financial institutions and so to benefit from a rise in productivity. This laid the foundations for 'Fordism' as an 'accumulation regime' – in the sense defined by Regulationist theory – and for what came to be known in English as the 'Social Democratic Compromise'. Last but not least, until the Federal deficit financing of the war in Vietnam made the pegging of the dollar to gold unsustainable, capitalism enjoyed a stable international monetary system.

The rise in the organic composition of capital, as first argued by David Yaffe,[17] and the emergence of overproduction within the boundaries of internationally interdependent but still autonomous, self-centred national economies, laid the ground for the first postwar 1974–6 economic crisis. Triggered by the encroachment on already declining profits of a jump in fuel costs following the sharp rise in the price of oil (the 'oil shock'), it sees the start of a downward trend in the annual rate of growth of GDP and investment in the industrialised countries. It undoubtedly marks the end of a first sub-period of particularly dynamic accumulation. Ernest Mandel names it soberly 'the first generalised recession of the [postwar] international capitalist economy'.[18] The years 1974–6 are often referred to by many authors as the starting point of the 'structural crisis of capitalism'. There are several difficulties with this, two of which are directly related. First, the use of the term 'structural crisis' immediately raises the question: was capitalism not structurally in crisis in the 1930s, and, moreover, so deeply that the response was world war?[19] Second, those who use the term make little mention of the very special historical conditions which had allowed the temporary establishment of the stable regime known as 'Fordism'. Nostalgia for the 'Glorious Age' ('les trente glorieuses') persists in part of the European left. These decades were simply a parenthesis. It ended once capital accumulation had led again to over-accumulation of productive capacities within national economies, the rate of profit had fallen, 'financial accumulation proper', as defined in this book, regained momentum and financial liberalisation was initiated with Britain's financial centre in the City as its hub.

---

17  Yaffe 1973.
18  Mandel 1982.
19  Duménil and Lévy 2011 have developed, on the sole basis of an analysis of US economic history, an idiosyncratic theory of class division totally alien to Marxism, in which managers are pivotal. Duménil and Lévy use the term structural crisis indeterminately (see notably 2011, pp. 19 and 267). The 1929 Great Depression, the 1974–6 crisis (with managers' shift of alliance from the popular classes to the upper class) and the ongoing Great Recession are all named in the same way.

### 1.1.1 The Bourgeoisie's Fight Against the Immanent Barriers of Capitalist Production

The terms 'structural crisis' or again 'relative stagnation' used by Andrew Kliman[20] do not capture the brutality of class aggression as expressed by Andrew Glyn's 'capitalism unleashed',[21] nor the measures deployed by capital in the 1980s and 1990s. As noted by McNally, 'for the most part, the approaches [that read the current crisis in terms of a decline in the rate of profitability] tend to be amazingly static, ignoring the specific dynamics of capitalist restructuring and accumulation in the neoliberal period'. As he points out, 'there is a particularly unhelpful tendency in many of these analyses to treat the entire 35-year period since 1973 as a "crisis", a "long downturn", or even a "depression"'.[22] The political context must not be neglected. In many countries, a few years before the 1974–6 crisis the bourgeoisie had just been confronted by strong working-class and student action. But domestic political relationships, as well as the working class's leeway for militant action, were still strongly affected in Continental Europe by the interests of the Soviet bureaucracy. A key moment was the containment of the French General Strike by the French Communist Party and the CGT in May 1968, followed by the crushing of the Prague Spring in August of the same year. This containment was reiterated in Italy in the autumn of 1969. This gave capital the opportunity to readjust strategically.

The way I have approached the analysis of capital's very strong reactiveness[23] takes its lead from Marx's observation that 'capitalist production seeks continually to overcome its immanent barriers, but overcomes them only by means that set up the barriers afresh and on a more powerful scale',[24] and from Engels's remark in his 1894 edition of Volume III of *Capital* that 'every factor, which works against a repetition of the old crises, carries within itself the germ of a far more powerful future crisis'.[25] These factors include ones related to technology: 'Since the last general crisis of 1867 many profound changes have taken place. The colossal expansion of the means of transportation and communication – ocean liners, railways, electrical telegraphy, the Suez Canal – has made a real world-market a fact'. In contemporary globalisation, strong technological factors have clearly also been at work. Cheaper and more reliable telecommunications, information management software and increasingly

---

20  Kliman 2012, pp. 9 and 48. This position is defended vigorously by Choonara 2009 and 2011.
21  Glyn 2006.
22  McNally 2009, pp. 42–43. See also his reply to Choonara (McNally 2012).
23  Chesnais 2006b.
24  Marx 1981, Vol. III, p. 358.
25  Footnote in Marx 1981, Vol. III, pp. 620–621.

powerful personal computers due to advances in information and communications technologies (ICT) have lowered the cost and increased the efficiency of coordinating international operations within and between companies. Containerised shipping and the standardisation, automation, and greater inter-modality of freight have facilitated trade in goods and reduced its costs (with the externalisation of environmental ones). They are correctly defined as enabling factors.[26] The decisive factors were political.

Between the late 1970s and the early 2000s, capital and state in the world system's core countries devised three main successive ways to sustain accumulation until 2007–8, albeit at an ever-slower rate. As argued by Panitch and Gindin, states must 'be placed at the centre of the search for an explanation of the making of global capitalism'.[27] The notion of 'informal empire' captures the role played by the US as the hegemon of the 'Western world' (Japan included)[28] from the 1940s onwards in the elaboration and implementation of economic policies with global reach. These were in the US's own interests and in those of capital as a whole as interpreted by them and rarely in dispute. In the period following the 1974–6 world recession and the further, less sharp international recession in 1978–80, the first response was the neo-conservative revolution planned by Friedrich Hayek and Milton Friedman and led by Margaret Thatcher and Ronald Reagan, which saw its first full-scale application with the 1973 Chilean military coup and the sanguinary Pinochet regime. This response involved from the beginning of the 1980s continuous steps towards the liberalisation, deregulation, and globalisation of finance, trade and FDI. NAFTA, the Washington Consensus, the Treaty of Maastricht and the Treaty of Marrakesh were key landmarks. From then on, the conditions were established for an increase in the rate of surplus value not as a development specific to given countries but as a global (though necessarily differentiated) worldwide process. It was permitted in particular by the growth of production and the increase in the number of low-paid, non-protected workers in semi-colonial 'developing countries'. The second course was the support given in the 1990s to the successfully managed reintroduction of capitalist production in China by the CCP and its incorporation into the world market, crowned by its co-option

---

26  See OECD, 1992, p. 211, and recently with reference to global value chains OECD 2013, p. 8.
27  Panitch and Gindin 2012b, p. 2.
28  Panitch and Gindin make no mention of the limits to the 'empire' in the form of the political setbacks suffered by the US outside its natural sphere of hegemony, notably the failure of its attempt to thwart revolution in China in 1948–9. It is true that following Nixon's visit to China in 1972 the US started correcting this.

into the WTO in December 2001. Direct investment into China was one of the responses given by the US in particular following the 1990–2 recession.

In contrast to these un-debatable expressions of strength, the third method used for sustaining accumulation and prolonging its duration marked the vulnerability of US growth. This was the recourse to credit creation after the 1997–8 Asian crisis[29] and 1998 Russian crisis, and yet more after the 2001–2 Nasdaq crisis, on such a scale that one could speak of a US 'debt-led growth regime', which spread later to several European countries. Bellofiore gives a good description of this regime: 'wage deflation, capital assets inflation and the increasingly leveraged positions of households and financial corporations were complementary elements where real growth was doped by toxic finance'.[30] It permitted the expansion of the automobile, housing and construction sectors and experienced its climax in 2003–6 in the US housing bubble. The overbuilding of houses and over-capacity in the construction industry were fuelled by debt-supported securitisation and unsustainable levels of leverage. Despite the financial crisis, it remains the growth regime to which finance capital aspires to return.

### 1.1.2 The Fall in the Rate of Profit and the Play of the Counteracting Factors

Challenging mono-causality does not imply a rejection of the research bearing on the rate of profit and in particular whether or not, after falling in the 1970s and 80s, it recovered in the 90s. The thesis of a falling rate of profit has been contested by some, notably by Michel Husson with his 'tendency for the rate of profit to rise in the principal capitalist countries'.[31] Most studies show a temporary recovery of the rate of profit in the 1990s followed by a new fall.

---

29   Underlying the 1997 foreign exchange and stock market crisis and the collapse of the housing and stock market bubble fed by foreign short-term capital inflows first in Thailand, then in Malaysia, Singapore, Indonesia and the Philippines, and subsequently in Korea and Taiwan, was high overproduction which existed in semiconductors and consumer electronics throughout the region and in Korea similarly in cars, steel and petrochemicals. See *inter alia* Hart-Landsberg et al. 2007, p. 11.

30   Bellofiore 2014, p. 16.

31   See Husson 2008 for a first presentation, reiterated in an article posted on the website of *A l'Encontre*, 'Le marxisme n'est pas un dogmatisme', 2009. This prompted a vigorous reply by Harman 2009. The most thorough critique in French is by Gill 2010. It is part of the debate launched by Alain Bihr's contention that the world crisis was principally due to an 'excess of surplus value'. The debate involved, at one point, Bihr, Louis Gill, Michel Husson and myself. Most articles can be found either at http://www.carre-rouge.org or on the Lausanne-based website http://www.alencontre.com. Husson has since plotted a different

An initial point must be made, namely that Marx's own discussion of the law of the tendency of the rate of profit to fall (LTRPF) includes a clear reminder of the fact that 'as the capitalist mode of production develops, so the rate of profit falls, while the mass of profit rises together with the increasing mass of capital applied'.[32] In the literature, little stress is put on the mass of profit. Yet it compounds the problems posed to capitalism by the fall in the rate of profit. The mass of profit turned away from productive investment and accumulated in the form of fictitious capital is only destroyed in the case of a crisis of great proportion left to run its course, an issue I return to later. The plethora of capital stemming from the sheer mass of capital accumulated over more than half a century is part of the current economic situation as much as the fall in the rate of profit.

Regarding the latter, in order to really intervene in the debate on the LTRPF, one should be capable of producing one's own figures. Since I myself am not able to do this, I will make reference to the data that I find most convincing. From the reading I have done, I have noted the following points. First, there is the ability to show that the data from which the profit rate is calculated really represent proxies for the Marxian categories. Andrew Kliman is the first to have clearly raised this problem.[33] It has been posed again by Harvey in the text discussed above. Second, one can argue, along with Fine and Harris, that Marx was dealing 'with an "abstract tendency" rather than an "empirical tendency"'.[34] It is the latter which is of importance even if it may be seen as remaining simply a 'stylised fact'. On account of the quality of the US statistical data, most calculations are made for that country. How far this drawback is compensated for by the US's position in the world economy is a question of debate. Those of Smith and Butovsky, which are less cited than others, come close to my understanding of the recent dynamic of accumulation, class struggle and contemporary imperialist domination.

---

curve in which there is a very strong fall from 1965 to 1980 which makes the recovery of the rate of profit all the more spectacular. See Husson 2013, Figure 1.

32   Marx 1981, Vol. III, p. 356.

33   'The data necessary to construct the Marxian rate of profit with any precision are not available. Marx's LTRPF pertains to the total social capital, which in our day is the capital of the world economy as a whole. But reliable profitability data for the world economy does not exist. There is also a sizeable discrepancy between surplus value as defined by Marx and profit as defined by the Bureau of Economic analysis' (Kliman 2012, p. 96).

34   Fine and Harris 1977.

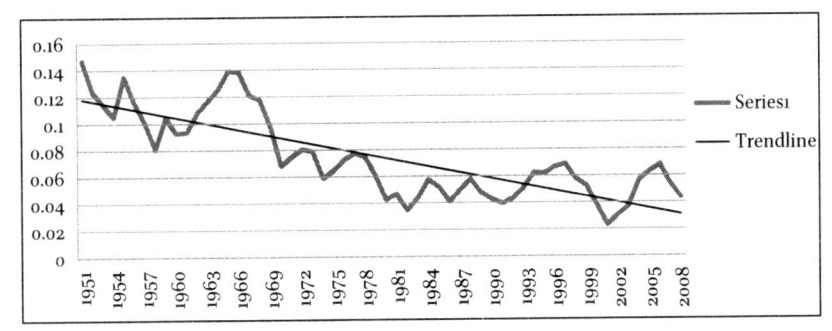

# THE HISTORICAL SETTING OF THE CRISIS AND ITS ORIGINAL TRAITS

FIGURE 1.1  *Non-Financial Corporate Rate of Profit (After-Tax), USA 1950–2008.*
SOURCE: SMITH AND BUTOVSKY 2012.

Pointing out that the real problem is that 'of explaining why this fall [of the rate of profit] is not greater or faster', Marx writes in this short chapter that 'counteracting influences must be at work, checking and cancelling the effect of the general law and giving it merely the characteristic of a tendency, which is why we have described the fall of the general rate of profit as a tendential fall'.[35] The importance of the counteracting factors to one another and their overall influence on the rate of profit must be discussed historically. Marx actually starts Chapter 14 by mentioning 'the enormous development in the productive powers of social labour over the last thirty years alone' (i.e. mid-1850s). The permanent feature is that once they feel that profit is falling, capital and state do not remain passive. The way they reacted after the 1974–6 world recession, which was preceded and partly prepared by the fall in profit, illustrates this perfectly. Accumulation as a process that has 'neither end nor limits' and the 'immanent barriers' it recurrently comes against create an equally recurrent imperative for corporations and governments to seek ways of overcoming the latter. It is these responses that shape the actual concrete course of capitalist development. Henryk Grossman, to whom a theory of capitalist breakdown is attributed simply on account of the title of his book,[36] in fact devotes a very long chapter to modifying countertendencies, stressing that

---

35  Marx 1981, Vol. III, p. 337. And later in the chapter: 'The latter do not do away with the law, but impair its effect. Otherwise, it would not be the fall of the general rate of profit, but rather its relative slowness, that would be incomprehensible. Thus, the law acts only as a tendency. And it is only under certain circumstances and only after long periods that its effects become strikingly pronounced' (Marx 1981, Vol. III, p. 346).

36  The origin of this is in Sweezy's partisan reading (Sweezy 1944, p. 209ff.).

[t]he capitalist mechanism is not something left to itself. It contains within itself living social forces: on one side the working class, on the other the class of industrialists. The latter is strongly interested in preserving the existing economic order and tries, in every conceivable way, to find means of 'boosting' the economy, of bringing it back into motion through restoring profitability.[37]

Grossman calls the six counteracting factors listed by Marx 'countertendencies internal to the mechanism of capital' as opposed to what, writing in the era of imperialism, he names 'restoring profitability through world domination'.[38] The six factors are: (1) the degree of exploitation of labour; (2) the depression of wages below the value of labour power; (3) relative overpopulation; (4) the cheapening of elements of constant capital; (5) foreign trade; and (6) the increase of the stock of capital. The first three all increase the rate of exploitation and the amount of surplus value appropriated compared to the capital invested. The cheapening of elements of constant capital and foreign trade work both ways. They both support and offset the tendency towards the falling rate of profit, each effect getting the upper hand according to circumstances. The last factor relates to the increase in share capital: 'As capitalist production advances and with it accelerated accumulation, one portion of capital is considered simply to be interest-bearing capital and is invested as such'.[39] The meaning that can be given to this today is discussed in later chapters. Here the analysis focuses on the first five factors.

Since the 1980s, the first and third factors have effectively tended towards raising the rate of exploitation in the advanced capitalist countries as elsewhere. Technological changes with strong effects on productivity, absolute surplus value obtained through the intensification of exploitation by management practices based on ITCs, and relative overpopulation in the form of the 'global industrial reserve army' which has emerged though trade and direct investment liberalisation have all been at work. With the crisis and the most recent forms of global production discussed below, the second factor, the

---

37   Grossman 1992 [1929]. Marx had already pointed towards this: 'Capitals invested in foreign trade can yield a higher rate of profit, because, in the first place, there is competition with commodities produced in other countries with inferior production facilities, so that the more advanced country sells its goods above their value even though cheaper than the competing countries' (Marx 1981, Vol. III, p. 345).

38   However, in his book, 'the economic function of imperialism' is reduced in fact to beating others in exports.

39   Marx 1981, Vol. III, p. 347.

depression of wages below the value of labour power, has reappeared in some countries, even in advanced economies. Smith and Butovsky write that on the basis of past experience, this may be 'ephemeral',[40] but the specific historical context of today and capitalism's difficulty in overcoming its immanent barriers make it a permanent feature. Carchedi is right in arguing that 'the view that the increase in the rate of exploitation cannot be considered a countertendency because it has lasted since 1987 is based on a misunderstanding. A countertendency is not defined by, and is independent of, its duration. It persists as long as the conditions for its existence persist, in this case the defeat of the US (and the world's) working class'.[41] In the context of a liberalised world economy, in which the effects of the 'global industrial reserve army' are central, global relations of power between capital and labour could only be altered by working class victories in key countries, in the US, of course, but also in China.

In the course of the 1990s, trade and direct investment liberalisation and the doubling of the world labour force (see below) activated the third factor listed by Marx. They opened up opportunities for industrialised countries' TNCs to raise their rate of profit both through exports, imports, and through FDI exploiting the working force *in situ* and exercising their competitive advantage *vis-à-vis* local capital by their direct presence in its domestic market. Marx already pointed to the effects of imports. When 'commodities are bought abroad and sent home (not only) is the rate of profit higher because it is generally higher in the colonial country, favourable natural conditions may enable it to go hand in hand with lower commodity prices'.[42] US imports from China and South and South-East Asia of cheap manufactured 'wage-goods' entering into the cost of the reproduction of labour power can be hypothesised to have had an effect on the movement of the US rate of profit. For core capitalist countries, this can be extended to flows of profit from FDI.[43]

The direction taken by the organic composition of capital depends on the relative price of the components of constant capital, which in turn depends on changes in technology and in production and logistics management. Gordon has plotted a regular long-term fall in the price of investment goods.[44] Nonetheless, the magnitude of the shift between constant and variable

---

40  Smith and Butovsky 2012, p. 47.
41  Carchedi 2011, p. 127.
42  Marx 1981, Vol. III, p. 346.
43  This is discussed by Norfield in his review of Kliman (Norfield 2012). See his note on 13 March 2012. http://www.economicsofimperialism.blogspot.fr/2012/03/number-of-beast.html.
44  Gordon 2012.

capital due to the labour-saving impacts of information technology suggests that today the fall in the cost of 'machines' (broadly defined), however important, will not be a factor offsetting the fall of the rate of profit in the coming period.[45] Attention must also be given to raw materials and energy, namely the 'non-fixed' or circulating component of constant capital, which are sometimes overlooked. It can be hypothesised that increasing scarcity and rising prices are likely to accentuate the fall of the rate of profit save for countries with specific endowments. Laurent Baronian, in a commentary on Chapter 6 of Volume III, points out that Marx only discusses given agricultural raw material components of circulating constant capital (cotton and wool) and only envisages their rise in price as a temporary, passing phenomenon.[46] The reverse is true today. The underlying tendency (despite their significant recent fall) in the rise in the price of energy, many minerals and other raw material inputs to production – in which China's huge demand has only acted as an accelerator of a much longer-term process – can be seen as a long-term influence acting on the LTFRP. Given resource endowments and political conditions may permit a country to increase its competiveness and reduce external dependency, as is the case for the massive exploitation of shale gas by the US.[47]

Figures 1.2 and 1.3 find a partial recovery of the rate of profit during the first half of the 1990s and again from 2002 to 2005. Given all that has just been said about the vigorous recourse by capital to several key offsetting factors, it would have been odd had it not recovered during the first period. The second

---

45    Carchedi and Roberts are very confident, more than most in any case, in their capacity to calculate the rise and fall of the organic composition of capital: 'the rate of profit in the G7 economies fell over 21 percent between 1950 and 2014 as the organic composition of capital rose over 60%, much faster than the rise in the rate of surplus value at 11%. In the neo-liberal period from 1982 to 2002, the rate of profit rose nearly 30%, while the organic composition declined by 5% and the rate of surplus value rose 22%. In the current "depression" period, the rate of profit has fallen 20% with the organic composition of capital up 41%, well ahead of the rise in the rate of surplus value at 7%'.

46    Baronian 2013, p. 190. One of the relevant passages from Marx is found in the chapter on price fluctuations in Volume III of *Capital*: 'the development of capitalist production, and, consequently, the greater the means of suddenly and permanently increasing that portion of constant capital consisting of machinery, etc., and the more rapid the accumulation (particularly in times of prosperity), so much greater the relative overproduction of machinery and other fixed capital, so much more frequent the relative under-production of vegetable and animal raw materials, and so much more pronounced the previously described rise of their prices and the attendant reaction. And so much more frequent are the convulsions caused as they are by the violent price fluctuations of one of the main elements in the process of reproduction' (Marx 1981, Vol. III, p. 214).

47    This point is made by Geier 2012.

short-lived recovery is due to a factor exterior to the working of the LTFRP, namely the artificial boosting of profits through the accentuated expansion of credit in the conditions discussed later in the book.[48] Duménil and Lévy identify recovery at both moments.[49] In their calculations, the profit rate then falls sharply in 2005 as in Smith and Butovsky. In light of this, their assertion that 'the crisis of neoliberalism, just as the Great Depression, cannot be interpreted as a "profitability crisis"',[50] is all the more bizarre.

## 2     A Crisis Which Has Not Been Allowed to Run Its Course

Crises express the contradictions of capitalist production and, in the case of great crises, its historical limits, but they also have the cathartic function of clearing the way for new accumulation. The vigour of true cyclical recovery and renewed expansion of accumulation depends upon the scale on which the destruction of capital and commodities has taken place in the crisis and whether the deck is cleared for new investment.[51] Over a part of its history, capitalism had enough strength and room for expansion to ensure that they played this role. In the case of the Great Depression, the clearing of the way was largely supplemented by the huge destruction provoked by the Second World War. The current configuration is quite different. The working class suffered major defeats, to which dates can be put in the UK and the US, following the progression of Thatcherism and Reaganism, but in other countries in Europe similar processes have been longer, more protracted and less conclusive. But now workers are suffering vicious attacks everywhere in the world, one region being Southern Europe since 2010. Yet the world bourgeoisie has assessed the combined configuration of internal and political relationships as excluding that the crisis be left to destroy fictitious and productive capital in the way that occurred in the 1930s. The speed and scale of government intervention in 2008 by the US and the major European countries in support of the financial system, and also, more temporarily and to a lesser degree, of the automobile industry, must be considered as expressing the direct pressure of the banks in defence of fictitious capital and that of US and European

---

48    See Chapter 7.
49    Duménil and Lévy 2012, figure 4.1 and the commentary to it, pp. 58–9.
50    This related to their assertion that 'if an overreaching explanation [of the crisis] must be sought it lies in the objectives of neoliberalism, the tools used in their pursuit and the contradictions inherent in these aims and methods' (Duménil and Lévy 2012, p. 34).
51    Kliman 2012, pp. 3 and 77.

carmakers to protect their position against Asian competitors. But it also signifies considerable political caution both domestically and internationally. The world bourgeoisie led by the US reckoned that it could not risk a world crisis of the magnitude of the 1930s. US government intervention has been well documented.[52] Central to this intervention has been the Fed, which resorted to unprecedented measures, such as buying the big US banks' toxic assets.[53] But more broadly, all the governments and ruling elites that met during the first conferences of the G20 shared the view that they could not afford the political consequences of a large scale purging of over-accumulation. This was particularly true for China where the bureaucratic-cum-capitalist elite still has a genuine fear of the proletariat. What must be briefly discussed at this point are the consequences in terms of the 'non-clearing of the decks' for a new take-off of long-term accumulation.

## 2.1   A Mountain of Fictitious Capital Alongside Over-accumulation and Overproduction

The success with which capitalism pushed back its immanent barriers over several decades, the scale of debt-creation resorted to after 2001, and the policies enacted in 2008–9 and after to contain the crisis help to explain the massive accumulation of fictitious capital in the form of claims on value and surplus value, engaging in innumerable speculative operations, alongside a state of global over-accumulation of production capacities and overproduction of a wide range of industries. Huge nominal amounts of interest-bearing and fictitious capital, in all its forms, hang over the world economic situation. They are the object of incessant trading in globalised financial markets and are lodged in very powerful financial conglomerates possessing the capacity to dictate their policies to governments through a variety of economic channels and political institutions. Their magnitude and their pace of growth in comparison to that of world GDP is shown in figure 1.2. It is based on one of the most reliable estimations of global financial assets, published regularly by the McKinsey Global Institute. The curve expresses the growth of four categories

---

52   Duménil and Lévy in particular provide a very detailed account of the period from August 2007 to the first quarter of 2009 (Duménil and Lévy 2012, Chapters 17 and 18).

53   Marx in the mid-nineteenth century had considered this possibility and thought it inapplicable: 'It is clear that this entire artificial system of forced expansion of the reproduction process cannot be cured by now allowing one bank, e.g. the Bank of England, give all the swindlers the capital they lack in paper money and to buy up all the depreciated commodities at their old nominal values' (Marx 1981, Vol. III, p. 621).

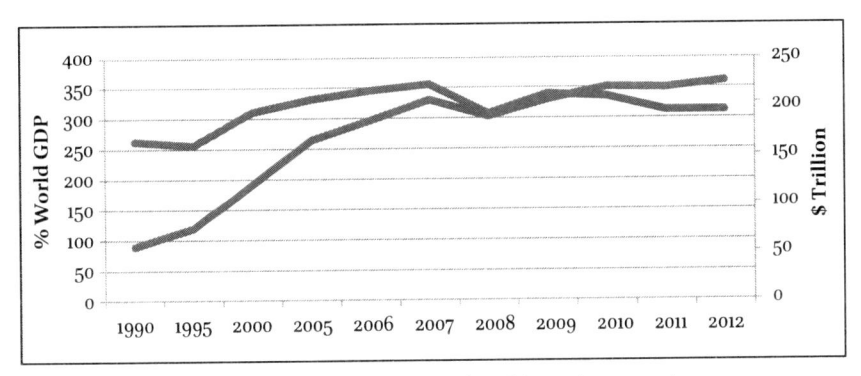

FIGURE 1.2  Growth of Global Financial Assets and World GDP (1990–2010).
Left Axis Global Financial Assets as % World GDP, Right Axis amount at 2011 exchange rates and in $ trillion.
SOURCE: MCKINSEY GLOBAL INSTITUTE 2012.

of assets: equity securities, private debt securities, government debt securities and deposits. Derivatives are not included. Even though the estimates only have the status of a proxy since market valuation is the basis of their calculation, they are impressive. For reasons discussed in chapters 2 and 7 they grew at a compound annual average growth rate of 9% from 1990 to 2007 with a sharp acceleration in 2006 and 2007 (+18%). That year the ratio of financial assets to world GDP rose to 359%.[54]

The twenty-year period of exponential growth of financial assets starting in the mid-1990s was brought to a halt by the 2007–8 financial crisis. In its 2013 report the McKinsey Global Institute expresses its concern that 'although global financial assets have surpassed their pre-crisis totals, growth has hit a plateau. Their annual growth has slowed to an anaemic 1.9 percent since the crisis'.[55] The authors are concerned that their indicators of financial globalisation (international flows of loans, cross-border holdings of bonds and equity, foreign direct investment) reveal a certain degree of 'retreat from globalisation'. However, it is the *degree of resilience* of the accumulation of fictitious capital, and the strength of the international and national institutions on which it is founded, that need to be explained, even if changes have taken place in the configuration of capital flows and in the relative strength of different banks and national banking systems. As a percentage of world GDP, global financial

---

54   McKinsey Global Institute 2009, pp. 8–9.
55   McKinsey Global Institute 2013.

assets continued to rise. The fall in stock market capitalisation was offset by pursued expansion of developing economies before it stalled in 2014–15, but also by an increase in government debt estimated by the McKinsey Global Institute to be $4.4 trillion.[56]

## 2.2  Global Over-accumulation and Overproduction with China as a Central Locus

Over-accumulation and overproduction at the global level can develop alongside declining rates of productive investment in given countries, even major ones, as was the case in the United States in the late 1990s and 2000s. The unique international monetary status of the dollar, as well as huge household and financial sector debt, made the US both 'consumer of last resort' and recipient of central bank reserves and private hoards (Sovereign funds from the Gulf) in search of a safe investment. In the industrialised countries, over-accumulation and overproduction are largely located in specific industries, notably automobiles, and sectors such as housing and construction. These industries and sectors have been the cornerstones of accumulation and, in the case of housing and construction, were the basis of the 2003–8 financial bubble. Ivanova has argued rightly that there is a close complementarity between the over-accumulation of capacity and 'surplus' (e.g. non-reinvested capital) in the industrial centres of the periphery, principally China, and the overproduction of housing in the US.[57] So as to offset domestic macro-economic effects of a very large-scale offshoring of production by US TNCs, with its consequences on domestic employment,[58] the real-estate, housing and construction sector (defined in broad terms) became the vector of internal accumulation with the engineering of fictitious securities to support the process.

The tendency towards over-accumulation and overproduction was already at work in China long before the 2009 world recession. Under Deng Xiaoping, from 1978–9 onwards, with an acceleration after Deng's 1992 'Southern Tour', China progressively embraced the model of export-led growth despite geoeconomic and demographic characteristics very different from those of South Korea or Taiwan: a continental economy and the world's largest population. This choice was the consequence of the relationships of production and distribution specific to China's single party oligarchical economic and social system and the place given to export-oriented foreign investment, notably by Japanese and US industrial and commercial corporations in manufactured goods. It is

---

56    McKinsey Global Institute 2011.
57    Ivanova 2011.
58    See *inter alia* Scott 2007.

estimated that if Wal-Mart were a country, it would rank as China's seventh-largest trading partner, sourcing over $18 billion worth of goods from the Chinese manufacturing sector.[59] More generally, in a liberalised global trading system, over-accumulation can temporarily be offset and masked by exports, as manufacturing capacity is destroyed by competition in other parts of the world economy. In the case of textiles, for instance, China's very pronounced turn to the world market, coupled with the total dismantling in 2005 of the Multi-Fibre Arrangement (MFA) in the WTO, seriously impacted the industry on both shores of the Mediterranean. Contradictorily, what Ho-Fung Hun names 'the miracle of prolonged over-accumulation in China', which 'at least until 2013 [lay] in its capacity to export excess capacity', expresses a critical dependence on world demand.[60]

In the 'old' industrialised countries, the economic crisis has exercised its classical function, destroyed industrial capacity, created high unemployment and strongly increased job precariousness. This occurred first in the United States and elsewhere in the OECD in late 2008 and 2009 and then again in many EU countries from 2011 onwards. In Europe, plant closures and intensive restructuring are continuing. This has not been true for the emerging countries, particularly China. Indeed, since 2008, the destruction of means of production in the US and Europe has been offset by the pursuit of Chinese capacity creation. China set the floor to world recession in 2008–9. Through very high investment outlays, it stopped the US 'Great Recession' from leading to global depression, in particular by ensuring a market for large primary product producers in South America and thus largely insulating them from contagion. In this way a brake was put on the sharp downward path of world trade. Despite some evidence regarding the fall in the rate of profit,[61] investment has continued to grow quickly while household consumption has remained almost unchanged.

There are systemic reasons for the high rate of investment. The communist-cum-capitalist elites entrenched in large cities and provinces are engaged in deep competition among themselves, the result of which has been the multiplication of investment in plant.[62] On the other hand, workers are refused the right to build independent trade unions of their own since the concession of this right by the Chinese Communist Party (CCP) would open the door to the building of independent political organisations. An increasing number

---

59   Data published by China Labor Watch. See also *inter alia* the *Guardian*, http://www.guardian.co.uk/business/2010/jan/12/walmart-companies-to-shape-the-decade.
60   Ho-Fung Hun 2012, p. 222.
61   See (in French) Gaulard 2009 and 2014, and (in English) Ho-Fung Hun 2012.
62   Aglietta made this point early on (Aglietta and Berrebi 2007).

of workers now organise local industrial action of different types, including strikes, but the working class does not exist as a force capable of altering the overall pattern of income distribution. The CCP is committed to growth, but since 2001, and again spectacularly in 2009, this has been based very heavily on gross capital formation, which includes investment in infrastructure and construction. The contribution of private consumption to GDP growth has remained low and has been accompanied by increasing inequality in income distribution.

Since 2013–14, the Chinese government recognises that industrial over-accumulation is a real problem. Fairly reliable estimates of overcapacity exist only for a very small number of industries. Steel is one of them. A recent study puts global overcapacity at 500 million tons.[63] The countries include China, Japan, Russia, South Korea, India, and the EU steel plants. China's overcapacity alone amounts to the whole of EU potential production.[64] Steel, cement and glass are cited by the head of the CCP, Li Keqiang, as industries in absolute overcapacity. Other Chinese reports focus on what they call 'overcapacity with respect to foreign demand'. A study made by industrial firms in Hunan unsurprisingly lists textiles, clothing and shoes. It foresees protectionist barriers for more sophisticated products such as windmill and photovoltaic equipment.[65] China is sufficiently dependent on exports to feel the changes in world demand. As this began to falter after the 2010–12 recovery, the huge accumulated savings of corporations and individuals turned to housing. This fostered the formation of a housing boom supported by political corruption and entailing the growth of an idiosyncratic form of shadow banking. The boom did not last long and the financial bubble was sufficiently small for the mid-2015 stock market and financial crash to be contained. There is a growing consensus backed by IMF data that the era of rapid growth is over,[66] that deleveraging in the housing sector will take a long time, and that the CCP will be confronted by the political and social problems postponed during the period of high growth rates.

---

63   'Surging Steel Imports Put Up To Half a Million U.S. Jobs at Risk', *Economic Policy Institute Briefing Paper*, no. 376, 14 May 2014.

64   http://www.ibtimes.com/china-steel-overcapacity-reaching-new-heights-beyond-imagination-1558026.

65   'Textile and Apparel: traditional external demand overcapacity in the industry, the development of counter-measures', 2012, <http://www.fyjhx.cn/en_US/news/html/18.html>. This study is also of interest because it details the respective responsibilities of central and local authorities.

66   IMF 2015b.

## 2.3 The Globalisation of the Labour Force, the Cornerstone of Capital's Strength

In the industrialised countries, despite the dead end of the debt-led growth model, no substitute has really been envisaged, still less put in its place. Since mid-2011, the process of capacity destruction has been launched again in most of Europe. Here high levels of unemployment and large precarious employment reflect simultaneously: domestic over-accumulation; the pro-cyclical policies immediately dictated by rentier capitalists holding debt – and the migration of industrial corporations to continents where markets still have a potential to grow, where labour is cheaper and largely unprotected by labour law and anti-pollution legislation is less stringent or non-existent. In the US, new investment has remained very low. The estimates of time horizons for the deleveraging of household debt and a reduction of Federal and other public debt to pre-2008 levels extend to 2018 if not further. Today China is asked to boost the world economy by seriously expanding its domestic market, but until political rights are recognised, notably that of setting up independent unions, this can only take place through the enrichment of the new middle class. However important it may be, its consumption cannot found the conditions of world growth.[67] So capitalism's problems remain unresolved. But so do those of the working class and the exploited. Workers have been unable to stop capital and governments from making the brunt of the economic and financial crisis fall on labour and on the most vulnerable people in society, not only in all the countries included under the name of emerging and developing countries, but also those in the erstwhile centres of the world system.

The single most important explanation is the following. Capital's greatest achievement during the past 40 years has been the creation of a 'global labour force', through the liberalisation of finance, trade and direct investment and the incorporation of China and India into the world market. This is often referred to as the 'great doubling of the global labour pool',[68] but can more properly be described as the potential global industrial reserve army. Its existence sets the conditions for the increase in the rate of exploitation and the configuration of the industrial reserve army in each national economy. The advent of 'structural unemployment', of a situation whereby the younger generations are denied employment and of the generalisation of short or very short work contracts, calls for the reappropriation and updating of the analysis proposed by Marx of

---

67  'China's consumers: Doughty but not superhuman', *The Economist*, 24 September 2015.
68  Freeman 2008 estimates an increase in the size of the 'global labour pool' from approximately 1.46 billion to 2.93 billion workers using the much clearer expression 'effective doubling of the world's now connected workforce'

the different strata of the industrial reserve army. These strata vary considerably in different countries owing to demography, the moment and conditions of accumulation, and the relationship to the world market. Harry Braverman sought to analyse the industrial reserve army in the US in the early 1970s and to identify its three classic strata.[69] This notion needs to be used fully by Marxist research today.[70]

Capital can pit workers against one another between and also within countries. In this context, information and communication technologies have been vectors of continuous increase in the rate of exploitation. In the advanced industrialised countries, across a number of industries and sectors, permanent employment has shifted to precarious jobs through outsourcing, extended use of employment agencies to provide 'short-term' contract employees and the classification of workers as 'independent contractors' or 'self-entrepreneurs' with employees passing from a wage-earning status to one of contractual service provision.[71] Consequently, in European countries, where remnants of earlier labour legislation exist, its repeal is high on the list of the 'reforms' demanded by capital.

The immense managerial opportunities created by ICTs, in particular for large transnational corporations – ranging from global network organisation and international and domestic outsourcing, to the new methods of work surveillance in production sites or the managing of outputting in its contemporary forms – have allowed the transfer of a growing range of manufacturing industries to low-wage countries. Commodities satisfying the requisites of socially necessary labour time needed for production and marketing in the world market are produced in countries where necessary labour time (the labour time required for the reproduction of the labourer's capacity to work and eventually the reproduction of his household)[72] is kept very low. The condition of millions of workers can thus be defined as that of 'super-exploitation'.[73]

---

69   Braverman 1974, pp. 382–388.
70   Smith 2010 and 2011 begins to do this. However, his analysis of 'relative surplus population' is placed in the theoretical framework of 'a new stage of the globalisation of the capital/labour' relation in which the dualism of oppressor and oppressed nations prevails and the relocation of surplus value production and appropriation is seen as the dominant way in which capital in oppressor nations offset the fall in profits. He even talks of 'a third form of surplus value'. I return to this in Chapter 6.
71   A major reference is Huws 2014.
72   At Foxconn and other factories, the overwhelming majority of workers are single and live in dormitories.
73   See Smith 2011, who rightly argues the need to ground the analysis of global capitalism on the theory of value, but proposes a very simplistic theory of 'super-exploitation'. I return to this in Chapter 6.

This occurs in the configuration of clearly imperialist relationships (Mexico, Bangladesh), but also in the political conditions specific to countries which overthrew imperialist domination, but have been reintegrated into world capitalism, as in the case of China. China does not suffer national domination, let alone national oppression. But it places its huge labour force at the disposition of foreign and domestic firms alike in a configuration different from that of 'classical imperialism'.

The industrial reserve army available to capital domestically can be increased through immigration. Recourse to this method has taken the form of great waves, as at the end of the nineteenth century, or in the 1920s after the First World War, and of targeted demands for different types of workers at different moments by specific countries (the US and Canada; many countries in Western Europe, notably Germany).[74] In a historical context of war as in the Near East, of increasing economic inequality and of climate change, advanced countries see migration as a threat, but for capital in the countries mentioned calling on the global industrial reserve army through targeted immigration is still topical.

The political choices made in 2008 and 2009 by G20 countries laid the foundations of the very slow growth regime which set in during the 2000s, now consolidated by the fall in China's growth rate since 2015. When a rate of profit insufficient for new accumulation to take place is accompanied by the organisational forms of worker exploitation discussed below in Chapter 6, this leads necessarily to the 'forced hoarding' of profits. This is one of the sources of financial accumulation. But other important factors and institutional mechanisms must be taken into account. In the next chapter, we begin to examine financial accumulation in a historical perspective.

---

74   In Chesnais 2004, I used the theory of the industrial reserve army in relation to immigration-related issues in France.

CHAPTER 2

# Financial Liberalisation and Globalisation from the 1960s onwards and the Return of Financial Crises

The notion of financial accumulation as distinct from 'actual accumulation, i.e., the expansion of the reproduction process'[1] will be discussed along with other key notions in Chapter 3. Here we start examining its growth. It is indissociable from financial liberalisation and globalisation. Over a period of 50 years the financial markets of different parts of the world have been integrated step by step within a single highly hierarchised space which permits the deployment and constant redeployment of interest-bearing capital across national boundaries without, or with the least possible, restrictions. Today partial restrictions on financial flows are still applied with less and less success by China and there is strong pressure to lift them. This chapter takes the process of financial accumulation from its start in the mid-1960s to the point where the growth curve of financial assets accelerates in the 1990s (figures 1.4 and 1.5 above). The 1929 crash on Wall Street, the devastating banking crisis of the 1930s in its wake and the Second World War led to the large scale destruction not only of productive but also of fictitious capital. With the notable exception of Switzerland of course, finance capital *qua* finance almost disappeared from the scene in a number of countries. In others it had to take a back seat, waiting for the moment to make its comeback. Even the power of the large banks receded while US shareholders' claims on value and surplus fell significantly. Industrial managers were in the driver's seat.

As established by Helleiner, far from resisting the endogenous tendency of financial markets to integrate across frontiers, governments played a decisive role, from the mid-1960s onwards with a jump at the turn of the 1980s, in adopting measures which dismantled the controls over capital movements.[2] The re-accumulation of interest-bearing capital could not have taken place without lifting the controls and legal obstacles on financial flows established in some cases in the 1930s and in most countries in the immediate post-Second World War. But the accumulation of interest-bearing capital was of course also the outcome of very powerful economic processes and of political and institutional mechanisms. Financial markets were first fuelled with surplus value

---

1 Marx 1981, Vol. III, p. 493.
2 Helleiner 1996.

in the form of non-reinvested profits and subsequently of interest on government debt in Third and First World countries alike, while benefitting from the regular flow of workers' saving created by market-based retirement systems.

1      Industrial Profits and the Eurodollar Market in the Resurgence of Concentrated Interest-bearing Capital

A focus on financial corporations and markets carries the risk of pushing industrial capital productive of value and surplus value to the back of the stage. Yet, as will be argued throughout this book, industrial corporations provide one of the principal foundations of the power of finance capital. They were particularly at the forefront of its postwar restoration. Up until the beginning of the 1990s, they were the most active agents of the internationalisation of capital. While the liberalisation and globalisation of financial flows took place much faster than those of trade and direct investment, industrial corporations were parties to this process, at some moments importantly so. In 1945, the United States and Switzerland (Sweden can possibly be included too) were the only advanced capitalist countries to come out of the Second World War with an unscathed and indeed reinforced industrial base, albeit in very different political circumstances and with a considerable difference in the rapidity of its effects on the international economy. Once the phase of reconversion to civilian production had ended in the United States and even after the re-launching of massive military expenditure for the Korean War, US corporations were confronted with problems of insufficient domestic demand. If they were to avoid domestic oligopolistic rivalry leading to price wars, they had to turn to the world market. Trade barriers made exports difficult if not impossible. From the early 1960s onwards, foreign direct investment in Europe and Latin America imposed itself on US corporations as the solution, even if until the liberalisation and deregulation of the 1980s, this meant negotiating with European host country governments and tolerating trade unions.

Faced with regulations at home on the repatriation of profits, US MNES entrusted their corporate reserves to banks in the City. They were key parties to the re-emergence in London of an international loan market. Attention must be paid to this source of financial accumulation. Whenever capital is not reinvested in production because firms consider the rate of industrial profit as being too low or final demand insufficient to justify new investments, a part of profit is hoarded and ends up fuelling financial accumulation. London also offered special advantages to foreign banks, notably US ones. British rentier capital had been forced to make contributions to pay back debt to the US contracted under the lend-lease agreements. The City suffered the effects of controls on capital flows as well as those of the recurring crises of the pound sterling. Despite all this, London had retained a part of its previous position. The importance acquired by the City, from the second half of the nineteenth century onwards, in the areas of foreign investment and global financial intermediation transactions, was a specific trait in the configuration of British finance capital. The opportunities derived from financial globalisation were a key part of the British bourgeoisie's view of normality. Recall what Keynes wrote in 1920:

> The inhabitant of London could order by telephone, sipping his morning tea in bed, the various products of the whole earth, in such quantity as he may see fit, and reasonably expect their early delivery upon his doorstep; he could at the same moment and by the same means adventure his wealth in the natural resources and new enterprises of any quarter of the world, and share, without exertion or even trouble in their prospective fruits and advantages; or he could ... proceed abroad to foreign quarters, without knowledge of their religion, language, or customs, bearing coined wealth upon his person, and would consider himself greatly aggrieved and much surprised at the least interference. But, most important of all, he regarded this state of affairs as normal, certain, and permanent, except in the direction of further improvement, and any deviation from it as aberrant, scandalous, and avoidable.[3]

Among the financial institutions that London had successfully preserved was the private gold market, which will be mentioned again below when discussing the demise of the Bretton Woods agreement. The City's accumulated financial expertise also explains why it was in London that the first phases in the re-accumulation of money capital took place, first between 1965 and 1973, and then on a massive scale from 1976 onwards. US domestic policy contributed to this. As will be discussed again in Chapter 7, for several decades after 1945, US banks faced numerous restrictions on their activities. These included limits on inter-state banking by bank corporations and the Glass-Steagall legislation dating from 1933, limiting affiliations between commercial banks and investment banks. Of special importance for the re-emergence of the City was Regulation Q, which remained in force until the 1980s.[4] It prohibited US banks

---

3 Keynes 1920, pp. 11–12.
4 The Interest Equalisation Tax of July 1963 was another measure restricting US financial markets. It aimed to discourage foreign issuance of dollar bonds in the US, and so to reduce long-term capital outflows.

from paying interest on demand deposits and also restricted the interest rates banks paid on other types of account. One of its effects was that of encouraging US funds held by banks to invest them in foreign locations offering higher rates and guaranteeing total mobility. With the help of 'benign neglect' on the part of the Labour government, the City set up in its precincts the Eurodollar market with offshore status and exemption from prevailing capital controls.[5] While their abolition only came with the Thatcher government, 'constitutionally so to speak, the market enjoyed the distinction of being free from restrictions and regulations from the very outset'.[6] American commercial and investment banks quickly held a large part of the market, which made loans to governments and large firms.[7] The participating banks were not subject to reserve obligations and were free to offer deposits at very short maturity. Consequently, they had lower costs to bear than national banks and therefore were able to offer higher rates on deposits. The unregulated 'offshore' status of the Euromarket made the City the principal force behind an increasingly global offshore economy starting with the Anglo-Norman isles, remnants of the British Empire in the Caribbean, then expanding with Singapore, the islands in the South Pacific, Bahrain and Dubai. Not only did the City play a central role in putting finance back in the saddle, but it helped to place an organised network of tax havens out of reach of regulation and taxation. Today London still holds the first position in international banking, giving loans to and taking deposits from outside a given national territory, and in foreign exchange trading in major currencies.[8]

## 2   The End of the Bretton Woods Monetary System and the Advent of Floating Exchange Rates

As financial accumulation took off, international financial crises reappeared. Their first form was that of foreign currency crises. The linchpin of the Bretton Woods system of fixed exchange rates was the US dollar's fixed value against gold, implying its capacity to meet demands by foreigners to exchange dollar

---

5   The Eurodollar market was initially created to accommodate Russian rubles and facilitate the financing of USSR foreign trade, but it quickly became a haven for any capital seeking to evade home country regulations.
6   Amato and Fantacci 2012, p. 102.
7   This leads Panitch and Gindin to argue along the lines of Gowan 1999 that the City 'switch[ed] its allegiance from the sterling to the dollar and [became] the Eurodollar satellite of Wall Street' (2012, p. 12). For a critique with which I concur see Norfield 2016.
8   Norfield 2016.

reserves for gold. From the early 1960s onwards, misgivings about this developed. The constant increase in military spending caused by the Vietnam War, coupled with the growth in government spending of Lyndon Johnson's 'Great Society' programmes strengthened the assessment that the dollar was overvalued *vis-à-vis* gold. The attacks against the dollar first took the form of trading in gold on the London gold market at prices well above those fixed at Bretton Woods, and were met by the setting up of the Gold Pool by eight central banks. This heralded many subsequent moments of crisis cooperation between central banks and was a first step in the creation 'of a conducive regulatory environment for the progressive liberalization of capital movements'.[9] However, the setting up of the Gold Pool did not have much weight in the face of continuing appreciation of the dollar against gold. The pace of withdrawals from the Fort Knox vaults accelerated. Over the same period other countries had episodes of foreign exchange crisis. The most notable were the pound sterling crises from 1964 to 1967 provoked by the UK's balance of payment deficit, not only that of trade deficit but that of the capital account.[10] Repeated speculative attacks culminated in the devaluation of 1967.[11] Since the pound sterling was the second most important international reserve currency,[12] this strongly increased the pressure on the dollar and contributed to Nixon's announcement in August 1971 that the US had decided to put an end to the Bretton Woods agreement on its own.[13] Financing of the Vietnam War was not the only reason for ending convertibility. The rapidly dwindling US trade surpluses – which were subject to the closing of the 'technology gap' and successful competition by Japan and Germany[14] – sooner or later would have made this necessary

---

9   Panitch and Gindin 2012, p. 123, quoting Andrews 2008.
10  'In the end, it was short-term capital outflow, not the trade performance, which had provoked the 1967 sterling crisis' (Newton 2010).
11  Bordo et al. 2009.
12  Schenk 2009 writes: 'in the 1950s the sterling area [35 countries and colonies pegged to sterling and holding primarily sterling reserves] accounted for half of world trade and sterling accounted for over half of world foreign exchange reserves. In the early postwar years, this share was even higher – the IMF estimated that official sterling reserves, excluding those held by colonies, were four times the value of official USD reserves and that by 1947 sterling accounted for about 87% of global foreign exchange reserves. It took ten years (1954) after the end of the war (and a 30% devaluation of the pound) before the share of USD reserves exceeded that of sterling'.
13  Panitch and Gindin 2012, pp. 129–131, give a detailed account both of Paul Volker's role and of the hesitation of the Nixon Administration in taking its decision.
14  Brenner 2002.

anyway with the build-up of trade surpluses and large dollar reserves.[15] Working-class and student militancy during the Johnson Administration, with the 1968 French general strike a landmark in Europe, spelt the end of the viability of Fordist accumulation for capital. A new phase was gestating: 'something much larger than the old compulsion to find markets for its products was chasing the bourgeoisie around the globe, and that was the imperative to restore profitability through a global restructuring of production and labor relations'.[16]

The status of the dollar as world money after the demise of the Bretton Woods arrangements is discussed below in Section 2.5. Here the focus is on the huge scope and new conditions for the valorisation of idle money capital. In the process of strengthening financial investors, the collapse of the Bretton Woods system was a milestone. McNally calls it 'the day world finance changed for ever'.[17] The onset of floating exchange rates from 1973 onwards and the emergence of an ever more important foreign exchange market (Forex) were a boon for banks. They permitted the day-to-day collection of financial profits through commissions for transactions on firms and households, interest on loans through interest arbitrage (buying currencies to exploit interest rate differences) and in the case of massive speculative attacks on a given currency, the appropriation of surplus value in the form of Treasury holdings and central bank reserves. The British government's Black Wednesday of September 1992, where successful speculation by George Soros first brought investment funds into the limelight, is a well-documented instance of this.[18] Alongside bonds and equity (e.g. shares or stock), currencies became a major form of asset in the portfolios of banks and funds. Countries that attempted, as in South-East Asia, to keep dollar-pegged rates after liberalising capital flows were the targets of concerted attacks in 1997–8. In OECD countries, speculation against national currencies gave financial investors a way of exercising pressure on governments' economic and social policies before public debt gave them as creditors a still more powerful lever to shape public policies. Floating exchange

---

15 Garber 1993 notes: 'reflecting the growing pressure on the system, the Deutsche Mark was revalued in 1969 in response to selling attacks on the Deutsche Mark and floated in May 1971 prior to the closing of the US gold window'. He adds: 'tangentially, internal political difficulties in France in 1968 caused the devaluation of the Franc'.

16 Ivanova 2013, p. 59.

17 McNally 2011, p. 88. Today this key event is often forgotten and its consequences overlooked. Its importance is also emphasised by Gill 2011.

18 Black Wednesday refers to 16 September 1992, when the British government was forced to withdraw the pound from the European Exchange Rate Mechanism (ERM) after it had failed to keep it above its negotiated lower limit. George Soros is said to have made over £1 billion profit by short-selling sterling.

rates also created the obligation for multinational enterprises to protect their operations by hedging on currency risk. This strengthened the position of financial departments in MNEs and accelerated the growth of the first major form of derivatives, namely currency forwards, options and swaps.

In 1975, about 80% of foreign exchange transactions were related to the real economy and 20% to financial speculation. By the beginning of the 1990s, the first category had fallen to about 3% and the second had risen to 97%. Even the inclusion of hedging by TNCs as an obligatory trade and investment-related practice, only added 20% to the economy-related total.[19] Until the very recent period, which will be discussed later, the main operators were large banks with offices in all countries of any importance and in particular in the UK, the US and Japan. They set up large specialised clearing houses, notably the City-based London Cleared House, the Paris-based Euroclear (they were to merge in 2003), and the Clearing House Interbank Payment System (CHIPS) in the US. Foreign exchange markets grew exponentially. During the period discussed in this chapter, the daily volume of trading (US$ billion at current prices) rose from $15 billion in 1982 to $207 billion in 1986, $620 billion in 1989, and $880 billion in 1992.

Several factors drove this growth. The first was the mechanical, cumulative effect of financial accumulation, through their continuous reinvestment in financial markets, notably the foreign exchange market. The second was technological, notably the 'electronification' of money and the computerisation of market systems. These lowered transaction costs dramatically. Placing a few billion dollars in foreign exchange started to cost very little, 20 or more times cheaper than a stock transaction, and foreign exchange also became home to truly 'twenty-four-hour markets'. A further important point is that the foreign currency market was for a long time the largest and deepest market of all. As explained in a study prepared for the International Forum on Globalisation:

> If you have a few billion dollars to place bringing them to the stock market is going to move the stock's value and tip off other traders as to what you are doing. This is also true in most bond markets (except for the US and some European markets because of their large size). In foreign exchange, even $5 or $10 billion won't make a blip. So if you have a substantial amount of money to move around, this is the place to do it. You can get in and out without affecting the market.[20]

---

19  Lietaer 1997.
20  Lietaer 1997.

## 3　The Recycling of Petrodollars and the Third World Debt Trap

The re-accumulation of a concentrated mass of interest-bearing money or loan capital would have been a long process and taken a long time without the intervention of public debt.[21] Rosa Luxemburg's chapter on international loans is the first major study of debt both as a value and surplus transfer mechanism, and a key means of political domination between imperialist and semi-colonial countries.[22] Her chapter is focused on loans to 'young capitalist countries'. They allow 'old' ones to capitalise realised value and export capital goods, while also giving those countries scope for economic and political domination. A part of loans is spent in arms, but for most of the young countries Luxemburg refers to the loans that were used in investments that directly or indirectly produced value and surplus value (railroads and harbours). Such investment, she argues, can heighten contradictions between new and old capitalist countries which belong to the 'imperialist era'.

> BOX 2.1: INTERNATIONAL LOANS IN ROSA LUXEMBURG'S
> *THE ACCUMULATION OF CAPITAL*
>
> Public loans for railroad building and armaments accompany all stages of the accumulation of capital: the introduction of commodity production, the industrialisation of capitalism's hinterland, the capitalist transformation of agriculture as well as the emancipation of young capitalist states. The international loan fulfils various functions: (a) it serves to convert the money of non-capitalist groups into capital … (b) it serves to transform money capital into productive capital by means of state enterprise railroad building and military supplies; (c) it serves to transfer accumulated capital from the old capitalist countries to young ones.
>
> The contradictions of the imperialist era are clearly expressed by the contradictions in the modern system of foreign loans. These loans are essential for the emancipation of young rising capitalist states and at the same time they are the surest way for the old capitalist states to maintain their influence, exercise financial

---

21　In his very broad survey, Lapavitsas 2011 makes little mention of public debt, but more so in his 2012 book.

22　For a long time this contribution was not fully recognised not only because of Luxemburg's economic theory which defines under-consumption as capitalism's key contradiction, but also because of her particular position in major debates in the Second International and above all because of her warnings about the possible course of the October Revolution.

control and exert pressure on the foreign, tariff and commercial policies of the young states. They represent the most efficient way of opening new spheres of investment for capital accumulated in the old countries but at the same time of creating new competition, of widening the field of operation for capitalist accumulation of capital while narrowing it at the same time.

These inherent conflicts of the international loan system are a classic example of spatio-temporal divergences between the conditions for the realisation of surplus value and the capitalisation thereof. While realisation of the surplus value requires only the general spreading of commodity production, its capitalisation demands the progressive supersession of simple commodity production by capitalist economy, with the corollary that the limits to both the realisation and the capitalisation of surplus value keep contracting ever more.

Realised surplus value, which cannot be capitalised and lies idle in England or Germany, is invested in railway construction, waterworks, etc. in the Argentine, Australia, the Cape Colony or Mesopotamia. Machinery, materials and the like are supplied by the country where the capital has originated, and the same capital pays for them.

At first sight the financial operations (which accompany the process in Egypt) seem to reach the height of madness. One loan followed hard on the other, the interests on old loans were paid by new loans, and capital borrowed from the British and French was used to pay for the large orders placed with British and French industrial capital. While the whole of Europe sighed and shrugged its shoulders at Ismail's crazy management, European capital was making profits in Egypt on an unprecedented scale – an incredible modern version of the biblical parable about the fat cattle which remains unparalleled in capitalist history. And each loan was an opportunity for a usurious operation, anything between one-fifth and one-third of the money ostensibly lent sticking to the fingers of the European bankers. Ultimately, the exorbitant interest had to be paid somehow, but how – where were the means to come from? Egypt itself was to supply them; their source was the Egyptian fellah.[23]

---

If chapter 30 of *The Accumulation of Capital* is read, as proposed by Harvey, from the standpoint of situations where capital over-accumulation exists both in the form of 'realised value' looking for investments and in the form of industrial capacity in the capital goods sector, then her presentation of the functions

---

23   Luxemburg 1913.

of international loans comes close to the ones performed by petrodollar recycling following the 1974–6 world recession.[24]

From 1974 onwards, vast quantities of money derived from rising oil prices started to swell the mass of capital flowing to the City. 'Petrodollar recycling', as the operations valorising the proceeds of oil rent as interest-bearing loan capital came to be called, was carried out from London. In 1970, the total long-term international debt of developing countries stood at approximately $45 billion or about seven percent of these countries' aggregate GDP. By 1987, it was close to $900 billion, corresponding to 30 percent of their aggregate GDP. The trap was set in two steps and cannot be dissociated from the semi-colonial relationship between core and periphery countries in the configuration of imperialism up to the turn of the 2000s. A major response by the Atlantic rim economies to the 1974–6 crisis was the recycling of petrodollars engineered in the City in the form of syndicated loans by consortiums of large banks. These included US banks still hampered by provisions of the 1933 Banking Act, but US banks also made some direct loans to Mexico in particular. The beneficiaries of the loans were politically and economically subordinate semi-colonial Third World countries and in some cases dictatorial political regimes. This was the origin of the revival of the notion of 'odious debt'.[25] The debt of developing countries multiplied by 12 between 1968 and 1980. It was spent on imports on arms in many countries and everywhere on investment in infrastructure largely benefitting foreign firms. Along with imports tied to bilateral aid and to inward foreign investment by TNCs, these imports helped industrialised countries to offset much of the effect of the recession. Private bank loans increasingly took the place of those organised through the Bretton Woods international financial institutions.[26] In the early 1970s, most international government debt was owed to bilateral or multilateral official creditors. In 1987, more than 50 percent of total long-term international government debt was owed to private creditors (mostly international banks) and about 25 percent of the total to multilateral institutions. Most importantly, syndicate loans were made not at fixed rates but at indexed international short-term interest rates.

---

24 'Few would now accept Luxemburg's theory of under-consumption as the explanation of crises. By contrast, the theory of over-accumulation identifies the lack of opportunities for profitable investment as the fundamental problem ... The gap that Luxemburg thought she saw can easily be covered by reinvestment which generates its own demand for capital goods and other inputs' (Harvey 2003, p. 139).

25 Besides articles posted on the CADTM website, see Howse 2007.

26 This 'privatisation' of North-South lending, as it was called at the time, has to be relativised given that the World Bank finances itself privately. The loans it makes come from issuing bonds or borrowing from banks.

The spectacular rise in US interest rates induced by the measures chosen by Volcker in 1979 to break the back of inflation and set one of the conditions for the flow of capital to the US from all over the world, immediately sharply increased the weight of interest shouldered by debtor countries. The event has been likened to a coup.[27] From being around 4–5 percent in the 1970s, real interest rates jumped to 16–18 percent if not higher on account of rises in risk premium that the debt crisis developed. At the same time, export receipts of developing countries suffered as commodity prices (including oil) began to fall, reversing the rise of the seventies and making debt servicing even more difficult. The start of the Third World crisis, as it came to be named, took place in August 1982, when the Mexican government suddenly found itself unable to roll over its debt given the high level to which interest rates had risen. Mexico changed almost one day to the next from the status of a net borrower to a debtor incapable of meeting its commitments. All Latin American and Caribbean countries underwent the same experience to varying degrees.[28] The debt trap closed on them.[29] It entailed much more than massive financial flows to US and European financial centres. The rescheduling of debt was subject to the enacting of 'structural adjustment' measures under the economic supervision of the IMF and the World Bank. These measures included fiscal austerity, dismantling of government aid, privatisation of state enterprises, market-fixed exchange rates and also, ahead of the end of the GATT Uruguay Round negotiations, import and direct investment liberalisation. They served as 'benchmarks' for developing countries more broadly and were codified afterwards by an academic advisor and observer under the term 'Washington consensus'.[30] With the start of the 2010 financial crisis of the Eurozone, advanced capitalist countries began to experience debtor-lender relationships akin to those of Latin American countries in the 1980s and 1990s, along with a type of supervision (the Troika) analogous to the one they were submitted to. But with a very important difference: they have (spectacularly in the case of Greece) been denied rescheduling, namely the necessary breathing space for true reforms and new investment to take place. The reason is the following. In 1982, the US could not afford to have neighbouring economies with insurmountable financial and social problems. Today, Germany considers that the economic health of Greece is of little if no importance for itself.

27  See inter alia, Duménil and Lévy 2004.
28  See Chesnais and Baronian 2014 for the case of Chile under the Pinochet dictatorship.
29  The expression was actually first used in the early 1970s by Cheryl Payer to characterise IMF loans which later seemed puny in the wake of the 1980 events. See Payer 1974.
30  Williamson 1989.

In the case of Mexico, creditor banks and their governments met in the so-called Club of Paris and started organising an orderly rescheduling of debt before the US came up with the Brady Plan (see Appendix 1 below), namely a mechanism for the trading of Third World country bonds on a specialised international financial market as well as the exchange of financial assets for real productive ones. Between 1982 and 2001, they paid $612 billion US dollars in interest payments to creditors (banks and international financial organisations). Their total debt almost tripled during the same period, rising from $202 to $660 billion US dollars. Net South-North transfers reached $236 billion US dollars.[31] The spectacular reversal of international capital flows from North-South to South-North was worsened by the flight of domestic money capital to New York and London, made possible by the liberalisation of financial flows. It is worth noting that in the stage of financialisation of the 1980s in which tax havens were still at an early stage of development, reasonably precise figures could still be put on capital flight. This has now become impossible.

TABLE 2.1    *Capital flight from developing countries (in billions of 1987 $US)*

|  | Flight Capital Assets | % of Long-Term Public and Publicly Guaranteed Debt |
|---|---|---|
| Argentina | 46 | 111 |
| Bolivia | 2 | 178 |
| Brazil | 31 | 46 |
| Chile | 2 | 17 |
| Colombia | 7 | 103 |
| Ecuador | 7 | 115 |
| Mexico | 84 | 114 |
| Morocco | 3 | 54 |
| Nigeria | 20 | 136 |
| Peru | 2 | 27 |
| Philippines | 23 | 188 |
| Uruguay | 4 | 159 |
| Venezuela | 58 | 240 |
| Yugoslavia | 6 | 79 |
| **Total** | **295** | **103** |

SOURCE: *JOURNAL OF ECONOMIC PERSPECTIVES*, 4, NO. 1 (WINTER 1990).

---

31    Hanlon 2006.

## 4    The Growth of Government Debt at the Heart of the System

The very sharp rise in US interest rates not only triggered the 1982 Mexican crisis and accompanying bank crises in the US itself; the high level of interest rates over several years also led to a qualitative jump in the speed of financial accumulation in the form of the servicing of government debt countries at the heart of the world economy. The high real interest financial regime of the 1980s permitted the financing of non-inflationary military spending, notably the 'Star Wars' programme by the Reagan Administration, which was also the first administration to make important tax cuts for high income tranches.

Table 2.2 shows the respective increase in US Federal and developing country debt and the strong shift in the ration between the two. From the early 1980s onwards, money capital seeking to invest in safe and initially highly remunerated government loans flowed into Wall Street from around the world. However, initially the principal beneficiaries of the transfer of value and surplus value channelled through the Federal budget were US institutional investors, headed initially by pension funds and insurance companies. External dependence for the financing of US Federal deficits came much later. In the 1980s, 17 percent of US debt was held by foreign investors and between 1990 and 1994 the figure was 20 percent. It is only from 1995 onwards that foreign holdings of T-Bonds become important.[32] Potential money capital had been accumulated by pension funds since the 1950s. The surge in US government debt offered them a safe and initially very lucrative form of financial investment. The financial firepower controlled by financial investors and financial markets in the form of pension funds increased qualitatively along with that of mutual funds (hedge funds were not yet identified as a separated category).

## 5    The Political Implications of Market-based Retirement Schemes

A word must be said at this point concerning the trap that financial market-based retirement schemes represent for workers.[33] Since they centralise pension contributions along with a particular type of 'employee savings', there is a certain reticence in describing pension funds as financial corporations bent

---

[32]    US Office of Management and Budget, *Analytical Perspectives, Budget of the United States Government, Fiscal Year 1999*, Table 13–16, p. 255. http://www.ny.frb.org/research/current_issues/ci4-5.pdf.

[33]    Denunciation of the pension trap ('le piège des fonds de pension') is, of course, easier when one comes from a country where pay-as-you-go retirement benefits still prevail. See Chesnais 1988, and London 2000.

TABLE 2.2  *United federal and developing countries debt 1982–95 (millions $US)*

| Year | US Federal Debt | Increase (100=1982) | DC Debt | Increase (100=1982) | DC/US Debt Ratio |
|---|---|---|---|---|---|
| 1982 | $1,142 | 100 | $ 481 | 100 | 42,1 |
| 1983 | $1,377 | 121 | $ 560 | 116 | 40,7 |
| 1984 | $1,572 | 138 | $ 595 | 124 | 37,8 |
| 1985 | $1,823 | 160 | $ 661 | 137 | 36,3 |
| 1986 | $2,125 | 186 | $ 756 | 157 | 35,6 |
| 1987 | $2,350 | 206 | $ 870 | 181 | 37,0 |
| 1988 | $2,602 | 228 | $ 873 | 181 | 33,6 |
| 1989 | $2,857 | 250 | $ 911 | 189 | 31,9 |
| 1990 | $3,233 | 283 | $ 962 | 200 | 29,8 |
| 1991 | $3,665 | 321 | $1001 | 208 | 27,3 |
| 1992 | $4,064 | 356 | $1030 | 214 | 25,3 |
| 1993 | $4,411 | 386 | $1102 | 229 | 25,0 |
| 1994 | $4,692 | 411 | $1238 | 257 | 26,4 |
| 1995 | $4,973 | 435 | $1334 | 277 | 26,8 |

SOURCE: AUTHOR FROM UNCTAD AND US BUREAU OF ECONOMIC ANALYSIS.

on appropriating surplus value as dividend and interest and hence dependent on direct and indirect worker exploitation. The fact that this serves to pay for pensions does not change this reality. Pension funds make workers dependent on financial markets. They have been important agents in financialisation. Due to the 'alchemy' proper to financial centralisation, the savings accumulated in administrators' hands transform into capital and give rise to the relationship described and decried by Marx as being no solution to the problems of the working class:

> The savings bank is the golden chain by which the government holds a large part of the working class. By it they not only acquire an interest in the preservation of the existing conditions. Not only does it lead to a split between that portion of the working class which takes part in the savings banks and the portion which does not. The workers themselves thus give into the hands of their enemies the weapons to preserve the existing organisation of society which subjugates them. The money flows back into the national bank, this lends it again to the capitalists and both share in the profits and thus, with the money borrowed from the people at a

miserable rate of interest – which only by this centralisation becomes a mighty industrial lever – increase their capital, their direct ruling power over the people.[34]

Many OECD countries other than the US also had market-based retirement schemes and needed to invest in bond markets. All had accumulated savings and growing income and wealth disparities. All were to follow the US on the path to financial liberalisation and deregulation and to budgetary financing through borrowing. Even in countries with pay-as-you-go retirement schemes, the idea took root that rather than tax the wealthy, one should borrow from them. It became the cornerstone of fiscal policy, and the ratio of public debt to GDP was increasingly shaped by the lowering of tax on profits, financial income and wealth.[35]

## 6     World Money Since the Demise of Bretton Woods

In Marx, money is discussed extensively in Chapter Three of Volume I of *Capital*. It is seen as having three main roles to play: as a measure of value, as a means of circulation, and as money proper ('money as money'), which, in turn, performs three distinct functions: as an instrument of hoarding, as a means of payment, and as world money.[36] 'World money' (Marx acknowledges Sir James Steuart's prior use of the term in a similar sense)[37] 'serves as the universal medium of payment, as the universal means of purchasing and as the universally recognised embodiment of all wealth'. He immediately adds that world money's 'predominant function is a means of payment in the settlement of international balances'.[38] Marx's theory of money is grounded in the theory of value. It is 'because all commodities, as values, are objectified human labour, and therefore in themselves commensurable [that] their values can be communally measured by one and the same specific commodity, and this

---

34   Marx at www.marxists.org/archive/marx/works/1847/12/31.htm.
35   This is well documented with respect to the French case. See Chesnais 2011.
36   The path-breaking presentation is that of de Brunhoff 1977. For shorter, clear presentations, see Vasudevan 2008 and Ivanova 2013.
37   In his 2013 Deutscher prize lecture, David McNally 2014 presented evidence that the theory had been hashed out at the end of the seventeenth century by the English bourgeoisie, with Locke as one of the protagonists. It was seen to be a *sine qua non* requirement of the acceptance of sterling coins in international trade.
38   Marx 1976, Vol. I, p. 242.

commodity be converted into the common measure of their values, that is into money'.[39] Two commodities asserted themselves historically as money in the face of all other commodities, namely silver and gold, which quickly prevailed in most of the countries participating in the incipient world market in the form of gold coins and bullion in the vaults of central banks.

In reality, as historians have shown, money as 'world money' on a system-wide scale only functioned in the brief period of the late 1890s during which capitalism expanded without too strong an inter-capitalist rivalry, making the settlement of international balances by bullion generally possible.[40] The classical gold standard prevailed in the industrialised economies and functioned reasonably smoothly, without any major convertibility crisis in the period from 1880 to 1914. The rule of the gold standard was to maintain the value of national currency in terms of a fixed weight of gold (known in some countries as the mint price). During a period of over 30 years, very few countries suspended convertibility. World War I brought this to a sharp end. In financing the war and abandoning gold, many of the belligerents suffered drastic inflations. Price levels doubled in Britain, tripled in France and quadrupled in Italy, forcing them and other countries to suspend or abandon convertibility. In Britain, at the outbreak of the war, treasury notes replaced the circulation of gold sovereigns and half sovereigns. Legally, the gold specie standard was not repealed. The Bank of England appealed to patriotism and urged people not to redeem bank notes for gold specie. The restoration of the gold standard was brief and hinged in particular on Britain's capacity to sustain it. It was only in 1925 that Britain returned to the gold standard, along with Australia and South Africa, creating through the 1925 Gold Standard Act a gold bullion standard which was to be swept away only six years later as the 1929 world crisis worsened.[41] In May 1931, runs on commercial banks shook Austria and then Germany. In July, Germany adopted exchange controls, followed by Austria in October. Speculative attacks on the pound started and the Bank of England lost much of its reserves. In September 1931, Britain was forced to abandon the gold standard. The gold standard has been blamed for worsening the Great Depression. Keynes argued against the return to the gold standard in 1920 and

---

39　Marx 1976, Vol. I, p. 188.
40　Labrinidis 2014a studies the historical process where gold is saved in domestic circulation and freed to perform as world money as bullion. Vasudevan 2009 discusses the contemporary situation where 'world money' rests on the currency of a dominant state in the form of credit money (fictitious capital) rather than bullion, thus easing the external constraint on its domestic monetary discipline.
41　This short-lived episode is documented in Norfield 2016.

again in 1925 in a famous pamphlet against Churchill.[42] Historians have argued that adherence to the gold standard by the US prevented the Federal Reserve from expanding the money supply to stimulate the economy, save insolvent banks and finance government deficits.[43] This ended with Roosevelt's 1933 Emergency Banking Act. As for the gold standard itself under the system adopted by the Gold Reserve Act of 1934, the United States continued to define the dollar in terms of gold. Domestically the dollar no longer represented a given quantity of gold. But bullion continued to be used for settlements with other countries' central banks.[44] This made the US unique and helped them impose the system devised at Bretton Woods.

Until 1971, countries with foreign trade surpluses and dollar holdings could redeem them into gold. Thanks to this link with gold, however tenuous, the dollar could be defined as 'quasi-world-money' until 1971. The question since is whether the term is still applicable.[45] On account of the overwhelming world position the dollar held, and continues to hold, as a means of payment, of purchasing and as reserve currency, it has retained this function. But the degenerated conditions in which it continues to play this role are now an important facet of the problems facing world capitalism. De Brunhoff argues that the dollar is simply a 'stand-in' for world money. It has 'benchmark status [which] requires a common assent from countries that compete with the USA. Since the end of the Second World War, this assent has had different aspects'.[46] Bretton Woods was already the result of a 'common assent' obtained despite Keynes's misgivings. After its demise there was a period, now forgotten by all apart from historians, when the US had to negotiate with other countries the Plaza (1985) and Louvre (1987) agreements so as to stabilise the dollar exchange rate, in particular *vis-à-vis* the yen, first upward and then downward. After that, without the need for formal meetings of heads of governments, the main central banks went on intervening from time to time. With financial liberalisation, the dollar regained a position both as the principal means of international payment and principal reserve currency of non-American central banks.[47] All the more so since in 1990–1 Japan was hit by a financial crisis so hard that the yen exchange rate ceased to cause the dollar a problem.

---

42    Keynes 1925.
43    Eichengreen 1995.
44    See Elwell 2013 for a history of US legislation on gold.
45    Lapavitsas 2013 and Labrinidis 2014b keep the term, as does Vasudevan 2009 (though with quotation marks).
46    De Brunhoff 2004.
47    Mid-2014, the dollar accounted for circa 62 percent of world currency reserves, the euro 23 percent, the sterling and the yen 4 percent each, and the Swiss franc circa 1 percent.

US financial markets became the indisputable world leaders in terms of depth and the liquidity this provides, thus qualitatively increasing the hoarding attributes of the dollar. US stock and bonds became the main haven of private wealth owners as well as a safe investment for trade surplus countries' central banks, praised by all on account of the returns offered to hoarded money. But the debate opened up again in 2003 during the dollar's transitory relative weakness against the euro and crops up periodically on account of the size of the US's trade deficit and external debt, with the need for financing by permanent foreign capital inflows. Recriminations over China's dollar-pegged exchange rate and the additional advantage this gave Chinese exports have been a subject of frequent complaint. In becoming 'consumer of last resort', the US's 'privilege of seigniorage'[48] has lost its lustre. An undoubted form of dependence on foreign capital inflows appeared with the renewed growth of the Federal deficit in the 2000s.

Nonetheless assent remains. The relation is one of interdependence and convenience. The international regime is not one 'of forced monetary circulation but of voluntary circulation in which all countries in their different ways are willing participants'.[49] Today, as the US debt has soared, there are periodic mutterings of threats to find a substitute to it as central bank reserve money. The euro was seen at one time as being able to play the stable role that the pound sterling had played transitorily during the postwar period. The recurrent crisis in the Eurozone makes this unlikely, at least for a long time. There have been very tentative steps towards some kind of East Asian monetary zone. Eichengreen has strongly challenged the idea 'of a cohesive bloc of countries called the periphery ready and able to act in their collective interest',[50] arguing that the Asian countries 'are unlikely to be able to subordinate their individual interest to the collective interest'. In fact, as long as China and export-oriented countries rely heavily on the US domestic market, they have, as Ivanova puts it, 'no choice but to play along. The mountains of US government debt accumulated by them are largely irredeemable, as they cannot be disposed of without triggering a global calamity'.[51] What is more, 'maintaining even the illusory value of their holdings compels these countries to support the value of the dollar with further purchases of US Treasury securities'. More than the dollar itself, these 'serve not only as a universal means of payment and reserve asset, but also as the key source of ultimate liquidity'. It is these securities that come

---

48   The most frequent use of this term has been in Guttmann 1994.
49   Amato and Fantacci 2012, p. 91.
50   Eichengreen 2005.
51   Ivanova 2013, p. 68.

the nearest to being what Marx named 'hard cash',[52] the assets to which capitalists from all over the world revert at moments of acute global financial crisis in what is known as 'flight to quality'. Thus in March 2016 BIS observes that 'In the midst of a global risk asset sell-off, a general flight to safety strengthened the US dollar'.[53]

## 7  The 'Semi-completion' of Financial Globalisation and the Financial Crises of the 1990s

In 1994, the McKinsey Global Institute published the first of its long series of reports on the global capital market. It mapped the strong changes in the relative weight of different categories of financial assets that had occurred in the space of just ten years as 'First World' government debt had grown from 18 to 25 percent of the total.

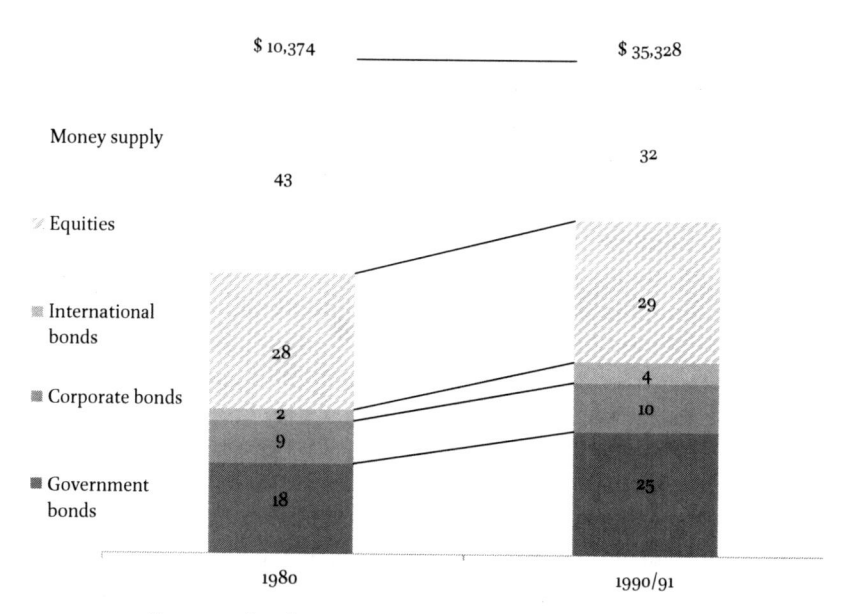

FIGURE 2.1  *Changes in the relative weight of global financial assets 1980–90/91 (US$ Billions).*
SOURCE: MCKINSEY GLOBAL INSTITUTE 1994.

---

52  'This sudden reversion from a system of credit to a system of hard cash heaps theoretical fright on the top of the practical panic; and the dealers by whose agency circulation is affected shudder before the impenetrable mystery in which their own economical relations are involved' (Marx 1904, p. 198).
53  BIS Quarterly Review March 2016, Chapter 1.

The McKinsey Global Institute considered that the process of formation of the global capital market was 'only half complete'.[54] In the wake of the formation of a liberalised foreign exchange market, the trading of short-term money across borders had taken off. At that time, bond markets, in particular domestic government bonds, had become internationalised. But equity markets had only just started to do so. Concerning banks, the development of securitisation was predicted to 'create instruments which could be traded and linked directly to the global capital market'.[55] This would lead to a surge in the foreign investment of bank deposits and link advanced capitalist countries' financial markets ever more closely. However, a significant part of the advance in financial globalisation would come from the integration of developing countries in Latin America and Asia. This indeed occurred but brought with it severe financial crises. As part of the 'Washington consensus', the financial systems of these countries were liberalised, e.g. opened up to foreign investments, and deregulated.

This saw the unwelcomed start of a new phase marked by the return of a type of financial crisis not known since the 1930s, with the triggering of mechanisms of international contagion both through finance and trade.[56] In 1982, Mexico was threatened by default on its sovereign debt. What came to be quickly known as the 'Mexican crisis' hit a number of countries on account of the common impact of the sharp rise in US interest rates,[57] but international contagion through production and trade remained small. This was not the case for the second Mexican crisis of 1994–5 and still less for the Asian crisis that followed. Their setting was that of global financial liberalisation.[58] In varying combinations, financial flows to these countries included portfolio investment in the form of different types of loans[59] to local private banks and firms as well as to governments (Mexico). In some countries, external financing led to housing and infrastructure bubbles (e.g. Thailand) and in others to industrial overaccumulation and overproduction (Korea in particular,[60] but also Taiwan). The sudden massive withdrawal of short-term speculative capital was preceded in some countries by the devaluation of pegged currencies. Contagion through

---

54  McKinsey Global Institute 1994.
55  Ibid.
56  See Chesnais 2000 for a preliminary discussion.
57  I have discussed the case of Chile (see Chesnais and Baronian 2014).
58  See Arestis and Glickman 1999 for a clear overview of financial liberalisation and its consequences in the region.
59  See Kregel 1998.
60  Hart-Landsberg Martin et al. 2007. See also Chang, Park and Yoo 1998.

trade affected all South East Asian countries, but Brazil and Argentina[61] also suffered the impact of the Asian crisis through a fall in trade. In October 1997, there was also a spectacular short episode of stock market crisis, a prefiguration of what was to occur in September 2008. It spread from Hong Kong to Wall Street, the fall being then relayed to Europe. Finally, in 1998, the Russian financial crisis provoked a new form of international crisis transmission requiring the rescue by Wall Street banks, under the auspices of the Fed, of the first large speculative fund to make the headlines, Long Term Capital Management. The seeds of the 2008 crisis and the global recession which followed had begun to be sowed and its scenario partly written.

Armed with an understanding of these historical elements of the initial phases in financial globalisation and the accumulation and centralisation of interest-bearing capital to the main financial centres that it drove, we can now turn to the theoretical presentation of the notion.

## Appendix: The 'Club of Paris' and Brady Bonds

Faced with the threat of international contagion following the Mexican default, the bank consortia, which had made the 1970 syndicate loans, enjoyed the full support of their home governments.[62] These had a strong interest both in the recovery of debtor countries and in the health of creditor banks and spared them the task of having to negotiate the rescheduling or partial cancellation of debt with debtor governments. In the case of Mexico, this was done for US banks by the Treasury and the Fed. But more generally, the interests of creditor financial institutions were taken care of by a regular committee of high-level Treasury officials meeting on a monthly basis in Paris. A well-documented UNCTAD study defines the Paris Club as a 'cartel of creditor countries' operating under an agreed set of principles: case-by-case treatment of debtor countries; consensus decision-making; conditionality in the form of the adoption by each debtor country of an economic adjustment programme; solidarity among members of the Club through the implementation of the 'Agreed Minute' of each

---

61  Griffith-Jones 1998.
62  A formal default occurred in the case of Mexico. In the case of other countries, when international capital markets dried up, they were unable to roll their debt any longer and had no option other than renegotiating payments. This was the case for Brazil, where there was no 'official' or formal default. Brazil negotiated with the IMF and the Club of Paris adjustment loans were used to pay part of its financial obligations. A first re-negotiation in 1983 was followed by two others in 1984 and 1986.

meeting.[63] Structural adjustment programmes were decided by the World Bank and the IMF, recreating or accentuating neo-imperialist external dependence. Debt constrained the Mexican government to accept the integration of the country into the liberalised and deregulated economic zone NAFTA (North American Free Trade Agreement). In numerous African countries and those in the Caribbean and Andean America, the necessity to export at any price in order to obtain foreign exchange and pay regular interest on debt was a vector in the transformation of food-producing agriculture into plantation agriculture under the aegis of the World Bank and subsequently of the WTO.

In the Mexican crisis, banks were not only given protection from further default. A plan was elaborated to allow them to remove bad debt from their balance sheets. It was essentially designed by the United States and known as the Brady Plan. It organised the repurchase by debtor countries of their debts at a discount by exchanging loans for bonds or by giving creditors equity in domestic firms. The repurchasing was made possible by aid paid from the government budgets of creditor bank home countries. At a time when Rogoff still took a critical stance on financial capital, he explained (taking the case of Bolivia as an example) that 'the main focus of the Brady Plan is precisely to ensure that the lion's share of officially donated funds reaches debtors'.[64] Brady bonds were negotiated in international bond markets, permitting the transfer of sovereign risk out of commercial bank portfolios into the financial system as a whole. During the six years that followed the launch of the plan, more than $200 billion dollars of defaulted syndicated bank loans were swapped into Brady Bonds. Two types of bonds were used most frequently: discount bonds, namely 30 year collateralised bonds with face value of about 30 to 35 percent less than the original claim, an interest rate above the LIBOR and a

---

63  Cosio-Pascal 2008, p. 12.
64  'Consider the Bolivian buy-back of March 1988. When the Bolivian deal was first discussed in late 1986, Bolivia's government had guaranteed $670 million in debt to commercial banks. In world secondary markets this debt traded at six cents on the dollar. That is, buyers of debt securities were willing to pay, and some sellers were willing to accept, only six cents per dollar of principal. Using funds that primarily were secretly donated by neutral third countries – rumored to include Spain, the Netherlands, and Brazil – Bolivia's government spent $34 million in March 1988 to buy back $308 million worth of debt at eleven cents on the dollar. Eleven cents was also the price that prevailed for the remaining Bolivian debt immediately after the repurchase. At first glance the buy-back might seem a triumph, almost halving Bolivia's debt. The fact that the price rose from six to eleven cents was interpreted by some observers as evidence that the deal had strengthened prospects for Bolivia's economy. A sober assessment of the Bolivian buy-back reveals that commercial bank creditors probably reaped most of the benefit' (Rogoff 1991).

single 'bullet' payment at maturity. The second type was par-bonds, similar to discounts but which were issued at face value and had a fixed interest rate of 6 percent.[65] The outcome of the Brady Plan was a sharp increase in the size of the international market for developing country debt and the accumulation in the IMF and the Club of Paris of experience valuable to financial capital on the restructuring and rescheduling of public debt. The figures given above concerning interest payments between 1982 and 2001 show the extent to which the banks profited from rescheduling.

---

65  UNCTAD 2008, p. 6.

CHAPTER 3

# The Notion of Interest-Bearing Capital in the Setting of the Present Centralisation and Concentration of Capital

This chapter assembles the different dimensions of the Marxian theory of interest-bearing capital which form – along with the key notions discussed in Chapter 1 – the theoretical foundations of this book. The setting is that of an extremely high degree of the centralisation of money capital and of concentration in banking and financial services. The notions of centralisation and concentration have a theoretical history for industrial capital as for financial capital alike. The history is sketched out in Appendix 1. The centralisation and concentration of industrial and financial capital became indissociable from the 1980s onwards, albeit at a different pace in the major capitalist economies.[1]

Marx defines interest as being 'nothing but a portion of the profit, i.e. of the surplus-value, which the functioning capitalist, whether industrialist or merchant, must pay to the owner and lender of capital in so far as the capital he uses is not his own but borrowed'.[2] Marxist scholars who have delved into the chapters of Part V of *Capital*, Volume III, have focused on interest-bearing capital as loan capital and mainly discussed the creation and allocation of credit by banks. My argument is that the channelling of surplus value in contemporary capitalism, through both the holding of government loans and the possession of stock, by a single small group of highly concentrated financial and non-financial corporations and private high-income-bracket asset holders, requires that several features of interest-bearing capital that were treated partly separately by Marx now be approached *in toto*. The traits which should now be taken in combination,[3] if only on account of the sheer scale of financial assets discussed above in Chapter 1, include the predominance of the viewpoint of 'capital as property' over 'capital as function', exteriority *vis-à-vis* production, and the continuous systemic reinforcement of a state of things where for shareholders and bondholders alike, 'it becomes a property of money to generate value and yield interest, much as it is an attribute

---

1   This point is well argued in Hoca 2012, even if he understates national differences.
2   Marx 1981, Vol. III, p. 493.
3   These are all considered, with differences in emphasis from my account, but in isolation so to speak and never as a whole, by Lapavitsas 2013, Chapter 5.

of pear-trees to bear pears'.[4] Dividends and interest are simultaneously divisions of profit and two of the three primary forms of fictitious capital (bank credit being the third). As pointed out by Marx in the mid-nineteenth century, '[in] all countries of capitalist production, there is a tremendous quantity of so-called interest-bearing capital or "moneyed capital". And by accumulation of money capital for the most part nothing more than an accumulation of these claims on production and an accumulation of the market-price, their illusory capital-value'.[5] Globalised and financialised capitalism has brought this process to unprecedented and unforeseen levels.

## 1 Steps in Approaching the Analysis of Financial Profits

### 1.1 'Money-dealing' Capital, Interest-bearing Capital and 'Financial Accumulation'

Marx distinguishes between 'money-dealing capital' and 'money-making capital' e.g. 'interest-bearing capital'. Since banks are engaged in both the distinction is all the more important. The operations of 'money-dealing capital' are required at the M and M' moments of the accumulation cycle. They give rise to special work and costs classified as costs of circulation. At a given moment in capitalist development, 'the division of labour requires that these technical operations, dependent upon the functions of capital, should be performed as far as possible for the capitalist class as a whole by a particular division of agents or capitalists as their exclusive function, that these operations should be concentrated in their hands'. 'A part of the industrial capital present in the circulation process separates off and becomes autonomous in the form of money-capital, its capitalist function consisting in that it performs these operations for the entire class of commercial and industrial capitalists'.[6] This occurs principally through the granting of commercial credit in the form of bills of exchange and other promissory notes. We will meet this process again later in this chapter.

Suzanne de Brunhoff suggests that the distinct process of money capital accumulation through operations pertaining to interest-bearing capital started in the late seventeenth century in Amsterdam. Referring to research findings

---

4  Marx 1981, Vol. III, Chapter 24. Harvey 2013 puts emphasis on the considerable topicality of the notion. This is also emphasised by Lapavitsas 2013, who missed this dimension in his first reading of the chapters on interest-bearing capital (Lapavitsas 1998).
5  Marx 1981, Vol. III, p. 599.
6  Marx 1981, Vol. III, Chapter 19, pp. 431–432.

by Barbour,[7] she writes that, on account of profits made from financing merchant capital and lending to foreign governments, one sees:

> a certain form of financial circulation developing for its own aims and permitting profits from speculation distinct from interest. This concerned partly money exchange but mainly stock market shares. One can thus say that M' detaches itself from C, according to the definition given by Marx of finance capital (M-M'), but from M itself both as silver and gold and as 'commercial money' and become part of a now partly autonomous financial circulation.[8]

With the industrial revolution, a quantum leap took place in the scale of appropriation of unpaid labour time and so in the mass of money appearing in the hoard form during the circulation process as 'latent money capital'.[9] Marx points out that 'this latent money capital may in the interval [before reinvestment – F.C.] exist in the actual shape of money that breeds money, e.g. as interest-bearing deposits in a bank, bills of exchange or securities of one kind or another', adding that this analysis 'does not belong here' (i.e. in Volume II).[10] Non-reinvested profits can retain the form of latent money capital, of potential 'capital as commodity', for more than simply short periods. As I started to argue and trace historically in Chapter 2 for the postwar period, 'the accumulation of capital in the form of loanable money capital' can become distinct from and not coincide, as Marx writes, 'with actual accumulation, i.e., the expansion of the reproduction process'. This is for the simple reason that 'the transformation of money into money capital for loan is a far simpler matter than the transformation of money into productive capital'.[11]

It is not only the hoarding of industrial profits that feeds the growth of interest-bearing capital. The power of banks (and today of funds) is also based on their capacity to centralise money coming from land rent and workers' savings. Long before the creation of market-based retirement schemes and savings entrusted to banks, pension and mutual funds and insurance companies, Marx observed that 'small amounts, each in themselves incapable of acting in the capacity of money capital, merge together into large masses and

---

7   Barbour 1966.
8   De Brunhoff 1973, p. 116. Here she expresses a different position from Harvey (1982, p. 283), who only talks of a circulation process centred on the credit system.
9   Marx 1978, Vol. II, Chapter 2, p. 158.
10  Marx 1978, Vol. II, Chapter 2, p. 164.
11  Marx 1981, Vol. III, Chapter 31, p. 626.

thus form a money power'.[12] Finally, as government debt grows, the probability that the accumulation of interest-bearing capital will not coincide 'with actual accumulation' continually increases. In the excerpt placed in Box 3.1, Marx lists a number of ways in which this was happening in his time, including speculation on price falls in government debt and interest rates.

> BOX 3.1: THE ACCUMULATION OF LOANABLE CAPITAL AS A SEPARATE FORM
>
> The development of the credit system and the tremendous concentration of the money-lending business in the hands of big banks must already accelerate in itself the accumulation of loanable capital, as a form separate from genuine accumulation. This rapid development of loan capital is therefore a result of the genuine accumulation... and the profit that forms the source of accumulation for these money capitalists is simply a deduction from the surplus-value that the reproductive agents extract (as well as an appropriation of part of the interest on the savings of *others*). Loan capital accumulates at the expense of both the industrial and commercial capitalists.... In the bad phases of the industrial cycle, the rate of interest may rise so high that it temporarily swallows up profits entirely for some branches of business, particularly those unfavourably located.
>
> At the same time, the prices of government paper and other securities fall. This is the moment when money capitalists buy up this devalued paper on a massive scale, as it will soon go up again in the later phases, and even rise above its normal level. They will then sell it off, thereby appropriating a part of the public's money capital. Those securities that are not sold off yield a higher interest, since they were bought below their price.... If the rate of interest is low, this devaluation of money capital falls principally on the depositors and not on the banks.
>
> As far as the monetary accumulation of the remaining classes of capitalist is concerned,... we shall simply consider the portion that is placed on the market as money capital for loan.... Here we have firstly the section of profit that is not spent as revenue, being rather designed for accumulation, but which the industrial capitalists concerned do not have any immediate employment for in their own businesses.... Its amount rises with the volume of the capital itself, even given a declining rate of profit.... [I]t constitutes loan capital as a deposit with the banker.... With the development of the credit system and its organization, the rise in revenue, i.e. in the consumption of the industrial and commercial capitalists, is

---

12   Marx 1981, Vol. III, Chapter 25, p. 529. Marx emphasises that 'this collection of small amounts, as a particular function of the banking system, must be distinguished from the banks' functions as middlemen between actual money capitalists and borrowers'.

expressed as an accumulation of loan capital. And this holds good of all revenues, in so far as they are only gradually consumed – i.e. ground-rent, the higher forms of salary, the incomes of the unproductive classes, etc. All of these assume for a time the form of money revenue and can hence be converted into deposits and thereby into loan capital.[13]

The systemic foundations of the contemporary accumulation of 'loanable money capital' as a distinct process ('financial accumulation proper') rest on institutional mechanisms still incipient in Marx's time but now extremely powerful (forced savings of workers in financial market dependent retirement schemes) and on financial globalisation. Today the amount of money taking the form of 'capital as commodity' originates in the processes dating back to the 1960s and 1970s discussed in Chapter 2. It is fed by the servicing of government debt in numerous countries, the play in Keynesian terms of the declining marginal propensity to consume of high income brackets, the accumulation of rent and surplus value in Middle East and Asian Sovereign Funds and, as accumulation falters, by non-reinvested corporate profits. The outcome is a global 'plethora of capital' expressing 'nothing more than the barriers of capitalist production' on a scale that Marx of course could not have anticipated.[14]

### 1.2   Credit and Debt as Creating Different Relationships

At the time he wrote *Limits to Capital*, Harvey still argued in favour of 'the need for the money capitalist as an independent power in relation to industrial capital'. Given that 'money capitalists absorb rather than generate surplus value, we may well wonder why capitalism tolerates such seeming parasites'.[15] The reason, according to Harvey, is that 'interest-bearing capital performs certain vital functions and the accumulation of capital therefore requires that money capitalists achieve and actively assert themselves as a power external

---

13   Marx 1981, Vol. III, Chapter 31, pp. 634–5.

14   'The plethora of loanable money capital proves nothing more than the barriers of *capitalist* production. The resulting credit swindling demonstrates that there is no positive obstacle to the use of this excess capital. But there is an obstacle set up by its own laws of valorisation, by the barriers within which capital can valorise itself as capital' (Marx 1981, Vol. III, Chapter 32, p. 639).

15   Harvey 1982, p. 261. Recall the way that Marx talks at the end of *Capital*, Vol. III, Chapter 33 of the 'allegedly national banks and the big money-dealers' as 'a class of parasites [having] a fabulous power not only to decimate the industrial capitalists periodically, but also to interfere into production most dangerously' (Marx 1981, Vol. III, pp. 678–9).

to and independent of actual production processes'.[16] Harvey lists the vital functions of the functioning of the credit system and the distribution of 'the common capital of the class' under 'six main headings',[17] namely (1) its role in the mobilisation of money as capital; (2) its efficiency in the promotion of monetary circulation and in the economisation on transaction costs; (3) its role in the formation and circulation of fixed capital; (4) its capacity 'to create fictitious capital in the form of flows of money capital not backed by any commodity transaction', flows 'in anticipation of future labour as a counter-value' aimed at being 'subsequently realised in real value form'; (5) the part it can play in the equalisation of the profit rate; (6) finally, the centralisation of capital as distinguished by Marx from the mobilisation of money. The extent to which these functions were carried out by banks rather than left to financial markets, and the degree to which credit creation supported industrial capital, differed from country to country. They are matters of historical study and are touched on in various ways in later chapters. However, taking Harvey's analysis as a starting point, with differences still existing among countries, financial liberalisation and globalisation have brought about what I name in Chapter 8 the degeneration of the credit system.

Credit and debt are generally presented as the two sides of a single relationship. I argue that the term credit should be used only for: (1) advances of money made by banks to facilitate or 'lubricate' the accomplishment of the full accumulation cycle (M-C-P-C'-M'); and (2) for loans, whether by banks or by industrial bond markets, in support of extended reproduction. The term debt should be used to designate creditor-debtor relationships which either were never related to the creation of surplus value but solely to their appropriation, or which ceased at some point to include or support closely the process of productive valorisation.

Advances of money at M and M' involve *ipso facto* the creation of credit money by banks. Loans in support of extended reproduction rest for a very small part on bank 'intermediation', e.g. putting 'savings' at the disposal of firms for investment. The largest part of such lending involves the opening of credit lines to firms and the creation of the particular form of fictitious capital discussed in Chapter 7. Loans can be of different maturity. Their purpose is the production of value and surplus which once successfully realised permit the repayment and the wiping-out of debt by firms. Barring moments of economic crisis, there will be no rescheduling. Firms will not remain debtors long. This has rarely been true for governments. The experience is that of hardened if

---

16   Ibid.
17   Ibid.

not permanent relationships of subordination short of true default as soon as debtor governments are forced to make new loans in order to pay interest and reimburse principal at redemption dates. This can be the case, as for instance in Brazil today, even when government bonds are held domestically. Precise financial interests are always parties to this relation. Marx observed the way in which during the July Monarchy,

> the faction of the bourgeoisie that ruled and legislated through the Chambers had a *direct interest* in the *indebtedness of the state*. The *state deficit* was really the main object of its speculation and the chief source of its enrichment. At the end of each year a new deficit. After the lapse of four or five years a new loan. And every new loan offered new opportunities to the finance aristocracy for defrauding the state, which was kept artificially on the verge of bankruptcy – it had to negotiate with the bankers under the most unfavourable conditions.[18]

As was discussed in Chapter 2, developing countries were the first to be trapped after 1982 into relationships of this type, with the rescheduling of debt allowing creditors led by the IMF and the World Bank to interfere in their internal affairs and impose 'structural adjustment'. In the context of early twenty-first-century world capitalism, this is now the case for countries classified as industrial countries. Today the relations are global and systemic. Today the balance sheets of many banks and funds depend on the security but also the permanence of the flows of interest rooted in surplus value created by government debt. The 'men in black' from the EU, the ECB, and the IMF are there to ensure this. A state of permanent indebtedness can also be experienced by households in the form of mortgage and consumer credit. Today, when contracted by the poorer layers of workers, this indebtedness assumes again the character of usury (level of interest payment and permanent threat of foreclosure by banks or landed money-lenders). Financial capital has put workers in a situation in which they face capital simultaneously as workers in their factories and offices, and as debtors in their daily life.

## 1.3  The Nature of Financial Profits

In national accounting systems financial profits refer to the profits of 'financial corporations', one of which are banks, today diversified financial conglomerates. Financial corporations' share of total profits grew from 15–20 percent in the late 1980s to 40 percent on the eve of the 2007–8 crisis. *Monthly Review* has

---

18    Marx 1850, Chapter 1, original emphasis.

consistently drawn attention to these figures, but remained rather vague about the sources and nature of these profits. However other Anglophone Marxists have engaged in a lively debate on this matter. As a result of the developments which will be discussed in Chapter 7, contemporary banking has undoubtedly moved significantly beyond the traditional business of managing deposits for the general public, providing commercial credit and making loans to enterprises through credit creation and earning interest on these operations.[19] The trading of financial assets, whether on behalf of customers or on the bank's own account (proprietary trading), along with services to very large corporations and to governments, now form a very important part of the profits of large banks. The thorough analysis of European banks prepared for the European Commission[20] identifies those banks that engage more in traditional commercial banking business and those banks, notably the large internationalised institutions, where profits depend on the size of trading operations. The same divide holds in the US between the small state banks and the Wall Street giant financial conglomerates. The question is how to relate all these developments to the theory of interest as a division of surplus value,[21] and more generally to the theory of labour value.

The core component of banking profit was traditionally founded on interest on loans (commercial credit and industrial credit) and determined by the degree of leverage, the scale of the credit created in proportion to the bank's own capital (owners' equity) and the high liquidity securities in its possession.[22] Regular, continuous 'proprietary trading' develops form the 1980s onwards. Interest is the core of financial profit.

The first point under debate concerns the nature of what are now named 'non-interest' banking profits. These profits come from fees and commissions, which include, in the case of services to industrial corporations, foreign exchange, investment banking and the organisation of M&As, and, in the case of services to rich households, brokerage, wealth management trading, and the management of mutual and insurance funds for customers. The growth of these sources is one of the factors behind the increase of financial profits as recorded in national accounts. Seen from the perspective of the appropriation

---

19  Dos Santos 2009, p. 183.
20  Liikanen 2012, p. 37.
21  Marx 1981, Vol. III, p. 480.
22  The term appears late in capitalist history, 'the noun leverage in the financial sense is attested by 1937 and the verb in American English by 1957'. http://www.thesaurus.com/browse/leverage.

of surplus value, these various commissions and fees paid to banks by corporations and high-bracket households clearly fall under the heading of interest.

The second point concerns 'profits' from speculation. Here one must simply follow Hilferding:

> Speculative gains or losses arise only from variations in the current valuations of claims to interest. They are neither profit, nor parts of surplus value ... They are pure marginal gains. Whereas the capitalist class as a whole appropriates a part of the labour of the proletariat without giving anything in return, speculators gain only from each other. One's loss is the other's gain. *'Les affaires, c'est l'argent des autres'*.[23]

One is in the presence of a process of division and re-division of previously created surplus value for which the term 'fictitious profits', used by Brazilian economists, is appropriate.[24] Or again the ones named 'dubious profits' by Duménil and Lévy.[25] What is new is that, due to the scale reached by such transactions by 2007, the 'loss to others' meant bankruptcy for Bear Stearns and Lehman Brothers (the processes are discussed below in Chapter 8).

Lapavitsas in a detailed manner[26] and Guillen[27] more briefly have discussed the contemporary relevance of Hilferding's theory of 'promoter's' or 'founder's' profit in relation to proprietary trading by investment banks in the stock of corporations for which they have organised the issuance of new shares or engineered M&As. Here again there is no creation but only a different distribution of surplus value.

The third point on which there has been a sharp confrontation of positions among Anglophone economists concerns – to use the terms in Lapavitsas and Dos Santos – the 'historically new, *exploitative* modes of appropriation from the independently secured income of wage-earners'.[28] These modes of appropriation are a result of 'significant class-defeats suffered by the working-class movement'. The first question concerns the novelty of this mode. In Chapter 36

---

23   Hilferding 1910, Chapter 8. On this point, see also Pollin 1996 who correctly defines financial profits from market transactions as a redistribution within the capitalist class – a zero-sum game resulting in no profit from financial transactions for the economy as a whole.
24   Carcanholo and Nakatani 2007; Sabadini 2008; Carcanholo and Sabadini 2008.
25   Duménil and Lévy 2011, p. 8.
26   Lapavitsas 2013, pp. 57–8.
27   Guillen 2013, p. 15.
28   Lapavitsas and Dos Santos 2008.

of Volume III of *Capital*, Marx uses the term secondary exploitation starting with rent paid to landlords: 'the renting of houses, etc., for individual consumption. It is plain enough that the working-class is swindled in this form too, and to an enormous extent, but this is also done by the petty trader, who supplies workers with means of subsistence. This is secondary exploitation, which proceeds alongside the original exploitation that takes place directly within the production process itself'. Then there is the question of generality. Today, in particular in the US, interest and fees on mortgage, credit cards, student loans, etc., are a component of the profits of financial corporations and account for part of their increase. Iren Levina defends the position held by Lapavitsas that lending to households is qualitatively different from lending to industrial and commercial capitalists and represents a reinstatement of essentially usurious relations within the capitalist mode of production.[29] With a totally privatised system in mind, she writes that 'households approach borrowing from the perspective of use-values in order to secure access to basic necessities, such as housing, education, healthcare, and consumer goods, whereas firms borrow from the viewpoint of value to embark on a circuit of capital and extract surplus value'.[30]

However the explosion of consumer credit and of student loans remains fairly specific to the US and to countries which have adopted the same model. The Liikanen report on European banks found that since 1999 the relative importance of 'customer loans' (loans to households for mortgage and consumer credit lumped up with loans to non-financial corporations) has fallen regularly and done so particularly rapidly after 2008. In the case of the UK, the ratio of such loans to the total assets of financial corporations has fallen to 4 percent and to 10 percent in Germany and France.[31] The increasing privatisation of health and education in EU countries corresponds certainly to defeats suffered by the working class and to the resurgence of 'secondary exploitation' on a scale it had not known since the 1930s. The notion of usurious relations is certainly applicable in some advanced capitalist countries with respect to the poorer and most fragile layers of the working class, as was the case for the US subprime mortgage crisis discussed in later chapters. The question raised

---

29  Lapavitsas 2009, p. 132.
30  Levina 2012 sees this position as being 'in line with Adam Smith's distinction between lending for production and consumption. For him, borrowing for production allows the borrower to "both restore the capital, and pay the interest, without alienating or encroaching upon any other source of revenue" while borrowing for consumption can "neither restore the capital nor pay the interest, without either alienating or encroaching upon some other source of revenue"'.
31  Liikanen 2012, p. 15, chart 2.3.9.

correctly by Norfield is the relation of 'double exploitation' to the labour theory of value. The interest paid to banks by wage earners must either represent a lowering of the value of labour power or be a deduction made by banks from the profits of productive capitalists.[32] It is clearly the first. It is worth recalling that Rosa Luxemburg tackled a similar question in relation to indirect taxation. She writes:

> [Indirect] taxation means that part of the purchasing power of the working class is transferred to the state. Now as before the variable capital, as a fixed amount of money, will put in motion an appropriate quantity of living labour, that is to say it serves to employ the appropriate quantity of constant capital in production and to produce the corresponding amount of surplus value. As soon as capital has completed this cycle, it is divided between the working class and the state: the workers surrender the state part of the money they received as wages. Capital has wholly appropriated the former variable capital in its material form, as labour power, but the working class retains only part of the variable capital in the form of money, the state claiming the rest.[33]

Taxation is thus analysed by Rosa Luxemburg as a levy on the value of labour power, a reduction of the level of wages. This applies to household debt in all its forms. The levy is made by banks and is a component of their profits. It can only be a small, if not a minute fraction, and cannot become, as was dreamed by financial corporations in the run up to 2008, a regular channel of surplus value appropriation which the financial innovations discussed in Chapter 8 might permit.

---

32  Norfield's full critique is the following: 'The argument against the notion that finance exploits the working class by taking a share of wages can be put simply. *If* one source of financial profit is a cut out of workers' incomes, in interest payments, fees, etc., then there are two alternative implications. *Either* this implies that workers are receiving a net income below the value of labour power once these deductions are accounted for, *or* these deductions are part of the value of labour power, paying for the "socially necessary" goods and services, some of which are delivered on credit. In the former case, where such deductions were persistent, this would imply that a lower value of labour-power was in place than otherwise. But, over time, this lower level would become the new norm. In the latter case, if workers are *not* being paid below the value of labour-power, then the cost of consumer credit, mortgages, etc., is a part of the regular wages that workers are paid. In neither case is there a systematic "financial exploitation" of workers. Instead, the financial profits are a deduction from the profits of productive capitalists' (Norfield 2014).

33  Luxemburg 1913, Chapter 32.

## 2 Interest-bearing Capital: Exteriority to Production and the Blurring of Lines between Profit and Interest

### 2.1 'Capital-as-property' and 'Capital-as-function'

The next notion which must be revisited when approaching financialisation is the distinction Marx makes between 'capital-as-property' and 'capital-as-function'. What Marx names a 'qualitative division' in some passages refers in fact to two situations. The first concerns the economic status of 'passive' and 'active capitalists', e.g. lenders and borrowers of money capital. Lapavitsas argues that the rentier implications of this opposition, about which he has reservations, are a dimension of a critique of rentiers that Marx shares with Adam Smith and Ricardo. Subsequently, it was taken up again by Keynes when he called for the euthanasia of the rentier defined as the 'functionless investor' in a context of stock market dominance. When idle money is centralised largely by banks, the issue is that of appreciating whether the pattern of credit allocation, e.g. banking policy, is shaped by the specific priorities of the owners of money capital.[34] The second concerns the distinction between 'capital-as-property' and 'capital-as-function' resulting from the growth of joint-stock companies and so the emergence of shareholders and managers as distinct groups. 'Stock companies', Marx observed, 'have an increasing tendency to separate the work of management as a function from the ownership of capital'.[35] Indeed,

> [the] capitalist mode of production has brought matters to a point where the work of superintendence, entirely divorced from the ownership of capital, is always readily obtainable. It has, therefore, come to be useless for the capitalist to perform it himself. An orchestra conductor need not own the instruments of his orchestra, nor is it within the scope of his duties as conductor to have anything to do with the 'wages' of the other musicians.[36]

The dividend and interest accruing to the firms' shareholders and creditors 'depend on the degree of exertion that such exploitation demands, and which he can shift to a manager for moderate pay. After every crisis there are enough ex-manufacturers in the English factory districts who will supervise, for low

---

34  Epstein and Jayadev 2005.
35  Marx 1981, Vol. III, Chapter 23, p. 386.
36  Marx 1981, Vol. III, Chapter 23, p. 385. Baronian and Pierre 2011 elaborate on this.

wages, what were formerly their own factories in the capacity of managers of the new owners, who are frequently their creditors'.[37]

The 'qualitative division', in its two approaches, has undoubtedly influenced the contemporary opposition between 'bad finance' and 'good industry', to which a considerable number of those engaged in the critique of financialisation have given importance, in the case of some authors at the macroeconomic level[38] and of others with respect to the margin of initiative left to managers. Marx's observation that interest and dividend-bearing capital is in a position of 'exteriority' to production acquired significance again in the attention paid to 'short-termism' during the 1990s, as the balance of power between shareholders and managers moved sharply in favour of the former. We return to this in Chapter 4.

## 2.2 The Blurring of Lines between Profit and Interest

The category of interest as a specific form should be kept and indeed developed on account of the surge of government and of household debt, but with regards to corporations the situation is more complicated. Part V of Volume III of *Capital* is entitled 'Division of Profit into Interest and Profit of Enterprise: Interest-Bearing Capital'. Early on in the renewal of Marxist research on money and finance, in which she played a key role, Suzanne de Brunhoff argued in respect to this division that a distinction should be introduced between firm size and corporate status:

> Marx indicates that there exists no economic rule for the distribution of surplus value between industrial profit and interest, this depending on the power relationships between borrowers and loaners, given change in the business cycle and the action of the central bank. The only exception, a very important one, is that of joint-stock companies, where because constant capital (material means of production) is 'huge' in relation to variable capital (wages), the whole of profits goes to the financial capitalist in the form of interest.[39]

Today ease or difficulty – if not impossibility – of access to corporate bond markets according to the size of firms is the key marker of power relationships between borrowers and loaners. When large corporations borrow money on the bond markets to increase dividends by share buy-backs, this involves

---

37  Ibid.
38  Stockhammer 2004 and 2008.
39  De Brunhoff 1973, p. 117.

money and asset circulation in favour of a common group of funds and banks. In his commentary Harvey is somewhat disturbed by Marx's drift, as the analysis in Part V of Volume III unfolds, towards a very broad definition of interest extending well beyond the remuneration of loans:

> Since owners of money are concerned primarily to augment their money by interest, they are presumably indifferent as to whom and for what purposes the money is lent provided the return is secure. This creates some difficulties, which Marx is aware of but brushes aside for plausible enough reasons. If, in the final analysis, all interest payments have to be furnished directly or indirectly out of surplus value, then the crucial relationship to be examined is that between interest-bearing capital and surplus value production.[40]

Given the level of concentration reached today this is now overwhelmingly the case. As a result of the deep changes brought about since the late 1980s by liberalisation and the globalisation of capital discussed in Chapter 1, the central antagonistic relationship is indeed one in which workers are placed in direct opposition to the demands of financial capital *in toto*. The unfinished state of the chapters on interest-bearing capital undoubtedly makes their reading difficult and opens the way for differing interpretations. The very broad definition of interest, which justifies Harvey's remark, is in Chapter 23 of Volume III. Marx posits that:

> Interest, then, is the net profit, as Ramsay describes it, yielded by property in capital as such, whether to the mere lender, who remains outside the reproduction process or to the owner who employs his capital productively himself. Yet it does not yield him this net profit in so far as he is a functioning capitalist, but rather as a money-capitalist, the lender of his own capital as interest-bearing capital to himself as functioning capitalist. Just as the transformation of money and value in general into capital is the constant result of the capitalist production process, so its existence as capital is in the same way the constant presupposition of this process. Through its capacity to be transformed into means of production, it always commands unpaid labour and hence transforms the production and circulation process of commodities into the production of surplus-value for its possessor. Interest therefore simply expresses the fact that value in general – objectified labour in its general social form – value that assumes the form of means of production in the actual pro-

---

40    Harvey 1982, p. 257.

duction process, confronts living labour-power as an autonomous power and is the means of appropriating unpaid labour; and that it is this power in so far as it confronts the worker as the property of another.[41]

Other passages contradict this, but today they should be set aside. One is where Marx talks about the 'ossification and individualisation of the two parts of the gross profit in respect to one another, as though they originated from two essentially different sources, [that] now takes firm shape for the entire capitalist class and the total capital. The profit of every capital, and consequently also the average profit established by the equalisation of capitals, splits, or is separated, into two qualitatively different, mutually independent and separately individualised parts, to wit – interest and profit of enterprise – both of which are determined by separate laws',[42] interest being determined largely by power relationships.

## 3    The Theory of Fictitious Capital

### 3.1    *Fictitious Capital: Bonds and Shares*

Before the outbreak of the financial crisis in 2007–8, Harvey, Robert Guttmann (very appreciative of this notion in Marx)[43] and Louis Gill[44] were among the few scholars to have explored the notion of 'fictitious capital'. When Marxist economists did use the term it was often limited to a simple quote from *Capital*: 'the formation of fictitious capital is known as capitalization'.[45] Before taking the theory forward in relation to the forms of assets which developed in the 1990s, one must start by reading Marx carefully. In Chapter 29 of Volume III, he applies the term fictitious capital to government loans and to shares. (The full quotes are given in Box 3.2). The first step is to put straight the nature of bonds and shares, namely drawing rights on previously produced surplus value, appropriated in the first case indirectly through the levying of taxes and the servicing of government debt, and in the second case, more directly, through the division of profit between what are today called retained profits and dividends. What the possessors of bonds and shares view as 'capital' is not analysable in these terms from the standpoint of accumulation. In fact the mass of surplus value appropriated by bond and stockholders can, in

---

41    Marx 1981, Vol. III, p. 502.
42    Marx 1981, Vol. III, p. 498.
43    Guttmann 1994.
44    Gill 1996.
45    Marx 1981, Vol. III, p. 597.

given macroeconomic conditions, affect accumulation negatively. The third characteristic of fictitious capital is the fluctuation of asset prices in financial markets, hence the possibility of speculating on their movement along with the advent of conditions in which assets become unsellable or sellable only at very low prices ('fire prices', in today's jargon).

> BOX 3.2: FICTITIOUS CAPITAL IN THE FORM OF GOVERNMENT BONDS AND STOCK
>
> Following the issuance of bonds,
>
> [the] state has to pay its creditors a certain amount of interest each year for the capital it borrows. In this case, the creditor cannot recall his capital from his debtor, but can only sell his claim, his title of ownership. The capital itself has been consumed, *spent* by the state. It no longer exists. It is illusory and fictitious capital. It is not only that the sum lent to the state no longer has any kind of existence. It was never designed to be spent as capital, and yet only by being invested as capital could it have been made into a self-maintaining value. As far as the original creditor A is concerned, the share of annual taxation he receives represents interest on his capital, just as does the share of the wealth of the spendthrift that accrues to the money lender.[46]
>
> When bond markets are functioning properly,
>
> the possibility of selling the state's promissory note represents for A the potential return of his principal. As for B, from his own private standpoint, his capital is invested as interest-bearing capital. In actual fact, he has simply taken the place of A and bought by buying A's claim on the state. No matter how these transactions are multiplied, the capital of the national debt remains purely fictitious, and the moment these promissory notes become unsalable, the illusion of this capital disappears.[47]
>
> However,
>
> for the person who buys the title of ownership, the annual income of £100 represents indeed the interest on his capital invested at 5%. In this way, all connection

---

46   Marx 1981, Vol. III, pp. 595–6.
47   Marx 1981, Vol. III, p. 596.

with the actual process of capital valorisation is lost, right down to the last trace; confirming the notion that capital is automatically valorized by its own processes.[48]

Marx then turns to shares, industrial stock. Here

> this security while not representing a purely illusory capital, as in the case of national debts, is still pure illusion.... The stocks of railways, mines, navigation companies, and the like, represent real capital, i.e. capital invested and functioning in these enterprises as capital.... It is in no way ruled out that these shares may simply be a fraud. But this capital does not exist twice over, once as the capital value of ownership titles (shares) and then again as the capital actually invested, or to be invested, in the enterprises in question. It exists only in the latter form, and a share is nothing but an ownership tittle, *pro rata*, to the surplus-value which this capital is to realise. A may sell this title to B, and B to C. These transactions have no essential effect on the matter. A or B then has transformed his title into capital, but C has transformed his capital into a mere title of ownership to the surplus value expected from this share capital.[49]
>
> The fictitious nature of bonds and shares and their vulnerability as income-yielding assets is accentuated by financial market transactions and fluctuations.
>
> The independent movement of the value of these ownership titles, not only of government bonds but also of shares, strengthens the illusion that they constitute real capital besides the capital or claim to which they may give title. They become commodities, their price having a specific movement.... Their market value receives a determination differing from their nominal values, without any change in the value of the actual capital (even if its valorisation does change).... [T]heir market value fluctuates with the level and security of the receipts to which they give a legal title.... The market value of these securities is in part speculative, since it is determined not just by the actual income, but rather by the anticipated income as reckoned in advance.[50]

Today one cannot follow Marx completely when he refers to government loans as 'never [having been] intended to be expended as capital', and when he says that 'only by investment as capital could it have been transformed into a

---

48   Marx 1981, Vol. III, p. 597.
49   Marx 1981, Vol. III, pp. 597–8.
50   Marx 1981, Vol. III, p. 598.

self-preserving value' (paragraph 1 in Box 3.2). Since the growth of the 'mixed economy' after the Second World War, a part of government loans have been spent in value and surplus-value production (state-owned industrial enterprises before their privatisation) and more largely and importantly in the close support of the accumulation process (government investment in transport, communication systems, R&D). On a much more limited scale, even after extensive privatisation, this remains true today, notably for basic research.

Bond and share trading is based on the capitalisation or discounting of anticipated income. As Marx stresses, 'promissory notes on states [can] become unsalable [and] the illusion of this capital disappear'. The same goes for shares. When financial markets collapse, then, seen from the standpoint of shareholders, 'wealth vanishes into thin air'. But this does not mean the collapse of the social relations of production on which the drawing rights on surplus value are founded. The truth of this fact is most notable when state power comes to the rescue of stock markets and governments give the highest political priority to the payment of their debt, whatever the effects on accumulation and whatever the social consequences.

### 3.2  *Bank Created Fictitious Capital in its Classical Form*

Credit creation takes two forms, commercial credit, the issuance of bills of exchange and other promissory notes, and 'banker's credit', e.g. the opening of credit lines to industrial firms. Regarding the first, Marx emphasises that 'bills of exchange, until they expire and are due for payment, circulate themselves as means of payment and they form the actual commercial money. To the extent that they ultimately cancel each other out, by the balancing of claims and debts, they function absolutely as money, although there is no final transformation into money proper'.[51] Here 'money proper' is, of course, gold, but the point holds for legal tender (fiat money).

Loans in support of extended reproduction have always only rested to a very small extent on the operations of banks acting as 'middlemen between actual money capitalists and borrowers', e.g. putting savings at the disposal of firms for investment. Banks have always lent far more than the deposits made with them, the savings they have collected and their own proprietary capital. 'Banker's credit' entails the creation of investment credit of some duration to industrial capitalists, namely the creation of fictitious capital.[52] If all goes right,

---

51  Marx 1981, Vol. III, p. 525.
52  As recalled by Bellofiore 1998, in his comment on de Brunhoff, this is what Schumpeter (1912, Chapter 22) names *ex nihilo* credit creation. It is important to add that Schumpeter used the term 'fictitious' and argued that the dynamism of the process of evolution

this represents such capital in its most innocuous form.[53] The production of value and surplus once successfully realised will permit the fictitious capital created by the loan to be wiped out. Excess credit creation and credit bubbles[54] have been inherent to the accumulation cycle as well as to the profitability of banks, which always depended on the amount of interest appropriated in their operations and so on the quantity but also the riskiness of the loans they made. Only the very largest could earn commissions through operations such as the search for capital required for the launching of joint-stock corporations. From the mid-nineteenth century onwards, crises of overproduction were fuelled by what proved every time *a posteriori* to be excessive credit creation for investment. Banks were at the heart of the euphoria leading up to crashes and crises, and these seemed on the surface always to be financial crises.[55]

An important point made by Marx is the interconnection between this form of fictitious capital and the other two. Bonds and stock are in fact discussed in Volume III, Chapter 29, in relation to the balance sheet of banks. A factor of vulnerability specific to banks is that part of their capital is

> invested in these so-called interest-bearing securities. This is actually part of the reserve capital and does not function in the banking business proper. The most important portion consists of bills of exchange, i.e. promises to pay issued by industrial capitalists or merchants. The final portion of the banker's capital consists of his money reserves in gold. Deposits, unless tied up for a longer period by contract, are always at the depositors' disposal.[56]

In contemporary capitalism, the process whereby 'with the development of interest-bearing capital and the credit system, all capital seems to be duplicated, and at some points triplicated, by the various ways in which the same capital, or perhaps even the same claim, appears in different hands in different

---

required that banks should not accumulate independently and be completely at the service of the entrepreneur in his role of 'fideicommis of productive forces' (Chapter 3.1).

53   See (in French) Chesnais 2006, pp. 83–6 and Durand 2014, pp. 64–7. De Brunhoff 1997 is unclear on this in her Palgrave Dictionary article and more generally on the relation between interest-bearing capital and fictitious capital. This is also true for Lapavistas 2013, p. 29. On the contrary, Guttmann 1996, pp. 76–7 has no hesitations.

54   These are often referred to as 'Minsky moments', on account of the author's theorisation of contemporary financial crises.

55   See the title of Kindleberger's 1978 book, *Manias, Panics, and Crashes: A History of Financial Crises*.

56   Marx 1981, Vol. III, pp. 599–600.

guises',[57] has taken proportions only vaguely guessed at by Marx. These remarks lay the foundations for the further analysis in Chapter 7 of derivatives, and in Chapters 8 and 9 of high-risk credit creation as developed in the 1990s and 2000s.

## 3.3   The Onset and Hardening of Money Fetishism

The main developments on the notion of money fetishism are in Chapter 24 of Volume 3 (see Box 3.3), but the basis is already set out in Chapter 21. Money fetishism is contained in the very relation whereby the capitalist owner of loan capital 'appears simply as the seller of a commodity and the buyer as the buyer of a commodity',[58] meaning that 'in the case of interest-bearing capital, everything appears in a superficial manner: the advance of capital as a mere transfer from lender to borrower; the reflux of the realized capital as a mere transfer back, a repayment with interest from the borrower to the lender'.[59] Despite the rooting of money fetishism in basic financial transactions, Marxist economists have given the notion little to no attention, leaving the field to Marxist philosophers. As with fictitious capital, they are ill-at-ease with the notion of fetishism which allows no common ground for discussion even with most heterodox economists. The only remotely related notion is that of 'irrational exuberance' developed outside of Marxism.[60] Yet with the fabulous expansion of fictitious capital and transactions on financial markets, money fetishism pervades contemporary capitalism. One welcome exception is Harvey in his *Companion to Marx*. He pleads for 'a deep internal and subjective understanding of the fetish's destructive and potentially destructive violent powers. We can, in short, now hope to get into the head of the Wall Street speculator. But who among us can truly claim that we are immune to the fetish siren of the pure lust for money... Can we now hope to understand what has entered our own heads too?'[61]

---

BOX 3.3: THE FETISH FORM OF CAPITAL

In interest-bearing capital, the capital relationship reaches its most superficial and fetishized form. Here we have $M\text{-}M'$, money that produces more money, self-valorizing value, without the process that mediates the two extremes.... $M\text{-}M'$.

---

57   Marx 1981, Vol. III, p. 601.
58   Marx 1981, Vol. III, Chapter 21, p. 463.
59   Marx 1981, Vol. III, Chapter 21, p. 478.
60   Shiller 2005.
61   Harvey 2012, p. 172.

We have here the original starting-point of capital, money in the formula $M$-$C$-$M'$, reduced to the two extremes $M$-$M'$, where $M' = M + \Delta M$, money that creates more money. It is the original and general formula for capital reduced to a meaningless abbreviation. It is capital in its finished form, the unity of production and circulation processes, and hence capital yielding a definite surplus-value in a specific period of time. In the form of interest-bearing capital, capital appears immediately in this form, unmediated by the production and circulation processes. Capital appears as a mysterious and self-creating source of interest – of its own increase. The *thing* (money, commodity, value) is now already capital simply as a thing, and capital appears as a mere thing; the result of the overall reproduction process appears as a property developing on the thing in itself; it is up to the possessor of money, i.e. of commodities in their ever-exchangeable form, whether he wants to spend this money as money or hire it out as capital. In interest-bearing capital, therefore, this automatic fetish is elaborated into its pure form, self-valorizing value, money breeding money, and this form no longer bears any marks of its origin. The social relation is consummated in the relationship of a thing, money, to itself.... Money as such is already potentially self-valorizing value, and it is as such that it is lent, this being the form of sale for this particular commodity. Thus it becomes as completely the property of money to create value, to yield interest, as it is the property of a pear tree to bear pears.

While interest is simply one part of the profit, i.e. the surplus-value, extorted from the worker by the functioning capitalist, it now appears conversely as if interest is the specific fruit of capital, the original thing, while profit, now transformed into the form of profit of enterprise, appears as a mere accessory and trimming added in the reproduction process. The fetish character of capital and the representation of this capital fetish is now complete. In $M$-$M'$ we have the irrational form of capital, the misrepresentation and objectification of the relations of production, in their highest power: the interest-bearing form, the simple form of capital, in which it is taken as logically anterior to its own reproduction process; the ability of money, or a commodity to valorize its own value independent of reproduction – the capital mystification in the most flagrant form.

Capital is now a thing, but the thing is capital. The money's body is now by love possessed. As soon as it is lent, or else applied in the reproduction process (in so far as it yields interest to the functioning capitalist as its owner, separate from profit of enterprise), interest accrues to it, no matter whether it is asleep or awake, at home or abroad, by day or by night.[62]

---

62    Marx 1981, Vol. III, pp. 515–17.

The most spectacular manifestations of money fetishism are of course those of financial investors in general and of traders in particular. There have been repeated spectacular examples of trader *hubris* associated with individual names. But more systemically it takes the form of what McNally calls 'number fetishism', namely the belief in the reliability of mathematical trading and risk management models.[63] The banker's and investor's aspiration to autonomy pervades twenty-first-century capitalism. But the autonomy of interest-bearing capital and the fictitious forms of capital it takes is necessarily but partial and temporary. This autonomy can never free itself from an ultimate dependency on the effective production and realisation of surplus value. This dependency is sheltered by the social and political power of financial capital and the protection it has received from governments. Money fetishism is pervasive. Backed by all the institutions and mechanisms which financialise our daily existence,[64] it generates conservative political and social behaviour on a scale that can only be broken by an economic and financial crisis of great magnitude. The ongoing crisis has not met this requirement.

### Appendix 1: The Centralisation and Concentration of Capital in Marxist Theory

Very high centralisation and concentration of capital in its three forms is a central feature of contemporary capitalism. Marx develops the interrelated notions of the centralisation and concentration of capital in Volume I of *Capital*. He returns to the issue fleetingly in Volume III,[65] where Engels adds a few paragraphs. Marx establishes a clear-cut distinction between concentration and centralisation which is very often ignored. The term concentration refers simply to capitalist production as such: 'every individual capital is a larger or smaller concentration of means of production, with a corresponding command over a larger or smaller army of workers'. However, 'not only are accumulation and the concentration accompanying it scattered over many points, but the increase of each functioning capital is thwarted by the formation of new capitals and the sub-division of old'. And two sentences later:

> This fragmentation of the total social capital into many individual capitals or the repulsion of its fractions one from each other is counteracted by their attraction. The attraction of capitals no longer means the

---

63  McNally 2011 pp. 108–9.
64  Konings 2010.
65  Marx 1981, Vol. III, Chapter 27.

simple concentration of the means of production and of the command over labour, which is identical with accumulation. It is concentration of capitals already formed, destruction of their individual independence, expropriation of capitalist by capitalist, transformation of many small into few large capitals. This process differs from the former in this respect, that it only presupposes a change in the distribution of already available and already functioning capital. Its field of action is therefore not limited by the absolute growth of social wealth, or in other words by the absolute limits of accumulation. Capital grows to a huge mass in a single hand in one place, because it has been lost by many in another place. This is centralization proper, as distinct from accumulation and concentration.[66]

Centralisation takes place through two mechanisms. The first is competition: the bankruptcy and simple disappearance of smaller firms as a result of competition or their acquisition by and merger with a larger firm. The second entails the role of finance in two forms, bank credit following the centralisation of loan money in their hands, and the formation of joint-stock companies. Here the relevant passages from Volume I are quoted *in extenso* with added emphasis by me on certain points:

> *The battle of competition is fought by the cheapening of commodities. The cheapness of commodities depends, all other circumstances remaining the same, on the productivity of labour, and this depends in turn on the scale of production.* Therefore, the larger capitals beat the smaller. It will further be remembered that, with the development of the capitalist mode of production, there is an increase in the minimum amount of individual capital necessary to carry on a business under its normal conditions. The smaller capitals, therefore, crowd into spheres of production which large-scale industry has taken control of only sporadically or incompletely. Here competition rages in direct proportion to the number, and in inverse proportion to the magnitude, of the rival capitals. It always ends in the ruin of many small capitalists, whose capitals partly pass into the hands of their conquerors, and partly vanish completely.
>
> Apart from this, *an altogether new force comes into existence with the development of capitalist production: the credit system.* In its first stages, this system furtively creeps in as the humble assistant of accumulation, drawing into the hands of individual or associated capitalists by invisible threads the money resources, which lie scattered in larger or smaller amounts over the surface of society; but *it soon becomes a new and terrible*

---

66   Marx 1976, Vol. I, pp. 776–7.

*weapon in the battle of competition and is finally transformed into an enormous social mechanism for the centralization of capitals.*

... Today, therefore, the force of attraction which draws together individual capitals, and the tendency to centralization, are both stronger than ever before. But if the relative extension and energy of the movement towards centralization is determined, to a certain degree, by the magnitude of capitalist wealth and the superiority of economic mechanism already attained, the advance of centralization does not depend in any way on a positive growth in the magnitude of social capital. And this is what distinguishes centralization from concentration, the latter being only another name for reproduction on an extended scale. Centralization may result from a mere change in the distribution of already existing capitals, from a simple alteration in the quantitative grouping of the component parts of social capital. Capital can grow into powerful masses in a single hand in one place, because in other places it has been withdrawn from many individual hands. In any given branch of industry centralization would reach its extreme limit if all the individual capitals invested were fused into a single capital. In a given society this limit would be reached only when the entire social capital was united in the hands of either a single capitalist or a single capitalist company.

*Centralization supplements the work of accumulation by enabling industrial capitalists to extend the scale of their operations.* Whether this latter result is the consequence of accumulation or centralization, whether centralization is accomplished by the *violent method of annexation* – where certain capitals become such preponderant centres of attraction for others that they shatter the individual cohesion of the latter and then draw the separate fragments to themselves – or whether the fusion of a number of capitals already formed or in process of formation takes place by *the smoother process of organising joint-stock companies* – the economic effect remains the same.

... But accumulation, the gradual increase of capital by reproduction as it passes from the circular to the spiral form, is clearly a very slow procedure compared with centralization, which needs only to change the quantitative groupings of the constituent parts of social capital. *The world would still be without railways if it had had to wait until accumulation had got a few individual capitals far enough to be adequate for the construction of a railway. Centralization, however, accomplished this in the twinkling of an eye, by means of joint-stock companies.* And while in this way centralization intensifies and accelerates the effects of accumulation, *it simultaneously extends and speeds up those revolutions in the technical composition of capital which raise its constant portion at the expense of its variable portion, thus diminishing the relative demand for labour.*[67]

The focus of the analysis in these passages is on industrial capital. Marx and Engels place strong emphasis on the relationship between centralisation and technological progress. They see monopolies as being possible stepping stones to socialism.

> The United Alkali Trust has brought all British alkali production into the hands of a single firm. The former owners of more than thirty individual plants received the assessed value of their entire establishments in shares to a total of some £5 million, which represents the fixed capital of the trust. The technical management remains in the same hands as before, but financial control is concentrated in the hands of the general management. The floating capital, totaling about £1 million, was offered to public subscription. The total capital is thus £6 million. In this branch therefore, which forms the basis of the entire chemical industry, competition has been replaced in England by monopoly, thus preparing in the most pleasing fashion its future expropriation by the whole of society, the nation.

In the case of interest-bearing capital, the distinction is made between its centralisation and concentration is not used. Marx speaks of the formation of a 'concentrated and organized mass [of money-capital]' which 'placed it under the control of bankers as representatives of social capital in a quite different manner to real production'.[68] But he does not consider the process of concentration in banking, which only took place at a much later stage in Great Britain.

Hilferding is interested in the joint-stock corporations less from the standpoint of the development of productive forces than from that of property rights and finance. He focuses on 'founders' profit' and dividends. The distinction between concentration and centralisation in *Finance Capital* is unclear. In Part III, he examines what he names 'concentration' essentially through the analysis of market power and the monopolistic (oligopolistic) pricing of commodities by cartels and trusts. It is in relation to this issue that he discusses the two-way relationship between concentration in industry and concentration in banking. He puts the process in industry first but stresses at the end of the quote the coercive role that banks can play in industrial concentration.

---

67  Marx 1976, Vol. I, pp. 777–80.
68  Marx 1981, Vol. III, Chapter 22, p. 491.

> The development of capitalist industry produces concentration of banking, and this concentrated banking system is itself an important force in attaining the highest stage of capitalist concentration in cartels and trusts.... In the relations of mutual dependence between capitalist enterprises it is the amount of capital that principally decides which enterprise shall become dependent upon the other. From the outset the effect of advanced cartelization is that the banks also amalgamate and expand in order not to become dependent upon the cartel or trust. In this way cartelization itself requires the amalgamation of the banks, and, conversely, amalgamation of the banks requires cartelization. For example, a number of banks have an interest in the amalgamation of steel concerns, and they work together to bring about this amalgamation even against the will of individual manufacturers.[69]

Lenin uses mainly the word 'concentration'. He places industrial concentration at the centre of his analysis, positing that 'the enormous growth of industry and the remarkably rapid concentration of production in ever-larger enterprises are one of the most characteristic features of capitalism'. Lenin then analyses the data he has collected mainly from German sources, presenting among other things the first analysis of what came to be known in industrial economics as 'vertical integration'. Concentration in banking is examined only once it has been for industrial production. Lenin then takes up this dimension in some detail. He notes the high level of bank concentration in France, citing Crédit Lyonnais, the Comptoir National and the Société Générale, and also in Germany Deutsche Bank and Disconto-Gesellschaft. Here he uses the term 'centralisation'.

> We see the rapid expansion of a close network of channels which cover the whole country, centralising all capital and all revenues, transforming thousands and thousands of scattered economic enterprises into a single national capitalist, and then into a world capitalist economy. The 'decentralisation' that Schulze-Gaevernitz, as an exponent of present-day bourgeois political economy, speaks of in the passage previously quoted, really means the subordination to a single centre of an increasing number of formerly relatively 'independent', or rather, strictly local economic units. In reality it is *centralisation*, the enhancement of the role, importance and power of monopolist giants.[70]

---

69   Hilferding 1910, Chapter 14.
70   Lenin 1917, Chapter 2.

CHAPTER 4

# The Organisational Embodiments of Finance Capital and the Intra-Corporate Division of Surplus Value

This chapter discusses a number of issues pertaining to the intermeshing of large global banks, transnational industrial and service corporations and giant retailers. It also examines one of the dimensions of inter-corporate rivalry, namely that between industrial corporations and large retailers. In its dealing with workers, both as producers of surplus value and as consumers or debtors, finance capital functions as a block, but on the world market oligopolies behave as rivals. The chapter starts with a very short historical perspective on bank-industry relationships in four major countries (I). It then turns to the relation between capital-as-property and capital-as-function in the contemporary context of corporate governance and shareholder value followed by a discussion of interlocking boards of directors in globalised capitalism (II). Taking up again the idea that large banks and industrial corporations represent differentiations within finance capital, examples are given of TNC involvement in financial operations and of investment banks in non-financial operations (III). The chapter then takes up the issue of 'profits from circulation'. It argues that the decisive notion is the inter-capitalist division of the total surplus value produced in the exploitation process. The amount of total surplus produced by industrial firms which commodity traders and large retail firms manage to pocket, obviously depends on their capacity to exploit their own employees and workers but is determined more decisively in the balance of oligopolistic and monopsony power along the circuit of capitalist production and realisation of value and surplus value (IV). A short discussion of natural resource and oil rent ends the chapter (V).

1  A Brief Historical Perspective on the Bank-Industry Relationship

The centralisation of money capital as a 'concentrated and organized mass placed the control of bankers as representatives of social capital in a quite different manner to real production',[1] raising the issue of the relations between

---

[1] Marx 1981, Vol. III, Chapter 22, p. 491.

banks and industrial firms. In the case of small and medium firms, the situation has always been that of a dependence entailing close subjection of credit for investment to the scrutiny of banks. There have been quite long periods during which this relationship worked well in advanced capitalist countries, a part of the banking system being composed of small entities. We return to this in Chapter 8. Here we are concerned with the question of the relations between large banks and large industrial corporations in the context of the centralisation/concentration of money capital and the concentration of industrial capital. I risk a rough characterisation in the late nineteenth century for the four leading capitalist countries.

1.1     *Germany: The 'Unification of Capital' and a Strong Bank Influence in Industry*

The history of German industry is that of concentrated stable shareholders led by banks. In an oft-quoted passage of *Finance Capital*, Hilferding sums up his analysis of the combined effect of concentration in banking and in industry by saying that finance capital 'signifies the unification of capital'. It is placed under the hegemony of banks and comprises a high degree of control over industrialists, an involvement in management.[2] The stakes banks have in corporations through the loans they make to them, the capital they raise on the stock market on their behalf, and the shares they own themselves lead them 'to establish a permanent supervision of the companies' affairs, which is best done by securing representation on the board of directors'. Banks try 'to work with as many companies as possible, and at the same time, to be represented on their boards of directors. Ownership of shares enables the bank to impose its representatives even upon corporations which initially resisted. In this way there arises a tendency for the banks to accumulate such directorships'. 'Personal union' takes also the form of industrialists' membership of boards of other corporations. Their aim is 'to establish business relations between the companies involved. Thus, the representative of an iron firm who sits on the board of directors of a colliery aims to ensure that his firm obtains its coal from this colliery. This type of personal union, which also involves an accumulation of positions on boards of directors in the hands of a small group of big capitalists, becomes important when it is the precursor or promoter of closer organizational links between corporations which had previously been independent of one another'. These links can be those of vertical or horizontal integration through mergers to form a bigger firm or of cartel formation. Of course there are also personal advantages: as 'member of the board of directors, the large shareholder receives a share of the profit in the form of bonuses' and can also

---

2   Hilferding 1910, Chapter 14.

'use his inside knowledge of the firm's affairs for speculation in shares, or for other business transactions. A circle of people emerges who, thanks to their own capital resources or to the concentrated power of outside capital which they represent (in the case of bank directors), become members of the boards of directors of numerous corporations'.[3]

Comparative historical research on corporate ownership and control has broadly confirmed these relationships' existence in Germany. First, from the 1880s onwards, the important role of banks in the expansion of joint-stock companies or limited-liability share companies (*Aktiengesellschaft* or AG); second, the 'increasing cooperation and integration between firms that led to cross-shareholding, community of interests and corporate groups'.[4] In the large majority of firms, majority stockholders and their representatives had 'primary control and managers had held the status of leading employees'. There were notable exceptions, however, whose names personify German heavy industry. They are where personal family equity on a sufficient scale in combination with personal authority allowed 'the likes of Krupp, Thyssen, Stinnes, Wolfff, Stumm, Klökner, Siemens and Bosch to maintain solid control of their concerns'. The formation of cartels at the turn of the twentieth century is well documented. Following the Second World War these were dismantled but the particular relationships between large banks and large corporations survived and only started to be eroded as some of the major banks, notably Deutsche Bank, became globalised financial service conglomerates along with other major European 'universal banks'. The modest role of the stock market in the governance of German corporations is attested to by looking at capitalisation as a percentage of GDP: 38% over the period 1990–2005 as compared with 113% for the US and 132% for the UK. Cross shareholdings among banks, insurance companies and industrial corporations thwarted hostile takeovers until the Mannesmann-Vodafone case.[5] In the 2000s, German corporations still enjoyed the advantages of what Porter named 'the permanent owner' and 'dedicated capital'.[6]

### 1.2   Money Trusts as the US Form of Finance Capital

US corporations in industrial, mining and railways were big from the outset and became increasingly large with concentration. Mergers between medium-sized companies started early, at the turn of the twentieth century.[7] The 1890

---

3   Ibid.
4   Fohlin 2005, p. 225.
5   Onetti and Pisoni 2009.
6   Porter 1992.
7   See Roy 1997.

Sherman and 1914 Clayton Antitrust Acts created in principle the basis for anti-trust action against corporations in production and transport, but their wording was vague enough to give the courts considerable leeway in their interpretation while recourse to legislation depended on the Administration.[8] Concentration in industry was paralleled by that in banking. An intermeshing of the two developed from the 1890s onwards in the form of 'money trusts', with JP Morgan and Company, but also the Rockefeller family owners of Standard Oil, at the core. The Pujo 1913 Congressional Committee on the 'concentration of the control of money and credit' defined the money trust as meaning 'an established and well-defined identity and community of interest between a few leaders of finance which has been created and is held together by stock-holdings, interlocking directorates and other forms of domination over banks, trust companies, railroads, public service and industrial corporations, and which has grown in a vast and growing concentration of control of money and credit in the hands of a comparatively few men'.[9]

A specifically US form of direct bank control over large industry undoubtedly existed in this period. US money trusts were investment banks in their first form, in which they played substantial roles on corporate boards. This form of association between finance and industry created conflicts of interest that investment bankers could exploit as insider information for themselves. Nonetheless for shareholders the system was beneficial. Investment banker representation on boards allowed them to assess the performance of firm managers, quickly replace those with unsatisfactory performances and signal to investors that a company was fundamentally sound. The money trusts, notably JP Morgan and Co. in a position to decide which corporations were allowed to issue stock.[10] When Morgan and his partners sat on the boards of the corporations in which they had large stakes, it was mainly to follow closely the operations of management in relation to output and pricing. Veblen contrasted engineers possessing knowledge of industrial processes and products to what he named 'absentee owners'[11] and stressed the latter's control

---

8   Even before the neo-liberal turn of the 1980s, the intensity of action by the Federal Trade Commission varied considerably. The record is one of failure (Faulkner 1960, pp. 444–6).
9   Report of the Committee Appointed to Investigate the Concentration of the Control of Money and Credit, 62nd Congress, 3rd Session, p. 130, quoted by Faulkner 1960, pp. 447–8.
10  O'Sullivan 2015 argues however from historical data that JP Morgan and Co.'s domination has been considerably overstated.
11  Veblen 1923a and 1923b, quoted by Lazonick 1991, pp. 341–2.

over output and prices. In 1910–12, the presence on one's board of directors of a partner in JP Morgan and Co. added about 30% to common stock equity value.[12] According to the Pujo Committee, in 1912 Morgan or his partners sat on the boards of 20 manufacturing, mining, distribution, transport, or utility corporations that in turn had quoted common stocks in three utilities, nine railroads, and eight other companies. Diversification by the New York Stock Exchange out of railroads really took off between 1898 and 1902.[13] The transformation by Carnegie of his steel enterprises into joint stock corporations and the announcement of his retirement allowed JP Morgan and Co. to acquire them in 1901 and found the US Steel Corporation, the first corporation in the world with a market capitalisation over $1 billion. In 1914, corporations controlled or influenced by JP Morgan as shareholder and board members, besides US Steel, included AT&T, International Harvester, Westinghouse and General Electric. The end of the First World War saw a very rapid growth of the stock market and a sharp increase in the number of shareholders. With the disappearance, in the case of most corporations, of a dominant shareholder came the issue of the separation of ownership and control and the ways in which shareholders, despite their dispersion, could prevent managers taking decisions in their own interests. In 1932, it is posed as follows in Berle and Means's famous book:

> In its new aspect the corporation is a means whereby the wealth of innumerable individuals has been concentrated into huge aggregates and whereby control over this wealth has been surrendered to a unified direction. The power attendant upon such concentration has brought forth princes of industry, whose position in the community is yet to be defined. The surrender of control over their wealth by investors has effectively broken the old property relationships and has raised the problem of defining these relationships anew. The direction of industry by persons other than those who have ventured their wealth has raised the question of the motive force back of such direction and the effective distribution of the returns from business enterprise.[14]

This question was to be the foundation of the theory of agency and its victory in the form of contemporary corporate governance. However, for a time as a result of the crisis and the political struggles of the 1930s, and then of the war

---

12   De Long 1991, p. 205.
13   See O'Sullivan 2015.
14   Berle and Means 1932.

economy, managers seemed to have things in hand and a 'managerial revolution' was deemed as having triumphed. We return to this below.

### 1.3 The Prevalence of Imperial Financing Priorities in Britain

The British situation in the late nineteenth and early twentieth centuries is clearly different from that of Germany and the US. With respect to domestic industry, the debate among historians hinges on the extent to which a 'conspicuous absence of a working relation between the banks and industry before 1914'[15] existed or not and whether this could account in part for the falling back of British industry despite its lead in the advent of the Industrial Revolution. A 1911 report to the US government on the situation of America's European rivals observes that in the case of Britain the 'complete divorce between stock exchange and deposits... causes another great evil, namely, that the banks have never shown any interest in the newly founded companies or in the securities issued by these companies, while it is a distinct advantage of the German system, that the German banks, even if only in the interests of their own issue credit, have been keeping a continuous watch over the development of the companies, which they founded'.[16] Some banks with a primary interest in long-term industrial investment did appear in the 1860s and 1870s, but with the exception of the National Provincial Bank of England their lives were brief. Another paradoxical factor may have been the successful adoption of the joint-stock company. The 1844 Joint Stock Company Act accorded this status to small companies. It is also argued that the establishment of local stock markets in industrial centres in the Midlands and the North may have contributed to hold up industrial concentration in Britain.[17] A number of historians consider that if Britain had employed at home the capital and labour that went abroad after 1850, domestic growth rates after 1870 could have been as high, or even higher, than those of the 'Mid-Victorian Boom'.[18] However, this line of argument may be overlooking the demand pull coming from investment abroad.

As the centre of the world gold-based monetary system, City banks made large profits from money-market and foreign exchange operations. In the centralisation of money capital for investment, the City also favoured financial operations which looked out to the world economy. The Stock Exchange

---

15  Garside and Greaves 1996.
16  Riesser 1911, quoted by DeLong 1991.
17  Thomas 2005.
18  Cain and Hopkins 1993, pp. 191–2, citing Kennedy 1982, Pollard 1985, and Eichengreen 1982.

attracted more foreign corporations than any other financial centre up to 1914. The data organised by Cain and Hopkins[19] include showing that only 600 of the 5,000 stocks quoted in London in 1910 were issued by British industrial and commercial companies and a good many of those were overseas-based concerns. Of the money raised for domestic-based projects, only about 18 percent went into manufacturing on average during the years 1865 to 1914. This represented roughly 6 percent of all the finance raised in London in these years. In sharp contrast, something like one quarter went into the financing of railway companies operating in the Empire or foreign countries. Indeed from 1870 to 1913, some 5 percent of British GDP was invested abroad and in 1914 a third of British assets came from foreign investments and loans. Another indicator is the use of savings. Their mass in Britain was not lower than that of Germany and the US, but while these invested about 12 percent of their annual income domestically, Britain put only 7 percent of its annual income back into the national economy and sent another 4 or 5 percent abroad.[20] The share of British as opposed to foreign companies in the loan capital raised in London was in fact falling before 1914. The City can be defined as having helped to build the British Empire as the first system of worldwide appropriation of surplus value in the form of profits and interest made abroad.[21] This started through the building of railroads in India and Canada and later Australia, and railroads and harbours in South America and South Africa. There the system involved the setting up of large firms only in mining (Rio Tinto and deBeers, for example). But a large part of British investment overseas was the doing of small 'free-standing companies' financed by capital centralised in the London stock exchange.[22] The very large manufacturing corporation appeared in Britain long after it did in Germany and the US. The flagship of mid-twentieth-century British industrial capitalism, ICI, was only founded in 1926.

What is certain is that over the same period Britain lost its technological lead. Lewis points out that at the end of the nineteenth century 'organic chemicals became a German industry; the motor car was pioneered in France and mass-produced in the United States; Britain lagged in the use of electricity, depended on foreign firms established in the US and took only a small share of the export market. The telephone, the typewriter, the cash register, and the

---

19   Cain and Hopkins 1993.
20   Pollard 1985.
21   The scale of and the contemporary conditions in which 'Britain uses the financial system to gain economic privileges by appropriating value from other countries while appearing to do them a favour' are examined by Norfield 2016.
22   Wilkins 1970.

diesel engine were all exploited by others'. Before that British production of steam locomotives had already been caught up by all its future rivals, while the full exploitation of the revolutionary Bessemer steel-melting technique took place in the US following Bessemer's licensing of his invention to an American firm in 1863.[23] Britain's 'comparative advantage' was to lie not in industry but in commerce and finance and in the role the City plays more than ever in the global financial system.

### 1.4   France: State Support to Industry and Large Foreign Government Loans

The French story is different again. As a result of class relations born from the French Revolution and from counter-revolution during the Restoration and the July Monarchy, banking developed in the form of the French variant of investment banking. This was the *Haute Banque* where the interests of landowners and conservative financiers converged, imprinting on French banking deep rentier traits. Fear of the working class (the silk workers' or Canuts' revolt in Lyon, the February 1848 Revolution in Paris and later the Paris Commune) led the bourgeoisie to maintain the social stability brought about by small land ownership,[24] to the detriment of an expansion of the domestic market. The pace of industrialisation as embodied by iron, steel and metallurgy took place very slowly[25] and was driven by the building of railroads and demand from state-owned military factories and shipyards.[26] During the Second Empire (1852–70), government financing and the creation of government-supported Saint-Simonian banks willing to challenge the *Haute Banque* was necessary in the financing of the railroad industry.[27] The only feat of the *Bourse des valeurs*, the Paris Stock Exchange, was the financing of the Suez Canal Company (*Compagnie universelle du canal maritime de Suez*) with the issue of shares starting in December 1858. Otherwise the data presented by Bouvier[28] showing the weakness of industry is startling: in 1845 banks represented 23 percent of Paris market capitalisation and railroads 53 percent, and in 1870 the

---

23  Lewis 1978, p. 130, quoted by DeLong and Grossman 1993.
24  Marx's book on mid-nineteenth-century France, *The Eighteenth Brumaire of Louis Bonaparte* (1852), remains a synthetic socio-economic and political analysis which subsequent research has substantiated. Readers pressed for time can go straight to the last chapter.
25  See Palmade 1961 and Caron 1979.
26  See Chesnais and Serfati 1992.
27  Notably Issac and Emile Peirere's *Crédit Mobilier* set up in 1852. See Plessis 1982 and Stoskopf 2002.
28  Bouvier 1961.

corresponding figures were 25 and 48 percent. During the period running from 1871 to 1918, banks made 35 percent of new domestic issues.[29]

During the first decades of the Third Republic, industry made such a limited call on finance that Henry Germain, the founder of the largest commercial bank Crédit Lyonnais, declared in 1876 that 'we are overburdened with money; we don't know what to do with it'.[30] So the banks sought foreign investment. France's capital exports, compared to those of other developed countries, were marked by a clear preference for loans (and to a lesser extent, for portfolio investments in government bonds) over direct investments in production.[31] After 1880, Russia became the leading destination of French foreign investments, accounting for more than 25 percent of them in 1914. The ill-fated Russian bonds were the culmination of this form of investment. But there were more successful loans to Argentina and Mexico.[32] The French colonies were the other recipient of French investment.[33] Once gunfire had ceased, finance took over, in Africa and the Far East, notably Indochina, not simply through trading posts but the setting up of plantation production and export (rubber in particular).[34] Very powerful entities were created, notably the Banque d'Indochine.[35] In Africa, the most powerful entity, the Banque Rivaud, survived political decolonisation. It is part of the Bolloré family group, still extremely active today in plantation production and the commodities trade in West Africa.[36]

Weak industrial investment and a low call of finance whether from banks or the stock market is a persistent trait of French capitalism in which family-owned firms enjoying privileged access to public markets and state-owned firms predominated. France did not miss the emergence of the automobile industry, but it is significant that the Renault family built the firm initially through self-financing and then from 1914 onwards with large government orders.[37] The creation by the government of the Caisse Nationale de Crédit Agricole in 1920 (now France's second largest financial conglomerate) reflected

29  Arbulu 1998, tables 2 and 7.
30  Quoted by Bouvier 1961.
31  Levy-Leboyer 1977.
32  Girault 1993.
33  The remark by Lenin 1916, Chapter 4, that unlike British colonial imperialism, French imperialism might be termed usury imperialism, underplays this activity.
34  The role of the conditions of production in Michelin's growth and profits are discussed in Panthou and Bình 2013.
35  See a Japanese scholar, Gonjo 1993.
36  The main references are Suret-Canal 1962 and Bouvier 1974.
37  See Fridenson 1972.

the bourgeoisie's aim at making farmers more than ever a pillar of social and political stability. The 1930s were characterised, notably by Albert Sauvy, as being years of demographic but also of 'economic Malthusianism'. Only nationalisation during the 1936 Popular Government, together with government financing, allowed the aeronautical industry to take-off. The postwar French industrial system, the system of innovation (with the development of atomic energy at its core) and the highly concentrated corporate system are the result of forceful government action and financing first in 1945–8 and again in the 1970s and in 1982.[38] They are an outcome of a particular political alliance and the industrial face of the social-democratic compromise. To finish with one of Hilferding's themes: France experienced a very particular and visible form of 'personal union', namely the two hundred largest shareholders of the Banque de France as decreed by the statutes enacted by Napoleon in 1803. Known as the *'deux cent familles'*, they included the *Haute Banque* investment banks and industrial family capital[39] (*inter alia* the Schneider, the De Wendel, and a little later the Michelin, Renault, Peugeot, Worms and Schlumberger families). They lost this particular privilege with the nationalisation of the Banque de France by the 1936 Popular Front government, but their economic and social power[40] only ended in 1945 with the fall of the Vichy government.

## 2 Contemporary Issues Regarding Corporate Governance and Interlocking Boards of Directors

With the development of financial accumulation, the emergence of pension fund capital and the full reestablishment of stock markets, the issue of ownership and control, more properly understood as the relationship between capital-as-function and capital-as-property, have come to the fore once again. Economic integration in Europe and globalisation have also spurred new interest in the configuration of interlocking boards of directors.

### 2.1 *Control Under Contemporary US Corporate Governance*
For US industrial economists belonging to the liberal left, there exists a sort of Golden Age (somewhat akin to 'les trente glorieuses' for the French left), when managers, as theorised and celebrated in particular by Galbraith (also

---

38  I have made a full analysis in Chesnais 1993.
39  The position of family controlled capital has only receded slowly. See 'To have and to hold: Family Companies', *The Economist*, 2015, Special Report, p. 5.
40  Trotsky writes about this in *Whither France?* (Trotsky 1934–6).

described critically by Baran and Sweezy in *Monopoly Capital*), were in almost complete command. A recent nostalgic review of Galbraith's *The New Industrial State* recalls the period of the 1960s when:

> managers (typically salaried employees rather than owner-founders or their heirs) had seen their power grow relative to that of shareholders, as these were far removed from being able to usefully observe and understand the intricate internal workings of companies, while their prospects for exercising detailed control over company operations were further diminished by the wide diffusion of stock ownership. The result was that, so long as a company continued to deliver an 'acceptable' level of profit, the technostructure enjoyed the degree of autonomy without which its elaborate planning was impossible. The 'new' CEOs, (by contrast to the generation of Henry Ford), were more willing to give expertise its due, and more pragmatic in their dealings with government and labor ... They were not unconcerned with profit, but maximizing it was not their sole or even primary object – in part because they were salaried personnel whose own income was less closely connected to company fortunes, and in part because other motives had come to the fore, in particular 'identification' with the company that gave them their privileged positions, and the satisfaction afforded by the 'adaptation' of the company in line with their own, particular ideas about its mission.[41]

As the stock market regained strength in the 1980s and attracted more and more capital following the fall of interest rates on government bonds (see figure 2.1), and as large industrial corporations became in some cases unwieldy and highly vulnerable conglomerates, the 'Industrial State' corporation came under attack before disappearing.[42] The 1980s witnessed a first wave of finance-dominated industrial restructuring fuelled by a first generation of high-yield high-risk bonds ('junk bonds') and the emergence of financiers bent on increasing their returns very quickly. With the 1990s and the arrival of pension funds controlling significant chunks of shares came the restoration of the power of shareholders and the elaboration of the shareholder value doctrine. Concern over, if not denunciation of, its consequences have not ceased since. In the second half of the 1980s, at the time when the subordination of corporations to finance was

---

41  Elhefnawy 2012.
42  Baronian and Pierre 2011 show that what they name the 'internal financialisation' of corporations facilitated the introduction of corporate governance, through changes in management structures and accounting systems.

beginning, even at the MIT and the Harvard Business School the list of identified consequences of financialisation included 'short-termism' in production and investment decisions, and low corporate outlays on R&D provoked by the rise of finance-prone management.[43] These studies were followed by more radical analyses on the consequences of the market for corporate control by Lazonick and O'Sullivan, notably 'downsize and distribute' dividend strategies.[44] De-industrialisation as measured by the place of manufacturing and the loss of competiveness by the United States – even in high-technology industries at a time when financial markets were flourishing – led to further research by non-mainstream economists on the effects of financialisation, in the form notably of shareholder value maximisation on investment and R&D.[45] Today the main umbrella expression used by what remains of the 'pro-industry' wing in US business school literature is the 'industrial commons', lost on account of finance-subordinated managerial practices.[46]

Relations of power in the global system and issues of competitiveness and technological advantage have always guided US discussion and set the context in which what has been at stake is capital-as-property and capital-as-function. The most radical assessment of the current US situation as set out by Lazonick is that of a transition 'from value creation to value extraction'.[47] This refers not to the outsourcing relations between large firms and their subcontractors discussed below in Chapter 5, but to the division of corporate profit to the advantage of shareholders and stock-option remunerated senior executives.[48] The maximisation of shareholder value is the common creed of the senior executives of the very large industrial corporations and banks alike. The methods used are stock buy-backs and the elaboration of strategies influencing the movement of stock-prices.[49] Since the late 1990s, first in the US and subsequently in other advanced capitalist economies, recourse to external methods of control through the stock market has been coupled with stock option-based

---

43   In the late 1980s, well-publicised US studies, notably MIT's *Made in America* (Dertoutzos et al. 1989) and Michael Porter's study *Capital Choices* (Porter 1992), were at least temporarily very critical of finance-bred short-termism.
44   Lazonick and O'Sullivan 2000.
45   Lazonick 2012. In this particular study, the effects of share buy-backs are examined but also tax privileges on profit made abroad.
46   Pisano and Shih 2009.
47   Lazonick 2014.
48   There is an awareness of the exploitation and overexploitation associated with this, but it is totally subordinated to the thrust of the argument.
49   Lazonick 2014 calculates that between 2003 and 2012, the S&P 500 used 54 percent of their earnings to buy back their own stock, while dividends absorbed another 37 percent. He names these strategies 'stock market manipulation'.

remuneration systems for corporate executives, aimed at creating a close common financial interest and perspective between managers and shareholders.[50] The senior executives of the very large industrial corporations, banks and financial holding companies (of which Berkshire Hathaway is the largest and best-known), as well as the large asset managers and hedge fund owners, are seen as equals. Under financialisation the 'dictatorship' is that of financial returns and concerns banks and corporations alike.

For financial and non-financial corporations, management norms are routinely set by benchmark targets, the most important being the rate of return on equity (ROE). The task of ensuring the respect of shareholder value is very largely delegated, even by pension funds, to asset-managing corporations. Hedge funds are entrusted with the task of putting pressure on corporations and indeed mounting public campaigns to remove senior executives. For some it is a specialty.[51] Shareholder activism led by hedge funds can force corporations as powerful as Apple to increase their distribution of income to shareholders through share buy-backs. Corporations still marked by a conglomerate-type range of operations will be asked to discard non-core activities. Only large banks and large hedge funds have their own expertise. The largest specialised asset-managing corporation working for investors is BlackRock. It is also the one for which the most amount of information is available. It has shares in many of the largest US corporations.[52] At its heart is an enormous data-processing system churning out indicators of corporate performance. BlackRock does not look at the management strategies of these companies, but because it 'is often their largest shareholder companies care what it thinks'.[53] Large investment banks with true expertise and seats on boards will offer corporations their advice, but the executives of, say, Goldman Sachs and JP Morgan will hardly tell those of Exxon, Wal-Mart and General Motors what they should do.

---

50   In 2012, for the 500 highest-paid executives in proxy statements, compensation came at a rate of 42 percent in the form of stock options and 41 percent in stock awards (Lazonick 2014).

51   The state of play of shareholder activism is presented in *The Economist*: 'The pressure on companies from activist shareholders continues to grow', 15 February 2014. Icahn Enterprises is cited as the leader of the pack. On Icahn and his shares in Apple see Lazonick, https://ineteconomics.org/ideas-papers/blog/what-we-learn-about-inequality-from-carl-icahns-2-billion-apple-no-brainer.

52   In December 2013, it held 25 percent of the stock of Apple, 22 percent of Exxon, 20 percent of Google, to name the largest US non-financial corporations in its portfolio, but BlackRock also held 19 percent of Berkshire Hathaway (Warren Buffet). ('The Monolith and the Markets', *The Economist*, 9 December 2013).

53   Ibid.

## 2.2 Cross-country Interlocking Boards of Directors and 'Transnational Capitalist Class Formation' in Europe

In the case of the US today, the importance of interlocking directorates is mainly that of ensuring the class cohesion necessary for full capitalist social and political domination. Domhoff, author of a major book on the structure of American class power,[54] writes that 'most corporate directors are not interlocking directors. Even when a large number of companies are included in the database, making the possibilities for interlocks much greater, only about 15–20 percent of corporate directors sit on two or more corporate boards. And even fewer, of course, sit on three, four, five, or six boards, although they are the people who tie the network together. They are "linchpins"'.[55] There is an 'upper-class control of corporations... seen in its over-representation on boards of directors along with a high degree of stability in interlocks. However the cooption by promotion of women and Afro-Americans to boards is an important way of broadening the basis of cohesion'. In the case of non-financial corporations, Domhoff sees the economic consequences of interlocking boards as being today mainly that of 'the easy diffusion of new management ideas'.

In the case of Europe, the growth of transnational corporations and the formation of the EU warrant a discussion of the available data and of academic findings in this area. In the context of global oligopolistic rivalry, slightly tempered at the national level by large firms in given sectors and moments of acute crisis, the relationship of corporation to state is one where each 'national' segment of financial capital will look for and obtain the support of its own government. As put by Serfati, the situation is one in which 'the anchoring of capitalist relations in a "home country" is both an economic and political necessity'[56] and one where different governments will seek, as far as they can, to evolve common policies in the interest of financial capital as a whole. He sees the formation of a 'transnational capitalist class' as being still a long way off. This is confirmed by data on interlocking boards of directors collected by William Carroll covering the period up to 2007.[57] He finds that only 29 percent

---

54 Domhoff 1967. In 2005, with an update in 2012, he summarised the data and the arguments of his 1967 book. http://www2.ucsc.edu/whorulesamerica/power/class_domination.html.
55 Domhoff 2013.
56 Serfati 2013, p. 155.
57 See Carroll 2013, p. 175: 'A relatively small inner circle of mainly European and North American men constitutes the network; a relatively small number of countries host most of the interlocked corporations, and within those countries a few cities predominate as command centres for global corporate power... the increasing number of South-based giant corporations were by 2007 only very tentatively linked into the elite network of

of the world's 500 largest corporations had one or more transnational interlocking director, the vast majority of those engaged in transnational interlocking being headquartered in the US and Canada[58] and in Europe.

In an essay published in 1970, and little quoted since, Mandel defended the hypothesis that mergers would take place between corporations from Common Market member countries. This would lead to a trans-border formation of truly European capital. A bourgeois 'United States of Europe' might even emerge and challenge North America.[59] An interesting study by Carroll, Fennema and Heemskerk[60] has taken up the hypothesis of the formation of a European capitalist class again. This is done through mapping the network of interlocking corporate directorates and its overlaps with the membership of the Brussels-based European Round Table (ERT), where large corporations meet to exercise influence on the policies of the EU. Capital centralisation/concentration is an underlying theme of the study. The mapping of this interlocking focuses exclusively on the European corporations listed in the Fortune Global 500 global league table, designated as 'corporate Europe'. The study covers the period from 1996 to 2006. Two types of interlocking are identified, interlocking within countries that 'bond' and interlocking between countries that 'bridge'. The authors also lay considerable stress on membership of the select European Roundtable of Industrialists (ERT). On the basis of their findings they consider that there has been a 'relative success' of capitalist class formation in Europe. Juggling the notions of class and 'community' (this is the unconvincing theoretical point of their study), they write:

> The consolidation of corporate Europe has been a conscious project, centered in organizations like the ERT and European Commission and in emergent norms favoring multinational representation on corporate boards. But within that institutional framework, community formation has also proceeded molecularly, as the by-product of an increasing volume of pan-European practices among Europe's major corporations. Coexisting as it does with the persistence of attenuated national corporate networks, consolidation of a European corporate community, integrated in no small measure by the ERT, is an important aspect of class hegemony. Even as it reproduces patterns of unequal representation,

---

corporate interlocks... only three G500 directors (all based in the global North) sat on Chinese corporate boards in 2007'.
58   Carroll 2008.
59   Mandel 1970.
60   Carroll et al. 2010.

this consolidation enables the leading segment of the capitalist class, the inner circle, to speak with one voice.[61]

It is obvious that within the EU, managers representing highly concentrated national capital find a consensus and speak when they meet in the ERT with one voice and seek to reinforce their class hegemony, especially on issues relating to capital-labour relations. But on issues pertaining to relations with other parts of the globalised economy, notably when international treaties are being negotiated, large corporations see to it that their national and sectorial interests prevail as far as possible. From the standpoint of the theory of finance capital, the study by Carroll and his colleagues contributes many useful findings. The sector with the highest domestic and intra-European transnational interlocks is finance qua finance. In 2006, seven banks and insurance companies ranked among the 21 corporations with five or more transnational interlocks. BNP Paribas in particular combined extensive bonding and bridging interlocking alike. The interlocking boards on which German banks and insurance companies sat remained within a national network, in which they occupied central locations, as were in France French banks other than BNP Paribas and the insurance companies (AXA). The Italian, Spanish, Belgian and Swedish banks and insurance companies attained centrality largely through European interlocking. The exception was the UK. Only three of the 13 UK large financial corporations had five or more interlocks, and their ties tended to be with other UK firms. Pursuing the analysis a step further, the research focused on executives who belonged simultaneously to the board of one or more financial institutions (banks or insurance companies) and one or more non-financial corporations, finding that bankers became less dominant. These executives 'create the institutional links that are typical of finance capital'. In 1996, such interlockers were 'national finance capitalists', directors of both industrial and financial companies domiciled within a single country. As bridging interlocks increased, so did 'transnational finance capitalists'; 'rather than bankers, it is *industrialists with financial connections* that form the core of the European corporate community'. 'Europe's corporate community is indeed organized around a financial-industrial axis, but the era of bank dominance is over'.[62] However this is not reflected completely in ERT membership. Of the 12 corporations that share multiple directors with the ERT, the tightest links are those of BNP Paribas and Allianz, each with four ERT members on board.

---

61  Carroll et al. 2010, p. 836.
62  Carroll et al. 2010, p. 830, emphasis in original.

The formation through intra-EU mergers of a truly European capitalist élite in the way hypothesised by Mandel has not taken place. The movement in this direction has been driven by governments rather than corporations. The European Space Agency (ESA) with its successful launcher Ariane (today Ariane 5) operated by the French corporation Arianespace has resisted intra-European industrial confrontations. Airbus is of course another example, but its history has been punctuated by moments of severe tension revealing how strong national interests remain even between countries that have been partners over a long period. In the defence industries, the absence of common interests is still greater – notable, for example, is the German veto on the planned merger between EADS and BAE. The history of Alstom and Siemens is that of bitter competition ending with the acquisition in 2014 of Alstom's power and grid divisions by General Electric. In the automobile industry, mergers and close strategic alliances have been between European and Japanese (Renault-Nissan and Volkswagen-Suzuki), European and US (Fiat-Chrysler), or Chinese corporations (Peugeot-DongFeng Motors).

## 3  Banks as Merchants and TNCs as Money Capitalists

One of the features of financialisation is the breaking down of the earlier separation of activities between the financial and non-financial operations of corporations. This will be illustrated by some examples.

### 3.1  The Operations of Financial Conglomerates in Commodities Trading and Production

Since the turn of the 1990s, the principal organisational or institutional form of financial capital *qua* interest-bearing capital is the large diversified financial service corporation, also named the financial conglomerate,[63] the core corporation of which may either be a commercial bank, an investment bank or an insurance company.[64] The other main forms of interest-bearing capital are investment funds – pension funds, mutual funds and hedge funds, which were initially an outgrowth of the former, before becoming very powerful

---

63   See Bank for International Settlements (BIS), *Principles for the supervision of financial conglomerates, www.bis.org/publ/joint27.pdf* and European Commission, The Financial Conglomerates Directive, http://ec.europa.eu/internal_market/financial-conglomerates/supervision.

64   The characterisation of 'banks' as diversified financial conglomerates is missing in Toussaint 2014.

independent entities. Banks remain in a special position among financial corporations. Through the credit-creating mechanism, they do not simply centralise loan capital, but they create it. The credit creating operations and speculative activities of financial conglomerates are discussed in Chapters 7 and 8. Here the focus is on one of their major ventures outside of banking, namely the trading and even the production of key basic commodities.

The scale of these operations really came into the limelight with the suits made against some of the largest Wall Street banks for manipulation of commodity markets on the grounds that they were simultaneously engaged in two major derivative markets, commodity forwards and futures, and in the physical trading and production of the very same commodities. The US Commodities Futures Trading Commission (CFTC) has initiated proceedings and private class-action suits filed in several Federal courts. The accusation of manipulation and so the identification of a 'conflict of interest' (to put it mildly) concerns in particular aluminium. In a hearing held by the US Senate Banking, Housing and Urban Affairs Committee in July 2013, an executive testified that 'the aluminium-warehousing system imposed waits exceeding 18 months and all "key elements" of the system for aluminium and base metals worldwide are controlled by the same entities, namely bank holding companies'.[65] The principal scholar to have studied the operations of financial conglomerates in this area is a law professor, Saule Omarova. She has published articles on the subject, but here and in Appendix 1 the data is taken from her extensive written testimony.[66] But Eric Toussaint has also enlightening pages which include information on major European bank entry in this field.[67] The possibility for 'financial holding companies' to enter this field was part of the 1999 Gramm-Leach-Bliley Act which definitively repealed the Glass-Steagall Act of 1933. It was also facilitated by decisions made by the Board of Governors of the Federal Reserve System in its capacity as regulatory agency, shedding light on the close relationships between the Fed and the large US banks.

Citigroup was the first financial conglomerate to receive, in 2003, the Fed's approval of its physical commodities trading as a 'complementary' activity. Citigroup was permitted 'to purchase and sell oil, natural gas, agricultural products, and other non-financial commodities in the spot market and to take and make physical delivery of commodities and to settle permissible commodity derivative transactions'.[68] In subsequent years, the Fed granted similar

---

65 'Metal bashing: Insinuations of market manipulation accelerate another upheaval in finance', *The Economist*, 17 August 2013.
66 Omarova 2013.
67 Toussant 2014, pp. 195–200.
68 All quotes in this and following paragraphs are from Omarova's 23 July 2013 testimony.

THE ORGANISATIONAL EMBODIMENTS OF FINANCE CAPITAL 111

orders authorising physical commodity trading to large non-US banks (UBS, Barclays, Deutsche Bank and Société Générale) allowing them to expand their worldwide physical commodities businesses by adding US operations. In 2005, JP Morgan Chase asked and was permitted in turn to engage in physical commodity trading activities as complementary to its financial derivatives business. In 2008, the Royal Bank of Scotland (RBS), still the UK's largest financial conglomerate, was authorised to do the same after acquiring a 51% stake in a joint venture with US utility corporation Sempra Energy. The joint venture, RBS Sempra Commodities, conducts physical trading in oil, natural gas, coal, and non-precious metals. The testimony notes that 'In the RBS Order, the Board [the Fed] significantly relaxed the standard limitations'. It 'authorized RBS to hire third parties to refine, blend, or otherwise alter the commodities... explicitly allowing RBS to sell crude oil to an oil refinery and then buy back the refined oil product'. It also permitted RBS to enter into long-term electricity supply contracts with large industrial and commercial customers.

The 2008 crisis had the twofold effect of changing the legal status of Morgan Stanley and Goldman Sachs into 'financial holding corporations' placed under the Fed's jurisdiction, and of leading to an increase in the degree of concentration of financial conglomerate activities in commodity shipping and production as it did in banking (cf. Chapter 7). Here the case in point was the acquisition by JP Morgan Chase of the commodity assets of Bear Stearns following its failure and collapse and of the shedding by RBS of its global commodities business following its rescue and nationalisation in 2009. The outcome is the domination of a highly oligopolistic sector by a core of three very powerful corporations. Omarova stresses the 'informational gap' which makes an exact assessment difficult. First, financial conglomerates report their assets, revenues and profits for a consolidated business in which the commodity-trading segment is only a part. Second, to the extent that financial-holding corporations include in their regulatory filings financial information specific to their commodities operations, it usually includes both commodity-linked derivatives operations and trading in physical commodities. As a result, most financial information reported under the 'commodities' rubric relates to the derivatives business, 'leaving one to guess what is going on in the firms' physical commodities businesses', and this makes less visible the fact that they act 'not only as dealers in purely financial risk but also as traditional commodity merchants'. The third difficulty stems from 'the inherently secretive nature of the commodity trading industry where a handful of large, mostly Switzerland-based commodities trading houses – including Glencore, Vitol, Trafigura, Mercuria, and Gunvor – dominate the global trade in oil and gas, petroleum products, coal, metals, and other products'. The testimony considers nonetheless that it is still 'possible to piece together enough data to get a sense of the *potential* significance of the Goldman Sachs, Morgan Stanley and JP Morgan Chase physical commodities businesses'.[69] This is summarised in Annex 4.2.

### 3.2    The Financial Operations of TNCs

Alongside their recognised productive and predatory activities, TNCs are strongly engaged in financial operations and thus show overall profits that include interest and gains from speculation. From the 1980s onwards, the scale of the hoards coming from non-invested and non-distributed profits led TNCs to set up their own financial departments or internal group banks with the purpose of valorising them in financial markets. A key notion is the holding company situated at the core of the corporate structure. Anglophone Marxist economists working in stock-market based corporate systems have rarely felt the need to reflect on the implications of the holding company as have French Marxist and heterodox economists with their early definition of large industrial firms as 'financial corporations principally engaged in industrial activity'.[70] Working in a government- and family-owned corporate system they were sensitive to the shift towards the US corporate form and paid particular attention to the operations of financial departments.

The management and valorisation by TNCs of non-invested and non-distributed profits blurs the lines between productive and interest-bearing capital. But the breakdown once identified also requires separate data collection and analytical treatment. In an early study little read by Anglophone economists, Serfati showed that at the level of the holding company, TNCs had all established financial departments, making a large range of short-term financial market, money market and foreign exchange market operations of non-negligible dimensions.[71] A number possessed affiliated banks at some point. In subsequent Anglophone research, Greta Krippner found that 'the increasing dependence of non-financial firms on financial activities as a source of revenue is critical for understanding these firms. Indeed, the very elusiveness of the control debate reflects the fact that the distinction between the forces acting "inside" and "outside" non-financial corporations is becoming increasingly arbitrary'. She emphasises that 'non-financial corporations are beginning to resemble financial corporations – in some cases, *closely* – and we need to take

---

69    JP Morgan Chase has since then sold its physical commodities affiliate to a Swiss commodity-trading house Mercuria; see 'Commodity-trading companies are growing and running more risks', *The Economist*, 6 September 2014.
70    Morin 1974.
71    Serfati 1996. See also (in English) Serfati 2008, but with much less detailed information.

this insight to our studies of corporate behavior'.[72] One of the findings of her meticulous article covering the period 1950–2000 is that the ratio of portfolio income – interest, dividends and capital-market-investment gains[73] – to cash flows, which she uses as her indicator of financialisation, grew from 20% in 1980 to 60% in 2001. It receded temporarily in the mid-1990s, which I interpret as a consequence of the momentary rise of profits from productive investment related to the New Economy. Within this portfolio income, the fall of the capital-market-investment gains component of the ratio in 2000 is more than compensated for by the increase of the interest component.[74] No studies or reports giving figures are available for the 2000s. Nor has there been academic work looking, as Serfati did in 1996, at the whole range of the interest-appropriating and speculative operations by industrial corporations and the way they integrated financial-type activities, including through the ownership of captive banks. In Appendix 2 examples are given of the place of financial affiliates in group structures focusing on General Electric, the automobile corporations and captive insurance, in the hope that this will encourage younger colleagues to explore this dimension of industrial corporations' activities systematically.

## 4  Concentrated Commodity or Merchant Capital and the Sharing Out of Total Surplus Value

In Volume II of *Capital*, Marx presents 'commodity-capital' as totally subordinated to industrial capital. Similarly, in 1910, Hilferding considers that 'the development of finance capital reduces the significance of trade both absolutely and relatively, transforming the once-proud merchant into a mere agent of industry which is monopolized by finance capital'.[75] The contemporary situation is radically different: even very large industrial corporations are forced

---

72  Krippner 2005, p. 202, original emphasis. I had seen Krippner repeatedly quoted as defining financialisation as 'a pattern of accumulation in which profits accrue primarily through financial channels rather than through trade and commodity production' (Krippner 2005, p. 174) – a position with which I, of course, disagreed, before discovering that her article was much better than the quote.

73  These are all appropriations of surplus value and appear as 'profits without production' *only* at the level of the individual firm. The problem is that Krippner's term was subsequently used by some Marxists to characterise contemporary capitalism more broadly.

74  Krippner 2005, figures 5 and 6.

75  Hilferding 1910, Chapter 14.

to abandon a part of the surplus value appropriated to highly concentrated commodity or merchant capital. In turn, analysing profits made by the latter helps to clarify the nature of financial profits.

## 4.1  The Notion of 'Profits in Circulation'

The idea that profits are increasingly being made in the circulation process rather than in the production process has been put forward unconvincingly and with a little hesitation by some authors.[76] The issue will be examined in Chapter 7 in relation to the operations of financial corporations and the sources of contemporary banking profits. Here it is discussed with respect to commodities and retailing.

The essential analytical framework is the circuit of capital: $M$-$C$-$P$-$C'$-$M'$. It has an inclusive analytical validity. At all five points there are common features, notably in that the share of any firm in the distribution of surplus value will depend on how cheaply it buys labour power and how efficiently it exploits labour power. But otherwise this share will depend on inter-corporate relationships as shaped by the state of supply and demand (whether a seller's market or a buyer's market) and by size. Degrees of monopoly and monopsony, even very relative ones, determine the 'bargaining power' of firms. All that is known about sub-contracting or outsourcing makes this perfectly clear. This is what 'value-chains' are about. The sub-contracting, outsourcing and offshoring operations as well as the operations of retailers are discussed at some length in the next chapter.

The key point, as put by Harvey, is that 'if there is no value and surplus value being produced in production in general, then these sectors (retailers and banks) cannot exist by themselves'.[77] Certainly, if we look at the corporations which collectively compose finance capital, at any given moment there is only a given amount of surplus value to be divided among them. Financial corporations, corporations engaged in the raw material constant capital component of $C$, and those engaged at the retail sales end in the transition of $C_1$ to $M_1$ will battle for as big a share as possible. Investment banks will likewise attempt to get corporations to concede to them large chunks of surplus value as fees for the organisation of M&As. Similarly, large manufacturers are permanently battling with giant retail firms on how much surplus value should remunerate

---

76  This hesitation seems to be the case in Lapavitsas's article for the Basque journal *Ekonomiaz*. The interesting analysis does not call for the title and first sentence of the abstract: 'Financialisation, or the search for profits in the sphere of circulation' (Lapavitsas 2009).

77  Harvey 2012, p. 11.

the organisation of the realisation of value and surplus value and the closing of the capital circuit. The configuration of the sharing out will depend on several factors, such as the skill of retailers in exploiting their employees, but more decisively on the balance of monopoly and monopsony in a given industry or branch. I see this approach as the only way of giving 'profits in circulation' at C and C' a Marxist meaning.

### 4.2  Large Commodities Traders

The place large commodities traders have created selling and transporting basic raw or semi-processed mining and agro-industrial inputs to downstream manufacturing corporations producing capital and consumer goods, is relevant both to the type of relationship analysed by Marx in his chapter on the history of merchant capital and to those analysed by writers on monopoly. The mix will differ according to the commodity and the country involved in transactions. The international copper cartel of the 1930s has been studied in this respect. In the 1990s, work was published identifying the groups which formed world cartels in the grain trade – Cargill (US), Continental (US), Louis Dreyfus (France), Bunge and Born (US, though rooted in Argentina and Brazil) and Andre (Switzerland)[78] – and more broadly in the food trade – the five first named plus Archer Daniels Midland (US grain), ConAgra (US meat), IBP (US meat) and the two huge diversified conglomerates Unilever (UK-Netherlands) and Nestlé (Switzerland).[79] All these firms date back to the nineteenth or the early twentieth century, growing later through domestic and international mergers and acquisitions. Several American firms grew following the migration to the US of capital, as well as networks and management experience originating in Holland and Switzerland. The first six grain corporations are family-owned and partly family-run. The sector is known for its secrecy.[80] The *Financial Times* has recently collected detailed case-study type data on the universe of commodities traders.[81] One reason for this interest is, of course, their interface with the derivatives market, and another is the

---

78   Morgan 1979.
79   Freeman 1995.
80   This is stressed in Saule Omarova's testimony to the US Senate committee: 'Commodities trading firms do not publicly report results of their financial operations and generally refrain from disclosing information about the structure or performance of their investments. Secrecy has always been an important attribute of the traditional commodities trading business, in which access to information is vital to commercial success and having informational advantage often translates into windfall profits'.
81   Javier Blas, 'Commodity traders reap $250bn harvest', *Financial Times*, 14 April 2013. The *Financial Times* reviewed 'thousands of pages of companies' filings and non-public

lateral oligopolistic entry since 2000 of new corporations, benefitting from massive financial support. The first ten groups[82] are Vitol (Swiss-Dutch), Glencore (Swiss), Cargil, Trafigura (Swiss), Koch Industries (US), Mercuria Group (Swiss, founded in 2004), Noble Group (Hong Kong), Gunvor group (founded in 2000 by a Swede and a Russian, registered in Cyprus with trading offices in Geneva, Switzerland, Singapore, Dubai and the Bahamas), Archer Daniels Midland and Bunge and Born. It is interesting to note that there are several almost unknown names and that familiar ones like Louis Dreyfus or Mitsubishi Trading are not in the first ten. The *Financial Times* notes that 'some companies are publicly listed and disclose financial information, but that most are privately-held and in some cases have never published data on profitability'. The documents in the review 'include filings in commercial registries from the Virgin Islands to Singapore'. Registration in tax havens is generalised and is recommended by consulting firms.[83]

Financial resources did not permit me to access the original data. Useful information and insights are given in the summaries provided by the *Financial Times* and other business publications. The first important insight is that the net income of the largest trading houses since 2003 (nearly $250bn over the last decade) surpassed that of Goldman Sachs, JP Morgan Chase and Morgan Stanley combined, or that of an industrial giant like General Electric. They made more money than Toyota, Volkswagen, Ford Motor, BMW and Renault combined, making the individuals and families that control the largely privately-owned sector large beneficiaries of the rise of China and other emerging countries. The commodities super-cycle caused by the industrialisation of China and other emerging countries strongly increased commodities trading volumes, but also increased the profitability of the trading groups' investment in oilfields, mines and farmland, permitting them to 'massively expand their influence'. The commodities trading sector, notes the *Financial Times*, is 'little understood and largely unregulated'. The publication of the study could 'heighten calls for greater transparency'. The sector's return on equity (ROE) attained 50–60 percent in the mid-2000s and still averages 20–30 per-

---

documents' and offers 'the first comprehensive account of the industry'. Access to the review is costly but the data seems to warrant thorough analysis.

82   Ginger Szala, '10 top global commodity trading firms: Smart money or bad boys?', http://www.futuresmag.com/2013/07/25/10-top-global-commodity-trading-firms-smart-money?t=financials&page=11.

83   KPMG, *Commodity Trade Companies. Centralizing Trade as a Critical Success Factor*, October 2012.

cent today, 'still large by any business standard'. The trading operations undertaken in the field of energy by the large oil, gas and utility groups – BP and Royal Dutch Shell, Total and EDF, the German Eon and RWE, and Lukoil and Gazprom overshadow those of other trading corporations. This is notably the case in oil. 'Industry estimates put the net income of those trading operations last year at about $5bn, well below the peak of 2008–9 of more than $10bn, but the exact level is difficult to ascertain'.

The large basic physical commodities traders or commodity trading companies are all holding corporations with a spectrum of financial services and financial investments. A recent study has shown that the proportion of commodity trading company revenues coming from such financial investments has been growing with respect to revenues derived directly from the trading of the physical commodity. 'Commodity trading companies have increasingly placed "risk management" at the centre of their core competencies, referring to in-house research departments and futures brokerages that cater for traders of physical commodities as well as financial investors looking to diversify their portfolios'.[84] In short, they have started invading the territory of investment banks.

### 4.3  Large Retailers

Today retail corporations are no longer the 'mere agents of industry', as Hilferding called them. Capital centralisation and concentration in the wholesale and retail trade,[85] coupled with slowing GDP growth and the transformation in urban and suburban lifestyles created by automobiles, has changed this situation radically. Large retailers, in particular general retailers, are major actors in the working of contemporary capitalism, in which control over access to final consumer markets has become crucial. They are a central component of finance capital and exert huge monopsony and monopoly power. Wal-Mart, Carrefour, Tesco and their like have also made employee exploitation a fine art, so to speak. The wages they pay, the hours they impose on their staff and the intensity of exploitation in the workplace have singled them out and made them a model for firms in other industries.

---

84   Kaltenbrunner et al. 2012.
85   Wrigley 2010.

TABLE 4.1    *Top 10 global retailers, net sales (2010)*
*(US$ million)*

| | |
|---|---|
| Wal-Mart US | 260,261 |
| Carrefour | 126,793 |
| Wal-Mart International | 109,232 |
| Tesco | 93,173 |
| Metro Group | 87,714 |
| Kroger | 78,834 |
| Costco | 78,394 |
| Schwarz Group | 76,339 |
| Seven & I | 70,959 |
| Home Depot | 68,002 |

SOURCE: BERG AND ROBERTS 2012.

A recent World Investment Report[86] calculates a 'transnationality index'. Wal-Mart is head and shoulder above the others. The ranking between Tesco and Carrefour is due to differences in strategy. Carrefour has fewer but much larger affiliates and higher foreign sales.

TABLE 4.2    *Top 5 TNCs in the retail industry, ranked by foreign assets, 2012*
*(US$ billion and number of employees)*

| Corporation | Country | Foreign Sales | Total Sales | Foreign Assets | Total Assets | Foreign Employees | Total Employees | Operating Countries | Transnat. Index* |
|---|---|---|---|---|---|---|---|---|---|
| Wal-Mart | US | 127 | 447 | 84 | 193 | 800 000 | 2 200 000 | 28 | 0.76 |
| Tesco | UK | 35 | 103 | 39 | 76 | 219 298 | 519 671 | 33 | 0.84 |
| Carrefour | France | 53 | 98 | 34 | 61 | 267 718 | 364 969 | 13 | 0.57 |
| Metro | Germany | 53 | 86 | 27 | 46 | 159 344 | 248 637 | 33 | 0.62 |
| Schwarz | Germany | 49 | 88 | ... | ... | ...... | | 26 | 0.56 |

SOURCE: UNCTAD 2014A, P. 16. (*THE TRANSNATIONALITY INDEX IS AN AVERAGE OF THREE RATIOS: FOREIGN TO TOTAL ASSETS, FOREIGN TO TOTAL SALES AND FOREIGN TO TOTAL EMPLOYMENT, EXCEPT FOR SCHWARZ GROUP WITH ONLY FOREIGN TO TOTAL SALES).

---

86    UNCTAD 2014a.

Giant general retailers, along with the major corporations in apparel, fashion and sportswear, are deeply engaged in global procurement and in direct forms of super-exploitation of labour in *maquiladoras* and Asian sweatshops. The dimensions of their operations and the intensity of the exploitation experienced by workers are discussed in the next chapter. Here the focus is first on inter-capitalist relations, namely the levy made by retailers on manufacturers for the task of organising the realisation of value and surplus value, and second on the role that skill in the exploitation of employees and the shortening of capital turnover time plays in increasing the degree of effectiveness of monopsony power. On account of the large amount of data available, the analysis focuses on Wal-Mart.

The amount of surplus value the farmer, the agribusiness or the consumer good manufacturing firm concedes to the retailer is a pure question of market power. This was always the case for farmers and small and medium enterprises (SMEs), but not, or much less so, for large firms. Up to the 1980s, the brand names built up by large US and European firms (the latter necessarily TNCs on the Nestlé and Unilever model) – through product innovation and large advertising outlays – allowed them to negotiate with retailers in favourable conditions. Then scale and power shifted in favour of Wal-Mart and the other very large global retail corporations. One visible indicator was the growth of the share of products under private (e.g. retailer) label. Today a study stresses that 'there are very few vendors that can compete with the global retailers in terms of scale: Wal-Mart International alone is now bigger than Nestlé and, indeed, Wal-Mart's annual expenditure on private labels – at over $100 billion – tops Nestlé's annual revenues'.[87] Focusing on Wal-Mart US, the same study reports survey results 'showing that around 120 vendors or service providers name Wal-Mart as a major customer, on average, for 21 percent of their total sales, with the proportion reaching as high as 55 percent'.[88] In 2010, Garanimals,[89] a large manufacturer of children's apparel, sold over 90 percent of its production through Wal-Mart. Among the corporations placed high in the survey of Wal-Mart dependency, the largest is Del Monte, the sinister and notorious seller of canned vegetables, fruit, tomato and pet care products operating in Mexico and all the Central Latin American countries. Not only does

---

87  Berg and Roberts 2012, p. 93.
88  Berg and Roberts 2012, p. 82.
89  Garanimals is a division of Garan Incorporated, wholly owned company by Berkshire Hathaway. http://www.fundinguniverse.com/company-histories/garan-inc-history/ (accessed 1 December 2013).

Del Monte sell its own brands through Wal-Mart, but it also produces Wal-Mart's private labels.

In the retailing sector, monopsony power is closely related to size. This is often the result of acquisitions. In the case of Wal-Mart this holds for its international operations, but in the US its growth has been almost exclusively endogenous. It has taken place by the creation of 'virtuous' profit-maximising feedback processes involving several factors, particularly a ruthless exploitation of its employees and a very successful use of information technology. Here Wal-Mart has been a pioneer and an example for its rivals in the sector. It has sped up capital turnover by the introduction of codes, scanners and computers to scrutinise point-of-sale consumer behaviour and minimise the size of inventories.[90] The revolution in logistics has allowed Wal-Mart US to eliminate wholesalers and other intermediaries (whom Wal-Mart executives name 'margin-takers') in its US base and severely reduce their place in global supply chains (see Chapter 5). It has also strongly reinforced Wal-Mart's position *vis-à-vis* its employees and has helped it to fight unionisation.[91] This has made Wal-Mart a 'model' which other corporations have sought to follow, shifting employment from stable medium-wage jobs to precarious low-wage ones in retailing, as well as other labour-intensive service sectors.

Arum Gupta has synthesised recent studies of Wal-Mart's effects on US local labour markets. The most detailed study he reports found that 'each Wal-Mart job cost 1.4 retail-sector jobs, or nearly 150 jobs on average in affected counties. There was a 2.7 percent reduction in retail employment attributable to a Wal-Mart store opening, as well as "declines in county-level retail earning of about $1.4 million, or 1.5 per cent"'.[92] The majority of Wal-Mart's employees are part-time workers who are paid the local minimum wage. Most employees are not entitled to any benefits, as it takes a part-time employee over five years to become eligible for benefits, profit-sharing, or other such compensation. There is a high turnover rate among these employees, which means most do

---

90  See Petrovic and Hamilton 2006.

91  A union named OUR Walmart, or Organization United for Respect at Walmart, was founded by employees in 2012. Some 500 of them backed by many thousands of others gathered at stores in December 2012 on the Friday after Thanksgiving (Wal-Mart officials name it 'Black Friday'). In 2014, leaked internal documents were published by OccupyWallSt.org and were confirmed as authentic by a Walmart spokesman, showing that Walmart's strategy for fighting to keep its workers from forming unions includes instructing managers to report suspicious activity and warning workers that joining OUR Walmart could hurt them. http://thinkprogress.org/economy/2014/01/16/3171251/walmart-leaked-powerpoint-unions/.

92  Gupta 2013, p. 5.

not reach the requisite level of seniority. In many cases the local minimum wage is far below the poverty line.[93] This is a consequence of Wal-Mart's war against unions. Wal-Mart has long tried to hold the upper hand over its workforce. They have repeatedly fought attempts by segments of their workforce to unionise. Several cases were brought to court in the 1990s by the United Food and Commercial Workers (UFCW). The US Congress held hearings about Wal-Mart's labour practices. 'Wal-Mart's policy has been one of delay and "terror" in the words of one union representative who has accused the company of old-fashioned union-busting tactics'.[94] Wal-Mart has paid its workers up to $3.50 an hour less than unionised supermarket workers. 'Thus if Wal-Mart has reduced consumer good prices for the entire US economy, it has also reduced wages and benefits for entire sectors. If a state had 50 Wal-Marts, which was the average in 2000, wages dropped 10 percent and health insurance coverage shrank 5 percent among all retail workers in that state'.[95] Unionisation in the giant retail firms is a little easier in Europe. In the UK, the Union of Shop, Distributive and Allied Workers posed problems for Tesco, while a large strike was successfully organised at Carrefour's French supermarkets in 2011. But the sector is one where struggles are exceptionally difficult.

## 5   Natural Resource-based Monopoly Profit and Oil Rent

Historically, land rent has fed the accumulation of money capital and the rentier traits it can naturally acquire when industrial capital is weak. In many countries, France in the nineteenth century, South American countries in the twentieth, large landowners and bankers have had close sociological and political affinities. In the case of the latter it has been consolidated further by mining rent. More generally and fundamentally the analysis of contemporary globalised capitalism calls for a discussion of revenues from the exploitation of energy and natural-based resources derived from large mining property and landholdings. The situation is that of a merging of rent and profit, with emphasis on the notion of surplus profit.[96] The revenues of agribusiness and mining corporations must be seen as based simultaneously on the ownership of agricultural land, possessing given endowments or of mineral resources and on

---

93   Quinn 2000, p. 47.
94   Quinn 2000, p. 45.
95   Gupta 2013, p. 6.
96   The notion of surplus profit is first raised right at the end of Chapter 10, Volume III, and then developed in Chapter 46 in Part VI.

antagonistic capital/labour relations. Firms in these activities derive surplus profit based simultaneously on the possession of natural resources and on the efficiency and brutality of the capitalistic organisation of extraction, which determines the productivity of the labour employed and the rate of surplus value. In *Capital*, the owners of natural-based resources and the capitalists that use these are still posited as different persons. The situation Marx analyses is one in which:

> wherever natural forces can be monopolized and give the industrialist who makes use of them a surplus-profit, be it a waterfall, a rich mine, fishing grounds, or a well situated building site, the person who by virtue of his title to a portion of the earth, seizes this surplus-profit from the functioning capital in the form of rent.[97]

Today, mining and primary raw material-processing corporations are proprietors of the natural resources they exploit. They appropriate surplus value in some of the harshest capital-labour relationships of global capitalism and collect the surplus profit permitted by monopolised ownership. The outcome of unceasing centralisation and concentration at a world level in oil and in most of metallic and non-metallic mining and processing industries is tight oligopoly. The long-term trend of diminishing supply allows corporations to establish pricing strategies that affect the production costs of industries which are dependent on their products as inputs to production. These numerous factors in combination place oil companies, and more generally mining and primary transformation corporations, among the richest and most powerful TNCs and make them a cornerstone of stock markets.

Revenues from oil are often referred to as rent and countries that enjoy them are named rentier states.[98] Yet in the case of advanced capitalist countries that possess and exploit oil (the US, the UK, Norway), such revenues are named monopoly profits and the countries are never referred to as rentier. While the characterisation of 'rentier states' is worth retaining when approaching the political economy of some present or former semi-colonial countries, among them Algeria,[99] in others, in particular the Gulf States, one is faced with a

---

97   Marx 1981, Vol. III, p. 908.
98   For a general approach, see *inter alia* Beblawi 1990.
99   For the widely-held position on Algeria as a rentier state cursed by oil revenue, see Dillman 2000 and Nashashibi 2002. The latter has quite convincingly been challenged by Henry 2004, who argues that while the connections between Algeria's oil wealth, its slide into the disasters of 1990s, the continued concentration of power around the army and deep corruption should of course be analysed, 'the original sin was a primitive form of French

specific variety of finance capital. Hanieh has studied the form of 'the Gulf capitalist class'.[100] He writes:

> the form taken by the capitalist class around these circuits is typically that of large capitalist conglomerates – often established by merchant families or individuals close to the ruling family – that are strongly interpenetrated with the state structures. These conglomerates are generally active across all moments of the circuit of capital – the productive circuit (construction, energy-rich commodities such as aluminium, steel, concrete); the commodity circuit (agents and distributors of imported commodities, malls and shopping centres); and the financial circuit (banks, investment and private equity companies). This class has emerged alongside the state itself, benefitting from state contracts, agency rights, land grants and positions within the government bureaucracy.[101]

We shall meet the Gulf States and the distinctive Gulf segment of finance capital again in the next chapter when examining Sovereign Wealth Funds.

Faced by a plurality of states in the Gulf, Hanieh does not attempt to identify a specific oil-based accumulation regime. Ashman, Fine and Newman do so for South Africa, with minerals as the material base. Pointing out that 'global accumulation and its shifts and restructuring are necessarily mediated by the structure of particular economies and forms of class rule',[102] they argue that 'in South Africa wider changes in the world economy and capitalist development driven by neoliberalism and financialisation have interacted with the legacy of the apartheid past'. This leads them to:

> characterize the system of accumulation in South Africa as a 'Minerals-Energy Complex' (MEC) where accumulation has been *and remains* dominated by and dependent upon a cluster of industries, heavily promoted by the state, around mining and energy – raw and semi-processed mineral products, gold, diamond, platinum and steel, coal, iron and

---

colonialism, not hydrocarbons. Before the oil revenues took off in the 1970s Algeria's trajectory was already conditioned by the intensity of the colonial occupation, the destruction of civil society and political intermediaries, the trauma of national liberation and a lingering identity crisis'. He points interestingly to the disastrous influence that the theory of 'industrializing industries' developed by economists, members of the French Communist Party, had on the early Algerian governments.

100   Hanieh 2012.
101   Hanieh 2012, p. 186.
102   Many Brazilian economists would do well to note this important methodological point. Paulani 2015a is a contribution in this direction.

aluminium. In the context of South African production, financialization has produced a particular combination of short-term capital inflows (accompanied by rising consumer debt largely spent on luxury items) *and* a massive long-term outflow of capital as major 'domestic' corporations have chosen offshore listing and to internationalize their operations while concentrating within South Africa on core profitable MEC sectors. The result, even before the impact of the current crisis, was a jobless form of growth and the persistence of mass poverty for the majority alongside rising living standards for a small minority, including new black elites.[103]

The massive outflow of capital in the form of the super-profits appropriated by MEC corporations is the South African accumulation regime's contribution to 'financialised accumulation' and to the consolidation of its 'global systemic nature'.[104] The configuration and the new instruments of exploitation of global capitalism are the object of the next chapter.

---

[103] Ashman, Fine and Newman 2011, p. 178, emphasis in original.
[104] Ashman, Fine and Newman 2011, p. 176.

## Appendix 1: Control in the ETH Zurich Studies

The term 'control' is used in two successive studies by a group of mathematicians based in Zurich.[1] The studies are highly sophisticated in their use of refined topological techniques developed in mathematics. On account of this neither their methodology nor their use of the term control have been discussed critically.[2] They exploit a huge database, built however on the very broad and almost meaningless official definition of TNCs, whether non-financial or financial.[3] Nodes are constructed on flows of dividends thus creating automatically the primacy of financial institutions as defined by NACE (including insurance companies and pension funds). The first study maps the topography of a universe of 43000 non-financial and financial TNCs which are interconnected through direct and indirect ownership. It then reduces it to a group of 1,300 companies with strong links to each other in a way that three-quarters of all the ownership ties remain in the hands of these firms themselves. This group is further refined to 737 companies that control 80% of the value of the initial 43,000 companies, then to the 'super-entity' of 147 companies, with near total control of over 40% of the value of all TNCs, and then finally to a list of 50 corporations. The second 2013 study focuses on nodes and breaks the data down into 'communities'. The two largest of these account together for about one fifth of all the nodes. The first biggest community is dominated by companies mainly located in North America (65%), in particular in the US (59%) and Canada (7%), while 10% of all the firms are located in three Asian countries (Japan, Taiwan and Korea). The second largest community in term of nodes belongs almost completely to European countries (89%), with Great Britain (42%) leading the other countries (Germany is represented by 9.6% of nodes, France by 6%, Sweden by 5% and Italy by 4%).

The collection and analysis of the ownership ties was completed in 2007. At that time, all 50 corporations were banks, insurance companies and other financial corporations; Lehman Brothers, doomed to collapse in 2008, was on the list. This puts the data in perspective and forces one to have a close look

---

1   Vitali et al. 2011; Vitali and Battiston 2013.
2   In their latest book, only available in French at the time of writing, Duménil and Levy 2014 give particular and totally uncritical importance to this study, even reproducing two of the figures drawn by the Zurich team. This stems from their focus on managers as an autonomous class and represents a follow up to the presentation of their theory of class struggle in which managers (cadres) decide whether their issue is favourable to capital or to labour. In a piece on imperialism today, Husson 2014 also quotes the data without discussing its methodology.
3   A firm that owns a 10 percent stake in more than two foreign countries.

at the term 'control'. It refers only to the pyramidal centralisation of surplus value resulting from portfolio investment. For the majority of the financial corporations listed, the term has no other meaning. Only a few banks, insurance companies and funds have the capacity to follow the operations of the non-financial corporations in which they have significant stakes in any detail. The tighter nodes express the concentration of reciprocal ownership relationships. The authors consider that at the heart of the entire core, there is a 'small subset of well-known financial players' and links between them which give 'an idea of the level of entanglement of the entire core' and that this finding raises 'two questions that are fundamental to the understanding of the functioning of the global economy'. The first concerns financial stability, where these nodes are seen as playing a central role in systemic international crisis contagion as in September 2008:

> It is known that financial institutions establish financial contracts, such as lending or credit derivatives, with several other institutions. This allows them to diversify risk, but, at the same time, it also exposes them to contagion. Unfortunately, information on these contracts is usually not disclosed due to strategic reasons. However, in various countries, the existence of such financial ties is correlated with the existence of ownership relations. Thus, in the hypothesis that the structure of the ownership network is a good proxy for that of the financial network, this implies that the global financial network is also very intricate... while in good times the network is seemingly robust, in bad times firms go into distress simultaneously. This *knife-edge* property was witnessed during the recent financial turmoil.[4]

The second concerns competition. Here concentration and oligopoly are not the result of the very process of accumulation, but again the result of ownership relations in a very deterministic way:

> Since many TNCs in the core have overlapping domains of activity, the fact that they are connected by ownership relations could facilitate the formation of blocs, which would hamper market competition. Remarkably, the existence of such a core in the global market was never documented before and thus, so far, no scientific study demonstrates or excludes that this international 'super-entity' has ever acted as a bloc. However, some

---

4  Vitali et al. 2011, p. 7.

examples suggest that this is not an unlikely scenario. For instance, previous studies have shown how even small cross-shareholding structures, at a national level, can affect market competition in sectors such as airline, automobile and steel, as well as the financial one. At the same time, antitrust institutions around the world (e.g., the UK Office of Fair Trade) closely monitor complex ownership structures within their national borders. The fact that international data sets as well as methods to handle large networks became available only very recently, may explain how this finding could go unnoticed for so long.[5]

So in the Zurich study one finally ends up with an embellishment of national anti-trust enforcement and a naive call for the establishment of a global anti-trust authority.

---

5  Vitali et al. 2011, p. 8.

## Appendix 2: The Three Major New York Investment Banks' Activities in Commodities[1]

Morgan Stanley's commodities business is run by Morgan Stanley Capital Group Inc. About half is reported to be in crude oil and oil products, and about 40 percent in power and gas. It owns physical assets in trading energy and commodities since the mid-1980s, before expanding its activities through acquisitions, first in 2006 the full ownership of Heidmar, a Connecticut-based global operator of commercial oil tankers. In 2006, it acquired full ownership of TransMontaigne, a Denver-based oil-products transportation and distribution company trading gasoline and all types of industry-specific fuels, asphalt, chemicals and fertilisers. It operates a vast infrastructure of crude oil and refined products, pipelines and terminals along the Gulf Coast, in the Midwest and Texas, and along the Mississippi and Ohio Rivers.

Goldman Sachs's commodities operations include both derivatives and physical trading. The derivate trading business goes back at least to 1981, when it bought J. Aron & Co., specialised at the time mostly in trading futures and options on precious metals and coffee. In the 1980s to 90s, Goldman Sachs built a dominant position in the energy futures and OTC derivatives markets and created the Goldman Commodity Index in 1991. In the context of the commodities boom it expanded into coal and shipping trading. In 2005, Goldman Sachs acquired Cogentrix Energy LLC, a large US power producer based in North Carolina. During the same period, Goldman made significant acquisitions in the oil and gas sector, including a large stake in Kinder Morgan, which controls approximately 37,000 miles of pipelines and 180 terminals handling crude oil, natural gas, and refined petroleum products. In May 2012, a $407 million deal was announced with the Brazilian corporation Vale, to acquire full ownership of Vale's Colombian coal assets and a coal port facility on Colombia's Atlantic coast. The deal also included an 8.43% equity stake in the railway connecting the mines to the port. In another sector Goldman's subsidiary, in 2010, GS Power Holdings, bought Metro International Trade Services, a metals warehousing company that owns and operates 19 warehouses in Detroit and warehousing facilities in Europe and Asia, including one of the largest metals warehouses in the network of storage facilities registered by the London Metal Exchange.

In 2005, JP Morgan Chase (JPMC) received the Fed's authorisation to trade physical commodities as an activity 'complementary' to its commodity derivatives business. In May 2008, along with the acquisition of Bear Stearns's banking operations, JPMC acquired its commodity trading assets and operations,

---

1  Taken from Omarova 2013.

including a large network of electric power generating facilities. As a result JPMC started trading physical oil. It became a very large operator in commodities when, as a result of the 2009 rescue and nationalisation of RBS, it bought the global oil and metals and the European power and gas businesses of RBS's large affiliate Sempra. In 2010, JPMC also bought RBS Sempra's North American power and gas business. In 2011, following the bankruptcy of a derivatives firm, Metal Futures Global, it became the London Metal Exchange's largest shareholder. As part of its Sempra deal, JPMC also controls Henry Bath, a UK-based metals warehousing company that owns and operates one of the largest LME-approved global metal storage networks.[2]

---

2   See 'Metal bashing', *The Economist*, 17 August 2013.

## Appendix 3: Three Examples of Industrial Corporation Ownership of Financial Corporations

Until the announcement made in April 2015 of its withdrawal from finance, the first most important example was General Electric. GE is better known as one of the world's main producers of aircraft engines and medical-imaging equipment. It also produces power turbines, oil pumps and locomotives and has announced its entry into 'green' alternative energies. But it had huge interest-bearing operations. The size of GE Capital was such that if it had been a commercial bank it would have been the fifth largest in the US.[1] In 2012, GE Capital accounted for 45 percent of the group's total profit after having reached 55 percent in 2007. Even after post-2008 job cutting, it employed 50,000 people. GE Capital presented itself as providing 'commercial lending and leasing, as well as a range of financial services' (health insurance notably). It claimed to 'focus primarily on loans and leases that it holds on its own balance sheet rather than on generating fees by originating loans and leases and then selling them to third parties'.[2] The story told by financial analysts was somewhat different:

> GE got into lending decades ago and grew steadily, leveraging the access to cheap capital that came with the conglomerate's triple-A credit rating. The financial crisis upended GE Capital's model. Funds that had been widely available in the short-term credit markets dried up overnight, forcing GE Capital to turn to government lending programs for help. GE's stock fell below $6 billion in March 2009. Unrealized losses in the real-estate division were estimated at $7 billion. GE was forced to cut its dividend for the first time in its history and its credit rating was downgraded by one notch to AA-plus, where it remains.[3]

In July 2013, the US government, through the Financial Stability Oversight Council created by the Dodd-Frank Act, added GE Capital to its list of 'systemically important financial institutions', on account of its being a 'significant source of credit to the US economy'.[4] The sale of a large part of GE Capital's operations to Wells Fargo and Blackstone in 2015 is interpreted as a sign of GE's

---

1 Kate Linebaugh, 'General Electric: Still a Bank', *Wall Street Journal*, 17 January 2013.
2 http://en.wikipedia.org/wiki/GE_Capital (accessed 21 September 2013).
3 Kate Linebaugh, 'General Electric: Still a Bank', *Wall Street Journal*, 17 January 2013.
4 *Financial Times*, 9 July 2013. The list includes JP Morgan Chase, Citigroup and Goldman Sachs. Corporations on the list are obliged, *inter alia*, to have higher capital reserves.

vulnerabilities as an industrial conglomerate and an imperative to focus on its core activities.

The second example is that of an entire highly oligopolistic industry, namely that of automobiles, where corporations have set up financial affiliates which represent important profit-centres in 'normal times'. In the case of General Motors (GM), its affiliate *GMAC (General Motors Acceptance Corporation)* operated in over 40 countries and had some 50,000 employees before 2009. The discussion here is limited to the three US corporations. Here the basic rationale is different from that of GE. It relates to the inter-capitalist distribution of surplus value, by way of providing loans and leases to car buyers and extending loans and lines of credit to dealers rather than have the banking sector do this. Given that in the context of slow growth and inherently insufficient demand, sales depend on credit, the object is not to let the lucrative business of auto loans fall into the hands of the banks, but to pocket them through the setting up of specialised financial affiliates fully owned, or as is now the case for Chrysler, a joint venture. As put with great clarity by a financial analyst, the configuration is the following:

> Think about the auto manufacturers and their finance companies as one entity. With auto financing, auto manufacturers can play a game between the cost of the auto and the financing. Even if they lose a little on the financing, they can make it up by selling the car at a higher price. They might be able to undercut the banks and worry less about risk since they can make it up in the price of a car.[5]

This yields high profits from interest and fees as long as the demand for cars does not collapse. In the period leading up to the 2008 financial crisis and the start of the US recession, without creating fully subprime auto loans, for which a specific brand of financial company exists,[6] GM and Chrysler had extended such large amounts of auto credit through their financial affiliates, *GMAC* and Chrysler Financial, that they both had to be bailed out during the TARP rescue plan. *GMAC* was spun off from GM and made into a separate bank named

---

5   Christine Dunn, 26 October 2012, http://www.boston.com/business/personal_finance/blog/2012/10/moodys_car_sales_and_loans_on.html.
6   The three best-known names in subprime lending are Bar None, JD Byrider and Autobytel. These companies have played a part in the more than 45 million used cars sold in the country, serving an estimated 40 percent of the population who fall in the subprime credit risk pool. See http://www.carsdirect.com/auto-loans/top-three-car-finance-company-reviews (accessed 3 April 2013).

Ally, which was then granted the status of a bank holding company by the Fed, along with the accompanying privileges, in particular of transferring bad assets to the Fed. Chrysler Financial was closed down before reopening in 2013 as a joint venture with Santander. For GM, the 'alliance' with Ally was not satisfactory. As soon as it returned to profits and was relisted on the New York Stock Exchange in 2010, it started to recreate its own captive finance company, first by acquiring a small financial company, AmeriCredit, in the US and then in 2013 by buying Ally's European operations. As the only constructor not to have asked for aid under TARP, Ford never lost its financial arm, Ford Motor Credit Company LLC (known as Ford Credit).

Inter-capitalist distribution of surplus value is also relevant to the third example. Captive insurance companies are companies set up by the parent corporation. They underwrite the insurance needs of the parent's operating subsidiaries. Oil and shipping companies were the first to set up 'captives', as they are referred to, used to insure and reinsure the risk of subsidiaries and affiliates, such as the risk of shipping fuel and commodities. The aim is to keep control over insurance fees and avoid litigation, i.e. not to give up too much surplus value to companies belonging to the insurance industry. Many large corporations in a large range of sectors followed suit. Even public pension funds, such as that of Michigan, have set up captive insurance firms. As succinctly put by a professional journal: 'Most were established to provide coverage where insurance was unavailable or unreasonably priced'. Offshore registration has been widely chosen, in the case of US groups in particular in Bermuda or the Cayman Islands. 'The risk management benefits of these captives were primary, but their tax advantages were also important'.[7] The US tax authorities repeatedly but unsuccessfully challenged captive insurance companies as subterfuges for non-deductible self-insurance within business and tax evasion. It gave up after the IRS lost a $600+ million challenge against a captive owned by United Parcel Service in 2001.

---

7   http://www.journalofaccountancy.com/Issues/2013/Mar/20126102.htm.

CHAPTER 5

# The Internationalisation of Productive Capital and the Formation of Global Oligopolies

The present moment in the internationalisation of productive capital must now be discussed. After the slowdown of the 1930s and the interruption of the Second World War, foreign direct investment and the international deployment of productive capital took off again before that of financial flows. In fact, as recalled in Chapter 2, the non-reinvested profits of US TNCs played a key role in the growth of the London Eurodollar market. Once a threshold of domestic centralisation and concentration of capital has been passed, for large firms the pursuit of growth outside their national borders through the setting up of foreign production operations is an opportunity and even a constraint. Today the mobility of concentrated capital, its access to domestic markets following the liberalisation of foreign direct investment and the high degree of freedom it has in exploiting largely unprotected workers in many parts of the world form a solid foundation for the appropriation of surplus by financial oligarchies, the other source being government debt. The deployment of industrial corporations will be examined in two steps. This chapter focuses on global oligopoly as the most general form of contemporary market structures. Chapter 6 sets out the new modes of global corporate management and worker exploitation by TNCs.

In the 1920s and 1930s, the encounter of monopolies belonging to several countries led to the formation of international cartels bounded by strict agreements. Since the 1970s, the process of centralisation and concentration at both the domestic and the international level has seen the emergence of a looser form of global monopoly capital, namely global oligopoly. It gives rise to specific forms of competition in the world market and is the seat of collective monopoly power. These issues are approached with the help of Marxist and non-Marxist theory and with the use of the scant available case study and statistical data.

1    The Internationalisation of Productive Capital: Theory and History

The internationalisation of productive capital designates the process whereby the production and appropriation of surplus value is undertaken by capitalists abroad, outside their base country. Taking the full accumulation cycle (M-C-P-C'-M') as the simplified analytical starting point, capitalists export M in the form of investment capital (they raised it *in situ* from the 1980s on). With respect to C, classically they buy *in situ* variable capital – the labour power component – and also, according to a given industrial sector, all or part of the raw material/energy component, but they generally import machinery and sophisticated inputs. P takes place *in situ*. The locus of C' can either be domestic or foreign markets, or a combination of the two. M' is repatriated to the home country as profit and dividend. As we shall see, this simplified representation gave way in successive stages to much more complex organisational patterns and more recently to the development examined in Chapter 6 of diversified forms of external TNC appropriation of surplus value alongside their production intra-muros.

### 1.1   Foreign Production of Surplus Value in the Classical Theory of Imperialism

The theoreticians of imperialism of the Second and Third Internationals all pay attention to what is then named the export of capital. They differ in the degree to which they specifically identify the production of surplus value abroad. Lenin's chapter on the export of capital is very general. He is mainly interested in rentier interest-bearing capital and cites the names of large corporations principally in relation to the formation of international cartels.

In her chapter on international loans, Rosa Luxemburg sees loans as a mechanism for appropriating surplus and exporting it back to home countries and also as the 'surest ties by which the old capitalist states maintain their influence, exercise financial control and exert pressure on the customs, foreign and commercial policy of the young capitalist states'. She does, however, contemplate its production not only by domestic capitalists but also by British or German companies having extended their operations abroad:

> Realized surplus value, which cannot be capitalized and lies idle in England or Germany, is invested in railway construction, water works and the like in Argentine, Australia, the Cape Colony or Mesopotamia. Machinery, materials and the like are supplied by the country where the capital has originated and it is the same capital that pays for them. Actually, this process characterizes capitalist conditions everywhere, even at home. Capital must purchase the elements of production and thus become productive capital before it can operate. Admittedly, the products are then used within the country, while in the former case they are used by foreigners. But then capitalist production does not aim at its

products being enjoyed, but at the accumulation of surplus value. There had been no demand for the surplus product within the country, so capital had lain idle without the possibility of accumulating.[1]

Hilferding tackles the internationalisation of productive capital squarely. He sees the export of capital as taking place in two different forms: 'it can migrate abroad either as interest-bearing or as profit-yielding capital'. In both cases they do so because the rate of profit is higher than in their home country:

> The precondition for the export of capital is the variation in rates of profit, and the export of capital is the means of equalizing national rates of profit. The level of profit depends upon the organic composition of capital, that is to say, upon the degree of capitalist development. The more advanced it is the lower will be the average rate of profit.... So far as the rate of interest is concerned it is much higher in undeveloped capitalist countries, which lack extensive credit and banking facilities, than in advanced capitalist countries. Furthermore, interest in such countries still includes for the most part an element of wages or entrepreneurial profit. The high rate of interest is a direct inducement to the export of loan capital.

The main focus of Chapter XXII of *Finance Capital* is industrial capital producing value and surplus value in foreign countries: 'By "export of capital" I mean the export of value which is intended to breed surplus value abroad'.[2] The foreign operations of firms are viewed by Hilferding from the standpoint of shareholder interests and put in neo-mercantilist terms not far removed from the way a part of US public opinion sees them today. He introduces an unexpected distinction between the *export* and the *transfer* of capital:

> It is essential from this point of view that the surplus value should remain at the disposal of the domestic capital. If, for example, a German capitalist were to emigrate to Canada with his capital, become a producer there and never return home, that would constitute a loss for German capital, a denationalization of the capital. It would not be an export of capital but a transfer of capital, constituting a deduction from the domestic capital and an addition to the foreign capital. Only if the capital used abroad remains at the disposal of domestic capital, and the surplus value

---

1 Luxemburg 1913, Chapter 30.
2 All citations in this section are from Hilferding 1910, Chapter 22.

produced by this capital can be utilized by the domestic capitalists, can we speak of capital export. The capital then figures as an item in the national balance sheet and the surplus value produced abroad each year as an item in the national balance of payments.[3]

The export of profit-yielding capital, as distinct from its transfer, is enhanced by 'the joint-stock company and a highly developed credit system'. Because they 'enable capital to migrate out of a country detached from the entrepreneur, ownership remains for a much longer time, or even permanently, with the capital-exporting country and the nationalization of capital [e.g. ownership in the host country – F.C.] is made more difficult'. Initiative in foreign operations belongs, in Hilferding, to banks and not to large corporations:

> As European capital has advanced to the stage of finance capital it has frequently begun to migrate abroad *in this form* [emphasis mine – F.C.]. Thus a large German bank establishes a branch abroad, which then negotiates a loan the proceeds of which are used to construct an electrical generating plant, and the construction work is assigned to an electrical company which is connected with the bank at home. Or the process may be simplified further, and the foreign branch of the bank establishes an industrial enterprise abroad, issues the shares at home, and orders raw materials, etc., from enterprises which are connected with the parent bank. Such transactions attain their largest scale when State loans are used for obtaining industrial supplies. It is the intimate connection between bank and industrial capital which is responsible for the rapid development of capital exports.

Besides touching on FDI as a way of equalising the rate of profit across national frontiers, Hilferding makes a number of observations which have a very modern ring to them, identifying processes that played a very important role in the spread of TNCs to Third World countries in the 1970s and 1980s:

---

3  Hilferding adds: 'From the standpoint of the capital-importing country, a further consideration is what part of the surplus value is used to pay interest. Interest which has to be paid on mortgage bonds held by foreigners involves sending part of the ground rent abroad, whereas interest on the debentures of industrial enterprises represents an outflow of part of the industrial profit'.

Entrepreneurial profit is also higher because labour power is exceptionally cheap, and what it lacks in quality is made up by unusually long hours of work. In addition, since ground rent is very low or purely nominal, owing to the large amount of free land resulting either from the bounty of nature or from the forcible expropriation of the native population, costs of production are low. Finally, profits are swelled by special privileges and monopolies. Where products are involved for which the new market itself provides an outlet very high extra profits are also realized, since in this case commodities produced by capitalist methods enter into competition with handicraft production.[4]

### 1.2   *The Internationalisation of Productive Capital in Contemporary Theory*

The internationalisation of productive capital and the operations of multinational enterprises have not received much attention by Anglophone Marxist scholars. Baran and Sweezy's classical work does not treat this aspect of concentrated capital. In France, research in this area by Marxists and heterodox economists familiar with or close to Marxism dates back to the first half of the 1970s.[5] It gave birth to a particular field of heterodox economics with differing degrees of Marxist influence from one author to the next. The dialogue that some began with Stephen Hymer was interrupted by his premature death in 1974. With the exception of a little research developed around *Monthly Review* his death left the field in Anglophone countries almost solely to non-Marxist scholars, notably John Dunning and his students.[6] Foreign production, as they call it, takes place through foreign direct investment in manufacturing, mining and agriculture carried out by multinational enterprises (MNEs) as they were termed in most academic research or by transnational corporations (TNCs) in the UNCTAD terminology. Here the two terms are taken as being synonymous. The appendix to this chapter discusses the many problems UNCTAD has in collecting FDI data. The theory of globalisation requires that the official OECD-UNCTAD definition of an MNE or TNC as an enterprise that owns or controls value-adding activities in more than one country be made more specific. Dunning defines it as a corporation that 'has substantial foreign

---

4   Hilferding 1910, Chapter 22.
5   Authors included Michalet, Palloix and a little later Andreff. For a history of this research and a range of contributions discussing its anticipation of contemporary critical work on globalisation, see Andreff 2013.
6   Notably John Cantwell and Rajneesh Narula.

commitments and pursues an integrated managerial strategy towards their domestic operations'.[7] The largest are listed each year in the Fortune 500.

### 1.3 Stages in the Internationalisation of Productive Capital

I have not found references to monographic material, although it could well exist, documenting the bank-sponsored value and surplus value production described by Hilferding. On the basis of the historical material at his disposal, Dunning estimates, in what remains the most comprehensive work on international production, that in 1914 about 55% of total FDI took place in primary material production (mining, plantations), 20% in railroads, 15% in manufacturing and 10% in service sectors, commerce and banking.[8] Foreign direct investment in the primary sector occurred under the conditions of colonial and semi-colonial economic and political domination, and a combination of the most extreme worker exploitation and appropriation of rent, stemming from the ownership of vital raw materials. Here one is in the presence of surplus value production and the capturing of rent in conditions of a high degree of monopoly. As will be discussed later in relation to 'extractivism', this is still the case in the primary sector today, even if the global configuration of political relationships between countries is not exactly that of imperialism in Lenin's time.

In the 15% of FDI estimated in manufacturing prior to 1914, US multinationals were dominant. Singer, Edison, Westinghouse, Eastman Kodak, General Electric, International Harvester all had plants abroad.[9] This was not only due to their product innovations, but also to their particular managerial experience. It was unique at the time and remained so for a number of decades, resulting from the establishment from the 1890s onwards of large multi-unit business enterprises in the physical space of a continent. Chandler, who later became the historian and theoretician of this novel type of firm, writes that the large US industrial corporation did not grow by producing something new or in a different way. It grew 'by adding on new units of production, by adding new sales and purchasing offices, by adding facilities for producing raw and semi-finished materials, by obtaining shipping lines, railroad cars, pipelines and other transportation units'.[10] In other words, it first grew through a process of duplication, even multiplication, within a fairly loose overall corporate management regime of stand-alone enterprises capable of carrying out the

---

7   Dunning 1992, p. 3.
8   Dunning 1993, p. 117.
9   Wilkins 1970.
10  Chandler 1990, p. 397.

full accumulation cycle M-C-P-C'-M' on their own, with little supervision by corporate headquarters. Division of labour between affiliates only came at a later stage.

1.4     *From Horizontal to Vertical Integration and the Intra-Corporate Division of Labour*

Given that until the early 1980s, the internationalisation of industrial capital took basically the form of an international extension of this 'multi-plant enterprise' model, US MNEs were thus naturally at the fore. As put by Hymer: 'In becoming national firms US corporations learned how to become international'.[11] The first generation of postwar MNEs were horizontally integrated. Foreign affiliates engaged in single or in joint-multiproduct production operations similar to those of the parent corporation. They did so on a scale corresponding to the host-country's domestic market, possibly extended to the host-country's 'natural export zone', hence the term 'miniature replica' given to these affiliates. Freeing US MNEs from this constraint was one of the reasons behind the US government's role as an active and supportive agent in the creation of the European Common Market. By the late 1960s, US MNEs in Europe were starting to reap economies of scale more easily by concentrating production for specific product lines in small numbers and often only in one EU country. As trade liberalisation in the Common Market and in the European Free Trade Agreement (EFTA) gathered steam, plant could service several domestic markets' countries, allowing US parent companies to start an initial division of work among their affiliates with single product specialisation for the whole regional-continental market (multi-product horizontal integration). They were, as noted by a French essayist, the first companies to be 'Europeanised'.[12]

Up until the gradual dismantling of tariff barriers in successive rounds of negotiation in GATT, one of the determinants of FDI and the setting up of foreign affiliates was trade barriers, as well as the need to compete with domestic firms, enjoying the protection that this provided. It was only once liberalisation and deregulation, as initiated by the Thatcher and Reagan governments, had started breaking down the prevailing trade regime of international interdependence between still partly autonomous national economies and opened the door to the establishment of the WTO that vertically integrated TNCs emerged. Transnational vertical integration consisted in the creation of affiliates in different countries, either by new investment or by acquisitions which then produce components according to an international division of labour,

11     Hymer 1972a.
12     Servan-Sheiber 1968.

decided by the parent corporation. MNEs developed what Michalet[13] names an integrated global 'space' marked by a complicated mesh of 'internal markets' ensuring the flow of products, of know-how, of financial resources and to a lesser extent of personnel within the boundaries of the corporation. It is an integrated space, since dozens of affiliates (production, R&D, financial, etc.) are under the supervision of the holding company's departments, which manage resources and capabilities according to the objectives most in line with prevailing criteria for the satisfaction of shareholders. The 'internal markets' of TNCs straddle national boundaries and circumvent many governmental regulations. From the 1980s onwards they have increasingly shaped the pattern of foreign trade. What came to be named intra-firm trade began to be measured statistically by the best-endowed national statistical offices.

### 1.5 The Ownership-Location-Internalisation Theoretical Paradigm

At the time when academic economics still included industrial economics and the study of MNEs in its curriculum, the dominant paradigm was the ownership-location-internalisation (OLI) 'eclectic theory' developed by Dunning.[14] In the void left by Anglophone Marxists, the theory of 'international production' could be couched in the framework of certain strands of mainstream economics. In order to legitimise the study of MNEs, the 'eclectic theory' uses the theory of internalisation developed by Hymer[15] from Coase's theory of transaction costs and market failure.[16] The 'eclectic theory' seeks to respond to, or rather to accommodate, Hecksher-Ohlin-Samuelson (HOS) neoclassical trade theory and to add the accumulation of 'ownership assets' to the Coasian theory of the firm. No suggestion is made that FDI takes place after a twofold domestic process of accumulation and capital centralisation and concentration, and that it is a response to the need for large firms to transcend the limits of domestic markets if profit-making is to be pursued effectively. Internalisation is the expression of monopoly power based on concentration and size, yet there is only a fleeting mention in 'eclectic theory' of monopolistic practices. Starting simply from the observation that MNEs exist, and that the recourse to foreign manufacturing operations through FDI and the setting up of subsidiaries as opposed to exports has to be explained, OLI theory basically states that the

---

13   Michalet 1985.
14   The first full presentation dates back to 1981. The final formulation is in Dunning 1993, Chapter 4.
15   Hymer 1972b.
16   Coase 1937.

corporation has 'firm-specific' or 'intangible' assets (O). These are notably in the form of technology and industrial know-how, from which it can reap greater advantages and profits by using them internally (I) rather than exploiting them through licensing, transfers and sales to other firms. The theory asserts that the greater the net benefits of internalising cross-border intermediate product markets, the more likely a firm will prefer to engage in foreign production itself rather than license the right to do so. To his credit, Dunning's analysis is dynamic and stresses that MNEs develop additional ownership and internalisation advantages and so *de facto* monopoly power, in the course of and as a result of internationalisation. These are related *inter alia* to the circulation of components, know-how and improvements on technologies as well as of financial liquidities within internationalised corporate structures. Implicit to this is that further 'market failure' is deliberately created. Other dimensions of firm-specific ownership advantages, which are marked by their cumulative nature, relate to corporate management experience in general. It also includes more precise 'know-how' such as hedging in foreign exchange markets, which ceased under MNE financial management to be a protective mechanism and became one of pure speculation. By the time the onset of full trade and investment liberalisation had taken place, with the setting up of the WTO in 1994, not only US but also Japanese and European MNEs had built up a huge amount of diversified management experience through their multi-domestic international operations.

Location (L) requires closer examination. In manufacturing and services, lower wages and lower (if not non-existent) social costs are obviously important factors in corporate decisions to set up production units in given foreign countries and so appropriate surplus value by the exploitation of workers other than those of the home country. It is these forms of exploitation which have evolved considerably and are discussed in Chapter 6. With trade liberalisation the location of foreign production has, on the whole, despite non-tariff barriers of various sorts which can be challenged through procedures in the WTO, ceased to be prompted by the need to overcome trade barriers. Of course, in addition to low wages and near to equivalent levels of worker training, 'classical' locational factors continue to include abundant availability *in situ* of raw materials, as well as preferential taxes and complementary investments offered by governments or regional authorities in competition for inward FDI. Since the late 1980s, however, the location of FDI has predominantly been shaped by the need to operate close to end markets in conditions of oligopolistic rivalry both with host country domestic firms and with other MNEs. Thus vertically integrated firms will possess affiliates with wide responsibilities for end-line adaptation and commercialisation. As global brand names are built and impose themselves, TNCs which possess them will regain a measure of freedom, the extent of which is determined by the degree of monopoly the brand name gives them.

## 2 The Collective Global Monopoly Power of Transnational Corporations

Today, the principal if not sole form of market structure in the world market is global oligopoly, with its specific mixes in different sectors and industries of rivalry and collusion and of huge collective global monopoly power.

### 2.1 Mergers and Acquisitions and the International Concentration of Capital

The liberalisation of trade, direct investment and financial flows opened the way for the acceleration of concentration (to use the generally accepted term) at the domestic level and subsequently as an international process. Domestically both the methods analysed by Marx under the notion of centralisation have been at work. The building of large national corporations has combined 'the violent method of annexation – when certain capitals become such preponderant centres of attraction for others that they shatter the individual cohesion of the latter and then draw the separate fragments to themselves' and 'the fusion of a number of capitals already formed or in process of formation by the smoother process of organising joint-stock companies'.[17] In the US, investment banks were very active as instruments of 'shatter', notably during the aggressive and highly speculative wave of junk bond LBO acquisitions in the 1980s. In the 2000s, they have served as go-betweens and often architects of 'smoother' mergers and acquisitions (M&As), ensuring that such operations satisfy all shareholders and receive the benediction of the Stock Market. Indeed, the fees for this activity are one of investment banks' largest and least risky sources of 'financial profits'.

Elsewhere, governments have played a very important role, whether by fostering, as in the 1960s and 1970s, the emergence of 'national champions' through state-organised and financed mergers, by restructuring and merging corporations through 'nationalisations' at critical moments or, from the late 1980s onwards, by selling them through privatisations. In Europe, France has

---

17    Marx 1976, Vol. I, Chapter 25.

been the clearest example of all three phases. In Latin America, at different moments, Mexico, Argentina and Brazil have been the terrain of strong government action both in the building of large firms and in their subsequent partial or total privatisation. Advanced country state-owned corporations undergoing what has been termed in France 'crawling privatisation' have been aggressive actors of cross-border M&As since the mid-1990s. France Télécom and GDF-Suez, which have been totally privatised, and EDF, which is still a majority state-owned corporation, are major examples.

For MNEs, M&As are instruments of 'strategic asset-seeking' FDI. In the earlier studies of FDI, this motive was only mentioned in passing. From the late 1980s on, it became all-important. The foreign firms targeted are similar to those targeted by domestic public offerings or engineered M&As (hostile takeovers or negotiated mergers). They are profitable or highly profitable enterprises and are coveted for their market shares and/or their 'firm-specific' or 'intangible' ownership assets, *inter alia* their national or regional-continental brand names. In the case of high-technology industries, they are targeted for their laboratories, plant and skilled personnel and their patent rights.

Cross-border M&As took off in the late 1980s, slowed down in 1990–2 during the US and international recession before picking up strongly again from the mid-1990s onwards. For European TNCs, one of the factors behind the process was the acquisition of privatised state-owned firms in the so-called 'transition economies'. In Latin America in telecoms, electrical power and water-provision the cross-border M&A process benefited strongly from the implementation of the 'Washington Consensus', which pushed for the privatisation of state-owned firms. With the 'shift to services' in overall TNC activity documented in several of UNCTAD's annual World Investment Reports,[18] international M&A operations reached another peak around 2004–6. Estimates published in a recent official US study indicate that global activity in mergers and acquisitions surpassed $5 trillion in 2015, about $2.5 trillion of which was in the US, 'the highest amount in a year on record'.[19] Deals surpassing $10 billion accounted for 37 percent of global takeovers in 2015, almost double the average of 21 percent for the previous five years. As will be seen below, cross-border M&As are also now the favoured route for the internationalisation of large corporations from emerging countries.

---

18   UNCTAD 2004.
19   Council of Economic Advisers 2016.

### 2.2 Scant Data on Domestic Concentration and Little to No on Global Concentration

UNCTAD estimates that TNCs represent about a third of total world exports of goods and services and that the first 100 TNCs alone account for over 15% of these.[20] The available data on trade involving TNCs is discussed in section 6 of the next chapter. In most industries, monopoly power is a collective power, exercised by the small group of corporations that has emerged from the process of centralisation, a process which today is taking place at a world level. This power is exerted *vis-à-vis* workers, suppliers and consumers. Monopoly and oligopoly are trivialised if they are simply discussed in opposition to competition, with intermediary categories such as imperfect competition added on. Monopoly power is the capacity to shape the trajectory of social life under capitalism in the most essential basic manner, such as in issues pertaining to energy and modes of consumption (the supermarket). One senses a high or very high degree of centralisation and concentration because it surrounds us, not least on the Internet (Apple, Google, Facebook) where concentration is particularly high, but one can rarely back up this perception with statistical data. Even at the national level, in most countries, data on industrial concentration has never been collected systematically. France has recently published significant overall data. The category named 'group firms' represent 2% of total firms but account for 64% of employment and 70% of value-added. 186 large firms account for 49% of export turnover and their affiliates another 33%.[21] The US situation is the only one to be fairly well documented. On account of anti-trust legislation dating back to the end of the nineteenth century, the 1890 Sherman Act, which remains the basis for special Congress investigations (as recently for Microsoft), it is the only country to publish 4-firm and 8-firm concentration ratios at regular intervals.[22] It is much less used in academic research than in previous periods.[23] Effective anti-trust action was severely reduced by the Reagan Administration in the mid-1980s,[24] but has been resorted to again following the increase in concentration and a renewed concern over monopoly power. An impressive academic review of US mergers and some of their effects on R&D, on market access of new products as well as other social costs[25]

---

20  UNCTAD 2012.
21  INSEE 2012.
22  http://www.census.gov/econ/concentration.html.
23  The last major economic treatise on oligopoly using 1963 US concentration ratios is Scherer 1970.
24  The story is told in Flynn 1988.
25  Brock 2011.

received little attention but the publication of a Congressional study on a very sensitive sector[26] and a Council of Economic Advisors' policy brief suggest a change in the political mood.[27]

Concerning world concentration ratios nothing even remotely approaching US Census data exists. Global data on concentration is not published by UNCTAD. The only data available comes from special industry reports or monographs. I have attempted elsewhere to collect these for the mid-1990s as completely as possible.[28] Scattered recent information includes automobiles, where in 2011 five corporations held 54% of world production and 13 held 87%.[29] Some estimates are available for pharmaceuticals, where in 2006 the top ten firms from the US and Europe accounted for nearly half the value of global sales.[30] They may be out-dated since a new wave of concentration in pharmaceuticals has been underway since 2009. The industry is one where monopolistic positions should ideally be calculated at the level of specific therapeutic categories, where they are often extremely high. The reasons for the current wave of mergers include expiring patents (the 'patent cliff') faced by some large corporations, the increasing cost of molecule screening, regulatory requirements and the demand for generic drugs where corporations from emerging countries have played a leading role. In pharmaceuticals, M&As between advanced country corporations[31] have developed alongside their search for acquisitions in emerging countries.[32]

Thanks to painstaking work by NGOs, agribusiness is the area where very good data is available. It is presented in box 5.1.

---

26  Shields 2010.
27  Council of Economic Advisers 2016.
28  Chesnais 1997, Chapter 4.
29  OICA (*Organisation Internationale des Constructeurs d'Automobiles*) is (*in English*) The International Organisation of Motor Vehicle Manufacturers.
30  OECD 2008.
31  In 2009, Pfizer acquired Wyeth, Merck bought Schering-Plough and Roche merged with Genentech. In 2014, Novartis, GlaxoSmithKline and Eli Lilly launched a complicated series of cross-product deals for a total of $25 billion. Novartis is trading its vaccine division for GSK's cancer drug business. Eli Lilly is acquiring Novartis's animal-health business. GSK and Novartis are also setting up a joint venture to produce and sell over-the-counter drugs, creating a global leader in that segment with brands like Excedrin and Panadol. Then there are Pfizer's so far abortive efforts to buy the Anglo-Swedish AstraZeneca for about $100 billion. See http://www.bloombergview.com/articles/2014-04-22/pharma-mergers-make-sense.
32  UNCTAD 2014a, pp. 13–14.

BOX 5.1: WORLD CONCENTRATION IN AGRIBUSINESS

SEEDS: The world's top three corporations – Monsanto, DuPont Pionner and Syngenta (Switzerland) – control over half (53%) of the world's commercial seed market; the top 10 control over three quarters (76%).

PESTICIDES: Just six corporations – Syngenta, Bayer Crop Science (Germany), BASF (Germany), Dow AgroSciences, DuPont and Monsanto – hold 76% of the global agrochemical market. The top ten companies control almost 95% of the world market.

FERTILISERS: The top 10 corporations control 41% of the global market.

ANIMAL PHARMA: Three corporations – Zoetis (formely Pfizer Animal Health), Merck Animal Health and Merial Sanofi (USA) – account for 46% of the global market. The top seven firms – all subsidiaries of multinational drug companies – control 72%.

LIVESTOCK GENETICS: Four corporations account for 97% of poultry genetics R&D (broilers, layers, turkeys). In swine genetics, four corporations account for two-thirds of industry R&D worldwide.

Source: ETC Group 2013.

The consequences of collective monopoly power differ across industries. In automobiles, non-price and price combination offers consumers some protection. In others where products are standardised, technology stabilised and consumers economically and socially dominated, the opposite holds true. The ETC Group study on agro-industries stresses that 'more disturbingly, the oligopoly paradigm has moved beyond individual sectors to the entire food system: the same six multinationals control 75% of all private sector plant breeding research; 60% of the commercial seed market and 76% of global agrochemical sales. The six companies are Monsanto, DuPont, Syngenta, Bayer, Dow, and BASF. BASF is not among the top 10 corporations producing seed. But it is heavily engaged in seed research and has partnerships with several of the other five companies and investments in several start-up enterprises'.[33] In the case of the fertiliser industry, data has been collected for countries rather than firms and the countries concerned are somewhat different. China, India, Russia and Canada have large domestic corporations so that the top five producer

---

33   ETC Group 2013, p. 3. The study contains data on many other sectors, notably animal breeding.

countries control between 47 and 77 per cent of the world's production capacity for all major products.[34] The merger between Lafarge and Holcim has placed the issue of concentration in the limelight. The merger aims at making the new corporation the new world leader, ahead of the present leader, the Chinese Anhui Conch. In 2013, the next four corporations in the world ranking were China National Building Material (CNBM), HeidelbergCement, Italcementi and Cemex (Mexico). Yet studies on concentration in the industry, which is characterised by a very high capital/labour ratio (e.g. constant to variable capital ratio) are very hard to find.[35]

### 2.3  Non-Price and Price Competition in Global Oligopolies

Oligopoly as a form of market structure is characterised by the recognition by the small number of firms in each industry of their mutual market dependence. This is the essence of oligopoly[36] and holds for the relationships among large and very large TNCs. In 1986, Porter still opposes multi-domestic industries in which for firms (e.g. groups) 'competition in each country or small group of countries is essentially independent of competition in other countries' and global industries 'in which a firm's competitive position in one country is significantly affected by its position in other countries'.[37] All industries are now global for reasons that have to do with profits and return on equity, but also with oligopolistic rivalry. The stock market's attention is riveted on overall performance as read in consolidated corporate accounts and most shareholders will consider that the corporation must draw profits from all its markets. All industries can now be seen as global in that rivalry comprises strategies where as one firm enters an important market, others will follow sooner or later. This has taken place recently for TNC investment in automobiles in China.

A key issue concerns the place of price competition in rivalry. Oligopoly is associated with behaviour which Baran and Sweezy, in a commentary on Schumpeter, were the first to characterise as 'co-respective',[38] now often referred to under the term 'mutual forbearance', in which firms only resort to price competition in the last instance. They seek to outpace and outdo

---

34  Hernandez and Torero 2011.
35  A very early French study by the geographer Yves Lacoste 1957 had already emphasised a high degree of concentration. The only contemporary study I have found is on India. Mukhopadhyaya et al. 2008, figure 1, found the first four firms had a ratio of 52 percent.
36  Caves 1974.
37  Porter 1986, p. 18.
38  Baran and Sweezy, p. 74, in a discussion of Chapter 8 in Schumpeter's *Capitalism, Socialism and Democracy*.

their rivals through the new products they launch, the scale and pace of their investments in R&D and production facilities, and their strategic choices with respect in particular to the servicing of given markets, by exports from given production platforms (now never that of the sole firm's home country) or by production for the host country domestic market. As long as overall macroeconomic conditions permit rival companies to forego price competition, the situation can be, as in automobiles prior to the start of the crisis, one where 'the higher the level of multimarket contact among competitors, the more one could expect to observe rivalry deterrence and the corresponding higher industry profitability'.[39]

Every time an industry undergoes centralisation/concentration, competition is weakened initially. At some point it reasserts itself. This has been shown in a number of instances during the last quarter of the twentieth century. The stable cosy US postwar domestic oligopolies with their recognised price leaders represented a passing phase. It ended with the entry of Japanese firms into the US market, not only on account of their own advances in technology and organisation but also of the opportunity offered to them by the complacency and sluggishness of US oligopolies. This was followed by 'cross-invasion' by European firm FDI. The loss of market shares by the US giants in all the industries not backed by Federal government resulted from their belief that for them the 'constraint of competition' was a thing of the past. A similar process is at work today in relation to China with the additional play of political relationships which gives Chinese capital a further competitive edge. Today it is certain that unless in the coming years massive class struggle destabilises Chinese bureaucratic capitalism, large Chinese corporations will fight their entry through foreign direct investment into a number of global oligopolies.

## 3   The Place of Emerging Countries' Corporations in the Global Oligopoly

Corporations from countries still listed by the UN as 'developing countries' are now part of many global oligopolies. In UNCTAD's annual World Investment Reports, its institutional and organisational embodiments fall under several headings: sovereign wealth funds (SWFs), state-owned enterprises, and TNCs. The centralisation of capital and its concentration both in the form of large banks and funds and large non-financial corporations has also taken root in

---

39   For a demonstration of this hypothesis in the automobile industry, see Yu, Subramamian and Cannella Jr. 2009, p. 129.

certain of them, especially those where since the late nineteenth century the possession of key primary resources had favoured accumulation in the particular form of non-land rent discussed above in Chapter 4. In 1938, Mexico was strong enough politically to resist US pressure and create its own state-owned oil corporation, Pemex. In Brazil and Argentina, Bonapartist governments followed suit. In the 1930s and 40s, they established state-owned enterprises in basic service industries and spurred the formation of national industrial capital in a few others, while calling in foreign firms in others in keeping with import-substitution policies theorised by CEPAL in the 1960s. The military dictatorships of the 1960s and 70s were also actively 'developmentalist'. Liberalisation and globalisation saw the entry of a number of these corporations into their respective global oligopolies.

One somewhat particular indicator of global oligopoly membership status exists in the form of the list of 'global challengers' that the Boston Consulting Group (BCG) started publishing in 2006. It published its fifth edition in 2013 adding 26 names to the 'member' list, plus seven 'graduates'.[40] The BCG selection criteria are exclusively financial, namely long-term value for shareholders, specifically total shareholder return (TSR) and so eligibility to be included in investor portfolios. BRIC countries (Brazil, Russia, India and China), where accumulation in oil, mining and manufacturing has really taken place and which were previously home to 84 challengers, are down to 69 in 2013. This points to finance *qua* finance as a major entry ticket.

The presence in global oligopolies of BRIC countries is ensured quite significantly by state-owned enterprises (SOEs). In 2012, there were 18 SOE among the world's top 100 TNCs. Since they are rarely fully government-owned, they are listed on stock markets. The government is the largest shareholder in China's 150 largest firms where SOEs represented 80 percent of stock market capitalisation. The figure for the Russian Federation is 62 percent, 38 percent for Brazil, and for India some 20 percent. Everywhere oil and natural gas companies are important (Petrochina, Gazprom, Petrobras, Indian Oil Corporation). In the case of India, they are almost wholly concentrated in public services and utilities (in India, coal and oil production, power generation, and distribution and telecoms account for 71 percent of the total). Given the low UN and OECD thresholds for qualifying as a TNC, these Indian corporations are listed as such. Closer examination concludes that their investments made abroad, and the dividends and interests accruing on such investments, are paltry.[41]

---

40  https://www.bcgperspectives.com/content/articles/globalization_growth_introducing_the_2013_bcg_global_challengers/.
41  Mishra 2009, p. 20.

In Brazil, the weight of the development bank BNDES, which manages financial resources larger than those of the World Bank, in the provision of investment loan capital to Brazilian firms, notably large ones, means that *de facto* government presence is larger.[42] BNDES actively supports Brazilian large firms' foreign investments. The loans BNDES makes go principally to large groups (83 percent in 2009). Those in mining and agribusiness received 27 percent of these loans and high-technology firms only 1 percent,[43] meaning that BNDES has done little to offset the shift to the primary sector which makes Brazil so tributary to Chinese demand.

### 3.1  Sovereign Wealth Funds

Sovereign wealth funds (SWFS) created by or on behalf of sovereign states with large export surpluses have become both important participants in global financial markets and the initiators of asset-seeking FDI. They are mainly portfolio investors, with the bulk of their funds held in relatively liquid financial assets in core financial centres. In 2011, only a small proportion of their value, estimated by UNCTAD to be in the order of $125 billion, took the form of FDI, accounting for one percent of global FDI stock. The largest part was directed to the advanced capitalist countries and highly concentrated in finance, real estate and upgrade services.[44] The fraction invested in developing countries is almost exclusively in natural resources. Four funds, Temasek (Singapore), China Investment Corporation, the Qatar Investment Authority and Mubadala (United Arab Emirates), accounted for almost the whole of such SWF investment.[45]

Appelbaum and Batt have synthesised analyses tracking down SWF investments. In the case of the US, private equity funds are targeted. The Abu Dhabi Investment Authority bought a 9 percent stake in Apollo Management and a 7.5 percent stake in the Carlyle Group. The Kuwait Investment Authority and the Government of Singapore Investment Corporation have stakes in Texas Pacific Group (TPG), and China Development Bank (CIC) is following suit.

---

42   For a full account of BNDES see Chandrasekbar 2016.
43   Paulani 2015b.
44   US examples include the Abu Dhabi Investment Authority holdings in Citigroup Inc. (4.9 percent), Apollo Management (9 percent), and Hyatt Hotels Corporation (10.9 percent). Istithmar World, the private equity arm of the Dubai World Fund, controls a 100 percent stake in Barneys New York, a 100 percent stake in Loehmann's, a 10 percent stake in Perella Weinberg Partners (financial services), and a 33.3 percent stake in Education Media and Publishing Group International (EMPGI). See Appelbaum 2012, p. 31.
45   UNCTAD 2013.

CIC's record in the US financial sector is impressive. Its investments include a $3 billion investment in Blackstone Group with non-voting rights in 2007 and a $5 billion investment in Morgan Stanley in the same year.[46] In early 2008, CIC launched a $4 billion private equity fund with JC Flowers & Co., primarily focusing on the US financial sector. It contributed about 80 percent of the capital. In 2009 and 2010, CIC invested $1billion in Oaktree Capital Management LP, which oversees more than $60 billion in assets and was one of the firms involved in the Public-Private Investment Partnership, the US government programme designed to rid banks of toxic assets. It also has a stake in BlackRock and joined a private equity partnership with Lexington Partners, Goldman Sachs and Pantheon Ventures.[47]

### 3.2  FDI by Developing-Country TNCs and Modes of Foreign Entry by China, India and Brazil

Over the last ten to fifteen years, in the large emerging economies, the centralisation and concentration of capital have proceeded apace, much like that of the industrialised countries, but the internationalisation of corporations has been somewhat slower.[48] In 2011, the assets of the 100 largest firms of developing and transition countries amounted to 39 percent of those of the 100 largest firms worldwide, but in the case of the former only 27 percent of assets were held abroad compared with 61 percent for the latter. Acquisitions have been a major form of entry to foreign assets and markets. In 2013, cross-border M&As by emerging countries accounted for 53 percent of total cross-border M&As. Half of cross-border M&As by Southern TNCs involved foreign affiliates of developed-country TNCs transferring their ownership into the hands of developing-country TNCs, notably in the extractive sector.[49] A number of acquisitions by emerging economies in the 'South' have been the consequence of developed-country TNCs divestments. Examples of this trend include very large acquisitions such as the Italian oil and gas group ENI's sale of its subsidiary in Mozambique to PetroChina, the oil and gas group Apache's (United States) sale of its subsidiary in Egypt to Sinopec (China) and

---

46   Singh 2008.
47   Appelbaum and Batt 2012.
48   For a very well documented analysis using the Dunning typology, see Andreff 2016.
49   Here the value of transactions involving sales by developed-country TNCs to developing-country-based counterparts represented over 80 percent of the gross value of acquisitions. In Africa as a whole, these purchases accounted for 74 percent of all purchases on the continent. Asian TNCs in particular have been making an effort to secure upstream reserves in order to satisfy growing domestic demand (UNCTAD 2014a, p. 8).

ConocoPhillips's sale of its affiliates in Algeria to an Indonesian State-owned company, Pertamina. This has also occurred in banking since the 2008 financial crisis and its 2011 extension in Europe. UNCTAD gives two examples.[50] In Colombia, Bancolombia acquired the entire share capital of HSBC Bank Panama from HSBC and in Egypt, Qatar National Bank, a majority-owned unit of the state-owned Qatar Investment Authority, acquired a 77 percent stake of Cairo-based National Société Générale Bank.

Following pressure by the IMF, the Chinese Ministry of Commerce published data on FDI for the years 2007–9. This shows a large part of it went to Hong Kong but also to tax havens such as the Cayman Islands and British Virgin Islands, from which capital was redirected to other unknown destinations. Part of FDI was round-tripping, even if an IMF study notes that estimations vary significantly.[51] The most reliable study is a US government report.[52] Leaving aside the flows to tax havens, in the period up to 2008, in emerging and developing countries FDI was directed largely to basic resources and in advanced countries to finance, wholesale and retailing, leasing and business services. There was a rapid acceleration after 2004. Seeking markets on the basis of geographical proximity and the opportunities offered by large local Chinese communities explains the rank of Australia, Singapore and Canada. In the case of the US, where M&A is the main mode of entry, sensitivity to Chinese investment in high technology made financial services the main target. Data collected for 2013–14 gives prominence to commercial real estate, shale gas and biotechnology.[53] In the case of Europe, the data collected since 2009 shows a trend towards an increase in Chinese FDI to countries struggling with government debt or corporate insolvencies. The acquisition of part of the harbour of Piraeus in Greece is a spectacular expression of this. Chinese capital will handle Chinese exports into Europe right down the line. China is also investing in the construction of the Southern Gas Corridor in the Balkans. For China, Portugal is still more strategic. Since the start of the Eurozone crisis, Chinese SOEs acquired major shares in strategic sectors of the Portuguese economy, such as the water, electricity, and communications industries. One example of such a purchase occurred in late 2011, when the Three Gorges Corporation acquired 22 percent of Energias de Portugal (EDP) for US$3.5 billion (nearly twice EDP's actual market value). In 2012, China State Grid bought 25 percent of Redes Energéticas Nacionais (REN) at 40 percent over the value of the stock

---

50   UNCTAD 2014a, p. 9.
51   http://www.imf.org/external/pubs/ft/pdp/2002/pdp03.pdf.
52   Salidjanova 2011.
53   See http://rhg.com/notes/chinese-fdi-in-the-us-2013-recap-and-2014-outlook.

at the time of the agreement. In 2013, Beijing Enterprise Water Group acquired Veolia Water Portugal from its French parent company for US$123 million. China Mobile also announced that it was considering acquiring a stake in Portugal Telecom. The picture must be completed by the massive amount of Chinese capital pouring into real estate.[54]

In the case of outward Indian FDI, a UNESCAP study found that despite highly publicised foreign acquisitions, such as Tata Motors' purchase of Jaguar and Land Rover in the UK during the period for which data was available, a very high percentage of India's overall 'approved FDI' had been directed towards financial centres: Singapore (22 percent), Mauritius and other tax havens (25 percent), and in the Eurozone the Netherlands (15 percent). In the case of M&As, which is the favoured form of internationalisation of Indian groups, the locational pattern was of course quite different. During the period examined, Canada was the first host country for India's foreign acquisitions: a 34 percent share with a concentration in resources, notably the acquisition of the large Canadian aluminium firm Novelis by Hidalco. The US came next with a 24 percent share in a range of sectors, notably finance. Another 16 percent were aimed at resource-rich countries (Russia, Egypt, Australia and South Africa) and the rest to the UK and Europe (17 percent). Besides Tata Motors' acquisitions, this included Tata Steel's purchase of the Anglo-Dutch firm Corus.[55]

Brazilian FDI breaks the pattern proposed above, with respect to the mode of expansion, in that greenfield investment is important. Most of Brazil's largest TNCs operate in natural resource-based sectors (mining, energy and agricultural commodities) or in services, mainly engineering and construction, with an incipient role for financial services in neighbouring countries.[56] Besides Petrobras, the largest TNCs are the mining corporation Vale, with investments in 33 countries in 2009 (and a very controversial one in Mozambique in 2011), and the steel manufacturer Metalurgica Gerdau, with affiliates in seven Latin American countries, the US, Canada, Spain and India in 2013. In food and drinks, major TNCs are the meat processors JBS,

---

54  Horta 2013.

55  Singapore and the Netherlands are attractive hosts for holding companies from India and elsewhere because of the low and simple tax rates and the large number of double tax treaties between the two countries and rest of the world. Tata Steel financed the Corus acquisition partly via a debt arranged by a consortium of banks for Tata Steel UK as well as through bridge finance obtained by its subsidiary Tata Steel Asia Singapore. As such the deal may not even have shown up in India's FDI statistics or could have shown up as being made via Singapore (Gopalan and Rajan 2010).

56  In 2009, the 20 largest Brazilian TNCs earned 25 percent of their revenues abroad, held 28 percent of their assets and 27 percent of their employees abroad. See Doctor 2010.

the largest multinational meat processing corporation in the world, producing processed beef, chicken and pork with 150 industrial plants around the world in 2012; Brasil Foods (BRF) created in 2013 through the merger of two already large firms; Sadia and Perdigão; and the brewing company Ambev, formally Companhia de Bebidas das Américas (in English: American Beverage Company, henceforth 'Ambev'), the biggest brewery in Latin America and the fifth biggest in the world, which is now part of the giant Anheuser-Busch InBev. In pulp and paper the list of Brazilian TNCs includes Suzano Papel e Celulose and Fibria Celulose, created by a 2011 merger. In engineering and construction, the largest TNC is Noberto Odebrech Construtora. It is part of the Odebrech conglomerate, which also controls Braskem, one of the largest petrochemical companies in Latin America. Brazil's largest firms do not operate in high-technology sectors, with the exceptions of the aerospace corporation Embraer and certain aspects of Petrobras's activities. Both are largely legacies of very active state support in the 1960s and 1970s. Embraer started as a purely military firm. It is known outside Brazil as the direct competitor of Bombardier as well as a manufacturer of small business executive planes, but it continues to produce military transport planes.

A 2015 report by the McKinsey Global Institute considers that emerging country corporations have become important contenders in global oligopolistic rivalry. The composition of the Fortune Global 500 shows that between 1980 and 2000, emerging country corporations accounted for roughly 5 percent of the Fortune 500. After that there was a strong acceleration driven by China among its own corporations but also through the impact of its global expansion, which allowed trade partners to become even bigger than they were before. The report cites the example of Vale. By 2013, the share of emerging country corporations had risen to 26 percent; that of US and Western European companies dropped from 76 percent in 1980 to 54 percent in 2013. The report emphasises that a number of the contenders threatening industrialised countries' positions in world oligopolies are diversified conglomerates combining the holding with strong centralised control stemming from state or family ownership.[57]

### Appendix: Recent Developments Affecting the Statistical Data on FDI

The collection of statistical data on FDI from national sources began in a specialised unit named UNCTNC at the United Nations headquarters in New York,

---

57  McKinsey Global Institute 2015, p. 50.

where the first World Investment Reports were published from 1988 onwards. The work was transferred to UNCTAD in Geneva with the setting up of a large Department on FDI and TNCs. The publication of annual World Investment Reports (WIR) is an important moment for all those who consider the analysis of TNC operations as crucial. In the 1980s, work on FDI started at OCDE in order to establish a framework for the collection of data by member countries. There have always been caveats about the data collected. In the case of the output, domestic sales, exports and employment of TNC affiliates, e.g. their 'material' activities, they have been considerably reduced. Some countries also undertake periodical surveys, which permit reasonable estimates of the size of intra-firm trade. On the contrary, the problems posed by the collection and interpretation of comparable data on the inflows and outflows of FDI and of profits from foreign investment, recorded by balance of payments statistics have always been important (few countries have data with the degree of reliability of that of the US Survey of Current Business). These problems increased significantly in the 2000s, particularly after 2007.

UNCTAD lists a number of factors which lead to inconsistencies in the data collection and reporting methods of FDI flows by different countries. Some have always existed, but new ones, specific to contemporary financialisation, have appeared. These include the changing nature and increasing sophistication of FDI-related transactions (e.g. investment through exchange of shares between investors and acquired firms or investment from indirect sources). Then there is the fact that as a result of financialisation 'the distinction between FDI transactions with "portfolio-like behaviour" and portfolio investment, including hot money, is blurred'.[58] Finally since 2007–8, increasing volatility in exchange rates makes the correspondence between home- and host-country reporting more uncertain. These problems are compounded by the rise in offshore finance.

### *Offshore Finance and 'Special Purpose Entities'*

Since the start of the world economic and financial crisis, the size of offshore finance in financial flows recorded as FDI has grown extremely rapidly. This finance takes two forms: flows to and out of 'offshore financial centres' (OFCs), the official and polite name for tax havens, and 'special purpose entities' (SPEs). These can either be specialised foreign affiliates set up by TNCs in low tax countries or countries that provide specific tax benefits for such entities, or they can be home-based affiliates with the status of financial holding companies (as in the US). UNCTAD has tried to keep track of flows to and from tax havens from 1990 onwards. The average annual FDI inflows to OFCs in the

---

58   UNCTAD 2011, Chapter 1, p. 6.

period 2007–12 were $75 billion, well above the $15 billion average during the years 2000–6. They peaked at nearly $90 billion in 2011, representing nearly 7 percent of global FDI flows. According to UNCTAD, 'a significant part of inflows consists of "round-tripping" FDI to the original source countries'. Thus the top three destinations of FDI flows from Russia (Cyprus, the Netherlands and the British Virgin Islands) coincide with the top three sources of foreign investment to Russia itself. 'Such flows are more akin to domestic investments disguised as FDI'.[59]

UNCTAD is now trying to track financial flows through SPEs. In the World Investment Report 2013, Luxembourg, the Netherlands and Hungary head the list of countries hosting SPEs on account of very advantageous tax treatment. But Portugal and Denmark have followed suit. In Asia, Hong Kong and Singapore are leaders. The role of these two centres for China is discussed above in section 3.2 Austrian SPEs, which account for one third of inward FDI stock, are used mostly for investments in Central and Eastern Europe. Mauritius, which concluded a double taxation treaty with India, has attracted foreign holding firms and, as a conduit for SPE FDI, has become one of the largest FDI sources for India. The sums involved are much higher than those of OFCs. Three countries alone (Hungary, Luxembourg and the Netherlands) reported more than $600 billion in investment flows to SPEs for 2011 compared with $90 billion to OFCs. 'Any change in the use of special entities, thus, would dwarf variations in flows to offshore financial centres'. In the 2014 report, the UNCTAD Secretariat publishes estimations for five countries, four of which are members of the EU, of FDI with and without SPEs.[60]

### *Foreign Acquisitions by Private Equity Capital*

Further difficulties in measuring FDI flows come from the surge of cross-border short-term investment by private equity firms. These are financial corporations raising pools of capital (private equity funds) and using them to acquire controlling positions in non-financial enterprises generally not traded in stock markets, with a view to restructuring and reselling them in a very short time. Private equity firms can either be independent corporations or affiliates of a large financial conglomerate. The largest firms are American and include The Carlyle Group, Kohlberg Kravis Roberts (KKR), Goldman Sachs Principal Investment Group, BlackRock and Bain Capital. But there are some big European firms such as the London-based CVC Capital Partners and the

---

59   UNCTAD 2013, Chapter 1, pp. 15–16.
60   UNCTAD 2014, p. 3.

affiliates of two French financial conglomerates, Paribas Affaires Industrielles (PAI) and Axa Private Equity (Axa PE).

Since the mid-2000s a growing proportion of private equity investments have been in foreign countries. In 2007, a third of trans-border M&As identified by UNCTAD were made by private equity, before falling to 15 percent in 2011.[61] After a period when large firms targeted big, publicly traded companies, from 2007–8 onwards, private equity has been predominantly aimed at smaller firms. The firms targeted in developing countries are largely concentrated in services and mining. In developed countries, private equity firms invest in a wide range of industries, from food, beverages and tobacco in the manufacturing sector to real estate in the services sector. With a nice sense of euphemism UNCTAD observes that the 'strategic motivations of private equity funds in international investment differs from FDI by TNCs with possible downside implications for the long-run growth and welfare of the host economies'.[62] Private equity funds seek short-run profits entailing layoffs and restructuring of companies. Acquired firms are held on average for five to six years, a period which has declined in recent years.

---

61   UNCTAD 2012, Chapter 1, p. 11.
62   UNCTAD 2012, Chapter 1, p. 12.

CHAPTER 6

# The Operational Modes of TNCs in the 2000s

The deep transformations in the activities of concentrated industrial capital associated with financialisation are not limited to the growth of the financial operations of large non-financial corporations. They concern the present forms of organisation of international production by TNCs or MNEs as well as the respective role in the production and appropriation of value and surplus value between FDI in the narrow sense and offshoring and what UNCTAD names the 'new non-equity modes'.[1] In the late 1980s, the 'new-style MNEs', as first named by Dunning,[2] started to extend subcontracting outsourcing relationships beyond their national economies, appropriating value created by smaller firms through offshoring on an international level. Milberg and Winkler argue that offshoring by TNCs reached a 'level of growth and depth [such as] to constitute a "new wave" of globalization'.[3] It bears a direct relation to financialisation.[4] It also leads to some important theoretical questions about 'super-exploitation' and the law of value. These are discussed at the end of the chapter.

## 1 Industrial Capital: From Internationalisation to Globalisation

Under the effects of growing trade liberalisation, the configuration of foreign production by TNCs evolved continually from the 1960s onwards. Then the combined liberalisation of trade and direct investment in the WTO opened the present phase of globalisation. It saw from the mid-1990s onwards the setting up of ever more complex 'global value chains', first among TNC affiliates and then increasingly through offshoring with medium and small firms, often

---

1  UNCTAD 2011, Chapter 3.
2  'The MNE is now increasingly assuming the role of an orchestrator of production and transactions within a cluster, or network, of cross-border internal and external relationships, which may or may not involve equity investment, but which are intended to serve its global interests' (Dunning 1988, p. 327).
3  Milberg and Winkler 2009, pp. 2–3.
4  Milberg is one of the very few authors to do this. In a vein similar to Lazonick, he writes: 'the enormous expansion of global value chains has ... coincided with a decline in manufacturing in most countries, and thus has permitted companies to return a greater share of net revenues to shareholders rather than reinvesting these revenues in new productive capacity' (Milberg 2004, p. 3).

situated in a large number of countries. Within their corporate boundaries, TNCs have continually reorganised, with the help of ICTs and the new modes of bulk transport, the international location and management of production operations. They have maximised the appropriation of surplus value at business-unit and plant levels and reduced transport cost through containerisation.[5] They have simultaneously developed or extended mechanisms for the appropriation of surplus value produced by other firms through subcontracting. Value and surplus value predation by global corporations has taken ever more diversified forms. The process is well summarised by UNCTAD:

> In the period immediately after the Second World War, an international political economy grounded in concepts of national independence, self-sufficiency and import substitution led to international trade essentially being conducted between autonomous enterprises, with TNC activity mostly in the form of 'multi-domestic', host-country-oriented affiliates. This began to change in the late 1960s and 1970s, with the initial footfalls of offshore production by Japanese, European and United States manufacturing TNCs in South-East Asia, pursuing cost-cutting strategies in the wake of recession and competitive pressures in their home (and later global) markets. Subsequent decades have inexorably built on the dynamic of these incipient global value chains (GVCs), with technological progress (ITT), political factors (e.g. liberalization and privatization policies, China's emergence as a global manufacturing base) and investor strategies (e.g. fine-slicing of operations and offshoring of every segment or sub-segment of their value chains, a greater use of cross-border non-equity modes) jointly and inter-connectedly leading to the trade-investment nexus of today.[6]

## 2   Value Chains in Business Management Theory

A notion used in varying ways by business management theory and international industrial economics is that of 'value chains'. One of the international organisations that now uses the notion is the World Bank. It states:

> value chain analysis is a method for accounting and presenting the value that is created in a product or service as it is transformed from raw inputs

---

5   OECD 2011.
6   UNCTAD 2013, p. 140.

to a final product consumed by end users. Value chain analysis typically involves identifying and mapping the relationships of four types of features: (i) the activities performed during each stage of processing; (ii) the value of inputs, processing time, outputs and value-added; (iii) the spatial relationships, such as distance and logistics and, (iv) the structure of economic agents, such as suppliers, the producer, and the wholesaler.[7]

Value chain analysis ignores the Marxist distinction between variable capital and constant capital in fixed investment. It takes constant capital as the starting point and successful commercialisation as the closing point, thus proposing an approximation of the M-C-P-C'-M' cycle as far as non-Marxist economics can go. A firm can encompass the whole cycle itself, including the in-house production of components and even of machines, as was the case at one time for automobile firms, or it can decompose or fragment the production process through subcontracting, keeping for itself the conception and design of products, their assembly and their marketing. In the case of TNCs, the process straddles across frontiers.

Well before the World Bank the analysis of commodity chains had been taken up in a progressive manner by Gary Gereffi[8] with emphasis on:

> two dramatic changes in the structure of the global economy. The first is an historic shift in the location of production, particularly in manufacturing, from the developed to the developing world.... The second is a change in the organization of the international economy. The global economy is increasingly concentrated at the top and fragmented at the bottom, both in terms of countries and firms.[9]

Gereffi proposed to distinguish between 'buyer-led' chains built by commercial groups and 'producer-led' chains by industrial corporations. Subsequently he argued that ICT was necessarily going to modify the configuration of value chains and blur the previous dichotomy between buyer-driven and supplier-driven.[10]

---

7   World Bank/FIAS 2007, pp. ix–x.
8   Gereffi 1994, 2001 and 2005.
9   Gereffi 2005, p. 50.
10  Gereffi 2001, pp. 37–8, sketches out three possible scenarios.

3    Buyer-Driven Global Commodity Chains

In conditions of slow or very slow growth, the most critical moment in the accumulation cycle is C', access to the market. This holds for large manufacturers *vis-à-vis* giant retailers, as was seen in Chapter 4. It is even more the case for the subcontractors of such monopsonies. The conditions in which firms sell determine how much of the value added along the chain will remain in their hands. Market access is decisive. Superior bargaining power as buyers allows firms to capture a part, in many cases a large part, of the value created by smaller ones. In the case of large retailers in consumer goods the relationship with smaller suppliers is easily identifiable as one of outright monopsony. In his path-breaking research on the large retailers, Wal-Mart, Carrefour, Tesco and their like, Gereffi[11] identified them as having succeeded in organising extensive 'buyer-driven global commodity chains' characterised by very strong predatory appropriation of value. Research led by Gereffi continues to be one of the main sources of academic case study data.[12] Business and NGO sources provide other important insights.

In Chapter 4, several facets of Wal-Mart US's domestic operations were examined. It is also heavily involved in global sourcing and has built specialised mechanisms for eliminating 'margin-takers' and for maximising the appropriation of downstream surplus value. An apologetic study exploring Wal-Mart strategies shows supply chains before and after restructuring:[13]

> **Traditional produce supply chain**: Grower → Pre-packer → Agent exporter → Agent importer → Supplier/packer → Regional distribution centre → Wal-Mart store.
>
> **Wal-Mart produce supply chain**: Grower → Pre-packer → Regional distribution centre → Wal-Mart store.

This organisational change entailed the creation of 'Global Merchandising Centers' (GMCs). The corporation's CEO boasts that 'by leveraging our scale and restructuring our relationship with suppliers, we will enable our businesses around the world to offer even more competitive pricing on merchandise and to provide our customers a clear and compelling assortment of better

---

11    Gereffi 1994.
12    See the very numerous references to Gerrefi and his colleagues in the footnotes to the chapter on GVCs in UNCTAD 2013, pp. 198–202.
13    Berg and Roberts 2012, p. 117.

quality products at lower prices'.[14] The full meaning of this was brought out by the rapid succession of catastrophes in Bangladesh: the Tazreen Fashions factory fire in November 2012, the Rana Plaza factory collapse in April 2013 and the November 2013 fire, all in Dhaka. Wal-Mart was implicated in all three. Besides Wal-Mart one can find in garments and apparel, sportswear and even fashion brands like Adidas, Christian Dior, Hugo Boss, Nike, Marks and Spencer's, Gap and H&M, which all thrive on workers, mostly women, paid wages far below even other sectors locally.[15] Approached descriptively, overexploitation or super-exploitation has been defined by NGOs as a gap relative to the wage levels of other workers. Table 6.1 illustrates this in the garment industry.

TABLE 6.1  *Wage levels in apparel in selected countries*

| Countries | Distance from local living wage | Distance from UK living wage |
|---|---|---|
| Bangladesh | 44% | 7% |
| China | 47% | 11% |
| India | 45% | 9% |
| Morocco | 60% | 25% |
| Thailand | 50% | 14% |
| Vietnam | 56% | 11% |

SOURCE: HTTP://WWW.LABOURBEHINDTHELABEL.ORG/ABOUT-US/ITEM/587-LETS-CLEAN-UP-FASHION-2007-UPDATE.

The 'business model' is one in which an indigenous capitalist (the Bangladesh Standard Group in the case of the Gazipur fire in November 2013), for instance, builds a factory building, buys machinery, hires workers and oversees operations in the workplace, while the US or European sub-contracting corporation chooses material input suppliers and provides designs and then handles the marketing in its chain of stores. The indigenous capitalist is a contemporary personification of the comprador bourgeoisie.

---

14   http://www.storebrandsdecisions.com/news/2010/02/02/wal-mart-creates-global-merchandising-centers-to-streamline-sourcing.
15   Smith 2010 has a similar table (Table 4.1) with data collected by US NGOs.

## 4 Outsourcing and Offshoring and Global Value Chains in Manufacturing

The lengthy chapters devoted by UNCTAD in 2011 to 'non-equity modes of international production' (NEMS), as it names them, and then again in 2013 to GVCs, provide invaluable detailed information on the extraordinary intensity of exploitation now taking place under corporate management operating on a global level. Taking advantage of evermore sophisticated information and telecommunication technologies and of increasing trade liberalisation, large corporations had started a course of 'vertical disintegration' and of externalisation of components and parts to networks of subcontractors from the late-1970s. In the 2000s, outsourcing and offshoring became central. An example of current business-school thinking on corporate strategies is given by professors at the Rutgers School of Business. In a definition – where the first sentence has almost a Marxist ring – they write that

> the relentless forces of competition and globalization are forcing firms to disaggregate themselves and reach for foreign inputs, markets, and partners. By disaggregating their value chain into discrete pieces – some to be performed in-house, others to be outsourced to external vendors – a company hopes to reduce overall costs and risks, while possibly also reaping the benefits of ideas from their contractors or alliance partners worldwide.[16]

The different facets and advantages seen from the viewpoint of corporate strategy are presented in box 6.1.

---

BOX 6.1: MOTIVES FOR OFFSHORING AND MOVING CORPORATE BOUNDARIES

*Outsourcing* can be both (1) in the home nation of the firm, as well as (2) abroad, and entails an organizational restructuring of some activities. Outsourcing is a conscious abdication (this is hardly the right word – F.C.) of selected value chain activities to external providers. *Offshoring* is restructuring the firm along another dimension, namely geography. It entails the relocation of operations from the home nation to a foreign location where the same company activities are performed under either (1) the multinational company's (MNC's) own subsidiary or

---

16   Contractor et al. 2010.

(2) allocated to a foreign contract vendor. At stake are not only low-end manufacturing and service activities, but increasingly, high-value company functions like R&D, design, and engineering that are being increasingly relocated to foreign locations.

The boundaries of many firms have therefore simultaneously shrunk organizationally and expanded geographically, while also becoming more permeable. We treat outsourcing and offshoring as two outcomes of the same strategic drivers that force companies to reconsider the configuration of their activities.

A cursory examination of outsourcing and offshoring would suggest cost reduction as a main driver. However, especially in recent years, two other strategy motivators have gained significance.

First, the knowledge accessing motive: with growing complexity of products and services, even the largest companies no longer have all the diverse components of knowledge within their own organization, or personnel, to be competitive in research, production, and marketing. Hence the need for external knowledge inputs and expertise. Organizationally and geographically distant knowledge can often be more valuable than internal or related-party knowledge.

Second, relocation of operations abroad helps the MNC to better understand and exploit foreign markets. Local value-added builds legitimacy with local customers and governments. Thus outsourcing and offshoring simultaneously help the firm in three strategic needs: (1) 'efficiency' or cost reduction; (2) 'exploration' or access to knowledge and talented people; and (3) 'exploitation' or development of foreign markets.

Source: Contractor et al. 2010.

---

The practice of outsourcing developed with industrial concentration and the ever deepening divide between large and smaller firms and contractors and sub-contractors. It was and is still used domestically before being globalised. Subcontractors are placed in intense competition with each other and more generally the costs and risks associated with fluctuations in demand are shifted to smaller firms and in turn on the workers they exploit. Consequently Milberg correctly talks about the term 'arm's-length' to specify clearly the nature of the outsourcing relationship. Smith follows this up by emphasising that while balance of payment data captures the return on FDI in the form of the repatriation of profits and intellectual property rights (revenue from licences, etc.), they cannot capture fully the nature and consequences of arm's-length outsourcing.[17]

---

17  Smith 2010.

## 5 'Non-equity Modes of International Production'

MNEs were already identified in the 1980s as beginning to use 'new forms of investment' (NFI) as distinct from FDI proper. These involved the use of intangible assets, such as technology or guaranteed access to central capitalist economy markets, as a counterpart for the recognition of capital property rights and management control in developing countries' joint-venture firms.[18] Case studies were made showing the range of arrangements.[19] They heralded the non-equity modes (NMEs) of today. UNCTAD does not attempt to give a precise definition, simply saying that they 'include contract manufacturing, services outsourcing, contract farming, franchising, licensing, management contracts and other types of contractual relationships through which TNCs coordinate activities in their global value chains (GVCs) and influence the management of host-country firms without owning an equity stake in those firms'.[20] According to UNCTAD, in the industries where they are used the most, their growth is now outpacing that of FDI proper. This is the case in electronics where major TNCs include Dell, Hewlett Packard and Apple. This growth is 'driven by a number of key advantages for TNCs: (1) the relatively low upfront capital expenditures required and the limited working capital needed for operation; (2) reduced risk exposure; (3) flexibility in adapting to changes in the business cycle and in demand; and (4) as a basis for externalising non-core activities that can often be carried out at lower cost by other operators'. To Marxists, these 'advantages' have a familiar ring.[21] The first is recognisable as one of the factors counteracting the tendency for the rate of profit to fall discussed above in Chapter 1. The second and third concern the shifting of risk onto subcontractors and component suppliers and the fourth is just a way of saying that the principal firm is using 'other operators' to increase absolute surplus value that it will appropriate. UNCTAD writes that

> concerns are often raised, especially with regard to contract manufacturing and licensing, that countries relying to a significant extent on NEMS for industrial development risk remaining locked in to low-value-added segments of TNC-governed global value chains, and remaining technology dependent. In such cases, developing economies would run a further

---

18  Oman 1984.
19  Oman et al. 1989.
20  UNCTAD 2011, p. 122.
21  UNCTAD's work is a starting point for fieldwork and analysis. See the footnotes to the chapter on NEMS in UNCTAD 2011 and on GVCs in UNCTAD 2013.

risk of becoming vulnerable to TNCs shifting productive activity to other locations, as NEMs are more 'footloose' than equivalent FDI operations.

In manufacturing US, Japanese and European corporations contract local intermediaries to do this work. These possess their own network of suppliers. They can be quite large firms and some are TNCs in their own right. The notorious Taiwanese corporation Foxconn operating in electronics, notably at its ill-famed huge factory in Shenzhen, is the best known of all. The principals with whom Foxconn works include Apple, BlackBerry, Cisco, Dell, Hewlett-Packard, Microsoft, Motorola, Nintendo, Sony, Toshiba and Nokia. Some specific cases have been analysed in the case of personal computers with the aim of demonstrating that global value chains spread wealth from innovation 'far beyond the firm whose brand appears on the product'.[22] In a Marxian approach, value-added represents at best a proxy, but it provides an idea of inter-corporate relationships in the context of global oligopoly and their relation to the appropriation of surplus by TNCs across countries. The existence of super-exploitation comes from the trend towards a global homogenisation of productivity levels through the diffusion of equipment, technology and on-site management methods, while the socio-political context is that of strong or very strong national differences in necessary labour time.[23]

Confronted with what has come to be regarded as an irreversible process given prevailing economic power relationships, between capital and labour as well as between firms that possess monopoly power and those that have none, the focus of much research has increasingly been on the 'best', least bad ways for firms in developing and even in 'emerging' countries to operate as segments of large MNE-dominated value chains.[24] This is foreseeably the position taken by UNCTAD. In the face of TNCs' capacity 'to fine-slice activities and operations in their value chains, and place them in the most cost effective location, domestically and globally', host countries must find ways to get something out of an 'inexorable' development. As the 2013 World Investment Report puts it:

---

22  Dedrickn, Kraemer and Linden 2008 in their work on Apple and Hewlett-Packard products set the standard for later case studies.
23  Value in its Marxian or Marxist meaning 'is enclosed neither by (specific) firms nor by value chains, all of what economists call value-added is actually value captured' (Smith 2011, p. 33). This takes place within the hierarchically structured network of inter-corporate relationships.
24  This has become largely the case *inter alia* of Deiter Ernst 2008 and 2009.

[While] some countries may decide not to promote GVC participation ... for the majority of smaller developing economies with limited resource endowments there is often little alternative to development strategies that incorporate a degree of participation in GVCs. The question for those countries is not so much *whether* to participate in GVCs, but *how*.[25]

But the only effective beneficiaries of what UNCTAD calls 'right policies' for developing countries are the indigenous capitalists (as in the Bangladesh garment industry) acting as intermediaries with advanced industrialised countries' TNCs, in sum the contemporary version of the comprador bourgeoisie.

## 6    TNCs and the Present Configuration of World Trade

The fragmentation of production processes and the international dispersion of tasks and activities within global value chains mean that about 60 percent of global trade consists of trade in intermediate goods and services that are incorporated at different stages in the production process before final consumption.[26] It is a major reason why over a period of 25 years the volume of international trade rose much more rapidly than world GDP. GVCs have been seen as central to the collapse of world trade in late 2008, which was more severe and rapid than trade collapses experienced in the past, including during the Great Depression, even if the fall in the latter lasted much longer. On the basis of US data, Milberg and Winkler attribute this to the fact that GVCs had made export-dependent developing countries highly vulnerable to changes in the level of world demand, and specifically demand from high-income countries.[27] These authors make an even more important finding, namely that 'South-South trade is also moulded to some extent by global value chains and the processing of intermediates to serve these chains. In this sense, the expansion of South-South trade depends still on the functioning of GVCs'.[28] This means that they are tributary to TNC strategies. UNCTAD estimates that about 80 percent of global trade (in terms of gross exports) is linked to the international production networks of TNCs, either as intra-firm trade, through NEMS (contract manufacturing, licensing, and franchising), or through arm's-length transactions involving at least one TNC.

---

25   UNCTAD 2013, p. xxiv.
26   UNCTAD 2013, p. 122.
27   Milberg and Winkler 2012, p. 1.
28   Milberg and Winkler 2012, p. 27.

In many economies only a relatively small fraction of the total number of firms participates in international trade. Available data on the concentration of exports collected by WTO is given in table 6.1. In the US, the top 10 percent of exporting firms accounts for 96 percent of total exports, where around 2,200 firms (the top 1 percent of exporters, most of which are TNC parent companies or foreign affiliates) account for more than 80 percent of total trade. In the US case, this concentration is obviously related to the limited exposure of the US to foreign trade. But the concentration of exports is extremely high in export-oriented developing countries. Data on intra-firm trade depends on surveys which only few countries carry out.

TABLE 6.2   *Share of exports accounted for by the largest exporters in selected countries*

| Country | Year | Top 1% | Top 5% | Top 10% |
| --- | --- | --- | --- | --- |
| United States | 1993 | 78.2 | 91.8 | 95.6 |
|  | 2002 | 80.9 | 93 | 96.3 |
| *European Countries* | | | | |
| Belgium | 2003 | 48 | 73 | 84 |
| France | 2003 | 44 | 73 | 84 |
| Germany | 2003 | 59 | 81 | 90 |
| Hungary | 2003 | 77 | 91 | 96 |
| Italy | 2003 | 32 | 59 | 72 |
| Norway | 2003 | 53 | 81 | 91 |
| United Kingdom | 2003 | 42 | 69 | 80 |
| *Developing Countries* | | | | |
| Brazil | 2009 | 56 | 82 | 98 |
| Mexico | 2009 | 67 | 90 | 99 |
| Turkey | 2009 | 56 | 78 | 96 |
| South Africa | 2009 | 75 | 90 | 99 |

SOURCE: WTO 2013, P. 82.

## 7  Overexploitation and the 'Global Law of Value'

We must begin by defining overexploitation. In a careful analysis on work in the information intensive economy centered on the advanced capitalist countries, Fuchs approaches the notion as follows:

> Capital can gain extra surplus value by overexploitation. *Extra surplus value* is a term coined by Marx for describing relations of production, in which goods are produced in a way that the 'individual value of these articles is now below their social value' (Marx 1867, 434). By employing illegal migrants, unemployed compulsory or illegal workers, students, and precarious and informal workers, capital can produce goods at a value that is lower than the average social value because its wage costs are lower than in a regular employment relationship. As a result the commodities produced contain less variable capital, but are nonetheless sold at regular prices so that an extra profit can be obtained.[29]

The theoretical issue of the global law of value was raised by the South American *dependista* theoretically closest to Marxism, Ruy Mauro Marini,[30] and Samir Amin[31] in the configuration of the world market at the time. In 2010, Amin revisited what he names 'the passage from *the law of value to the law of globalized value* based on the hierarchical structuring – itself globalized – of the prices of labor-power around its value'. He argues that 'linked to the management practices governing access to natural resources, this globalization of value constitutes the basis for *imperialist rent*'.[32] This is not very helpful since the processes just discussed have nothing to do with rent, but with profit-seeking corporate strategies. Later in his book Amin develops his theory as follows:

> Capitalism is the United States and India, Germany and Ethiopia, taken together. Consequently labour-power has but a single value, that which is

---

29  Fuchs develops a number of very important ideas which include (2010, p. 190) the free consumption by corporations of the 'commons of society that consist of nature, educational knowledge, entertainment knowledge, practical knowledge, technological knowledge, and public infrastructures (labor in the areas of health, education, medical services, social services, culture, media, politics, etc.)'; the privatisation by capital of the 'general intellect' (2010, p. 192); Internet produsage as an extreme form of exploitation, in which the producers work completely for free and are therefore infinitely exploited (2010, p. 191).

30  Marini 1973.

31  Amin 1976.

32  Amin 2010, p. 11 (author's emphasis).

associated with the level of development of the productive forces taken globally (the *General Intellect* at this level).[33]

This is terribly vague. The major problem is that Amin skips Volume I of *Capital* where the locus of the appropriate notions is to be found and goes straight on to Volume II. Smith also retains the term imperialist rent.[34] He does discuss Volume I but concludes that on account of offshoring and international outsourcing, Marx's analysis does not correspond to the situation of today. He discusses 'international differences in the value of labour power, in the rate of exploitation', which he names super-exploitation, in an over-simplified way:

> If the working day comprises two parts, necessary labour-time (the time a worker takes to replace the values consumed by the proletarian household) and surplus labour-time (the time spent producing *surplus value* for the capitalist), the *rate of exploitation* is the ratio between them. For the purposes of this paper, *super-exploitation* signifies a higher rate of exploitation than the prevailing average domestic rate of exploitation within the imperialist economies.[35]

This definition is accompanied by a theoretical construct whereby 'wage arbitrage-driven globalisation of production processes is the *third form of surplus value* (the others being absolute and relative surplus value)' and '*the driver of the global shift of production to low-wage nations*'.[36]

My position is that one must stick to Marx closely and start from the notion set out in Volume I of 'socially necessary labour time' defined as 'the labour time required to produce any use-value under the conditions of production normal for a given society and with the average degree of skill and intensity of

---

33    Amin 2010, p. 84.
34    Smith 2010 and 2011.
35    Smith 2011, p. 11.
36    Smith 2011, p. 23. Examining the recourse to domestic outsourcing by large corporations in Brazil, Antunes 2015 chooses the term overexploitation. He writes: 'there has been a real epidemic of outsourcing in the last two decades, one that has contaminated industry, services, agriculture and public services, and that has affected production as well as support activities. In the various forms of outsourcing, one observes new working conditions that define workers in "primary" and "secondary" categories, and reveal distinctions or conditions of inferiority and inequality. These differences are yet more apparent in long shifts, the pace and intensity of the work, high levels of turnover, low wages, unsafe conditions and health hazards, among many others'.

labour prevalent in that society'.[37] Today the relevant 'society' is that born from the full accomplishment of the 'world market' and the total liberty of movement of productive capital. What remains specific to each country and very different from one to another is, as for every other commodity, the labour time required for the production and consequently the reproduction of labour-power. In the setting of globalised industrial investment production and trade, TNC direct investment in some countries and closely monitored outsourcing in others have resulted in the global diffusion of the 'average degree of skill and intensity of labour' (worker productivity) in some cases for the production of highly complex goods or commodities (high-skilled software programmes in India)[38] and to others for that of very simple one (garments, cheap shoes in Bangladesh or Vietnam). All these countries have a common characteristic, namely that with differences from country to country and industry to industry the cost of the reproduction of labour power is – whether for engineers or manual workers – lower and often qualitatively lower than in the advanced capitalist countries. Naming the outcome of wage differentials rent or extra surplus value is secondary. Bringing through the controlled transfer of technology by TNCs or the use of that made available by 'host countries' with true innovation capacity in given sectors (China, India) and productivity levels on a par with those of industrialised ones, does not of course preclude the recourse by capital, both foreign and indigenous, to methods of absolute surplus value extraction in countries where economic and political conditions are weighted in favour of capital still more than elsewhere. But this helps one to understand the de-industrialisation of nearly all the old advanced capitalist countries and avoid presenting a hierarchical configuration of global capitalism in which class relations are relegated to a second rank, subsumed by the centre-periphery issue. This is less true for Amin,[39] but Smith does

---

37   Marx 1976, p. 127. Or again Marx's formulation in 'Value, Price and Profit', Chapter 6, Value and Labour, 'the quantity of labour required to produce a commodity in a given state of society, under certain social average conditions of production, with a given social average intensity, and average skill of the labour employed'.

38   See the note by Engels to the third German edition of *Capital*, Volume I: 'Today, thanks to the competition on the world market which has grown up since then, we have advanced much further. "If China," says Mr Stapleton, M.P., to his constituents, "should become a great manufacturing country, I do not see how the manufacturing population of Europe could sustain the contest without descending to the level of their competitors" (*The Times*, 3 September 1873, p. 8). The desired goal of English capital is no longer Continental wages, oh no, it is Chinese wages!' (Engels, in Marx 1976, Vol. I, p. 749).

39   'Our reading of the twentieth and twenty-first centuries can be nothing other than that of the emergence – or of the "reawakening" – of peoples and nations peripheric to the globalized capitalist/imperialist system' (Amin 2010).

not examine even in passing the specific place of China, India and Brazil in world capitalism and makes no mention of their TNCs. The notion of subimperialism developed by Marini with respect to Brazil is reduced to a diversion from true issues,[40] while Chinese corporate strategies when investing in Africa or relocating to Vietnam are not discussed and characterised.

---

40   See Smith 2010, pp. 57–8, in his polemic against Callinicos 2009.

CHAPTER 7

# The Further Globalisation of Financial Assets and Markets and the Expansion of New Forms of Fictitious Capital

This chapter takes up the process of financial accumulation and globalisation where the analysis left off in Chapter 2. It examines successively cross-border capital flows involving principally the US and the EU; the growth of trade in derivatives and their characterisation; and finally, selected issues pertaining to developing countries' debt.

## 1  Factors Underlying the Growth of Global Financial Transactions

The McKinsey Global Institute's 1994 assessment that financial globalisation was only half way to its full development proved correct. The compound annual growth rate of cross-border capital flows from 1990 to 2006 was 14.6 percent and that of 2007 19 percent higher than the previous year. Cross-border bank deposits and bank lending experienced the highest growth. Table 7.1 shows the growth of assets held abroad and their simplified overall structure up until the financial crisis.

TABLE 7.1   *Estimated global foreign ownership of financial assets (1998–2007)*

| Asset | 1998 Value | 1998 % | 2001 Value | 2001 % | 2004 Value | 2004 % | 2007 Value | 2007 % | % of growth 1998/2007 |
|---|---|---|---|---|---|---|---|---|---|
| Equity securities | 4.0 | 23.5 | 5.2 | 22.9 | 8.7 | 22.3 | 17.6 | 26.1 | 340.0 |
| Debt securities | 4.0 | 23.5 | 7.5 | 33.0 | 14.6 | 37.3 | 22.7 | 33.7 | 467.5 |
| Deposits | 8.9 | 52.3 | 0.0 | 44.1 | 15.9 | 40.7 | 27.1 | 40.2 | 204.5 |
| Total assets | 17.0 | – | 22.7 | – | 39.1 | – | 67.4 | – | 296.5 |
| Foreign assets as % of total assets | 20% | | 22% | | 27% | | 32% | | – |

SOURCE: MCKINSEY GLOBAL INSTITUTE 2009.

Gross capital flows rose from around 10 percent of world GDP in 1998 to over 30 percent in 2007. The expansion of global gross flows resulted largely from flows *among* advanced economies. The bulk of this expansion reflected flows among advanced economies, despite a decline in their share in world trade. Flows between, or from, emerging market economies were much smaller. In the case of the US, operations by European banks and by Sovereign Wealth Funds for the acquisition of securities were the largest single category and took the form principally of non-Treasury securities. In the case of the Eurozone, acquisition of foreign debt resulted from bank lending by German and French banks to Irish and Spanish banks, and real-estate corporations drove the growth of cross-border capital flows.

### 1.1    On the Driving Forces of Financial Accumulation Again

The sharp increase in the indicators of financial globalisation in this period is again both the result and the cause of financial accumulation. When the rate of profit begins to fall, the mass of profit continues to grow and a growing fraction seeks a rate of return as interest-bearing capital. This is the last of the counteracting factors listed by Marx in Volume III of *Capital*. A careful reading shows that it is not truly a counteracting factor and that the paragraph concerns in fact the intra-capitalist distribution of profit.[1] The apparent 'diversion of investment' to financial markets marks the decline in profitable investment opportunities. As liberalisation progresses and with it the globalisation of the industrial reserve army, class relationships shift in favour of capital and along with it come changes in income distribution in favour of the upper bracket groups as well as the ever increasing divergence in the accumulation of patrimonial wealth in favour of the rich.[2] The creditor-debtor relation and the associated snowball effect in the growth of debt, notably government debt, are accompanied by a similar process in the accumulation of interest-income accruing to and fed by upper-bracket groups. However much the rich and the

---

1   Marx 1981, Vol. III, p. 347: 'As capitalist production advances and with it accelerated accumulation, one portion of capital is considered simply to be interest-bearing capital and invested as such. This is not in the sense in which any capitalist who loans out capital is content to take the interest, while the industrial capitalist pockets the entrepreneurial profit. Nor does it affect the general rate of profit, for as far as this is concerned, profit = interest + profit of all kinds + ground rent, its distribution between these categories is a matter of indifference. It is rather in the sense that these capitals, although invested in large productive enterprises, simply yield an interest, great or small, after all costs deducted, so-called dividends'.
2   See Piketty and Saez 2006 and Piketty 2012.

very rich spend,[3] Keynes's theory of the falling propensity of consumption asserts itself, meaning that a part of their income is continually pumped back into financial markets. All this has been linked to and intensified by specific economic conditions in the global economy. Since the beginning of the commodities boom in the early 2000s, revenues accumulated by primary producer countries in Sovereign Wealth Funds have not only been used for M&As but have directly flowed into the US and British financial markets. The case of oil revenues from the Gulf States, notably when prices soared in 2007–8, has been documented by Marxist research.[4] More broadly, the flow to the US of interest-bearing capital from countries with current account surpluses, notably China, accounted for the increase in global financial flows and the foreign ownership of assets.

### 1.2    Capital Flows In and Out of the United States

From the mid-1990s onwards these flows became one of the most important constituent features of macroeconomic relations at the world level. Consequently a part of the debate on the causes of the 2008 financial crisis focused on them. The assertion by Bernanke that Asia's and in particular China's and Japan's 'global saving glut'[5] was largely responsible for the crisis led to research showing that this factor has been significantly overstated. A detailed analysis published by senior BIS staff members concludes that attention must 'shift from current account balances to the gross financing flows that underpin economic activity; here monetary and financial factors take centre stage. A core question is whether the global economy has anchors in place that can prevent the overall expansion of credit and of external funding more generally, from fuelling the unsustainable build-up of financial imbalances. By financial imbalances we mean overstretched balance sheets, typically on the back of rapid increases in credit and asset prices'.[6] Indeed the bulk of gross inflows into the United States originated not in the government but in the private and the mortgage-related sectors. Acquisition of US securities overwhelmingly took the form of securities – not of T-bonds, but bonds issued by the Government Sponsored Enterprises (GSE) active in mortgage loans, Fannie May and Freddie Mac.

---

3  Duménil and Lévy 2011 spend a lot of energy trying to make them pillars of effective demand.
4  Hanieh 2012.
5  Bernanke 2005.
6  Borio and Disyatat 2011, p. 24.

TABLE 7.2   *Capital inflows into the United States, 1997–2012 (in billion US$)*

|      |         |                  | Private assets |                  |                      |                        |             |        |
|------|---------|------------------|---------|---------------------|----------------------|------------------------|-------------|--------|
| Year | Total   | Official assets  | Total   | Direct investment   | Treasury securities  | Corporate securities   | US currency | Other  |
| 1997 | 704.5   | 19.0    | 685.4   | 105.6 | 130.4 | 161.4  | 22.4  | 265.5  |
| 1998 | 420.8   | −19.9   | 440.7   | 179.0 | 28.6  | 156.3  | 13.8  | 62.9   |
| 1999 | 742.2   | 43.5    | 698.7   | 289.4 | −44.5 | 298.8  | 22.4  | 130.5  |
| 2000 | 1,038.2 | 42.8    | 995.5   | 321.3 | −70.0 | 459.9  | −3.4  | 287.6  |
| 2001 | 782.9   | 28.1    | 754.8   | 167.0 | −14.4 | 393.9  | 23.8  | 184.5  |
| 2002 | 795.2   | 115.9   | 679.2   | 84.4  | 100.4 | 283.3  | 18.9  | 192.3  |
| 2003 | 858.3   | 278.1   | 580.2   | 63.8  | 91.5  | 220.7  | 10.6  | 193.7  |
| 2004 | 1,533.2 | 397.8   | 1,135.4 | 146.0 | 93.6  | 381.5  | 13.3  | 501.1  |
| 2005 | 1,247.3 | 259.3   | 988.1   | 112.6 | 132.3 | 450.4  | 8.4   | 284.3  |
| 2006 | 2,065.2 | 487.9   | 1,577.2 | 243.2 | −58.2 | 683.2  | 2.2   | 706.8  |
| 2007 | 2,129.5 | 480.9   | 1,648.5 | 275.8 | 66.8  | 605.7  | −10.7 | 711.0  |
| 2008 | 534.1   | 487.0   | 47.1    | 319.7 | 196.6 | −126.7 | 29.2  | −371.8 |
| 2009 | 314.4   | 480.3   | −165.9  | 150.4 | −15.5 | 1.9    | 12.6  | −315.4 |
| 2010 | 398.2   | 353.3   | 205.8   | 297.8 | 139.3 | 28.3   | 63.0  | 189.9  |
| 2011 | 211.8   | 158.7   | 234.0   | 240.9 | −56.4 | 55.0   | 6.6   | 348.2  |
| 2012 | 373.6   | 347.9   | 174.7   | 123.6 | 76.7  | 57.1   | 925.0 | −399.0 |

SOURCE: JACKSON 2013. ORIGINAL SOURCE: SCOTT, SARAH O., US INTERNATIONAL TRANSACTIONS FOURTH QUARTER AND YEAR 2012, BUREAU OF ECONOMIC ANALYSIS, BEA-13-09, 14 MARCH 2013.

Columns 7 (corporate securities) and 9 (other assets, e.g. debt and mortgage-backed securities) represent 67 percent of total capital inflows in 2005 and 62 percent in 2006. Corporate securities include liabilities to private foreign investors by US banks. 'They were large and grew substantially after 2002. By far the most important source of capital inflows into the US was Europe, which accounted for around one-half of total inflows in 2007, more than half coming from the UK and roughly one-third from the euro area'.[7] The setting in of

---

7  Borio and Disyatat 2011, p. 14. See also the figures in Jackson 2013.

an 'excess financial elasticity', e.g. a highly permissive monetary regime,[8] was equally true for the Eurozone and its truly 'independent' central bank.

### 1.3 Intra-Eurozone Interbank Lending

The EU in general and the Eurozone in particular saw the rapid increase in cross-border flows in the form of interbank lending within member states, through wholesale markets and to a lesser extent as a result of cross-border bank-branch penetration. It was driven by financial accumulation in large banks experiencing concentration, both domestic and trans-border, notably the acquisition of the Banca Nazionale del Lavoro (BNL) by BNP Paribas in 2006. The increase of cross-border flows was the result of a combination of factors, the deregulation of global financial markets and of domestic credit-mortgage markets, as well as the low interest rate regime which prevailed in the 2000s. Some were specific to the EU and the Eurozone. Two are of special importance. The first concerns the European Central Bank (ECB). The Maastricht Treaty conferred it a status of absolute independence, allowing it to reduce consultation with governments to a bare minimum before being forced to do so intensively when the 2010 European financial crisis broke out. It also gave the ECB a priority mission of controlling inflation, written into the Treaty. The ECB interpreted inflation in a narrow way and ignored financial-asset inflation, including inflation in housing, which is both a commodity and a financial asset. The second specifically European factor was the German labour and wage policy of the Schroeder government's Agenda for 2010,[9] which led to stagnant German domestic demand and high savings seeking profitable financial investments. The choices made by capital and government in Ireland and in Spain to base growth largely on housing, real estate and construction from 2003 onwards gave the German banks the opportunity to 'recycle' excess German private household and corporate savings.[10] The large banks are highly internationalised, some largely within the EU (Société Générale and Crédit Agricole), others mainly outside Europe (Santander) and others both within the EU and globally (Deutsche Bank, Barclays and BNP Paribas). On account of the extreme concentration of the French banking system coupled with the

---

8   Borio names this the 'Achilles heel' of the international monetary and financial system, the outcome of which, compounded by the resort to quantitative easing, is today's 'debt trap' (Borio 2013).

9   http://www.transform-network.net/yearbook/journal-112012/news/detail/Journal/german-capitalism-and-the-european-crisis-part-of-the-solution-or-part-of-the-problem.html.

10  This is well documented by a Deutsche Bundesbank study (Buch, Koch and Koetter 2011).

country's weak GDP growth, the banking oligopoly was to look to its Southern neighbours in the Eurozone for financial profits in the form of interest and commissions. French bank exposure to the 2010–11 banking crisis, especially in Spain, was very high.[11] The seeds of Eurozone recession were sown. We enlarge on all these questions in Chapter 8 and 9.

### 1.4  The Growth and Present Organisation of Foreign Exchange Trading

Table 6.3 gives data showing that trading in foreign exchange and derivative markets has become by far the most widespread type of global financial transaction. Dividends and bonds are major instruments of surplus value appropriation by banks and funds. It is thus understandable that stock and bond markets remain the best-known form of financial markets. Stock markets are thermometers of investor moods and thus receive the most attention in the media. Yet trading in these markets is puny in comparison to trading in currencies and derivatives. Table 7.3 offers a broad idea of their relative size.

TABLE 7.3  *Overall composition of global financial transactions: 2002–8 (in trillion US$)*

|  | 2002 | 2003 | 2004 | 2005 | 2006 | 2007 | 2008 |
| --- | --- | --- | --- | --- | --- | --- | --- |
| Organised Forex | 23.8 | 220.6 | 379.5 | 545.8 | 714.3 | 940.6 | 1,0150 |
| Organised Derivative | 693.1 | 874.3 | 1,1523 | 1,4069 | 1,8080 | 2,2080 | 1,6600 |
| OTC Derivative | 385.7 | 524.0 | 545.2 | 557.8 | 144.3 | 147.5 | 820.4 |
| Bonds and Stock | 38.0 | 42.7 | 53.9 | 64.0 | 84.1 | 128.1 | 132.6 |
| Total | 1,172.9 | 1,698.6 | 2,172.5 | 2,619.3 | 2,799.1 | 3,478.5 | 3,688.1 |

SOURCE: MORIN 2011.

The evolution of foreign exchange markets is tracked by the Bank of International Settlements. Reasonably precise data is available and the growth of these markets is well documented. Surveys are done every three years. In its December 2007 Triennial Central Bank Survey, BIS found that average daily turnover had grown 69 percent since 2004. BIS calls this 'an unprecedented

---

11   Merler and Pisani-Ferry 2012.

growth, much stronger than the one observed between 2001 and 2004. Even abstracting from the valuation effects arising from exchange rate movements, average daily turnover rose by 63%'.[12] Financial accumulation under fund management and the fall in interest rates drove this growth. Pension funds, hedge funds and insurance companies were responsible for half of the growth in transactions with 'reporting dealer banks'.[13] The Staff study noted that 'foreign exchange markets have offered investors with short-term horizons relatively attractive risk-adjusted returns'.[14] During the years 2004–7, overall financial market volatility was very low by historical standards. 'This allowed longer-term investors, such as pension funds, to contribute to the increase in turnover by systematically diversifying their portfolios internationally'. In the 2010 Survey, BIS reported a further 20 percent increase in transactions since the one in 2007. The Staff study commented that 'against the backdrop of the global financial crisis of 2007–9 and the turmoil in European sovereign bond markets, the continued growth [of foreign exchange markets] demonstrates the resilience of this market'. In 2010, average global daily transactions reached $4.0 trillion against $880 billion in 1992. In 2013, they rose to $5.3 trillion a day representing a further 35 percent increase. The 2013 survey finds that in the main trading centres, London and New York, close to two thirds of all deals now involve non-dealer financial counterparties. The growth 'appears to have been mostly a by-product of the increasing diversification of international asset portfolios... With yields in advanced economies at record lows, investors increasingly diversified into riskier assets such as international equities or local currency emerging market bonds'.[15] There are obvious overall explanations for this continuous growth: the limited destruction of fictitious capital in 2008, the continued injection of liquidity by the Fed and other central banks, and the reduced attractiveness of bond markets, notably that of the US, on account of low interest rates.

---

12   BIS 2007, p. 1.
13   Reporting dealers are a small group of large bank and a few old specialised firms. In the case of the US the list is: Bank of America, Bank of Montreal, The Bank of New York, Bank of Tokyo-Mitsubishi, Barclays Capital, BNP Paribas, Citigroup, Canadian Imperial Bank of Commerce, Calyon, CSFB, Deutsche Bank AG, Goldman Sachs & Co., HSBC Bank USA, JP Morgan Chase Bank, Mizuho Corporate Bank, Morgan Stanley, Royal Bank of Canada, Royal Bank of Scotland, Skandinaviska Enskilda Bank, Société Générale, Standard Chartered, State Street Corporation, Sumitomo Mitsui Banking Corporation, UBS Bank, Wells Fargo Bank N.A. http://www.newyorkfed.org/fxc/volumesurvey/dealers.html (accessed 30 October 2013).
14   King and Rime 2010, p. 27.
15   Rime and Schrimpf 2013, p. 2.

Technological change has been at work.[16] Traditionally, a firm needing to deal in foreign exchange would phone its bank, which would make a transaction with a dealer bank. Prime brokerage,[17] notably for smaller banks, was a source of profits in the form of fees and commissions. Then interbank dealing began to shift to electronic systems. Reuters Dealing and EBS (Electronic Broking Services) both introduced electronic interbank trading platforms in the early 1990s. The uptake of electronic brokerage was relatively slow at first, but by the late 1990s these platforms came to dominate interbank trading flows. In 2007, they were estimated as accounting for about 90 percent of interbank trading in most major currency pairs. Data processing technology has led to the use of algorithmic trading. Investors connect their computers directly with electronic communication networks (ECNs).[18] These changes have opened up the foreign exchange market to retail investors. Trading by hedge funds and individuals from high-income groups (exchange trading now taking place from any office or home) occurs through a new form of financial corporation, the *retail aggregator* (BIS cites the US-UK FXCM, FX Dealer Direct, Gain Capital and OANDA, in Continental Europe Saxo Bank and IG Markets, and in Japan Gaitame.com).

The other key driver in the continuous growth of foreign exchange has been the entry of a large diversity of new actors, from high-frequency traders, using computers to implement trading strategies at the millisecond frequency, to the private individual investor. Retail aggregator platforms allow end users and dealers to connect to a variety of trading venues and counterparties of their choice. The traditional market structure based on dealer-customer relationships has given way to a trading network topology where both banks and non-banks act as liquidity providers.[19] Forex is dominated by what is now termed 'hot potato' trading. This is algorithmic-based high frequency trading (HFT) characterised by holding periods at the millisecond level and a vast amount

---

16   Barker 2007.
17   Prime brokerage is a service offered by banks that allows a client to source funding and market liquidity from a variety of executing dealers while maintaining a credit relationship, placing collateral and settling with a single entity.
18   'Examples of ECNs in FX markets are electronic broking systems (such as EBS and Thomson Reuters Matching), *multi-bank trading systems* (such as Currenex, FXall and Hotspot FX) and *single-bank trading systems*. A computer algorithm then monitors price quotes collected from different ECNs and places orders without human intervention. *High-frequency trading* (HFT) is one algorithmic strategy that profits from incremental price movements with frequent, small trades executed in milliseconds' (King and Rime 2010, p. 29).
19   Rime and Schrimpf 2013, pp. 1–2.

of offers often cancelled shortly after submission. HFT strategies can both exploit tiny, short-lived price discrepancies and provide liquidity at very high frequency, benefitting from the bid-ask spread.

A first example of the resulting increase in financial instability came in January 2015 when the central bank of Switzerland abandoned its support for a ceiling on the value of the franc against the euro without notice. The franc rose as much as 41 percent against the euro and some participants refused to quote in the currency. Foreign exchange liquidity overall collapsed. The IMF reports:

> the access of leveraged retail investors to foreign currency brokers allowing bets against the Swiss franc exacerbated the price surge. In many cases, heavily leveraged positions involved little coordination or oversight by authorities. Many retail investors were either unaware of the risks or had explicit or implicit guarantees from their foreign exchange brokers that they could not lose more than their deposits. However, when the franc suddenly and sharply moved against their positions, their high degree of leverage generated losses far greater than their account equity.[20]

## 2  The Growth of Global Transactions in Derivatives

While foreign exchange transactions had the highest growth rate between 2002 and 2008, the trading of derivatives both in specialised exchange markets and in over-the-counter (OTC) transactions became, during the same period, the most important form of international financial transaction. An unambiguous overall assessment is given by an OECD Secretariat paper. It states that 'derivatives do not fund real investments yet carry all the bankruptcy characteristics of debt'. It continues:

> Some of this mountain of derivatives is for socially useful purposes, such as end-users hedging business risks. However, in the past decade socially less useful uses of derivatives have abounded. Notable in this respect is the use of derivatives for tax arbitrage (e.g. interest rate swaps to exploit different tax treatment of products). Credit default swaps (CDS) have also been used extensively for regulatory arbitrage to minimize the capital banks are required to hold.[21]

---

[20]  IMF 2015a, p. 33.
[21]  Blundell-Wignall 2012, p. 6.

## 2.1 *A New Form of Fictitious Capital*

A derivative is a security, the price of which is dependent upon or derived from one or more underlying assets. It has no intrinsic value in itself.[22] The derivative itself is merely a contract between two or more parties. Its price is determined by changes in the price of the underlying asset (or, as in the case of mortgage debt, its very existence). The two main initial forms were futures and forwards (options came later, and were always a small part of the market). The first main underlying 'assets' were currencies and the interest rates on deposits and bonds, where they were used early on by TNCs, and commodities traded in specialised markets in Chicago and London. The 'straight-forward' categories of derivatives will be discussed first. As put by Norfield: 'in the case of bonds or equities, the underlying security's price is *already* the capitalised value of expected future revenues – what Marx called "fictitious capital"'.[23] Derivatives are fictitious capital once removed. A clear definition is given by Ivanova:

> Capital cannot and does not exist twice; thus, securities are not real, but fictitious capital, as they represent mere claims on future income associated with the underlying asset. Shares of company stock are still 'genuine titles to real capital'. This, however, is not the case with the bulk of the products of modern-day financial innovation – derivatives being a prime example – which represent claims on previously established claims.[24]

The frontier between 'legitimate, necessary hedging' and speculation is impossible to establish. Used to hedge, a 'put' or a 'call-option' represents a form of insurance. The corporation buys enough puts to cover its holdings of the underlying asset so that if there is a serious fall in its price, it has the option of selling them at the higher strike price.[25] As a speculative instrument it is a bet, a pure gamble. 'The buyer of a call option purchases it in the hope that the price of the underlying instrument will rise in the future. The seller of the option either expects that it will not, or is willing to give up some of the upside (profit) from a price rise in return for the premium (paid immediately) and retaining the opportunity to make a gain up to the strike price'.[26] Buyers are

---

22   Norfield 2012, p. 105.
23   Norfield 2012, p. 106, original emphasis.
24   Ivanova 2013, p. 60.
25   The strike price (or exercise price) is the fixed price at which the owner of the option can sell (in the case of a put) or buy (in the case of a call) the underlying security or commodity.
26   http://en.wikipedia.org/wiki/Derivative_(finance) (accessed 15 October 2013).

overwhelmingly financial corporations. Nonetheless, 'distinguishing "financial" from "non-financial" dealers does not capture the motives for the transaction. Financial companies themselves may also be using derivatives to hedge their risks, rather than simply to make a bet on price-movements. Banks and other financial companies – not just industrialists – are exposed to changes in interest-rates and exchange-rates'.[27]

This means that the scale of derivatives trading is simultaneously an expression of 'casino finance' in its purest form, and an indicator of the extremely high uncertainty which characterises the environment of financialisation, even for the financial corporations that contributed toward bringing it about. A very clear presentation for non-specialists echoes Hilferding's remark about the trading of assets, 'One's loss is the other's gain'. 'With a derivative, one party to the contract's gain is the other party's loss. Consequently, derivatives losses neither create nor destroy wealth – they redistribute it. In many instances, this redistribution has no impact beyond the parties involved in the derivatives contract'.[28]

## 2.2 The Underlying Assets of OTC Derivatives and the Particular Features of CDSS

A part of derivatives trading takes place on organised markets.[29] Another is party-to-party, trader-to-trader trading known as 'off the counter' (OTC) and is absolutely unregulated. It is typically 'fictitious capital to the *nth* degree'.[30] BIS collects and publishes data on OTC derivatives under the following categories: interest rate derivatives, exchange rate derivatives, credit default swaps, equity derivatives and commodities derivatives. What is known as their 'notional amount' has been of the order of $680 trillion since 2008, following a previous very rapid climb from 2000 onwards. The last BIS estimations are that it fell by 9 percent between end-June 2014 and end-December 2014, from $692 trillion to $630 trillion. Another indicator is gross market value. This stood at $21 trillion at end-December 2014. It represents the maximum loss that market participants would incur if all counterparties failed to meet their contractual payments and the contracts were replaced at current market prices. Since bank and non-bank financial corporations can reduce their exposure to

---

27  Norfield 2012, pp. 112–13.
28  Stulz 2009, p. 67.
29  See Wang 2009. The main markets are the Chicago Mercantile Exchange, the London International Futures and Options Exchange (LIFFE) and the Tokyo International Futures Exchange (TIFFE).
30  Chesnais 2007.

counterparty credit risk through netting agreements and collateral, BIS calculates a third indicator which is that of 'gross credit exposure'. For the market as a whole it stood at $3.4 trillion at end-December 2014, up from $2.8 trillion at end-June 2014. In the second semester of 2008, it had reached an all-time record of $4.5 trillion.[31] Financial risk linked to derivatives varies according to categories and to the level of risk incurred by specific individual banks. As a Bank of France staff paper explains:

> Derivatives that are traded OTC have characteristics that make them critical from a systemic risk perspective. First, given the bilateral nature of trading, there is no central place where OTC trades are captured and handled. The effective monitoring of market activities is therefore more difficult and effective risk management may be hampered by different or even inconsistent practices. Second, OTC derivatives are instruments tailored to the needs of the relevant counterparties. Accordingly, their risk profile can be very unique and their implications for the overall distribution of risks across the financial system can be difficult to determine.[32]

To date, the most extreme form of 'underlying assets' traded OTC have been credit default swaps, notably those known as multi-name, carrying by far the highest risk. Bear Sterns and Lehman remain up to now the banks to have pushed their level of credit exposure through leverage further than any other and AIG the insurance company to have insured the highest amount of CDS issuance. A credit default swap is an agreement that the seller of the CDS will compensate the buyer – the creditor of the reference loan – in case of a loan default by the debtor. This is to say that the seller of the CDS insures the buyer against some reference loan defaulting. The buyer of the CDS makes a series of payments (the CDS 'fee' or 'spread') to the seller and, in exchange, receives a payoff if the loan defaults. If a bank is large and strongly interconnected with other financial corporations, risk exposure in the form of the issuance of CDSs on very risky loans will have systemic impacts. In September 2008, systemic crisis was triggered by Lehman's issuance of CDS contracts on subprime pooled liabilities. The 'underlying assets' were not equity or interest rates, but 'structured' mortgage securities and were traded OTC. We return to this in Chapter 9.

---

31   BIS 2015.
32   Russo 2010, pp. 102–3.

## 2.3　The Theory of Derivatives as the 'Contemporary Form of World Money'

Dick Bryan and Michael Rafferty have argued the need for an 'adaptation' of Marx's theory of money to contemporary financialised capitalism and in particular have given derivatives a central role in the elaboration of their new theory. The initial formulation dates back to 2006, reflecting thinking developed well before the crisis of 2007–8. Their position, which argues that commensurability gives derivatives the status of a contemporary form of world money, only attracted full critical attention after the publication of Norfield's 2012 article just discussed. Bryan and Rafferty's response to Norfield throws a clearer light on their overall attitude to Marx than did their initial article, all the more so since their reply includes considerations on capital's post-crisis future. Their characterisation of '"interest-bearing" capital as a quaint term in the current era'[33] and their off-hand dismissal of the notion of fictitious capital obviously make me critical of their approach. Particularly enlightening is their attack on Norfield's 'agenda [which] is that an understanding of derivatives be placed at the service of theories of crisis and the falling-rate-of-profit tendency'.[34] Their conclusion – namely that the securitisation of household debt still belongs to capitalism's 'frontier' and continues to be an expression of 'capital's emerging capacities to self-transform and re-load a class-based, financially-centred accumulation'[35] – is in radical opposition to the assessments in the present book. Their thinking is light years away from any notion of the crisis as expressing capitalism's historical limits.

The claims Bryan and Rafferty make about the role of derivatives in the 2006 article are all-embracing. Derivatives

> take the connection of money to both commodity exchange and accumulation to a new level. It is not just, as with credit, that derivatives are used as advances for capitalist accumulation. Financial derivatives are themselves an expression of capitalist accumulation. Nor is it just, as with notes and coins, that derivatives facilitate the exchange of commodities. Derivatives are themselves commodities. They are produced and traded, not just as titles to ownership, but as packaged systems of conversion

---

33　Bryan and Rafferty 2012, p. 108. They regret that Lapavitsas still uses the notion.
34　Bryan and Rafferty 2012, p. 107.
35　See their concluding section 'Politics beyond the crisis' and its first sentence: 'There need not be a single frontier, of course, but in relation to finance we see it in the capacity of financial innovation to constitute more and more of the contingencies of daily life as capital assets' (Ibid.).

between different forms of assets (or revenue streams). Derivatives are distinctively capitalist money, and a recognition of their role serves to transform debates about Marxist theories of money.[36]

Much has been said in this book about financial accumulation. Even the most ardent bourgeois champions of financialisation do not include derivatives in their estimations of its size (see figure 4 in Chapter 1). Likewise they intuitively introduce gradations in the ladder of fictitious capital (brushed aside by Bryan and Rafferty) and make the difference between hard claims (interest and dividends) and claims-on-claims.

Turning specifically to their analysis of derivatives as the contemporary form of world money in 2006 (the 2012 article retreats to the very fuzzy term of 'moneyness'), Bryan and Rafferty start by bypassing the necessary discussion of the status of the dollar and the place that it continues to play as a means of payment, not only in foreign trade, to which the US is a partner, but also between economies more generally and in certain commodities like oil exclusively as such. They equally dismiss any consideration of the special status of the US state and so of the securities it issues as representing a very particular and degenerate form of hoarding. For Bryan and Rafferty, the context is not that of a hierarchically structured global state system still organised around the dollar as best as it can still be in the area of money (see Chapter 2, section 5), but rather that of

> a monetary system, where money cannot be explained by reference to the state – where volatile shifts in exchange rates are inexplicable and beyond state regulatory capacity – and where derivatives, particularly interest-rate and cross-currency interest-rate swaps,... provide what nation-state fiat money could not provide on a global scale: they secure some degree of guarantee on the relative values of different monetary units.[37]

Starting from an erroneous postulate, they are unwilling simply to recognise like others that after Bretton Woods exchange rates became highly volatile and that derivatives offered hedging facilities which reduce the costs of exchange-rate volatility for individual capitalists.[38] They then develop the theory whereby,

---

36  Bryan and Rafferty 2006, p. 77.
37  Bryan and Rafferty 2006, p. 87.
38  Bryan and Rafferty try to give their analysis a sophisticated turn in their reference to trust. The previous foundations of trust provided by governments and central banks having

'in terms of money, derivatives perform the role in international finance that gold played in the nineteenth century: they anchor the global financial system. While gold was a fixed anchor (all national currencies and commodity prices had to adjust to gold), derivatives provide a floating anchor; an on-going, flexible web of conversions that binds the world's asset markets'.[39] The role claimed for derivatives as similar to gold turns out to be only 'the capacity to commensurate different forms, locations, and temporalities of capital. They are thereby commodities that play multiple monetary functions'. Readers are confronted here, as in many other passages, with very confused and certainly confusing relationships between derivatives as money, commodities and capital. In the system as it worked until 1914, gold was primarily used as a means of international settlement or payment and an instrument of hoarding. Derivatives can play neither function.

In the 2012 article, under the fire of critical commentaries, Bryan and Rafferty shift their argument significantly and put forward the notion of 'moneyness':

> Our proposition is not that derivatives *are* money, as if they have jumped inside some pre-given definition of money. It is that derivatives have moneyness and the conception of money needs to be loosened to take account of how financial markets are working. What do we mean by moneyness? Essentially, we mean liquidity – the ability to be converted to something else with minimum loss of value or time. Cash is therefore the core measure of liquidity for goods and services, but asset markets may be different. Because derivatives involve an exposure to the performance of an underlying asset, but are unencumbered by the necessity of legal or physical ownership of the underlying asset, they are innately readily transferrable; that is, highly liquid. So liquid, indeed, that they embody money-like attributes.[40]

Pursuing this track, they write:

> derivatives on exchange rates and interest rates offer some inter-temporal guarantees of a unit of measure – they are a store of value in a world without a stable unit of measure. They may only store value for a short time – perhaps three months; or only for hundredths of a second in

---

        disappeared, derivatives, while not actually creating 'trust in currency values, neutralised the consequences of this loss of trust'.

39    Bryan and Rafferty 2006, pp. 89–90.
40    Bryan and Rafferty 2012, p. 99.

high-frequency electronic trades. They may also have their own vulnerabilities to crisis. But, however brief and fragile, they provide in aggregate an important, liquid store of value. That sounds like a money role.[41]

Some may accept this contradiction in terms, but for me it is untenable. Bryan and Rafferty also liken derivatives to bank credit and interest-bearing assets, taking notably mortgage-backed securities (MBS) as an example. MBS were certainly considered as high-risk/high-return financial assets, but only in Bryan and Rafferty's theoretical construct can they become the 'equivalent of money'.[42]

## 3  Financial Globalisation and Developing Countries in the 2000s

This chapter ends with an account of the present situation of developing countries' debt and the place of some large South American countries in financial globalisation. In the context of a relative slowdown of financial globalisation, these countries have again become attractive to financial investors. A few selected facets will be discussed: the apparent internalisation of government debt in Brazil, the partial repudiation of its debt by Ecuador and the default by Argentina in 2002, both of which have been seen as offering models for heavily indebted countries such as Greece.

### 3.1   *The Diminution of External Debt and the Renewed Attractiveness of Developing Countries*

Three major trends are apparent in table 7.4. The first is that, viewed as a whole, the external debt situation of developing countries has improved. The second is that the level of debt held by private capital doubled between 2005 and 2010, while that held by public entities rose at the modest rate of 8 percent. The third is that the increase in debt by banks and funds was accompanied by a parallel increase of similar magnitude in short-term as opposed to long-term debt.

---

41   Bryan and Rafferty 2012, p. 100.
42   Bryan and Rafferty 2012, p. 101. In his rejoinder, Norfield 2012 discusses this point at length.

TABLE 7.4  *External debt of developing countries 2005–10 (billion $US and selected ratios)*

|  | 2005 | 2006 | 2007 | 2008 | 2009 | 2010 |
|---|---|---|---|---|---|---|
| **Total External Debt Outstanding** | 2,514.1 | 2,675.3 | 3,220.5 | 3,449.2 | 3,639.6 | 4,076.3 |
| Long-term (including IMF) | 2,013.2 | 2,081.5 | 2,456.5 | 2,739.7 | 2,866.4 | 3,039.9 |
| Public and publicly guaranteed (including IMF) | 1,332.1 | 1,266.2 | 1,371.3 | 1,423.2 | 1,530.4 | 1,647.2 |
| Private non-guaranteed | 681.1 | 815.4 | 1,085.1 | 1,316.5 | 1,336.0 | 1,392.7 |
| Short-term external debt | 500.8 | 593.8 | 764.0 | 759.5 | 773.2 | 1,036.4 |
| **Ratios** | | | | | | |
| External debt outstanding to GNI (%) | 26.6 | 23.9 | 32.2 | 21.0 | 22.4 | 21.0 |
| External debt stocks to exports (%) | 75.9 | 66.1 | 65.6 | 59.3 | 77.0 | 68.7 |
| Reserves to external debt outstanding (%) | 78.7 | 97.8 | 114.9 | 118.7 | 132.9 | 137.1 |
| Short term debt to imports (%) | 15.3 | 15.2 | 16.0 | 13.0 | 16.2 | 17.2 |

SOURCE: WORLD BANK 2012, P. 2.

In its 2013 'retreat or reset' report, McKinsey found that developing countries had continued to see strong capital inflows, some $1.5 trillion in foreign capital in 2012. This was near or above the 2007 pre-crisis peak, for all regions save the ex-Soviet Union bloc and the Middle East. In 2012, they accounted for 32 percent of global capital flows in 2012, up from just 5 percent in 2000.[43] The report points to the improved macroeconomic and political stability in many of these countries, which has led to upgraded credit ratings. Another factor, which also underlies high-risk hedge fund strategies, as will be seen in Chapter 7, is that in the context of very low interest rates in the advanced economies, investors are turning to emerging markets in search of higher yields. The average US mutual fund investing in emerging-market debt (mainly government bonds) returned 10.4 percent a year since 1998. 'That beats the gains of emerging-market stock funds (8.2%) and dwarfs those of big American stocks (4.3%). The average

---

43  McKinsey Global Institute 2013, p. 34.

mutual fund investing in long-dated foreign Treasuries has returned 7.8% a year over the past 15 years'.[44] In 2012, developing countries represented 38 percent of global GDP and 27 percent of global FDI, but only 7 percent of foreign investment in equities and bonds and 13 percent of global foreign loans. The assessment is that emerging markets are 'under-weighted in investor portfolios', meaning that they could and should 'become vastly larger in the years ahead'.[45] One major investment bank where these investments are certainly not under-weighted is JP Morgan, which offers its clients the services of an emerging market equity fund as well as that of an emerging market investment trust.

### 3.2 The 'Internalisation' of Government Debt: The Case of Brazil

Major changes have taken place in the holding of government debt. This debt now takes the form of internal or domestic debt. In large part it only appears to be so. It is internal but in foreign hands. The change results from the pressure put on developing countries from the mid-1990s onwards by the US and international Washington-based financial institutions to open up their financial markets. As put by UNCTAD in relation to the context of financial liberalisation and open capital accounts, the 'distinction between external and domestic debt, makes less and less sense'.[46] International investors are present in the domestic markets of 'emerging' countries and the larger financial and non-financial corporations from these countries hold equity and bonds issued in New York and London. In 1995, external debt represented more than 50 percent of their total debt. By 2000, internally-held debt had overtaken it. Data from JP Morgan suggests that by the end of 2013 the ratio of internal to external debt will be one to six.[47] The history of Latin American countries from the 1994–5 second Mexican debt crisis onwards shows that they are highly vulnerable financially whatever the composition of debt. This was demonstrated again by their sensitivity in 2013 and 2014 to slight rises or even hints of future rises in the Fed's benchmark US interest rate on their bond and foreign exchange markets.

---

44  'Sovereign Debt Markets, An Illusory Haven, What lessons should investors learn from the Argentine and Greek restructurings?', *The Economist*, 20 April 2013. The data quoted is from Morningstar, a financial consultancy firm specialising in this market.
45  McKinsey Global Institute 2013, p. 36.
46  Panizza et al. 2010, p. 6. Paulani 2015c argues that consequently the only indicator of the interest flows from government debt is the financial account which also includes interest from private debt, dividends and profits.
47  'Sovereign Debt Markets', *The Economist*, 20 April 2013.

The question then is: who holds the internal debt? The answer requires a country-by-country analysis. In the case of Brazil, where internal government debt is among the highest in the world, it is held by both national and foreign institutions. The massive entry of foreign banks in Brazil started with the Color government as one of the measures of the financial liberalisation process later accelerated by the Cardoso government. The justification given was that competition would lead to lower interest spreads (the difference between lending and borrowing rates) and increase the accessibility of loans to corporations and households. Only the upper segments of the middle class have access to credit. The largest part of domestic corporate investment is supported by loans from the state-owned development bank, BNDES. Large private or public corporations like Petrobras can borrow in international loan markets. Thus the main effect of foreign entry was to accelerate the concentration of the banking sector, leading to the formation of a tight oligopoly between a very small number of private banks and one public Brazilian bank and three international financial conglomerates. The five private banks include Bradesco, Banco do Brasil, Itau-Unibanco, Safra and Votorantim, the latter having mainly the profile of an investment bank. The public bank is Caixa Economica Federal. The three foreign groups are Santander, HSBC and Citibank. The concentration process initially concerned the privatisation and acquisition of regional banks belonging to state governments. Itau became strong enough to buy BankBoston from Bank of America in 2006. Further concentration occurred in the course of the global financial crisis with the acquisition by Santander of the Latin American operations of ABN Amro Bank and the merger between Itau and Unibanco. All these banks are diversified financial services conglomerates referred to in Chapter 3.

This oligopoly of Brazilian and foreign banks is, along with market-based pension institutions also created as part of financial liberalisation and foreign portfolio investment funds, the beneficiary of a permanent flow of interest derived from the servicing of government debt. The funding of government expenditure has long been through debt more than through taxation. This always entailed high interest rates, but successive Brazilian governments established it as a permanent regime. Between 1999 and 2013, the average interest rate was 16.06 with a peak of 45 percent in March 1999 and a record low of 7.25 percent in October 2012. Since then it has continually risen. In January 2016 it stood at 14.25 percent. The percentage of Brazil's federal budget that goes to the servicing of government debt (interest plus payment of principal on expiry of loans) is extremely high: 45 percent in 2011 and 47 percent in 2012.[48]

---

48   Fattorelli and Ávila 2013.

As to the ratio of debt servicing to GDP over the years 2011–13, the interest paid on internal debt averaged 5.25 percent. If interest paid by the Lula government is added in the eleven years of government by the PT, the average level is 6.4 percent of GDP.[49] One of the many perverse features of the system is that the development bank BNDES is funded with money borrowed at these extremely high rates to the benefit of financial investors. The Brazilian financial account balance has been negative since 1972, with a first accentuation in 1994–8 and a second sharper one from 2006 onwards, worsened in 2011.[50] This has been long compensated by a trade surplus which started to collapse in 2010 before giving way to a deficit in 2014.

### 3.3   *The Audit and Cancellation of Illegitimate Debt by Ecuador*

Ecuador has been the only country to call upon the theory of odious debt[51] and to cancel a part of its debt following a public audit. In an international finance-dominated economic and political system, the possibility of countries to question, investigate or audit the debts undertaken by their rulers, in order to evaluate their legality or illegitimacy, is severely constrained. The behaviour of the ANC post-apartheid government is characteristic of the fear of questioning successor debt despite its traits of odious debt (see Box 7.1). This is why the audit carried out by Ecuador is noteworthy even if the losses incurred by creditors were puny.

> Box 7.1: A counter-example to Ecuador: The non-cancellation of apartheid debt by South Africa
>
> Advocates of repudiation of debt incurred by the apartheid South African regime argue that apartheid was the equivalent of a racial dictatorship, condemned as such by the international community for many years. South Africa was forced to leave the Commonwealth in 1961. In 1973, the United Nations called apartheid a crime against humanity. The struggle of the South African people was recognized as a struggle for national liberation. In 1977, the United Nations imposed a mandatory arms embargo and in 1985 the United Nations Security Council imposed trade sanctions on the apartheid regime. Despite this, the regime continued to borrow from private banks throughout the 1980s.

---

49  Marques and Nakatani 2015. The article is surprisingly optimistic about Brazil's 'strengths'.
50  Paulani 2015c.
51  See the discussion and references above in Chapter 2.

After being elected president of South Africa (1994), Nelson Mandela and the African National Congress came under heavy pressure not to renounce apartheid debt. The new Government distanced itself from calls to nullify its apartheid-era debts. It was considered important not to default on debts in order to attract critical foreign investment. However, Hanlon (2006) is typical of observers who argue that the promise of foreign investment has not been kept. 'Foreign direct investment has been tiny – only two thirds of the profits repatriated by companies on investments they made in the Apartheid State. And new lending has not kept up with repayments – over six years South Africa paid out $3.7 billion more than it received. Thus, promises have not been kept and policy advice was wrong. If South Africa had frozen profits on apartheid-era investments and simply repudiated the odious apartheid debt – or even if it had demanded a ten-year moratorium – it would have been $10 billion better off. Foreign aid during this period was only $1.1 billion, so even if aid had been cut off, South Africa would have profited by $8.9 billion'.

However on 12 November 2002, a suit was filed in the New York Eastern District Court for apartheid reparations against eight banks and 12 oil, transport, communications technology and armaments companies from Germany, Switzerland, Britain, the United States, the Netherlands and France. The suit was filed on behalf of the Khulumani Support Group, representing 32,000 individual 'victims of state-sanctioned torture, murder, rape, arbitrary detention and inhumane treatment', by the Apartheid Debt and Reparations Campaign of Jubilee South Africa. The suit was brought pursuant to the Alien Torts Claims Act (ATCA) which allows any non-United States citizen to bring a claim for damages against any other person who has violated customary international law.

The Government of South Africa continues to distance itself from the popular movement to cancel the apartheid debt. For example, its top ministers denounced the lawsuit seeking reparations from banks that loaned to the apartheid regime because 'we are talking to those very companies named on the lawsuits about investing in post-apartheid South Africa'.

Source: Howse 2007, p. 13.

---

On being elected in 2007, the new President Rafael Correa refused to recognise successor debt. Ecuador's military dictatorship (1974–9) had been the first government to lead the country into indebtedness and debt had continued to grow as a consequence of the mechanism recalled above. Correa declared a moratorium and set up a Public Credit Audit Commission (CAIC) 'to examine and evaluate the process of contracting and/or renegotiating public debt ... in order to determine its legitimacy, legality, transparency, quality, effectiveness and efficiency'. In November 2008, after an examination of the whole of commercial, multilateral, government-to-government and domestic debt from 1976–2006, it found much of Ecuador's foreign debt to be illegitimate. Debt restructuring had repeatedly forced the country to roll over debt, often at much higher interest rates. It did what very many other countries could have done. It charged that the US Fed's early 1980 interest rate policy constituted a 'unilateral' measure which had raised global rates and aggravated Ecuador's debt burden. It recommended that Ecuador default on $3.9 billion in bonds resulting from debts restructured in 2000 after the country's previous 1999 default. This represented a little less than 20 percent of Ecuador's total debt. The Commission singled out the Wall Street investment bank Salomon Smith Barney, subsequently acquired and merged by Citigroup, as having handled the 2000 restructuring and set 10 and 12 percent interest rates without proper consultation with the government. The Commission was also very critical of multilateral debt, showing that many IMF and World Bank loans were used to advance the interests of transnational corporations.

The timing of the report was particularly favourable since it took place in the midst of the 2008 financial crisis at a moment when US investment banks and hedge funds were very vulnerable. A financial journalist at Reuters has given a good account of the policy adopted. Ecuador announced that it was defaulting on its 2012 international bonds at exactly the time that three huge hedge funds holding the country's debt were being forced by their prime brokers to liquidate their holdings. As a result, Ecuadorean bonds fell from 70 to 20 cents almost overnight. The government then made sure that they would not be bought by vulture funds. The large Ecuadorean bank Banco del Pacifico was ordered to start buying bonds at levels above 20 cents on the dollar.

> That was just high enough that the vultures didn't want to amass a large position, and ensured that any future restructuring would face little organized opposition just because Ecuador's bondholders were so fragmented. Ecuador's next clever step was to pay cash for its defaulted bonds, rather than trying to do a bond exchange. And of course it also helped that Ecuador was so small. Even with the bonds at par, they accounted for only about 0.5% of the emerging-market index. You could fight them in the courts, but when your portfolio is down 20% for other reasons, what's the point.[52]

---

52   http://blogs.reuters.com/felix-salmon/2009/05/29/lessons-from-ecuadors-bond-default/.

## 3.4  The 2002 Argentinian Default

The Ecuadorian case also contrasts with that of Argentina where rescheduling and partial cancellation took place, but could have been much larger if a public audit process had been previously organised. In 2001–2, Argentina was the theatre of a radical political movement, characterised even as pre-revolutionary by many on the left. However, no particular attention was paid to public debt. No campaign was waged for repudiation at the time, nor in later years for a democratic audit. An Argentine government document can proudly write that no repudiation took place there and that foreign investors were only very slightly hurt given that 60 percent of allegedly foreign public debt was in fact held by domestic investors.[53] The latter certainly did not belong to the Argentinian working class which suffered loss of real wages, high unemployment, and the effects of massive privatisation under the Menem and de la Rua governments. Behind the façade of an exchange-rate-based stabilisation system known as the 'convertibility plan'[54] aimed at containing chronic inflation, a fiscal regime of low taxes and a new recourse to debt was established. As in other Latin American countries, the twofold repercussions of the Asian and Russian crises on exports and interest rates accelerated this process with the difference that the IMF considered Argentina as its 'best student' and granted it two new loans in 2001 just before the crisis. Public debt increased from 35 percent of GDP at the end of 1994 to 64 percent at the end of 2001, just before 'unpegging' took place, nearly all of it denominated in dollars. With the end of 'convertibility', the ratio of debt to GDP jumped to 166 percent.

The story of the *piqueteros* and the 'argentinazzo' has been written by authors of the left.[55] It is vividly described by the Argentine Embassy in Washington, pleading that the Dualde government had no choice but to default:

> Argentina's GDP declined by more than 20 percent between 1998 and 2002; unemployment reached more than 25 percent, poverty soared to 50 percent, banks failed, and depositors lost their savings. As a result, unprecedented social unrest shook the country, with dozens dead and hundreds injured in street riots as the country went through five presidents in a matter of weeks. Capital flight and the large devaluation of the

---

53  Embassy of the Argentine Republic 2012. This is confirmed by Panizza 2008.
54  Under this system, the Argentine peso was pegged to the US dollar at 1:1 while the Central Bank was required to back at least two thirds of its monetary base with hard currency reserves.
55  See *inter alia* Chesnais and Divés 2002.

> peso evaporated Argentina's wealth nearly overnight. The scale and magnitude of Argentina's problems made it impossible to fulfil its debt obligations. Argentina faced a true inability to pay. Thus, Argentina's default was neither a discretionary nor an easy-to-make decision aimed at repudiating its debt obligations. In light of the most unprecedented social and economic crisis ever experienced in our recent history, our country had no other option and was forced to cease all its debt payments in order to guarantee minimum social and economic cohesion. Against this background, there was no other feasible choice at hand.[56]

Default is not cancellation or repudiation. Successive Argentine governments never ceased to recognise their debt and rescheduled it as soon as they could. Thus in 2005, 76 percent of the defaulted bonds were exchanged for others, worth 35 percent of the original ones and at longer terms. The offer was accepted by three quarters of bondholders. The commentary made by *The Economist* is enlightening:

> Bond-holder groups think it a travesty. But even in a default, there is money to be made. So-called 'vulture' funds pick over the non-performing bonds discarded by disheartened investors. In the summer of 2002, a few months after Argentina stopped honouring its debts, a brave buyer could have purchased a distressed bond in the secondary market for 20 cents on the dollar or less. On February 25th, he could have swapped it for crisp peso-denominated paper worth 35 to 37 cents: a tidy annualised return of 25% or more.[57]

A true model of successful speculation! Nonetheless, some vulture funds considered that they could do better than that. A few creditors, led by a hedge fund named NML Capital, bought up the cheap defaulted debt in order to chase payment of full principal plus interest in the New York courts, under whose law the original bonds were written. In 2014, a protracted legal battle edged Argentina towards another minor default. In 2012, a ruling by a New York district-court judge banned Argentina from paying the creditors who held the exchanged bonds if the country did not also pay NML what it wanted. In June 2014, the US Supreme Court refused to hear the case, leaving the 2012 ruling intact and Argentina with the choice of paying NML the $1.3 billion plus interest awarded by the court and negotiate a settlement with other hedge

---

56   Embassy of the Argentine Republic, 2012.
57   Argentina's debt restructuring: A victory by default? *The Economist*, March 3rd 2005.

funds,[58] or stop paying the holders of exchanged bonds.[59] The ruling included wording that Argentina's deposit with Bank of New York Mellon to pay bondholders who had renegotiated their debt with Argentina was 'illegal', and ordered the bank to hold onto the funds. Argentina is technically again in default. The final outcome of this battle will depend on the balance of class and state power relationships in the context of today's global systemic financial instability. Unfortunately they are weighted in favour of capital and states wielding economic and political power. On 29 February 2016, the new Argentinean government agreed to make a settlement with four hedge funds and pay them $4.65 billion.[60] At that date there were still two settlements to come, those with the initiators of the New York legal proceedings.

---

58   These are led by Elliott Management and Aurelius Capital Management. See http://www.globalresearch.ca/argentina-and-wall-streets-vulture-funds-economic-terrorism-and-the-western-financial-system/5407073.

59   For a severe criticism of the New York court ruling, see http://www.nytimes.com/2013/08/30/business/fears-of-a-precedent-in-argentine-debt-ruling.html?pagewanted=all.

60   'One fund, Bracebridge Capital from Boston, will make about $950 million return on its original principal amount of $120 million, about an 800% return. Billionaire Paul Singer and his firm NML Capital – the leading firm in the case – will rake in $2.28 billion on principal and interest payments. That's a huge payday considering NML's original amount of only $617 million. That's a 370% return'. http://money.cnn.com/2016/03/02/news/economy/hedge-funds-argentina-debt/.

CHAPTER 8

# Financialisation and the Transformation of Banking and Credit

This chapter and the next aim at explaining the forms taken by the financial crisis in September 2008 and by the subsequent European banking crisis of 2010–11. They were preceded by extremely deep changes in the credit system. The process of capitalist production depends on the proper functioning of the credit system. This system has experienced deep changes since the 1980s and has suffered a process of degeneration rooted in the excess of money capital looking for financial profits. It is strongly marked by 'adverse selection', to use a term from mainstream economics. While banks lend intensively to one another, medium and small enterprises access credit with difficulty. They can experience outright 'credit starvation' in times of crisis. As shown by US data, the financialisation of credit saw the spectacular increase in the level of indebtedness of financial corporations, e.g. intra-sectorial borrowing within the financial system between its participating entities, banks and funds.[1] During the run up to the 2008 financial crisis, this increase was higher than even that of the household debt that financial innovation was funding in ways which would lead to systemic panic.

TABLE 8.1   *United States: Indebtedness by sector, 1980–2008 (as % of GDP)*

| Sector | 1980 | 1990 | 2000 | 2008 |
|---|---|---|---|---|
| Households | 49 | 65 | 72 | 100 |
| Non-Financial Corporations | 53 | 58 | 63 | 75 |
| Financial Corporations | 18 | 44 | 87 | 119 |
| Government | 35 | 54 | 47 | 55 |
| Total | 155 | 221 | 269 | 349 |

SOURCE: FEDERAL RESERVE BANK, FOFA.

1   McKinsey 2013, p. 3, estimates that between 1990 and 2007 globally 'bonds issued by financial institutions to fund lending activities and other asset purchases grew roughly five times the value of bonds issued by non-financial companies'. Michel Aglietta is the first French author to have reflected on the implications of lending between financial corporations in lectures given in 2009.

The mechanisms behind this process (securitisation and forms of trading between financial entities specific to shadow banking) and their relationship to household debt are one of the subjects of this chapter. Table 7.1 shows further that the degree of indebtedness of non-financial corporations rose rather slowly as profits were accumulated and hoarded. Far from placing brakes on this process, the US and Eurozone central bank and government monetary policies were marked by, for example, permissiveness toward banks building up unsustainable levels of credit. In the US, the transformations in the credit system started with disintermediation as a consequence of the entry of funds, the responses to this by banks, the first phase of financial liberalisation by Government (Fed and Congress), and a new spurt of bank concentration (section 1). Banking systems in Europe followed their own processes of liberalisation and concentration, the outcome of which was the full restoration of 'universal banks' (section 2). A qualitative leap in the scale and consequence of changes in the organisation of credit occurred from the late 1990s onwards with the development of securitisation in the US financial system, the adoption of the 'originate-to-distribute' banking model and the consequent formation and rapid globalisation of the shadow banking system (section 3).

## 1       The Transformation of Banking in the United States

The onset of financial liberalisation saw major changes both in the configuration of loan capital and in the provision of credit. Since the turn of the 1980s, the main driving factors have been the entry of important new actors in the centralisation-mobilisation of money capital, notably Pension Funds and Mutual Funds, the disintermediation of credit, and the ever-increasing use of securitisation.

### 1.1     *'Traditional' Banking and Credit Intermediation*

'Traditional banking' implied, as put by Harvey, 'the existence of some degree of personal trust and credibility... [I]f the bank was to maintain the quality of its own money it must retain the right to refuse bills it regards as risky or worthless'. The extension of credit to firms entailed the relationship named by JP Morgan as 'character banking' – making a loan based on a judgement of personal character rather than a balance sheet – but of course it involved what Henwood calls 'classic credit scrutiny'.[2] In turn, the bills of individual banks were freely convertible into central bank money through discount windows

---

2   Henwood 1997, p. 82.

only when the central bank was 'satisfied as to the quality or soundness of the individual bank money'. In times of economic and financial crises, 'central banks were there to do what they could'[3] (in fact quite little) to dampen these processes and they had the responsibility of saving the banking system from collapse through 'lending of last resort'.

In the US, where the changes were first to take place, this way of presenting bank-based credit creation still corresponded largely to the situation prevailing at the time Harvey wrote. In what Guttmann names 'post-Depression finance', the US credit system 'was built around three pillars'. The first was the direct result of the 1933 Glass-Steagall Act. 'Commercial banks specialized in taking liquid deposits and in making short term loans to businesses. Insurance companies which enjoyed illiquid liabilities and actuarial predictable outflows could afford to provide businesses with long term loans. And investment banks organized financial markets as underwriters, brokers and dealers of marketable securities'. Commercial banks dominated the processes of credit intermediation and credit creation: 'they could pool many small deposits into one loan package and satisfy the need of corporate borrowers or large-denomination credit ... A large portion of the deposits consisted of transactions from accounts which they alone could offer as issuers of private bank money'. Finally, because they possessed a monopoly over money creation, commercial banks were subject to special regulations, notably reserve requirements. 'For the same reason they also had certain privileges, most notably to the Fed's discount window, to the nation's external payment system and to deposit insurance'.[4]

### 1.2   The Start of Deregulation and the Transition to a Market-Intermediated Credit System

'The slow death of commercial banking', as Guttmann puts it, goes back to the mid-1970s, which saw the start of the 'disintermediation' of loans to corporations following the arrival of pension and mutual funds and the renewed importance of the corporate bond market. Historically it had always played a much greater role in the US than in Europe, but the accession of funds gave it a huge impetus. Increasingly corporations, even of medium size, accessed finance by floating bonds. Investment banks, in their capacity as underwriters for large issuances, profited from this change, and commercial banks lost. A new type of short term credit intermediation (to be discussed fully below in section 3.1) developed in the form of money market mutual funds, called money market funds for short (MMFs), further depriving commercial banks

---

3   Harvey 1982, p. 247.
4   Guttmann 1994, pp. 261–262.

of a part of their business. The response of commercial banks was an increasing diversification out of traditional activities. The process was reinforced by every new step taken towards liberalisation and deregulation. The shift in the relations of power between banks and funds, and so the pressure on banks to make ever deeper changes in their functions and structure, was accelerated by the accompanying measures which caused a rise in US interest rates. Of particular importance were the abolition of Regulation Q, which placed a ceiling on interest rates, and the 1981 International Banking Facilities Act, which gave Wall Street the same legal off-shore status as the City.[5] These measures not only attracted large amounts of foreign as well as US money capital, but also sped up domestic changes in the configuration of the financial sector. The turn of the 1980s marks a qualitative turning point. It is then that the assets held by security broker-dealers[6] – acting on behalf of pension and mutual funds and wealthy individuals – start to outpace all other forms.

The decline in bank intermediation carried out in the direct relation with borrowers and the growth of intermediation through financial markets saw the emergence of the new figure of the fund manager. He was not only central to the introduction of corporate management but was the first of a new breed of financier. The growth of non-bank-based intermediation and domestic and international corporate bond markets was also facilitated by the new ITC technologies which permitted both electronic trading in 'virtual' space and the possibility for fund managers to access computerised information networks.[7] Banks responded to the loss of a large part of their corporate loan business by offering corporations seeking reasonably large loans a new credit instrument, namely certificate of deposits (CDs).[8] A specialised segment of money markets arose, allowing these to be sold by issuer banks. Further types of negotiable credit instruments were created for the purpose in particular of facilitating inter-bank loans, so freeing banks from the constraints of having to keep large

---

5  See Gowan 1999, p. 26. An International Banking Facility (IBF) is a separate account established by a US bank or a US branch/subsidiary of a foreign bank to offer services to only non-US residents and institutions.
6  A security broker-dealer is a financial company that trades securities on its own account or on behalf of its customers. Broker-dealers may be independent firms solely involved in broker-dealer services but most are now business units or subsidiaries of investment or commercial banks. When executing trade orders on behalf of a customer, the entity is said to be acting as a *broker*. When executing trades for its own account, it is said to be acting as a *dealer*.
7  Guttmann 1994, p. 263.
8  These must not be confused with CDSs which are discussed at length.

reserves of cash and very liquid securities.[9] The road was opened up for large-scale leverage, the effects of which were already felt during the US banking crises of the 1980s and early 1990s.

The commercial banks' response to the threat to their profitability was a drive towards dis-compartmentalisation and diversification. They created mutual funds for their customers, offered management services to pension funds and started to invest in hedge funds. But they were still at a disadvantage with respect to investment banks for security issuance. So they campaigned for more than a decade to secure the relaxation and finally the repeal of the Glass-Steagall provisions.[10] These included measures written into legislation that limited the securities-dealing operations of commercial banks and the affiliation between commercial banks and securities firms. The demands of commercial banks were supported by the Fed. It undertook to give interpretations of the Glass-Steagall provisions and make authorisations that increasingly reduced the wall between commercial and investment banking. One key authorisation concerned the creation of bank-holding companies, and the permission given in April 1987 to three of these – Bankers Trust (acquired by Deutsche Bank in 1998), Citicorp (now Citigroup) and JP Morgan & Co – to establish a type of subsidiary forbidden by Glass-Steagall to underwrite and deal in residential mortgage-backed securities (RMBS) and municipal bonds. At the time, the Fed put a 5 percent limit on the profits from underwriting and dealing in these types of securities. It later added to the list 'asset-backed securities' backed by pools of credit card accounts or other 'consumer finance assets'. Formally, the Act was respected: bank holding companies, not commercial banks directly, owned the affiliates, but from there the way was paved for the outright repeal of the Glass-Steagall Act in 1999. The largest banks, known since the 2008 crisis as the 'systematically important banks' (SIBs), became 'diversified financial service corporations', e.g. financial conglomerates.

### 1.3  US Bank Concentration in the 1990s

Historically the US banking industry has been and remains to some extent marked by a sharp divide between Wall Street banks, along with a few others, and myriad small state banks, chartered, supervised, and regulated at both the

---

9   Guttmann 1994, p. 264.
10  One of the conclusions of the Financial Crisis Inquiry Report is that 'widespread failures in financial regulation and supervision proved devastating to the stability of the nation's financial markets' (US Government Printing Office 2011, p. xviii). Part II provides an easily readable account of the deregulation process and the emergence of the shadow banking system.

state and federal level. The passing of the first National Bank Act at the end of the Civil War gave federal charters to banks that had enough capital and would submit to strict regulation. Banknotes issued by National banks had to be uniform in design and backed by substantial reserves invested in federal bonds. The Act prohibited interstate banking and limited branching activity within states. The Act put an end to 'wildcat banks'[11] but led to the proliferation of state banks. As depression began to spread through American agriculture in the 1920s, bank failures averaged over 550 a year. With the Great Depression, the wave of bank failures threatened the collapse of the entire system. But the Glass-Steagall Act had to leave state banking as it was. The system was stable in the prosperous postwar years, but when inflation took off in the late 1960s, it began to break down. Despite the Savings and Loans (S&Ls) crisis, thrifts were saved, on account of their political influence, and not forced to merge or liquidate. In 2001, almost three out of every four US banks were still chartered and regulated at both the state and federal level.

With the new legislation of the 1990s authorising and implementing interstate banking, mergers began to develop and some centralisation of bank capital began. A Federal Bank Staff study on the 1994–2003 period reports that most deals involved the acquisition of a small organisation with operations in a fairly limited geographic area. Overall these small mergers accounted for a relatively small share of the assets, deposits, and branches. In contrast, the few acquisitions of very large banks accounted for a large share of the banking acquisitions made over the period, and were responsible for many of the changes to the banking industry caused by consolidation. Fifteen banks were acquirers in the 25 largest acquisitions. Four of them – First Union, Fleet (and its successor, FleetBoston), NationsBank, and Washington Mutual – were acquirers in three of the top 25 mergers and two – Firstar and Chemical (and its successor, Chase Manhattan[12]) – were acquirers in two. Chase Manhattan diversified spectacularly into investment banking with its acquisition of JP Morgan. But the targets of the largest deals were banks with large retail operations. In these transactions, the acquirers increased the size of their branch networks and obtained large retail customer bases. But in 2002 there still remained more than 8,000 insured commercial banks and about 1,500 insured savings institutions in operation. In 1995, very large banks with more than $100 billion in assets (in 2010 dollars) controlled 17 percent of all banking assets. By 2005, their

---

11   So-called for being situated in towns 'out among the wildcats'.
12   Although Chemical was the acquirer, the merged company took the Chase name because it was better known, particularly outside the US.

share had reached 41 percent. The increase was at the expense mainly of banks with assets between $10 billion and $100 billion.

Further concentration has taken place as the result of the financial crisis of 2007–8, starting with the acquisition by JP Morgan Chase of Bear Stearns in March 2008, and of Washington Mutual in September of the same year, and that of Merrill Lynch by Bank of America the same month. In 2011, three of the five largest US banks – Bank of America, Citigroup and Wells Fargo – combined commercial and investment banking. Outside the sphere of the investment banks and the disappearance of Bear Stearns and Lehman Brothers, the most important chain of mergers involved the acquisition of a large thrift, the World Savings Bank, by Wachovia in 2007 and the acquisition of the latter by Wells Fargo in 2008. It is now estimated that the loan market share (measured on a national level) of the top 10 banks increased from about 30 percent in 1980 to about 50 percent in 2010, and deposit market share of the top 10 banks increased from about 20 percent in 1980 to almost 50 percent in 2010.[13] Meanwhile, the share of the market held by community banks and credit unions, local institutions with less than $1 billion in assets, fell from 27 percent to 11 percent. These represent all that really remains of 'relationship banking'. Their disappearance has affected notably small 'Latino' credit unions.[14]

## 2   Financial Liberalisation in Europe and European 'Universal Banks'

As an outcome of the Maastricht Treaty, the European banking system is an interconnection of fragmented domestic systems marked by a higher level of bank concentration than in the US. Europe is at once home to the largest banks in the world and one of the most vulnerable segments of the global financial system. Several aspects of its make up complete the picture: the lack of a Federal state, the extremely narrow and conservative mission for the ECB written into the Treaty, and so its status as a genuinely 'independent' central bank, the only one in the G7 not to have to account for its policies to political authorities. This is not the case for the Bank of England, although the UK banking sector does not differ much from that of Continental Europe, regarding the level of concentration and the dependence of small and medium firms on

---

13   Council of Economic Advisers 2016.

14   Mitchell 2015. Each of the biggest US banks Bank of America, JP Morgan Chase, Citigroup, and Wells Fargo, is estimated to have become larger than all of the nation's community banks put together.

banks, bank credit being the main source of finance for the private sector as a whole in the EU.

### 2.1  The Course of Financial Liberalisation in Continental Europe

In the aftermath of the Second World War and up into the 1970s, European governments exercised a close surveillance over credit creation. Nationalised banks were the rule. While few governments exercised the right to allocate investment credit as part of indicative planning, as in the case of France, all watched over banks carefully. As recalled in Chapter 2, the creation of the Eurodollar markets came as a step on the 'road out of serfdom' for the larger banks. The loosening of regulations on capital flows and the first regulatory changes, including the status of central banks, took place in the 1970s.[15] Although individual countries liberalised capital flows earlier, agreements to abolish capital controls on a European-wide level and enact common legislation were only adopted with the signing of the Single European Act in 1986. This gave governments the political and legal support for the privatisation of the state-owned banks.[16] Full implementation into national law was only achieved in the 1990s in the majority of countries following the Maastricht Treaty. The Second Banking Directive, which became effective in 1993 eliminated, among other things, the need among Member countries to get a local banking charter for branches in another country, as well as the need for foreign branches to hold a certain amount of endowment capital. It subjected foreign branches to home country supervision.

However, until the Eurozone started to function in 1999, despite the deregulation of cross-border banking, the direct presence of foreign banks (branches plus subsidiaries) on domestic markets remained low for most EU countries. In 2002, a study found that compared to total domestic credit, bilateral financial linkages among EU countries still remained small. Notable exceptions were the claims of Germany, as the largest creditor in the Eurozone, on a number of smaller member countries and at a lesser level of France. Since there was not a political understanding of this at the time, this study announced the problems the Eurozone was to face.[17]

---

15   In the case of France, this occurred in a law passed in January 2003. The President at the time was Georges Pompidou and the Finance minister Giscard d'Estaing. The law was known as the 'Loi Rothschild' on account of Pompidou's association with the bank.

16   Again in the case of France, Paribas, Société Générale and Suez were privatised in 1987, and BNP in 1993. Because of the financial scandal and the state of its accounts, Crédit Lyonnais waited until 1999.

17   Buch and Heinrich 2002. The paper was written for a European Financial Services Roundtable project. In retrospect it showed considerable foresight. The Eurozone is one

### 2.2 Three Types of Banks in the EU

In the EU there were some 8,000 banks in 2011, also divided as in the US but in a different way, into three groups.[18] In 2011, the first very large group consisted of small banks operating on a regional level. Germany, Austria and some other Member States had many small savings and co-operative banks with assets of less than €1 billion. In total, there were nearly 4,000 small cooperative banks in the EU. These only represented 3 percent of total EU domestic bank assets. A second group making up 22.4 percent of EU domestic bank assets consisted of medium-sized banks with assets ranging from €1 billion to €100 billion. These banks operated on a countrywide scale. Among the Spanish savings banks, the *cajas*, there were a majority of small firms but also several with nationwide operations. The third group consisted of the 'large banks' as defined by the ECB,[19] having assets that exceed €100 billion (up to €2 trillion). While doing a significant part of their business abroad, large banks made up about three quarters of total domestic bank assets in the EU. They also provided the largest part of lending (69 percent of total loans by EU domiciled banks). The nine largest European banks had total assets exceeding €1 trillion at the end of 2011 and are headquartered in the UK, Germany, France and Spain. For some, total assets are well in excess of the national GDP of the county in which they are headquartered. Even in comparison to total EU GDP, those banks appear large in global terms. Half of the world's largest 30 banks by total assets (as reported in 2011) are EU banks. There are 15 EU banks in the group of 29 global 'systemically important banks' (considered G-SIBs), identified by the Financial Stability Board (FSB) and the Basel Committee on Banking Supervision by virtue of their size, complexity, substitutability and degree of cross-country activity.

### 2.3 The Full Restoration of the European 'Universal Bank'

Over the whole of the twentieth century, European countries possessed banking systems marked by high concentration and the dominance of the 'universal bank' model. It was this that gave banks the status of 'commanding heights' and, in the postwar period, of handy instruments in the service of industrial

---

where 'countries which are closely linked financially might expose themselves to spillovers of financial crises. Monetary and fiscal policies are constrained by the interregional mobility of capital'.

18 Liikanen report 2012, pp. 34–5.

19 ECB consolidated banking data as of the end of 2011 in which 'large' EU banks are defined as having a share of more than 0.5 percent of total EU bank assets (i.e. more than approximately €200 billion based on 2011 data).

policy. In Continental Europe, liberalisation and privatisation took the form of the full re-emergence in the 1990s of large universal banks,[20] a number of which were to quickly become highly internationalised. The process involved large mergers, among which was the merger of BNP (itself the outcome of commercial banking concentration) with Paribas, one of France's oldest 'haute finance' institutions. The same process of concentration took place with mergers and some reshuffling of cards in the United Kingdom. In the wake of US deregulation and financial innovation, the European universal banks quickly entered into hedge-fund-type activities pioneered in the US. In the years leading up to 2007, holders of portfolios under private wealth management were offered high-risk investments. French citizens only started hearing about bank diversification into hedge-fund-type activities when BNP Paribas announced the failure of two of its hedge fund affiliates.

The largest EU banking groups offer the whole range of banking services, ranging from deposit-taking and management, credit card and real-estate lending to deposit holders and traditional commercial and industrial credit to investment banking activities, including securities trading, market-making, underwriting, risk management for corporations and private wealth management. The larger investment-focused banks have customers requiring a wide range of banking and capital market services (the larger industrial firms) or having demands for specific capital market services (governments placing bond issues or smaller corporations seeking access to the corporate bond market). An idea of the relative profitability and so attractiveness of traditional banking, investment banking and wealth management is provided by figure 8.1, which shows estimates of returns on equity for the main product segments. This data also provides evidence of the growth of 'non-interest' sources of banking profits.

The Liikanen report shows that the mix can vary considerably even among large banks. It found that while some banks had limited assets held for trading, for others they reported more than 20 percent of their balance sheet. It quotes Deutsche Bank, Royal Bank of Scotland (RBS), Barclays, BNP Paribas and Société Générale as being the five banks with the highest proportion of assets (more than 30 percent) held for trading in 2011, reaching 50 percent in the case of Deutsche Bank and RBS. The same banks are referred to when

---

20   The Second Banking Directive adopted a broad definition of credit institutions, taking German universal banking as its model. Thus banks, investment firms and insurance companies may hold unlimited reciprocal equity participations, meaning that there are no limits on the formation of financial conglomerates.

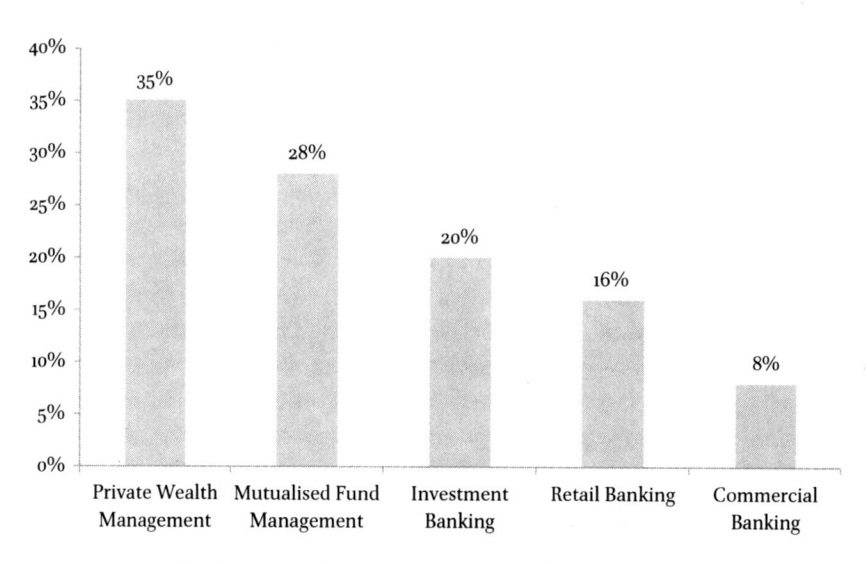

FIGURE 8.1  ROE for the main product segments in European banks in 2003.
SOURCE: PASTRÉ 2006.

looking at assets held for trading and available for sale in 2011. The report found that the balance sheet share of these assets fell for some banks after the 2007–8 crisis (RBS and Barclays), but for others (Deutsche Bank, BNP Paribas and Société Générale) it increased.[21] The frontiers between trading on behalf of customers, and proprietary trading are impossible to trace. Professionals estimate that in the case of EU banks proprietary trading is high and one of the factors contributing to their systemic fragility.[22] Several banks – Deutsche Bank, Barclays, BNP Paribas and RBS – had particularly high notional amounts of derivatives outstanding relative to the size of total assets.

Since mid-2015, the European universal banking model is under strain. Intense rivalry with US banks and in Asia with China's rising banks, in an overall context in which falling GDP growth rates throughout the world economy means weakening surplus value creation and appropriation, is forcing the largest banks, headed by HSBC and Deutsche Bank, to shorten sail and cut

---

21  Liikanen report 2012, p. 44, and charts 3.4.5, 3.4.6 and 3.4.7.
22  This comes out of the Liikanen report and is stressed by Naulot 2013. The author was a senior banking executive for 37 years and served the last years of his career as a member of the Autorité des marches financiers (AMF), the French equivalent of the US SEC.

back both on retail and investment bank activities and the extent of global activities.[23]

## 3   Securitisation, the Originate-to-distribute Model and the Shadow Banking System

Banks did not just concentrate and increase their scope for the centralisation of money-as-capital. US-led financial deregulation and financial innovations, aimed notably at increasing the scale of mortgage loans, led to the adoption of a new banking model. The two credit mechanisms discussed up to this point in the chapter have been: (1) 'traditional banking', on which small and medium firms throughout the OECD continue to depend, as well as, in many countries, household mortgage loans and; (2) corporate bond markets. They both entail easily analysable relationships: one is 'face-to-face' and the other operates through quite straightforward market mechanisms. The recourse by the Fed and the George W. Bush administration to housing as an instrument for recovery after the 2000–1 collapse of Nasdaq, and then as a pillar of GDP growth, saw the gradual emergence and then the full expansion in the mid-2000s of a new 'originate-to-distribute' banking model. It entails long and complicated chains of transactions bearing on very particular forms of assets, many of them created in a way that made their risk un-assessable. This was notoriously the case for certain categories of 'structured assets' containing so-called subprime mortgage loans. New patterns of relations ranged under the term 'shadow banking system' emerged. They involved banks, through specialised affiliates and a range of funds and financial investors. After receding under the impact of the 2008 crisis, the network of combined, regulated, and unregulated financial operations has grown yet further.

### 3.1   *The 'Originate-to-distribute' Banking Model and Securitisation*
The originate-to-distribute banking model is one where banks extensively resort to the opportunities created by securitisation, e.g. the pooling of assets and their subsequent sale to investors. Direct trader-to-trader – named 'over-the-counter' (ODT) – transactions are the rule. Securitisation dates back to the early and mid-1980s. Data began to be collected by the Securities Industry and Financial Markets Association (SIFMA) in 1980 for government-sponsored mortgage enterprises (GSE) and so-called 'private label' mortgage-backed

---

23   'Restructuring continues at two of the world's universal banks', *The Economist*, 13 June 2015.

securities (MBS), and in 1985 for asset-backed securities (ABS) backed by auto loans and credit cards. The years 1991 and then 2005 were acceleration points in the growth of private-label MBSs. ABSs only reached significant levels in the late 1990s. If the annual volume of total collateralised loan obligations (CLOs) is considered, it rarely surpassed $20 billion before 2003. Then loan securitisation grew rapidly, total annual issuance surpassing $180 billion in 2007.[24]

The analysis of the originate-to-distribute banking model lagged seriously behind its penetration into day-to-day practice. It was only after 2008 that studies began to be published. A 2012 Federal Reserve Bank of New York discussion paper defines the originate-to-distribute model as a method that 'enables banks to remove loans from balance sheets and transfer the credit risk associated with those loans. It involves selling the loans to a third party (the loan originator and the borrower being the first two parties)'.[25] 'Traditional loans' remained on the asset side of balance sheets. On the contrary, securitised loans are taken off the balance sheet and sold to another bank or fund, which is free in turn to sell the assets bought to yet another financial investor.

---

BOX 8.1: SECURITISATION

Securitization is the issuance of bonds that are repaid by the payments on a pool of assets, where the assets also serve as collateral. Securitized bonds backed by mortgages (MBS) are issued by either government-sponsored entities (the GSEs that issue MBS are Fannie Mae and Freddie Mac) or private financial firms such as commercial and investment banks (private-label MBS). A mortgage can get into the pool by several paths. The most direct path from origination to securitization is when a bank pools the loans it originates and makes them the collateral for a securitization it issues. But, only a handful of the largest banks originate enough mortgages to do this. Many of the mortgages in the pools backing private-label MBS come from banks other than the issuing bank. It is possible that a mortgage is sold several times before ending up in an MBS pool. It is the ability of lenders to easily make this first sale that made the OTD business model possible. Of course, the first sale is aided by the fact that the participants know that, in the end, the mortgage is likely to end up in an MBS pool.

Source: Rosen 2010.

---

24   Rosen 2010.
25   Bord and Santos 2012.

The 'production and circulation process' of debt-based securities is shown in figure 8.2. 'Normal' banks create specific affiliate companies with the US legal form of trusts, named 'conduits' or more generally 'special purpose vehicles' (SPVs). These are charged with pooling the assets and issuing them on appropriate markets. The rationale of special purpose or special investment vehicles (SIVs)[26] is to allow the risk of investing in separately worthless assets to be diversified. These can include not only payments from credit cards, auto loans, and mortgage loans, but also cash flows from aircraft leases, royalty payments and film revenues. Most mortgage and all consumer credit assets in particular are small and illiquid and cannot be sold separately. Pooling the assets into financial instruments which rating agencies assent to give a rating to, allows them to be sold to investors, including (as discovered by ordinary depositors in 2007–8) the high-risk affiliates of banking conglomerates. The pooled assets are issued as bonds and bought by investors. This is referred to either as 'offloading', 'risk-switching' or 'risk-stripping'.[27] Mortgage-backed securities (MBS) and asset-backed securities (ABS) are the most frequent. The special purpose vehicle issues bonds in layers called 'tranches', each with different risk characteristics. Senior tranches are paid from the cash flows from the underlying assets before the junior tranches and equity tranches. Losses are first borne by the equity tranches, next by the junior tranches, and finally by the senior tranches. Returns obey the inverse hierarchy.

The scale on which the operations shown in figure 8.2 can be carried out depends on access to finance. The profitability of an SPV and so of the larger parent-institution depends on leverage. It is here that MMFs enter the picture.[28] These funds can be both stand-alone asset-management financial corporations (such as Reserve Primary Fund, Vanguard Group, BlackRock and Schwab), or affiliates set up by banking conglomerates (JP Morgan, Bank of America, Wells Fargo).[29] Their growth dates back to the 1980s. They collect from funds and institutional investors ensuring them a stable net asset value (NAV) per share (traditionally $1.00 in the US)[30] and use them for short-term loans with differing risk profiles. In the lead up to the subprime crisis, the major rating agencies

---

26  The term special investment vehicle (SIV) is also often used.
27  This last term is used by Bhatia and Bayoumi 2012, p. 7.
28  Money market mutual funds (usually referred to as money market funds or money funds) invest in short-term, fixed-income securities, known as money market investments. Like other mutual funds, money market funds are pooled investments that allow investors to participate in a diversified portfolio managed by professionals.
29  See below for the major European conglomerates in this business.
30  If a fund's NAV drops below $1.00, it is said that the fund 'broke the buck'.

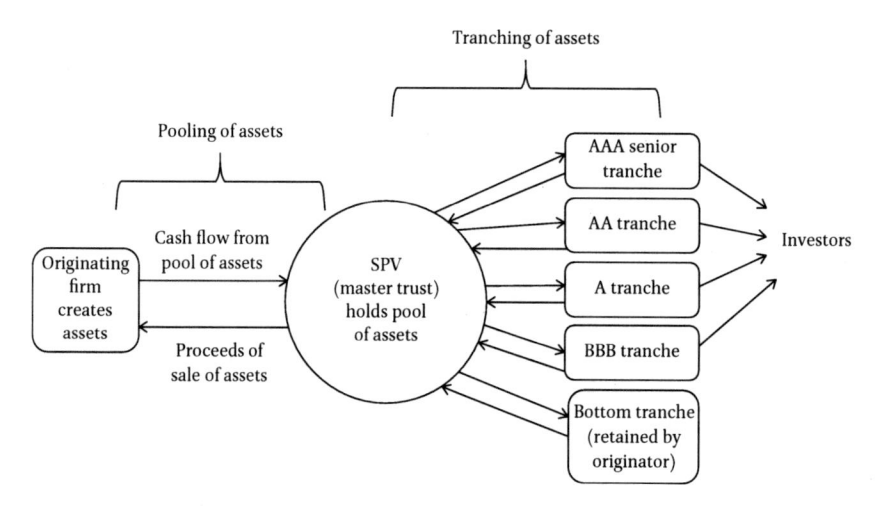

```
                    Tranching of assets
                  ┌─────────┴─────────┐
                              ┌──────────────┐
                              │  AAA senior  │
   Pooling of assets          │    tranche   │
 ┌────────┴────────┐          └──────────────┘
                              ┌──────────────┐
          Cash flow from      │  AA tranche  │──→ Investors
┌──────────┐ pool of assets   └──────────────┘
│Originating│─────────────→  ┌─────┐
│   firm    │                │ SPV │ ┌──────────────┐
│  creates  │                │(master trust)│ A tranche │
│  assets   │                │ holds pool │ └──────────────┘
└──────────┘ Proceeds of    │ of assets │
            sale of assets   └─────┘ ┌──────────────┐
                                     │ BBB tranche  │
                                     └──────────────┘
                                     ┌──────────────┐
                                     │Bottom tranche│
                                     │ (retained by │
                                     │  originator) │
                                     └──────────────┘
```

FIGURE 8.2 *The securitisation process.*
SOURCE: GORTON AND METRICK 2012.

gave high ratings to the risk/return profiles of pooled assets. All they were doing in fact was simply relaying the marketing operation of SPVs, giving sustenance to the financial system's collective hubris (Greenspan's 'irrational exuberance'), the degree to which it was carried away by the fetishism of money.

### 3.2 The Large-Scale Build-Up of Fictitious Capital on Household Mortgage

Securitisation and leverage allow the formation of $n$th degree fictitious capital in a new guise and on a huge scale. Housing bubbles and busts have been a recurrent feature of US economic history, but no bubble has been so long and no bust so devastating as the recent one. Between 1997 and 2006 (the peak of the housing bubble), the price of the average American house increased by 124 percent. From 1980 to 2001, the ratio of median home prices to median household income fluctuated from 2.9 to 3.1. In 2004, it rose to 4.0, and by 2006 it had reached 4.6. US household debt as a percentage of annual disposable income was 77 percent in 1990 and 127 percent at the end of 2007. This spectacular expansion of household debt after 2003 could not have taken place without the particular form of financing centred on the issuance of mortgage-backed securities (MBS) and collateralised debt obligations (CDO). The Fed's low interest policy and the government discourse about the 'proprietary society' made the bubble initially supply-driven, but from a certain moment onwards (from 2004–5) self-reinforcing mechanisms became all-important.

In the case of upper- and middle-class households, speculative borrowing in residential real estate became important.[31] In 2005, 22 percent of homes purchased were for investment purposes, with an additional 14 percent purchased as vacation homes. In 2006, as the boom began to falter, these percentages fell to 28 percent and 12 percent, respectively. Thus, nearly 40 percent of homes purchased were not intended as primary residences.

Nonetheless, the central feature of the length and dimension of the bubble was the rise in subprime lending, e.g. lending which represents a risk of insolvency, by contacting households. Such lending had always existed in the US, but this time the percentage of lower-quality subprime mortgages rose from the historical 8 percent range to approximately 20 percent from 2004 to 2006, with much higher ratios in some states and municipalities. This lending was supply-driven. The system ran from mortgage brokers to local and regional banks and then to the financial corporations who were in a position to issue opaque assets while keeping high ratings with the very concentrated oligopoly of rating agencies (Standard & Poor, Moody's and Fitch).

Mortgage brokers are a US institutional invention, extended to the UK and countries like Canada and Australia. But their systemic function is specific to the US,[32] as is their capacity to sell their mortgage titles to banks and for these banks in turn to remove them from their balance sheets. Brokers offered 'no income, no asset' (NINA) borrowers adjustable-rate mortgages (a below-market interest rate for some predetermined period, followed by market interest rates for the remainder of the mortgage's term). Adjustable rates transfer part of the interest rate risk from the lender to the borrower who benefits if the interest rate falls, but loses and is threatened by foreclosure if the interest rate increases. The income brackets targeted and the terms of the contracts fall under the 'reinstatement of essentially *usurious* relations within the capitalist mode of production',[33] while the interest paid by poor and very poor workers to brokers and banks fall within the labour theory of value.[34]

The capitalist class relations underlying mortgage-based securitisation are well illustrated by the contrast between the treatment of borrowers and of investors. The first suffered foreclosure and were chased from their homes.

---

31   Duménil and Lévy 2011, p. 178, correctly note that 'although the notion of a subprime crisis points to the rising indebtedness of households pertaining to the lower income brackets, most loans were contracted by high income brackets'.

32   See Vazire 2009 for a jurist's reading of subprime systemic relations. The French only learnt of their existence at the very outset of the subprime crisis, according to Jorion 2007.

33   Levina 2012.

34   Norfield 2014.

The second initiated legal action, which led to bank investigations by the US Securities and Exchange Commission (SEC). Foreclosure proceedings by banks began in 2007 on nearly 1.3 million poor households' properties. This increased to 2.3 million in 2008 and to 2.8 million in 2009, some 15 percent of all the homes bought through the mortgage. Ten states accounted for 74 percent of the foreclosure filings during 2008; the top two (California and Florida) representing 41 percent.[35] No mortgage broker has ever been investigated for having sold to or hoodwinked poor workers. Trust in the financial system necessitated that the most blatant of investor abuse be (benignly) punished. The latest report by the SEC on its enforcement actions[36] led to successful charges, first in 2010 against Goldman Sachs for 'defrauding investors by misstating and omitting key facts about a financial product tied to subprime mortgages as the housing market was beginning to falter'. The firm paid a record $550 million settlement. In the case of Citigroup's principal US broker-dealer subsidiary, charged with 'misleading investors about a $1 billion CDO tied to the housing market', a settlement of $285 million was returned to harmed investors. Charged with 'misleading investors in a complex mortgage securities transaction', JP Morgan agreed to pay $153.6 million in a settlement that enables harmed investors to receive their money back. Lower penalties for basically the same type of fraud have been paid by Merrill Lynch, Wachovia, Wells Fargo, RBS and UBS, as well as to smaller US regional banks and financial funds.

### 3.3  The Shadow Banking System

The shadow banking system is a combined offshoot of the centralisation of 'money as capital' by pension and mutual funds, and of securitisation. In the 1990s, pension funds created hedge funds with varying high-risk profiles. In order to remain profitable the larger banks followed their example. Alongside the holding of bonds and to a much lesser extent of stock, fund managers entered into 'over-the-counter' (OTC) trader-to-trader transactions in the new pooled assets with banks, while banks increased their 'off-balance' operations using the same trader-to-trader relationships. This resulted in the rapid growth from the mid-1990s onwards of the 'shadow banking system', as it came to be known again after 2008. The 'system' was global, more precisely transatlantic, from the outset. The major European universal banks were part of it as much as the US investment and very large commercial banks.

According to the Financial Stability Board (FSB), the term shadow banking system 'started to be used widely at the onset of the financial crisis, reflecting

---

35   http://www.stat.unc.edu/faculty/cji/fys/2012/Subprime%20mortgage%20crisis.pdf.
36   http://www.sec.gov/spotlight/enf-actions-fc.shtml (accessed 15 May 2015).

an increased recognition of the importance of entities and activities structured outside the regular banking system that perform bank-like functions'.[37] One finds considerable nuance both in the definitions proposed of shadow banking and in the stance taken towards it by financial institutions, including the IMF and the World Bank. The system's existence is considered to be irreversible but there is an array of positions on its usefulness and legitimacy. The closest to an official definition is that given by the FSB. The shadow banking system is stated as being 'a system of credit intermediation that involves entities and activities outside the regular banking system, and raises (1) systemic risk concerns, in particular by maturity/liquidity transformation, leverage and flawed credit risk transfer, and/or (2) regulatory arbitrage concerns'.[38] These 'entities' include financial companies[39] (notably non-bank mortgage lenders offering NINA mortgage), so-called special purpose vehicles (SPV) or entities (SPE) established by investment banks and hedge funds. Thus the shadow banking system is the result of the generalisation of the originate-to-distribute intermediation model throughout the financial system along with an increase in the off-balance operations of commercial banks.[40]

The issue is what entities are considered to be outside the 'regular banking system', notably with respect to 'commercial banks', and so whether 'regular' and shadow banking are in fact parallel.[41] Through their affiliates, 'proper banks',

---

37   Financial Stability Board 2011, p. 1. The Board, set up at the 2009 London G20 summit, almost apologises for using the term: 'some authorities or market participants prefer to use other terms such as "market-based financing" instead of "shadow banking". It is important to note the use of the term "shadow banking" is not intended to cast a pejorative tone on this system of credit intermediation. However, the FSB has chosen to use the term "shadow banking" as this is most commonly employed and, in particular, has been used in the earlier G20 communications'.

38   Ibid.

39   A finance company is an organisation that originates loans for both businesses and consumers. Much like a bank, a typical finance company acts as a lending entity by extending credit. However, the main difference between a bank and a finance company is that, unlike a bank, a finance company does not accept deposits from the public. Instead, a finance company may draw funding from banks and various other money market resources (http://www.investorglossary.com/finance-company).

40   In this model, 'the four key aspects of intermediation are 1° maturity transformation: obtaining short-term funds to invest in longer-term assets; 2° liquidity transformation: using cash-like liabilities to buy harder-to-sell assets such as loans; 3° leverage: employing techniques such as borrowing money to buy fixed assets to magnify the potential gains (or losses) on an investment; 4° credit risk transfer: taking the risk of a borrower's default and transferring it from the originator of the loan to another party' (Kodres 2013).

41   This was the initial academic position, see Farhi and Cintra 2009.

e.g. US conglomerates combining retail and investment banking activities and European 'universal banks', are inside the system. Citibank would not have had to be rescued in September 2008 otherwise, nor the large European banks saved from major difficulties. A Federal Reserve of New York staff paper emphasises that 'operations of many shadow banking vehicles and activities are symbiotically intertwined with traditional banking and insurance institutions. Such inter-linkages consist in back up lines of credit, implicit guarantees to special purpose vehicles and asset management subsidiaries, the outright ownership of securitized assets on bank balance sheets, and the provision of credit puts by insurance companies'.[42]

Despite its indeterminate boundaries, estimations of the size of the shadow banking system have been made. They vary quite considerably while telling the same basic story. A Federal Reserve Bank of New York staff report estimated a year later that the net liabilities of the shadow banking system had exceeded those of the formal banking system from 1997 on, passed the $10 trillion bar in 2004 and reached a peak of some $16 trillion in 2008. They had then fallen to some $13 trillion in 2011.[43] The IMF gives much higher figures. It reports that shadow banking had started growing again and that it was $65 trillion in 2011, compared to $26 trillion in 2002. In 2011, it represented on average 25 percent of world financial assets and 11 percent of aggregate world GDP. 'The U.S. has the largest system. For a variety of historical reasons, it has a very developed non-bank asset management complex, in contrast to countries with more bank-based systems. Accordingly, investors and asset managers in other countries, such as European pension and hedge fund managers, also choose to use the U.S. system for their needs. Today, however, two-thirds of shadow banking now occurs outside the U.S., notably in the euro area and the U.K., with rapid growth in many emerging markets'.[44]

The FSB discusses the advantages that 'intermediating credit through non-bank channels can have'. These advantages are very vague and express from the outset the Board's very limited ambitions and scope for reform: 'the shadow banking system may provide market participants and corporations with an alternative source of funding and liquidity...some non-bank entities may have specialized expertise that enables them to provide certain functions in the credit intermediation chain more cost-efficiently'. The FSB is forced to admit 'that the risks in the shadow banking system can easily spill over into the regular banking system as banks often comprise part of the shadow bank-

---

42  Adrian and Ashcraft 2012.
43  Figure 1 in Adrian and Ashcraft 2012.
44  Claessens, Pozsar et al. 2012, p. 6.

ing credit intermediation chain or provide support to shadow banking entities. These risks are amplified as the chain becomes longer and less transparent'.[45] This is what occurred in 2008 when the shadow banking system provided the terrain for very rapid systemic contagion (discussed in the next chapter). Yet it has not only survived the crisis; in 2012, it started to grow anew.

### 3.4  Global Systemically Important Financial Institutions and the Global Banking Oligopoly

Recognition of an internationalised shadow banking system was followed by the actual naming of the banks that comprise it. A list of 29 global systemically important banks (G-SIBS) was established by the FSB with the help of BIS in 2011, 26 of which were American or European. Given in particular the place of the US insurer AIG in September 2008, it was completed by a list of nine global systemically important insurance companies (three American and five European). Both lists were revised in 2013.[46] Global systemic importance is 'measured in terms of the impact that a failure of a bank can have on the global financial system and wider economy'.[47] The names are determined on the basis of a number of indicators proposed by BIS: size, 'cross-jurisdictional activity', 'substitutability' and 'complexity'. BIS observes that 'banks vary widely in their structures and activities, and therefore in the nature and degree of risks they pose to the international financial system'.[48] Size is the outcome of centralisation and concentration and determines the degree of exposure to shocks. 'Cross-jurisdictional activity' is an indicator of trans-border interconnectedness e.g. the density of the direct or indirect linkages between financial corporations that can be channels for the transmission of the effects resulting from their affiliates' financial difficulties. The definition of 'substitutability' was initially developed by the US monetary and financial authorities. It concerns the extent to which in case of failure other banks can provide similar financial services (such as brokerage and underwriting) and the effects of a bank's withdrawal from a particular market. It is measured by the value of underwritten transactions in debt and equity markets. Complexity refers in particular to the amount of OTC derivatives held by a bank at their notional value. It is

---

45   Financial Stability Board 2011.
46   Changes between 2011 and 2013 include the disappearance of three European banks, notably Dexia and the addition of two Chinese banks.
47   BIS 2011, p. 4.
48   Hence the presence on the list of a very discrete and rather small US bank, State Street, on account of the size of its operations in global markets.

compounded by size.[49] 'Global systemically important banks' are 'too-big-to-fail' banks[50] once financial globalisation has fully taken place. They enjoy an 'implicit government subsidy'. As put by the Liikanen report on the European banking system, an implicit subsidy exists 'for banks that are "too systemic to fail". 90% of all implicit subsidies are channeled to the largest institutions and much less so to medium-sized and small ones'.[51]

The corporations listed by the FSB as G-SIBs form what can be named the global banking oligopoly.[52] As argued in Chapter 5, the specific mix of huge collective global monopoly power, of oligopolistic rivalry and of collusion among corporations[53] must be analysed sector by sector. In banking, the global oligopoly is still, much more so than in manufacturing industries, a market structure where the pertinence of analysing the consequences of domestic oligopoly remains important. In the UK, Lloyds, Barclays, HSCB and RBS and in France BNP Paribas, Crédit Agricole, Société Générale and BPCE hold three quarters of the domestic banking market. True rivalry only really occurs around the acquisition of small banks. Each group has its portfolio of corporate customers, each of whom can negotiate for themselves fees on foreign exchange. Some degree of competition exists in wealth management but fees to retail banking customers are on par.

Moving to the global oligopoly, acute corporate rivalry exists for the engineering of M&A deals, advisory services to transition and developing countries' governments and the floating of government loans in the international bond market. The three remaining and yet more powerful Wall Street investment banks after the 2008 financial crisis, Goldman Sachs, JP Morgan and

---

49    The Financial Crisis Inquiry Report emphasises that 'much of the risk of CDS and other derivatives was concentrated in a few of the very largest banks, investment banks, and others – such as AIG Financial Products, a unit of AIG – that dominated dealing in OTC derivatives. Among U.S. bank holding companies, 97 percent of the notional amount of OTC derivatives, millions of contracts, were traded by just five large institutions (in 2008, JPMorgan Chase, Citigroup, Bank of America, Wachovia, and HSBC) – many of the same firms that would find themselves in trouble during the financial crisis. The five largest US investment banks were also among the world's largest OTC derivatives dealers' (US Government Printing Office 2011, p. 46).
50    OCDE 2011 names them as such.
51    Implicit support is, amongst others, evident from the credit ratings of banks, which typically involve a 'stand-alone rating' and a (higher) 'support rating'.
52    See (in French) Morin 2015.
53    See above Chapter 5, section 2.

Morgan Stanley, are competing European banks out of many businesses.[54] Dominant positions in certain markets, notably foreign exchange and derivatives, are being contested by successful attempts to enter by mutual funds and hedge funds.[55] Tight oligopoly can create the conditions for collusion and market rigging to the benefit of participants. This occurred with the rigging on certain days in 2008 of the London Interbank Offered Rate LIBOR benchmark interest rate, in which Barclays, UBS, RBS, Deutsche Bank, JP Morgan, Citigroup, and Bank of America have been investigated and have started to be fined. There have been great outcries of indignation but the banks have, as with other forms of fraudulent behaviour, had the power to smother it and negotiate settlements.[56]

---

[54] 'Europe's dithering banks are losing ground to their decisive American rivals', *The Economist*, 17 October 2015, pp. 75–7.

[55] See below Chapter 10, the analysis by the IMF.

[56] Eric Toussaint (Toussaint 2014) offers an extensive list of fraudulent behaviour by large banks. He also provides an analysis of financial speculation on food resources.

CHAPTER 9

# Global Financial Contagion and Systemic Crisis in 2008

The financial crisis of 2008 is said to possess 'the distinction of being the first "post-securitization" credit crisis'.[1] In October 1929, the start of the financial crisis was a massive stock market crash. Banking crises only came later. In September 2008, there was immediately a banking crisis of huge dimensions marked by the 'withdrawal of credit'[2] between financial corporations. It was triggered by the failure of a major investment bank and saw a brutal contraction of trading in the short-term money market funds loan market. Likewise the channels of international financial contagion differed significantly from previous financial crises, including those that came with financial globalisation in the 1990s. This chapter begins by examining two major forms of financial corporations which have not yet been discussed, namely investment banks and hedge funds, as well as the scale of their use of leverage (section 1). It examines the changes in the modes of international financial contagion from the 1990s to the 2007–8 financial crisis (section 2). The chapter then turns to the particular vulnerability of European banks as illustrated by the 2011 crisis in the Eurozone (section 3).

## 1    Investment Banks and Hedge Funds

The previous chapter focused on banks as providers of credit. It discussed the deep transformations in the mechanism and main beneficiaries of credit, as banks became diversified financial conglomerates. The ground was laid for understanding the new channels of international financial contagion. Investment banks and hedge funds must now be examined for the *dramatis personæ* of the 2007–8 financial crisis to be complete. They were in fact the immediate protagonists of this crisis and it was among their ranks that the most spectacular casualties occurred.

---

1   Greenlaw et al. 2008, p. 54.
2   Recall Marx's emphasis on this notion above in the Introduction.

## 1.1 High-Risk Leverage Driven by Low Profitability

The years leading up to 2007 saw a spectacular increase in leverage. Banks have always resorted in some degree to leverage.[3] It allows a bank or other financial institution to increase the potential gains or losses on a position or an investment beyond what would be possible through its own funds. What has changed with the development of shadow banking is its level and traceability. Leverage starts to have serious implications when it is off-balance sheet and takes the form of market-dependent future cash flows. Leverage becomes lethal when banks begin to hold securities or exposures that are themselves leveraged. This is named 'embedded leverage',[4] a situation in which assets are held by a bank with high leverage in an equity fund that is itself funded by loans. Embedded leverage is what brought down Bear Stearns and Lehman Brothers. It is

> extremely difficult to measure, whether in an individual institution or in the financial system. Most structured credit products have high levels of embedded leverage, resulting in an overall exposure to loss that is a multiple of the initial investment in the underlying portfolio. Two-layer securitizations or re-securitizations, such as in the case of a collateralized debt obligation that invests in asset-backed securities, can boost embedded leverage to even higher levels.[5]

A tendency to resort to leverage in these more and more pernicious forms developed in parallel with the rapid growth of hedge funds (in particular after 2001), the creation of hedge-fund-like affiliates by formerly commercial banks, and the shift to proprietary trading by investment banks.[6] These were expressions of a single underlying process, namely the decline in the flow of value and surplus faced by the growing mass of interest-bearing capital on account of the fall in the rate of accumulation and the constraint put on fund managers to devise forms of 'investment' that amount to redistributions of already centralised value and surplus. Couched in non-Marxist language, this point is stressed by Aglietta: 'Because of the important fall in stock markets in the wake of the 2001 bursting of the Internet bubble and the fall in long term interest rates,

---

3   Whenever a financial entity's assets exceed its equity base, its balance sheet is said to be leveraged.
4   D'Hulster 2009, pp. 1–2.
5   Ibid.
6   Proprietary trading (called 'prop trading' or PPT) refers to the trading by firms in their search for profits on their own capital and not simply their customers' money.

institutional investors looked for other sources with higher returns'.[7] Or again, as put by McNally in an innovative way which may disturb some Marxists: 'the key problem for the banks (and shadow banks like hedge funds) was the classic dilemma of the falling rate of return. Too many banks were turning out much of the same stuff and profit margins were falling'.[8] A report by the European Parliament Socialist Group (PSE/EP) points to the effects of 'the enduring monetary policy of low interest rates, coupled with a deep-seated imbalance of world trade flows, resulting in massive growth of liquidities seeking attractive yields'.[9] In this context hedge funds grew, with their offer of high-yield high-risk 'alternative investments' and a 'business model' adopted to varying degrees and greater or less success by commercial and investment banks.

The principal types of leverage used by hedge funds are margin loans, securities lending and repos. They are all variants of the starting point in a chain of transactions in which hedge funds make what amount to bets on the rise or the fall of targeted assets, staking either their own money or that supplied by other financial corporations, principally investment banks, which in making such loans are in fact betting that the loaner's bets will come off and so are putting themselves at risk (as did Bear Stearns and Lehman Brothers). As discussed in the section on derivatives in Chapter 6, margin loans provide access to funds for the financing of leveraged purchases and short selling. They have no specified payback period but are characterised by a contractual stipulation that if, owing to market fluctuations, the loaning corporation considers that its loan is at risk, it can issue a 'margin call'. This requires immediate repayment by the borrower in cash, security deposit or the liquidation of existing securities.[10] Repos and reverse repos are contracts whereby one entity sells securities and agrees to repurchase them at a future date (repo) and the other buys the securities and agrees to sell them back in the future (reverse repurchase).

### 1.2   *Investment Banks*

The part played by the high-risk positions taken by certain Wall Street investment banks in the 2008 episode of the global economic and financial crisis is notorious. Today only a very small number of financial corporations are still referred to as investment banks. The term supplanted the British name mer-

---

7    Aglietta et al. 2010.
8    McNally 2014, p. 106.
9    European Parliament Socialist Group (PSE/EP) 2006.
10   The 2011 movie *Margin Call*, directed by JC Chandor with Kevin Spacey and Jeremy Irons, illustrates this situation quite well.

chant banks[11] and the French name *banques d'affaires* in the 1980s. The largest ones are American: Goldman Sachs, JP Morgan and Morgan Stanley; and Swiss,[12] notably the two giants, Crédit Suisse and UBS. Chapter 4 above discussed their activities in the production and transport of commodities. As with the failures in 2008, the New York investment banks had in fact very different profiles, notably with respect to investment and operations outside of finance in the strict sense (Goldman Sachs own very large tracts of land, particularly in South America), and to the extent of their involvement in the issuance and trading of asset-backed securities. In their banking activities, investment banks make profits as advisors and intermediaries.[13] Their revenue takes the form of fees from four types of activities: advisory and go-between services between corporations during M&As, advisory services to governments (famously Goldman Sachs for Greece) and the underwriting of corporate and government bonds (investment banking proper); fees for broking (facilitating the buying and selling of financial products for investors speculating in stocks and other securities); fees for non-proprietary trading and investments on behalf of wealth owners or smaller financial firms; finally, fees for wealth-owner asset management. From the 1990s onwards, the Wall Street investment banks engaged increasingly in proprietary trading on a large scale both in 'classical' assets and in derivative markets. They became involved in the pooling, tranching and sale of CDOs as intermediaries but some also held these speculatively in large quantities. The authors of the Commodity Futures Modernization Act of 2000 had ensured that derivatives remained unregulated. In 2004, the Securities and Exchange Commission (SEC) relaxed the net capital rule, enabling investment banks to increase the level of debt assumed.[14] They set up specialised divisions which established close relations with hedge funds. These divisions were responsible for the development of overall levels of debt of the order of 25 percent to 32 percent, exposing the banks even to small falls in the price of critical assets. The disappearance of Bear Stearns and Merrill Lynch as independent entities and the failure of Lehman Brothers were due to holding the assets of hedge funds exposed to similar levels of risk in the same categories of securities.

---

11   Cogan 2009.
12   The growth of the large Swiss banks was built on the advantages of Swiss neutrality (non-military siding) during the two World Wars (money safeguarded, intermediation for financial transactions between belligerents, etc.) and its tax-haven behaviour (strict banking secrecy), which has just started to break down.
13   See the second point in Chapter 3, 1.6.
14   Lin and Treichel 2012.

### 1.3  Hedge Funds: The Absence of Regulation as a Key Enabling Feature

Just as shadow banking is difficult to define, so too are hedge funds. This is not surprising since shadow banking is their world and their business is speculative operations on assets representing fictitious capital. Hedge funds are marked by high mortality rates. In a typical year (2011, 2012, 2013), about 1,000 are created and some 800–900 go bankrupt.[15] The stability of the well-known big names gives a distorted picture. Several semi-official definitions of hedge funds have been proposed. In 2005, an ECB publication defined a hedge fund as 'a fund whose managers receive performance-related fees and can freely use various active investment strategies to achieve positive absolute returns, involving any combination of leverage, long and short positions in securities or any other assets in a wide range of markets'.[16] In 2009, a Government Accountability Office (GAO) testimony in the US Congress named such a fund as 'a pooled investment vehicle that is privately managed and often engages in active trading of various types of securities and commodity futures and options (exempted from) US securities laws and regulations, including the requirement to register as an investment company'.[17] In 2010, lawyers involved in the preparation of the Dodd-Frank Act stated: 'the term "hedge fund" is difficult to define for legal purposes, since it does not appear to be defined anywhere in federal securities laws. No single definition of the term appears to be used by industry participants, but perhaps one of the most useful definitions of a hedge fund is that it is "any pooled investment vehicle that is privately organized, administered by professional investment managers, and not widely available to the public"'.[18] Thus lack of regulation, opacity and very high levels of personalised risk management typically characterise hedge funds. The ECB study lists the Caiman Islands, the British Virgin Islands, Bermuda and the Bahamas as being 'the most popular offshore financial centres', along with the

---

15   Data is available at http://www.hedgefundresearch.com. However, 'estimating the hedge fund mortality rate is everything but straightforward, since hedge fund managers report to databases on a voluntary basis. Managers naturally tend to stop and delay their reporting when performance turns really ugly. Thus delays in reporting do not necessarily mean that the funds are in the process of liquidation. Managers may wait several months for the performance to improve before reporting again'. http://www.thehedgefundjournal.com/node/6748.
16   Garbarivicius and Dierick 2005, p. 5.
17   GAO 2009.
18   Ruane and Seitzinger 2010.

Channel Islands for EU hedge funds.[19] Box 9.1 sets out the key features of hedge funds identified by a report by the Socialist Group of the European Parliament.

---

BOX 9.1: KEY HEDGE FUND CHARACTERISTICS (PSE/EP 2006)

**Investment strategies:** Position-taking in a wide range of markets. Free to choose various investment techniques and instruments, including short selling, leverage and derivatives.

**Return objective:** Positive absolute returns under all market conditions. Usually managers also commit their own money, because preservation of capital is important.

**Incentive structure:** Typically a 2% management fee. And a 20% performance fee, often conditioned by a certain hurdle rate which must be exceeded before managers receive any performance fees.

**Subscription/Redemption:** Predefined schedule with quarterly or monthly subscription and redemption. Lock-up periods for up to several years until first redemption.

**Domicile:** Offshore financial centres with low tax and a 'light touch' regulatory regime, as well as some onshore financial centres.

**Legal structure:** Private investment partnership that provides pass-through tax treatment or offshore investment corporation.

**Managers:** May or may not be registered or regulated by financial supervisors. Managers serve as general partners in private partnership agreements.

**Investor base:** High net worth individuals and institutional investors (pension funds, insurance-institutions and others). Not widely available to the public. Securities issued take form of private placements.

**Regulation:** Generally minimal or no regulatory oversight due to their offshore residence or 'light touch' approach by onshore regulators; exempted from many investor protection requirements.

**Disclosure:** Voluntary or very limited (in many cases no) disclosure.

Source: PSE/EP 2006.

---

19   Garbaravicius and Dierick 2005, pp. 12–13.

The PSE/EP report points out that 'it would be inaccurate to assign the extensive use of short-selling, leverage and derivatives exclusively to hedge funds, since other financial companies, including banks and other registered and unregistered investment companies, also engage in such operations. The key difference is that hedge funds do not have any restrictions on the type of instruments or strategies they can use owing to their unregulated or lightly regulated nature'.[20] The PSE/EP report dwells on the differences between mutual funds and hedge funds. Mutual funds are highly regulated and restricted in their choice of investments. They are measured on relative performance provided by market indexes or the returns on other funds. By contrast, hedge funds promise and are expected to deliver absolute returns. Mutual funds remunerate managers based on the percentage of assets under management, while hedge funds remunerate managers with very high fees that are geared to performance – fees are based on two components: a 2 percent management fee charged on an asset-under-management (AUM) basis, plus a performance fee of 20 percent. Hedge funds make much higher, indeed qualitatively higher, minimum investment requirements (an average $1m) than do mutual funds. Finally, very little of the investment manager's own money is usually invested in mutual funds, while hedge fund founders, particularly those of almost all the numerous small ones, stake their personal fortune.

The number of funds seen as composing the 'hedge fund industry' in the narrow sense (stand-alone corporations) trebled from 1998 to early 2007, the estimated number of funds growing globally from more than 3,000 to more than 9,000, and assets under management from $200 billion to more than $2 trillion globally. In 2007, $1.5 trillion of these assets were estimated to be managed by US proprietors.[21] After a brief period of retreat following the 2008 financial hurricane, this sum has grown again. In April 2012, their estimated size was $2.13 trillion.[22] By 2005, approximately a quarter of the money managed came from pension funds and significant amounts from other institutional investors, ranging from insurance companies to academic foundations. Pension funds purport to generate long-term flows of income to meet their commitments, implying in principle that highly risky forms of investment should only be a marginal activity. The losses they suffered in 2008 resulted not only from the sharp fall of stock markets but also from their investments in assets handled by investment banks and hedge funds.

---

20   PSE/EP 2006, p. 5.
21   GAO 2009.
22   *Wall Street Journal*, 19 April 2012.

TABLE 9.1   *Top ten US and European hedge funds (2007)*

| Top 10 US hedge funds | Assets under management in billion dollars | Top 10 European hedge funds | Assets under management in billion dollars |
| --- | --- | --- | --- |
| JP Morgan / Highbridge | 33.1 | Barclays Global Advisors | 19.0 |
| Goldman Asset Management | 32.5 | Man Group/AHL | 18.8 |
| Bridgewater | 30.2 | GLC Partners | 15.8 |
| D.E. Shaw | 27.3 | Landsowne Partners | 14.0 |
| Farallon | 26.2 | Brevan Howard | 12.1 |
| Renaissance Technologies | 26.0 | Blue Crest Capital | 11.2 |
| Och-Ziff Capital | 21.0 | Sloane Robinson | 11.1 |
| ESL Investments | 17.5 | HSBC | 10.9 |
| Tudor | 14.9 | Marshall Wace Investments | 10.9 |
| Citigroup Alternative Investments | 14.1 | | 9.6 |

SOURCE: *ALPHA MAGAZINE*, 'TOP 100 HEDGE FUNDS, 2007'.

Despite the large number of hedge funds, the activity is in fact highly concentrated in all its facets. Three quarters of all funds are US-owned and three quarters of European funds are UK-owned. In 2006, the largest 200 funds with assets under management (AUM) superior to $2 billion accounted for three quarters of the total. For a number of years, the top funds had AUM ranging from $50 to $130 billion (the figure claimed by Bridgewater).[23] Two of the big Wall Street investment banks were in the US list: JP Morgan Asset Management and Goldman Asset Management. Citigroup Alternative Investments is not far behind. Three other truly stand-alone funds have their founder's name. Bridgewater Associates is the exception, not named after its 1975 founder Ray Dalio who was CEO until 2011, and remains one of the company's three chief investment officers. Today one of the most prominent hedge funds is Paulson & Co., set up by its founder and President, John Paulson, in 1994.[24] The ten

---

23   Hedge Fund Industry Trends, http://www.allaboutalpha.com/blog/.
24   Several of the entries in Wikipedia concerning these funds have been quite obviously vetted by the firms concerned. The one on Paulson & Co. is a case-in-point and quite helpful

European funds were in fact British, two of which belonged to the UK's largest diversified financial conglomerates, Barclays and HSBC. A large corporation like Paulson has some 50 professionals. But the smaller funds are manned by no more than ten traders. Risk management decision-making is carried out in-house, but particularly in small funds operational tasks are entrusted to other financial firms. Accounting, investor services, and performance measurement are often outsourced to specialised firms.

### 1.4 Highly Leveraged Speculative Investments Alongside 'Vulture' Hedge Fund Operations

Studies on hedge funds identify an extremely wide range of casino operations comprising different levels of risk and returns. The oldest, so to speak classical, operations are named 'directional hedges', where managers try to anticipate market movements and offer returns on derivatives, foreign exchange and equity markets. Macro hedge funds follow a 'top-down' approach and try to take advantage of major economic trends or events. Funds focusing on emerging markets and directional hedge funds with a regional focus use a 'bottom-up' approach of 'asset-picking' in given markets and search for inefficiencies in others, notably developing markets. The second type of classical operations are those of so-called 'market neutral funds' (also referred to as 'arbitrage' or 'relative value' funds), which look for relative value or arbitrage opportunities to try to exploit various price discrepancies while avoiding exposure to market-wide movements. Returns show lower volatility, but their implementation requires medium-to-high leverage in order to benefit from small pricing distor-

---

with regard to information. It specifies: 'Paulson & Co. Inc. ("Paulson") was established by its founder and President, John Paulson, in 1994. It is an investment management firm, employee-owned (e.g. partner-owned)... It provides services to investment vehicle pools and manages accounts for banking institutions, corporations and pension and profit sharing plans. Since founding, the firm has continued to develop its investment capabilities and infrastructure and as of June 13, 2012, had approximately $24 billion dollars in assets under management. Paulson employs approximately 120 employees in offices located in New York, London and Hong Kong. There are approximately 50 investment professionals in the firm, including John Paulson who is the Portfolio Manager for all funds under management... Members of the Paulson advisory Board include Alan Greenspan, former chairman of the Fed and the Harvard professor Martin Feldstein. External investors in the Paulson funds are financial institutions, corporate and public pension funds, endowments, foundations and high net worth individuals... All of the firm's strategies are based upon the same underlying investment philosophy and objectives of capital preservation, above average returns, low volatility, and low correlation to the broad markets'. http://en.wikipedia.org/wiki/Paulson_&_Co (accessed 03 November 2013).

tions, particularly in bond and other credit markets. There are also operations with predator-like features, coming under the heading of 'event driven strategies'. The PSE/EP report writes that they

> try to take advantage of 'special situations' in a company's life, such as mergers and acquisitions, reorganizations or bankruptcies. These strategies lie somewhere in the middle of the volatility spectrum, with corresponding medium volatility and low to medium leverage. Some event driven hedge funds, specializing in securities of distressed companies, try to exploit the fact that it is difficult to value such securities and that institutional investors are prohibited from investing in them.

Such funds have come to be named 'vulture funds', waiting to pick over the remains of a rapidly weakening company. In this area hedge funds work hand-in-hand with private equity corporations, the latter doing the 'on-site' job of restructuring targeted firms before re-selling them. Hedge funds have not only preyed on industrial corporations near bankruptcy, but have also targeted developing country government securities in situations close to default,[25] as well as other less lucky hedge funds.

As noted *inter alia* by an OECD study,[26] it is difficult to find hard data on hedge fund leverage. Estimates range from very conservative ones in the order of 1.5 percent by fund management industry spokesmen[27] to extremely high ones in the order of 140 percent by some financial analysts.[28] The figures examined by the OECD study suggest that 'about 25% of gross returns are absorbed by fees paid to hedge fund managers and around 20% are absorbed by execution costs to prime broker dealers, so about 45% in all'. Thus for the 11.3 percent return reported in 2006, hedge funds would have earned 20.5 percent from their operations. Earning gross returns of 20 percent or so implies recourse to quite high leverage. 'On average in 2007 it was in the order of 4, but differed considerably according to fund styles and assets. It was in the order of 19 for fixed income arbitrage and considered to be very high for derivatives'.[29] Subsequently it was this magnitude that turned out to be right. The World Bank

---

25   See the entries under the word 'vulture' on the CADTM website.
26   Blundell-Wignall 2007.
27   http://www.hedgefundfacts.org/hedge/statistics/leverage/.
28   Gross leverage in the hedge fund industry averaged 143 percent from 2005 onwards according to a financial consultant citing Bloomberg data from Morgan Stanley. http://www.thinkadvisor.com/2013/01/08/eight-hedge-fund-trends-in-2013?page=1.
29   Blundell-Wignall 2007, pp. 45–46.

study already cited estimates that at the time of the collapse of the subprime asset market, the riskiest funds had a debt-to-equity ratio of 20 to 1.[30]

### 1.5 Investment Banks' Proprietary Trading and Prime Brokerage for Hedge Funds

After 2001 and increasingly in the run up to 2007–8, the 'directional hedges', e.g. the pure gambles, made by hedge funds in anticipation of market movements, moved from foreign exchange and stock markets to pooled mortgage-backed and asset-backed securities. The funds required for leverage were largely provided by the small group of investment banks operating in New York and London. By the mid-2000s, hedge funds had become very important as counter-parties to traders at investment banks. Acting as prime brokers to hedge funds, investment banks earned a range of high fee services including transaction execution, financing, securities lending, etc. On the basis of available data, the PSE/EP report estimated that in 2006, approximately 30 percent of total US equity trading commissions in the US came from orders handled for hedge funds and that the situation was similar for Europe (in fact the City). Along with fees for other services, hedge fund related activities represented about 15–20 percent of investment bank profit. The report notes that this meant that if hedge funds were to face strong difficulties, so would investment banks. But the investment banks had started to develop proprietary trading and even to extend it to the business of asset pooling. In certain instances they had a particularly high degree of exposure, not only as the result of liquidity creation to highly leveraged hedge funds, but also on account of their own proprietary trading on the hedge fund model.

This was the case for Lehman Brothers, whose balance sheet was examined by the Federal Reserve Bank of New York after its failure.[31] At the end of 2007, the two largest classes of assets were long positions in non-proprietary and proprietary trading. Collateralised lending reflected Lehman's role as prime broker to hedge funds in the form in particular of reverse repos;[32] much of this

---

30   Lin and Treichel 2012, p. 11.
31   Adrian and Shin 2009.
32   A practice in which a bank or other financial institution buys securities or assets with the proviso that it will resell these same securities or assets to the same seller for an agreed-upon price on a certain day (often the next day). This is done in order to raise short-term capital. It is the equivalent of a short-term loan with the securities or asset serving as collateral. A reverse repurchase agreement is the same as a repurchase agreement from the perspective of the buyer rather than the seller. It is also called a matched sale transaction or simply a reverse. http://financial-dictionary.thefreedictionary.com/.

was short-term, often overnight. The cash holding was extremely small, a little over 1 percent of the total balance sheet. Lehman's own liabilities were also short-term. The largest component was collateralised borrowing, including again repos. Short positions in financial instruments and other inventory positions sold but not yet purchased was the next largest component. Long-term debt only represented 18 percent of total liabilities. They included the cash deposits of Lehman's customers, especially its hedge fund clientele. Hedge fund customers' deposits are subject to withdrawal on demand and proved to be an important factor in Lehman's collapse.

In another report, some more general, revealing observations are made by Federal Reserve Bank of New York staff members about the overall constraints placed on investment banks, notably 'the pursuit of shareholder value by raising return on equity', which drove them to take ever-higher risk in the mortgage-backed securities (MBS) market.

> For a bank, expanding its balance sheet means purchasing more securities or increasing its lending. But expanding assets means finding new borrowers. Someone has to be on the receiving end of new loans. When all the good borrowers already have a mortgage, the bank has to lower its lending standards in order to capture new borrowers. The new borrowers are those who were previously shut out of the credit market but who suddenly find themselves showered with credit.[33]

The turn in the housing market saw a downward accelerating cumulative process, the fall in real-estate prices leading to a rapid increase in default rates by borrowers with adjustable-rate mortgages (see Chapter 8), which made the position of hedge funds and investment banks, engaged deeply in subprime assets and even in higher quality MBS, an untenable one. The effects of 'embedded leverage', assets held by a bank with high leverage in a hedge fund that is itself funded by loans, came back into play with a vengeance.

Aglietta calls this the 'cumulative interplay' of credit risk by banks, having granted high-risk loans, and liquidity risk by hedge funds, having borrowed heavily to attain high leverage. This interplay can become systemic in a matter of hours. Highly leveraged financial institutions rely on short-term debt to sustain their capital and are at the mercy of lenders. Their capacity to roll over this debt can vanish at the slightest hint that they will be unable to repay. Any rumour of asset or derivatives losses may be enough to drive a financial corporation to collapse. In the case of a bank possessing systemically important

---

33   Adrian and Shin 2010.

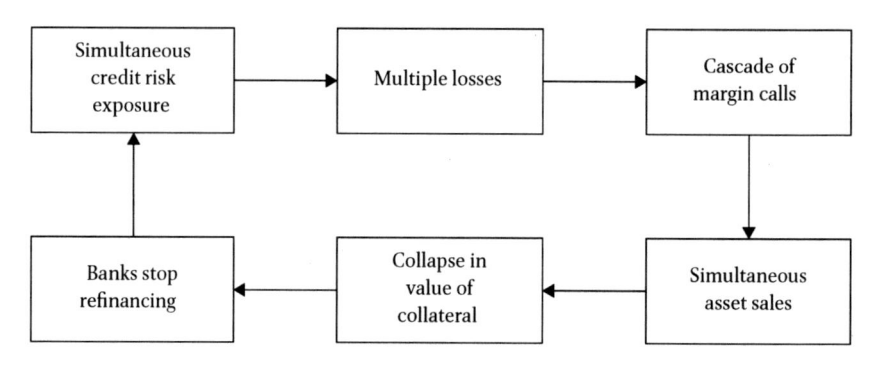

FIGURE 9.1 *Interplay of credit and liquidity risk.*
SOURCE: AGLIETTA ET AL. 2010, P. 175.

features, this will have contagious effects per se, but it can also dry up entire loan markets, notably short-term ones such as the New York money market funds (MMFs). The cross-Atlantic shadow banking system makes this contagion international.

## 2      The Channels of International Financial Contagion

The 2007–8 crisis witnessed forms of international financial contagion specific to securitisation and shadow banking. They are best understood when approached historically. The development of financial globalisation saw the emergence from the 1980s onwards of international financial crises, each successive phase marked by partly overlapping forms of financial contagion and its different channels. None have been entirely global, affecting specific points in the global financial system each time.

### 2.1     *The Channels of International Financial Contagion in the 1990s*

The most satisfactory introduction to financial contagion available in the literature is that of Kaminsky, Reinhart and Végh, who define it as 'episodes in which there are significant *immediate* effects in a number of countries following an event – that is, when the consequences are *fast and furious* and evolve over a matter of hours or days'.[34] This definition is based principally on work related to contagion during the second 1994 Mexican crisis, the 1997–8 Asian

---

34    Kaminsky, Reinhart and Végh 2003, p. 55, original emphasis.

crisis, and the 1998 Russian-provoked LTCM episode on Wall Street. During this period the determinant financial linkages were cross-border capital flows initiated by large international commercial banks. Crises were marked by the calling of loans and the withdrawal of credit lines. Contagion, in particular from Mexico to South American countries, and later from Asia, also occurred quite strongly through what is named 'common-creditor contagion', which takes place when banks cut back on loans to one or several countries, or funds withdraw from national bond markets which were not initially in difficulty. This was accentuated by investor behaviour, notably the phenomena of herding which has now been well analysed.[35] Hong Kong's financial markets were badly destabilised by speculative operations on the part of mutual funds and hedge funds.[36] The recessionary impact on production, trade and employment came through credit crunches as local banks in turn withdrew credit lines to local firms.

Abrupt changes in investor behaviour also took the form in 1998 of a sudden recognition by banks of risks due to high levels of leverage. The need felt by a number of large Wall Street banks to come to the rescue of Long Term Capital Management heralded measures taken in 2008 to avoid the bankruptcy of Bear Stearns. An early Fed staff study on this recue suggested that a strong role was played by the fear on the part of banks in the rescue group[37] that their own high credit risk exposure to LTCM was likely to be the case for others. Suspicion on the part of banks about the state of each other's balance sheet situations anticipated the particular type of credit crunch experienced in 2007 and 2008, as did the temporary cutting off of lending by money markets to hedge funds. In 1998, the difficulties were sufficiently confined so as to enable a consortium of private banks (at the request of the Fed, of course) to steer through the crisis by collective action. In 2007 and 2008, this was no longer so. The explosion of securitisation and the growth of transatlantic shadow banking had made it impossible.

---

35   The first formulation of herding is by Keynes regarding investor behaviour in stock markets, using the beauty contest metaphor.
36   For a survey of the evidence concerning the important role played by highly leveraged funds in speculative attacks against the Hong Kong dollar in August of 1998, see Kaminsky et al. 2003.
37   The consortium of lenders that met to bail out LTCM included Goldman Sachs, Merrill Lynch, JP Morgan, Morgan Stanley, Dean Witter, the Travelers Group, Union Bank of Switzerland, Barclays, Bankers Trust, Chase Manhattan, Credit Suisse First Boston, Deutsche Bank, Lehman Brothers, BNP Paribas, and Société Générale.

```
        ┌─────────────────────┐
        │   European          │
        │   Global Banks      │
        │   High Risk Affiliates │
        └─────────────────────┘
       ↙          ↓          ↘
┌──────────┐  ┌──────────┐  ┌──────────┐
│   U.S.   │  │   U.S.   │  │   U.S.   │
│Money Market│→│   SIVs   │→│   MBS    │
│  Funds   │  │Investment│  │   ABS    │
│  [MMFs]  │  │   Banks  │  │   CDO    │
└──────────┘  └──────────┘  └──────────┘
```

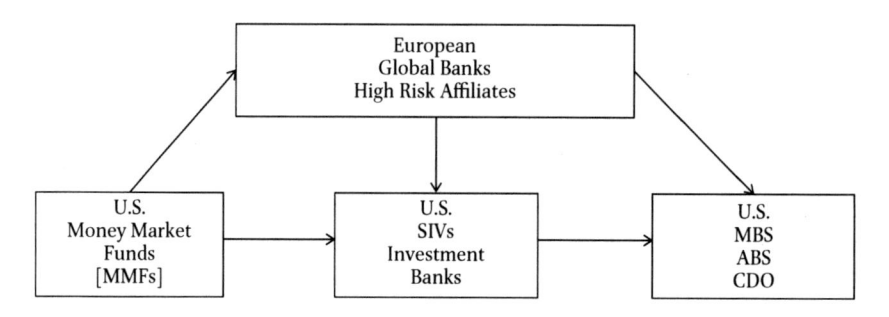

FIGURE 9.2 *European Banks within the Global Shadow Banking System.*
SOURCE: AUTHOR.

## 2.2  Contagion Through the Transatlantic Shadow Banking System

Since circa 2012, several large emerging countries have been caught up again by financial contagion in the new forms discussed in the last chapter. However, in 2007–8, the terrain of the crisis was the transatlantic shadow banking system. A popular story told by European politicians, certainly by French ones, is that the financial crisis of 2007–8 and the subsequent world recession were solely of US making and responsibility. European banks were, on the contrary, willing buyers of ABS and MBS and active participants in the shadow banking network of financial transactions. When the subprime market collapsed they had massive holdings of dubious high-risk assets. Critical nodes of contagion in the transatlantic network were also the London and New York interbank markets and the New York MMF markets.

The active involvement of European banks – some as speculators with their teams of trained traders, others as inexperienced portfolio managers with client savings to invest – was confirmed by the course of events in the summer of 2007. They warrant a brief recall. Bear Stearns announced losses on MBS in hedge-fund-like affiliates on 16 July and in the same period a medium-size German bank, Deutsche Industriebank (IKB), was unable to rollover part of its ABS. On account of its low international profile, not much notice was taken. This was not the case when BNP Paribas announced on 7 August that it had frozen two funds. Then three German banks of an unexpected category, namely Lander banks, announced their exposure to the US subprime market and requested help from the Bundesbank. Systemic reciprocal suspicion by banks about the state of each other's balance sheets set in, with London as its epicentre. In the interbank or LIBOR (London Interbank Offered Rate) market where banks make unsecured, short-term (overnight to three-month) loans to each other at rates agreed among themselves, very large, well-known banks refused overnight loans. The LIBOR average interest rate for loans made a huge leap as did the spread of the Fed-secured overnight interest rate at which New York banks lend to each other to meet the central bank's reserve requirements.

The financial crisis also saw new form of runs, notably on short-term money markets. A bank is run when its depositors withdraw their savings, as occurred with Northern Rock in September 2007. Since deposit insurance has severely limited runs on commercial banks, this proved to be the only case. But runs can occur on other financial institutions. Bear Stearns experienced essentially a run in March 2008 when hedge funds, which typically entrust a sizable amount of 'money-like' assets to their prime brokers, pulled out their liquidities. As defined by a Federal Reserve Board discussion paper, a market can be characterised 'as being run when it does not issue new paper during a week despite having a substantial share of its outstanding paper scheduled to mature'.[38] This happened first to the US asset-backed commercial paper (ABCP) market which suffered a $190 billion contraction in August 2007 and a further $160 billion fall by the end of the same year. There was another contraction in March before the sale of Bear Stearns to JP Morgan. The culminating point of the crisis in September 2008 saw the most spectacular episode of collective financial run. It took place in MMFs markets and concerned different types of short-term debt (repos, ABCP, MMF shares). These were initially perceived as safe and 'money-like', but then found to be imperfectly collateralised. In the days following Lehman's failure, one money market fund holding Lehman commercial paper, the Reserve Primary Fund, 'broke the buck', that is, marked the net asset value of the fund below the $1 per share that investors normally expect. Within a few days, the panic spread to other money market fund managers. When investors randomly chose funds to run from, they create self-fulfilling market collapses. Faced with a run, most MMFs sold assets at fire-sale prices. The speed and intensity of contagion revealed that following the advent of securitisation and of shadow banking, previously unsuspected degrees of interconnectedness had become a truly central feature of the global financial system.

## 3  Specific Systemic Vulnerability in the European Banking System

In the US, the measures taken by the government and the Fed to contain the financial crisis can be considered to have met their objectives inasmuch as US

---

38   Covitz et al. 2009.

financial markets have not experienced any new phase of turmoil. A major reason is that the Fed acted from 2008 to 2014 as 'dealer of last resort',[39] transferring to its balance sheet huge amounts of what were no more than 'junk bonds'.[40] Quite extensive restructuring and consolidation, e.g. concentration, took place. The US Treasury and the Fed have also seen to it that the government bond markets remain the largest and certainly the safest and most liquid bond in the world, guaranteed by the US government's 'full faith and credit'. The Eurozone, on the contrary, experienced a second major banking crisis in 2010 related to the quasi-collapse of regional banks and the sky-rocketing of government debt in Spain and to Greece's difficulties in serving its debt. As of late 2015, concern has grown about several major banks. These recurrent events reflect the vulnerability of the bank-dominated European financial system and the considerable politico-institutional deficiencies of the EU and the ECB. This requires a brief review of the politico-institutional setting.

### 3.1 The Maastricht Treaty Construction

During the first two years of the financial crisis, the discourse of European governments was that their banks were victims of a situation for which the US bore the essential responsibility. This could no longer be sustained for the subsequent banking crisis known under the misleading term of the 'sovereign debt crisis'. The 2010–13 events exposed the true nature of the European financial and banking system, namely the juxtaposition of national banking systems, both totally open and yet each different from the others, and the juxtaposition of banks of very differing strengths, banking models and geographical scope, all within the context of globalised capital flows. The very narrow mandate of the ECB, with control of inflation as almost its sole task, on which much debate had for a long time focused, hid a construction with much deeper flaws.

The Euro area is a monetary union amongst 17 countries out of 25, with non-Members still having their say. These 17 countries are marked by strong differences in economic structure which the Maastricht and subsequent treaties have constantly aggravated. The issue is not simply the absence of 'federal government', but the priority given in the treaties to 'free and undistorted competition' as the base of the whole construction. This has bred

---

39   Mehrling 2010.
40   Under the large-scale asset purchase program (LSAP), the Fed bought not only government bonds but also a wide range of longer-term private securities, including mortgage issued or guaranteed by the government-sponsored agencies (Fannie Mae and Freddie Mac). http://www.federalreserve.gov/faqs/what-are-the-federal-reserves-large-scale-asset-purchases.htm.

'non-cooperative' behaviour among governments as among firms. Truly European projects such as the ICT project Esprit have long been dismantled. EU and Eurozone decisions are painful compromises that never mask divergences that have increased over the last years and in which a dimension of diktat by certain countries has crept in, not to speak of the increasingly strong influence of corporate lobbies in EU decision-making (as discussed above in Chapter 4). In the Eurozone, the banking crisis in a single currency area has made direct and indirect labour costs the main if not the sole variables of economic policy. The highly 'non-cooperative' arena paved the way for financial speculation on interest rate differentials and, as the 2010 banking crisis broke out, worsened the politico-institutional deficiencies. It took two years for the ECB to take 'state-of-emergency' measures in 2012 in support of creditor banks and funds in a commitment to provide them with unlimited support through the buying of their insecure government bonds. A little later the same year, the European Stability Mechanism (ESM) and the European Financial Stability Fund (EFSF) were set up to basically organise the transfer of debt from private creditors to Eurozone governments. Another important point is the lack of a similar degree of authority over banks of the ECB and the European Banking Authority as witnessed in the weak reliability of stress tests due to inexact bank reporting.[41]

### 3.2  Asymmetric Intra-European Bank Relationships and the Effects of Shadow Banking

As indicated previously, European domestic banking systems are highly concentrated and the large banks are highly internationalised, some principally within the EU (e.g. BNP Paribas and Société Générale), others mainly outside Europe (Santander) and others both within the EU and globally (Deutsche Bank and Barclays). In the EU, internationalisation, often incorrectly named 'integration', has taken three forms. The first is that of mergers and acquisitions. BNP Paribas has been particularly active with the acquisition of the big Italian bank BNL in 2006, and of Fortis in Belgium in 2008. The second form is the establishment of branch offices where, as documented by the Liikanen report, the intensity of cross-border bank-branch penetration differs

---

[41] The most spectacular example is that of Dexia that required a first bail-out in 2008, passed the EBA's stress test in the summer of 2011 but three months later, in October, required a further rescue from the French and Belgian governments and then yet a further one a year later. Well before becoming a minister Yanis Varoufakis denounced this situation. http://yanisvaroufakis.eu/2014/10/27/the-ecbs-stress-tests-and-our-banking-dis-union-a-case-of-gross-institutional-failure/.

significantly between countries.[42] The lowest degrees by assets are those of Germany (5.2 percent) and of France (3.3 percent). The report comments caustically that these countries 'tend to export banking services to other Member States and are home to large banking groups'.[43] In other EU countries, on the contrary, the retail banking sector is dominated by foreign banks from other European countries. In some cases they possess more than 80 percent or 90 percent of total assets. The third form was, up to 2012, that of large inter-bank credit flows from the UK, Germany and France to banks and real-estate and building firms in Ireland and Southern Europe, particularly Spain, coupled with transactions in OTC markets in which non-bank financial corporations were involved.

In the absence of institutions possessing the mandate, authority and money-creating firepower of the US Treasury and the Fed, the fusion of commercial and investment banking, including hedge-fund-type high risk investments by the affiliates of very large banks heightened the risks associated with the shadow banking system for Europe. Contrary to what is often thought, this system is global and the EU has a massive share. In 2011, the US had the largest share of 35 percent with assets of $23 trillion, but it was down from 44 percent in 2005. The Financial Stability Board estimates the euro area share to be about the same with some $22 trillion assets, in addition to that of the UK with $9 trillion of estimated off-balance sheet assets.[44] The incapacity of ECB and Eurozone Member central banks to impose on banks stress tests with a degree of rigour approaching that of the Fed was seen in 2009, again in 2010, and notoriously so in 2011.[45] An OECD study points to the particular lack of 'transparent accounting', considering that 'risk exposures in large [European] SIFIs cannot be properly quantified let alone be controlled'.[46]

### 3.3 From Imported to Self-Generated Financial Crisis in the EU

The expressions are those used by the Liikanen report when discussing the 2008 and the 2010 crises. The involvement of European banks in the international shadow banking system makes the word 'imported' highly debatable, but it will be used at this point. When the crisis broke out in September 2008,

---

42  Liikanen report, table 2.3.2, p. 17.
43  Liikanen report, p. 18.
44  Jeffers and Plihon 2013. They quote another estimation by Bouveret 2011 in which the size of the European shadow banking system is $13 trillion.
45  The EBA press releases published on its website following the stress tests carried out since 2009 are remarkable exercises in cant.
46  Blundell-Wignall 2012, p. 19.

the price of bank shares on stock markets fell brutally, bringing these markets down with them even before the start of the US recession proper. The degree to which the collapse had hit the derivative markets was un-assessable. It became difficult for even the biggest and strongest banks to access either short- or long-term funding. Banks strongly funded in the short-term money market faced liquidity crisis. Massive injections were made by G7 central banks, but in the EU many banks with liquidity problems ran out of eligible collateral for central bank support. In some EU countries, smaller banks or savings institutions were creditors to larger banks, often across borders as in the case of Germany's northern European neighbours. 'The amounts lent exceeded in many cases the capital of the lending institutions. The government-led bailout of larger banks thus became imperative. Without it, many smaller banks would also not have survived the fourth quarter of 2008 unaided'.[47] So the UK, Germany and France followed the example of Paulson and mounted a rescue programme of similar dimensions. Banks that did not receive explicit state aid from European governments benefited from that of the US. This was the case of AIG creditors who had insured obligations of many financial institutions, including European banks, through the use of credit default swaps (CDS), and proved unable to meet its calls as the crisis progressed. As observed by the EU report: 'Had the US allowed AIG to fail, it is not at all clear how any of the banks exposed to AIG counterparty risk would have fared faced with the additional losses (EU banks included), the drain on their capital, and the indirect effects of the turmoil that would have followed in the markets to which they were exposed'.[48] Banks inside the shadow banking system passed on their difficulties to customer banks. Eastern European countries suffered 'common-creditor contagion'. This takes place when banks cut back on loans to one or several countries, or funds withdraw from national bond markets not initially in difficulty. Such withdrawal triggers credit crunches affecting industrial and service firms. In 2009, the denial of credit rollover by major European banks to entire banking systems in the Baltic countries sent them into recession.

Since 2010, 'endogenous' financial crisis has characterised the European and particularly the Continental banking system. Within the institutional conditions recalled above, the EU and the ECB bear the responsibility for the Euro-centred second crisis episode of the financial system, on a number of counts. The large European banks had developed investment portfolios by 2007 which already contained both US ABS and MBS and European public debt. They had also made large loans to Irish and Spanish banks allowing these in turn to make

---

47  Liikanen report, p. 6.
48  Liikanen report, pp. 21–2.

massive loans to firms and households during the housing and construction bubble. In the wake of the 2008 crisis, European banks kept junk assets on their off-balance accounts and under-provisioned for irrecoverable debt.[49] With the exception of the UK, little or nothing was done to reduce the opacity of large bank management despite the support that governments were giving to them. Then they were given leeway to escape true stress tests. In October 2009, the month before the threat of Greek default came to be known, the European Banking Authority reassured investors and governments that:

> Should economic conditions be more adverse than currently expected... the potential credit and trading losses over the years 2009–10 could amount to almost €400 bn. However, the financial position and expected results of banks are sufficient to maintain an adequate level of capital also under such negative circumstances... This resilience of the banking system reflects the recent increase in earnings forecasts and, to a large extent, the important support currently provided by the public sector to the banking institutions, notably through capital injections and asset guarantees, which has augmented their capital buffers.[50]

Yet a year and a half later, in the middle of the 'sovereign debt' crisis, the report on the new tests stated that 'in total, eight banks of the 90 participating in the EBA 2011 stress test exercise had a CT1 ratio under the adverse scenario below the set 5% benchmark... mitigating measures have been put in place for all banks with a post stress capital ratio below 5%, and deemed sufficient'.[51] Dexia, Bankia, the bigger Spanish *cajas* which had to be saved only a little later, all satisfied the EBA benchmarks.[52] In the case of big banks, notably the French ones, exposure to the sovereign debt crisis came from under-provision of loans to banks in Southern Europe, notably Spain, which themselves held irrecoverable corporate loans as unemployment and the effects of Troika policies pushed countries into recession.

In the first months of 2010, access to debt capital markets started to close, as in 2008, for all but the strongest European banks. By May 2010, CDS spreads were already higher than after the collapse of Lehman (rising to even higher

---

49  The IMF September 2011 Global Financial Stability Report emphasises this.
50  http://www.eba.europa.eu/risk-analysis-and-data/eu-wide-stress-testing/2009.
51  http://www.eba.europa.eu/risk-analysis-and-data/eu-wide-stress-testing/2011.
52  Financial analysts expressed high scepticism, so much so that the EBA had to undertake new tests only six months later. See www.ft.com/intl/cms/s/0/04993d2a-ef6f-11e0-941e-00144feab49a.html#axzz3HjjU5WXn.

levels in 2011 and 2012). The most affected were smaller and medium-sized banks, in Portugal, Spain and Italy. In Greece, all banks lost their access to capital markets. As the crisis developed, US investors, mostly hedge funds, fearing that European banks would have to write down a big portion of their Greek debt, began to reduce their exposures in the Eurozone. In its 'crisis narrative', the Liikanen report reveals the structural dependence of European banks on US MMFs. At the height of the crisis in 2011, 'most European banks, lost their access to US funding. The ECB's swap line with the Federal Reserve in the USA provided emergency assistance... In September 2011 the debt capital markets both in Europe and the United States were closed to even the strongest banks and would not open for the rest of 2011'.[53] The August 2011 edition of the *Economist* quotes a US money fund manager saying: 'it is just easier to say to clients "we don't have any exposure to Europe" than to try to explain the differences'. Academic research on decisions by MMFs in 2011 documents the way that 'financial intermediaries transmit distress across firms' (other financial corporations).[54]

The 2010–11 sovereign debt cum banking crisis put a halt to the little financial integration that had taken place. The Liikanen report expresses its concern over further fragmentation. 'There has been a decline or even a reversal of some cross-border credit flows; banks have increasingly focused on their home markets'.[55] A new ECB stress test and examination of compliance with Basel rules regarding banks' own equity (3 percent) was organised in 2014. The ECB has negotiated a new extension with the BIS for the enacting of the rules

---

53   Liikanen Report, p. 10. The OECD study provides further details: 'US money market funds (MMFs) have been huge creditors to EU banks – funding more than US$ 650bn in this way. As solvency concerns rose, they have shortened the maturity of lending and cut exposures sharply. It is for this reason that coordinated dollar swap arrangements have again been put in place by major central banks in September 2011 and more forcefully at the start of December 2011'. The study emphasises 'the interconnectedness of US banks to Europe in the case of CDS derivatives [which] underlines how the EU crisis could quickly return to the United States in the event of insolvencies within Europe' (Blundell-Wignall 2012, p. 5 and p. 13).

54   See Chernenko and Sunderam 2012. Their results demonstrate *inter alia* that 'problems at some firms raising financing from an intermediary can be detrimental to other firms raising financing from the same intermediary, that creditworthy issuers may encounter financing difficulties because of risk taking by the funds from which they raise financing and that money market fund risk taking may have spillover effects to the broader economy'.

55   Liikanen report, p. 11.

and has allowed banks to pursue what is called the 'risk-weighting of assets'.[56] This is the weighting by banks themselves of the risks of their different forms of off-balance exposure. As an OECD study puts it: 'risk-weighted asset optimisation has made nonsense of the Basel rules ... Systemically-important banks are permitted to use their own internal models and derivatives to alter the very risk characteristics of assets to which the capital weighting rules apply'.[57] The Liikanen report's recommendation for a stricter approach has not been followed. The results are, in the language of mainstream economics, excessive risk-taking, misallocation of public resources to the banking sector and the distortion of competition. Yet the European Commission, so given to ensuring 'level playing fields', waives this where large banks are concerned.

### 3.4  Greece as an in vivo Political and Social Experiment

The presentation in the media of the two successive loans made to Greece in 2010 and 2012 is that they were mainly aimed at keeping the bankrupt Greek state afloat, maintaining its basic operations and paying the salaries of its overpaid public workers. In fact only 11 percent of the total funding was used for the Greek state's operating needs and Greece has been running a primary budget surplus (i.e. its revenues have exceeded expenses) since 2013. The loans went to Greek banks and foreign creditors, mostly French and German banks. More than 80 percent of the bailout funds were used to bail out, either directly or indirectly, the financial sector (both Greek and foreign) and not the Greek state.[58] A central mechanism has been that of loans by the ECB to Greek banks at low interest rates followed by lending by these to the Greek government at much higher rates. Greek treasury bonds were the target of particularly intense speculation in the form of 'naked CDS purchases', whereby financial corporations (generally hedge funds) take insurance on bonds without actually owning them in the expectation that their price will quickly fall, letting them repurchase them at a lower price.[59]

---

56  'Regulators go easy on Europe's overstretched banks', *The Economist*, 18 January 2014.
57  Blundell-Wignall 2007, p. 3.
58  Fazi 2015.
59  In November 2012, regulatory measures were adopted by the EU. A Thomson Reuters' Business Law Currents Report characterised them as follows: 'The new European short selling regulations are dressing naked short sellers in a regulatory straightjacket, but ill-fitting provisions may leave investors with skin in the game. The regulations were supposed to curb naked short selling and to provide transparency on those trading against European sovereign debt. However, with gaps between short selling methods and alternatives popping up in exchange traded futures and synthetic forms, the holes are already

Parallel to this, following the activation of the European Stability Mechanism (ESM) and the European Financial Stability Fund (EFSF), the major part of Greek government debt was shifted from the private sector to the public sector, with other Eurozone governments now holding around 65 percent of Greece's debt, with another 20 percent in the hands of the ECB and IMF. Two successive punitive austerity programmes were imposed on Greece, leading to a fall in GDP of close to 25 percent since 2010, a rise in unemployment to a level unseen since the 1930s, and impoverishment of large parts of the Greek population.[60] The official narrative is that the intense austerity imposed on the Greek population is inevitable and in the end will bear fruit. A full independent inquiry into Greece's debt is now underway. It will challenge the legitimacy of this debt examining its origin, growth and consequences.[61]

### 3.5   Unresolved European Bank Vulnerabilities

The start of 2016 has seen a further development in the serious difficulties of European banks.[62] One of the factors is common to banks throughout the OECD, namely the 'zero interest crunch' on their profits due to zero-bound or negative interest rates. But others are specific to Europe. They confirm earlier doubts about the veracity of the information provided during stress tests and shed light on the consequences of split responsibilities between the ECB and the EU political authorities. The most critical situation is that of Italian banks. They were resilient to the first wave of the financial crisis in 2008, due to their low exposure to US high-risk securities and to the fact that, contrary to Spain and Ireland, there was no housing bubble to burst. But when the financial crisis turned into a euro sovereign debt and banking crisis, their situation started to deteriorate. Italian banks are burdened by some €360 billion of bad loans, the equivalent of a fifth of the country's GDP. Collectively they have provisioned for only 45 percent of that amount. In most countries bank bonds are held by big institutional investors, but in Italy some €200 billion of bank bonds

---

becoming apparent'. http://blogs.reuters.com/financial-regulatory-forum/2012/12/04/europes-naked-short-selling-ban-leaves-investors-with-skin-in-the-game/.

60   See inter alia: 'Greece's health crisis: from austerity to denialism', *The Lancet*, 22 February 2014 http://www.thelancet.com/journals/lancet/article/PIIS0140-6736(13)62291-6/abstract.

61   Truth Committee on Greek Public Debt (Debt Truth Committee), Preliminary Report, May 2016 http://cadtm.org/Preliminary-Report-of-the-Truth.

62   'A tempest of fear: European banks are in the eye of a new financial storm', *The Economist*, 12 February 2016.

are held by small investors.[63] They have placed the savings of a whole life in this form of fictitious capital. For them the implementation of the recent EU 'bail-in' rules written for institutional investors would wipe out their savings. Shares in Italy's biggest banks have fallen by as much as half since April 2016, a sell-off that intensified after the Brexit vote. The biggest immediate issue is the solvency of Monte dei Paschi di Siena. According to Bloomberg, credit-default swaps on the bank's low-grade bonds suffer a 63 percent probability of default within five years. The riskiest securities of UniCredit and Intesa Sanpaolo, Italy's two biggest lenders, have also fallen.

Several major universal banks have reported the poor performance of their investment bank operations. This is notably true for Deutsche Bank. A new bizarrely-named security has appeared in the daily financial press.[64] In order to meet the capital requirements, in case of losses, required by the Basle III agreement, banks have since 2013 issued a new security with the name contingent convertible bonds (CoCos).[65] They pay a fixed coupon, but they convert to equity or can be written off when losses force a bank's capital below a certain threshold. They also allow the issuer to miss coupon payments. CoCos have been bought by individual investors and private banks in Asia and Europe, US institutional investors looking for new investment instruments and European non-bank financial institutions. CoCos are the riskiest debt issued by banks, with only a quarter of the eurozone market judged investment-grade by the rating agency Fitch in 2015. Consequently yields are 6–7 percent. In early 2016 Deutsche Bank's €1.75bn coco bond was trading below 75 cents on the euro, its lowest level, a 19 percent fall in price over a year. Similar security issued by Unicredit and the Spanish bank Santander were faring only a little better. The prospect of further bank crises in Europe is just one dimension of the situation of the world financial system, to which we turn in the next chapter.

---

63  http://bruegel.org/2016/01/bad-banks-and-rude-awakenings-italian-banks-at-a-crossroads/.
64  www.theguardian.com/business/2016/feb/10/market-turmoil-what-are-cocos-banks-bonds.
65  For a full analysis, see the BIS staff paper: Avdjiev et al. 2013.

CHAPTER 10

# Global Endemic Financial Instability

The outcome of a situation in which the rate of profit is too low and investment opportunities insufficient for accumulation to take off again is that much of the proceeds of non-financial corporations' relentless exploitation of workers and of poor farmers across the world are not reinvested. Instead, they serve to increase the mass of money capital seeking to make profits through financial investments. At the same time, government debt increases the amount of financial securities on offer, while government austerity and pro-employer labour policies set ever higher barriers to the realisation of the mass of surplus value produced and the completion of the full accumulation cycle. The result is the slowdown from year to year of world GDP growth, capital's principal economic indicator. Yet institutions such as life insurance and, more significantly, pension funds constantly increase the mass of money seeking valorisation. Hence there is a plethora of capital in the form of money capital centralised in mutual funds and hedge funds, bent on valorisation through the holding and trading of fictitious capital in the form of assets more and more distant from the processes of surplus value production. Financial profits are harder and harder to earn. Sharp competition takes place around interest-like commissions and fees, notably in mergers and acquisitions. In financial markets, each bank or fund manager seeks to gain a minute fraction of surplus value at the others' expense, moving continually and rapidly from one type of asset to another. The outcomes are the unabated intensity and a diversity of asset trading and endemic global financial instability. These are compounded when quantitative easing, including central bank buying not only of government bonds but also of risky private securities, becomes the major instrument of economic policy.

The Bank of International Settlements' (BIS) observation about the 'puzzling disconnect between the financial markets' buoyancy and underlying economic developments globally'[1] was quoted in the introduction. The BIS Annual Reports are untitled but its latest March 2016 Quarterly is: 'Uneasy Calm Yields to Turbulence'. The IMF's annual Global Financial Stability Reports all bear a title. The April 2012 edition bore a very vague one, 'The Quest for Lasting Stability', and the April 2013 edition, 'Old Risks, New Challenges'. In October 2014, the title was precise and worded almost as a slogan: 'Moving

---

1 BIS 2014, p. 1.

from Liquidity-Driven to Growth-Driven Markets'. The theme chosen by the IMF was the perverse effects and dangers of continuous massive injections of money by the Fed and other central banks through quantitative easing and 'unconventional monetary policies' and also the difficulty of bringing them to an end: 'In advanced economies, financial markets continue to be supported by extraordinary monetary accommodation and easy liquidity conditions', without contributing to 'an environment of self-sustaining growth, marked by increased corporate investment and growing employment'.[2] The report focused on the financial vulnerability of a number of emerging economies and the activities of mutual fund managers. Despite a new rather vague title, 'Navigating Monetary Policy Challenges and Managing Risks', the April 2015 GFSR expressed great concern over the rise in global financial stability risks and the fact that 'these risks have also been pivoting away from banks to shadow banks, from solvency to market liquidity risks, and from advanced economies to emerging markets'.[3] The October 2015 report pursues these issues, particularly that of emerging markets' non-financial corporate debt, while discussing the Chinese situation and its possible repercussions in the wake of the July–August 2015 stock market crash.

1      The Effects and Potential Backlashes of Quantitative Easing

Quantitative easing and 'non-conventional' central bank measures have had practically no impact on growth. They have simply comforted what is called investor 'risk appetite', e.g. the search for high-risk speculative investments. The BIS and IMF record that from 2013 on, this appetite began again to be very 'robust'.[4] In stock markets, the cyclically adjusted price-to-earnings ratio (Shiller P/E ratio) is high. The IMF considers that 'further liquidity-driven boosts in asset prices could force overvaluation and lead to the development of bubbles' in stock markets. This was the case in October 2014 and again in the spring of 2015. Quantitative easing has allowed US financial corporations,

---

2  IMF 2014, p. 1. The IMF reports contain comments on the situation in Japan, but here as throughout Chapters 7 and 8 the focus is on the US and European financial system.
3  IMF 2015a, p. 1.
4  As defined by the Institute for International Finance, 'risk appetite is the amount and type of risk that a company is able and willing to accept in pursuit of its business objectives. Risk appetite in this sense is linked to but conceptually separate from "risk capacity", which is the maximum amount of risk a firm is technically able to assume given its capital base, liquidity, borrowing capacity, and regulatory constraints' (Institute for International Finance 2009).

'including those rated as speculative, to refinance and recapitalize at a rapid pace'. Banks are noted for having rebuilt their capital (mainly through retained earnings). However, despite an improvement in aggregate profitability, 'many banks face lingering balance sheet weaknesses from direct exposure to overindebted borrowers and more generally the drag of debt overhang on economic recovery'. In the European case, there has been much talk of the ECB's March 2015 quantitative easing programme. It is supposed to support cyclical recovery in the Eurozone, but there is no guarantee either that more credit will reach medium and small firms or that demand will be sufficiently strong to encourage them to invest again. Banks are taking the opportunity to strengthen their balance sheets. Contrary to official government and media assertions, the October 2015 GFSR observes that 'euro area banks are struggling to generate sustainable profits, partly because of their high rates of nonperforming loans'.[5] The greatest challenge regarding a rise, sooner or later, of the Fed funds interest rate concerns investor behaviour in emerging economies, both by US mutual funds and hedge funds, and by emerging countries' governments and corporations. It is discussed later in this chapter.

## 2  The Very Long Continuous Fall in Interest Rates and the Growth of Debt

The 2015–16 BIS Annual Report focuses on the movement of global interest rates since 1986.[6] It emphasises that they have never been so low for so long both in nominal and real (inflation-adjusted) terms and against any benchmark:

> Between December 2014 and end-May 2015, on average around $2 trillion in global long-term sovereign debt, much of it issued by euro area sovereigns, was trading at *negative* yields. Policy rates are even lower than at the peak of the Great Financial Crisis (2008–9) in both nominal and real terms. And in real terms they have now been negative for even longer than during the Great Inflation of the 1970s. Yet, exceptional as this situation may be, many expect it to continue.[7]

Very low interest rates over a long period create problems for funds prohibited from making high-risk investments. This is the case for European mid-sized

---

5   IMF 2015b, p. 17.
6   BIS 2015, p. 8.
7   BIS, 2015, p. 7.

life insurers. It is estimated that almost a quarter of insurers may be unable to meet their solvency capital requirements in the future, if low interest rates persist. With a portfolio of 4.4 trillion dollars in assets in the European Union in the hands of life insurers,[8] weak insurers create a source of potential risk as they move 'to new investment strategies and increasingly offload risks onto their customers'.[9] Pension funds have equally responded to declining asset returns by increasing their exposure to 'so-called alternative investments. These include real estate, hedge funds, private equity and commodities. Industry estimates reveal that the share of such investments in pension fund asset portfolios has risen – from 5% in 2001 to 15% in 2007 and 25% in 2014 – mirrored by a 20 percentage point drop in the equity share'.[10]

Given its long trajectory, the fall in interest rates is not just the result of quantitative easing. According to BIS, 'market interest rates are determined by the interplay of central banks' and market participants' decisions'. The latter 'reflect many factors, including risk appetite, views about profitable investments, regulatory and accounting constraints and, of course, expectations about what central banks will do'. The reference to profitable investments is the nearest BIS gets to the relation between interest rates and the pace of production and accumulation. And the closest it comes to explaining how the long fall of market rates might be due to the sheer plethora of capital is when it observes: 'interest rates are low today, at least in part, because they were too low in the past. Low rates beget still lower rates. In this sense, low rates are self-validating'.[11] What is certain is that they fuel debt. They did so from 2003 in the run up to the financial crisis. The movement shown in Graph 1.2 of the BIS report[12] is that during the period 2008–14, while interest rates moved from 2 percent to zero percent, global government and private non-financial debt rose from circa 230 percent to circa 260 percent of global GDP. The BIS sees low interest rates as 'the most remarkable symptom of a broader malaise in the global economy: the economic expansion is unbalanced, debt burdens and financial risks are still too high, productivity growth too low, and the room for manoeuvre in macroeconomic policy too limited'.[13]

While government debt rose in a number of countries, e.g. the US and the UK, the majority of Eurozone Member states and many countries ranked as

---

8   IMF 2015, p. 24.
9   BIS 2015, p. 101.
10  BIS 2015, p. 116.
11  BIS 2015, p. 17.
12  BIS 2015, p. 8.
13  BIS 2015, p. 1.

developing countries, the growth of private non-financial debt has been particularly rapid in emerging countries.

3     Non-bank Financial Corporations and Systemic Contagion Risks Today

In 2008, the financial authorities had no theory of risk and contagion in a system dealing with fictitious capital once or several times removed – MBS, derivatives, and even a derivative of MBS. Work by US Federal bank staff began with the postmortem of the Lehman bankruptcy. Since then a lot of work has been commissioned. It is sifted and synthesised by the IMF in the October 2015 GFSR, which identifies three forms of liquidity and studies 'contagion' as spillovers from one market to others. The forms of liquidity identified are market liquidity, namely 'the ability to rapidly execute sizable securities transactions at a low cost and with a limited price impact'; funding liquidity, which is the ability by market participants to obtain funding at acceptable conditions and monetary liquidity (as used in relation to monetary aggregates).[14] Given the place that funds of many varieties (leveraged hedge funds, money market funds, mutual funds and exchange-traded funds) offering or seeking liquidity occupy in a system dominated by securitisation, the first is by far the most important. 'Two aspects of market liquidity must be considered: its level and its resilience. Low levels of liquidity may foretell low resistance to shocks. But measures of the level in normal times may be insufficient to assess the risk that a shock will produce if liquidity "freezes." A well-known characteristic of market liquidity is that it can suddenly disappear during periods of market stress, causing asset prices to strongly overreact to unexpected events'. Now as to contagion:

> Market illiquidity and the associated financial stress can spill over to other asset classes. Liquidity shocks may propagate to other assets, including those with unrelated fundamentals, for a variety of reasons. These reasons include market participants' need to mark to market and rebalance portfolios, which can affect their ability to trade and hold other assets. The propagation of liquidity shocks (known as liquidity spillovers) could be amplified when market participants are highly leveraged. In addition, when asset fundamentals are correlated, spillovers can be larger: investors may perceive a sharp price correction in certain assets as conveying

---

14    IMF 2015b, p. 53.

information about the valuations of their own securities. As a result, they may start fire sales and cause liquidity to freeze up.[15]

The assessment of the IMF and BIS alike – namely that risk has moved from banks to funds – must be read in the light of these considerations. The IMF observes the way in which 'risks have been pivoting away from banks to shadow banks',[16] more precisely to the non-bank component of the shadow banking system. There have been some measures to regulate banking, and the constraints of a return to specialisation has de facto led to some separation of commercial and investment banking, but there remain worthless assets in the balance sheets of Eurozone banks in particular. Such banks are not lending to medium and small enterprises, and they are not borrowing massively on the money markets as they did in 2007–8 and again in 2010. Mutual funds and hedge funds have taken their place. 'Market-based intermediation has filled the gap left by strained banks; the asset management sector has grown rapidly. Even when asset managers operate with low leverage, their investment mandates can give rise to leverage-like behaviour that amplifies and propagates financial stress'.[17] The IMF writes: 'inflows into mutual funds have provided an illusion of liquidity in credit markets, but changes in market structure may exacerbate illiquidity in times of stress'. It points to the deterioration of underwriting standards 'with covenant-light loans now accounting for two-thirds of new issuance of leveraged loans'; the 'near-record rate of issuance of other types of lower-standard loans, such as second-lien loans' and the rise in leveraged buyouts in mergers and acquisitions.[18] All in all, 'US high-yield issuance over the past three years is more than double the amount recorded in the three years before the last downturn (that of 2007–8)'. As measured by rising ratios of net debt to assets, leverage has grown: 'a combination of lower dealer inventories, elevated asset valuations, flight-prone investors and vulnerable liquidity structures have increased the sensitivity of key fixed-income markets to increasing market and liquidity risks'.[19] The growing role in bond markets of mutual funds that offer daily redemptions to retail investors, coupled with signs of increasing herding and concentration among market participants, has made market liquidity more vulnerable to rapid changes in sentiment.

---

15   IMF 2015b, p. 56.
16   IMF 2015a, p. ix.
17   BIS 2015, p. 101.
18   IMF 2015a, p. 31.
19   IMF 2015a, p. 26.

The top 500 world fund managers are estimated by the IMF to be at the head of some $76 trillion worth of assets (100 percent of world GDP and 25 percent of global financial assets). They include stand-alone mutual funds and large hedge funds, but also still the high-risk affiliates of some global systemically important banks (G-SIBs). The consequence of a huge amount of assets being managed by a small number of institutional investors in sharp competition among themselves is that changes in the consensus of market operators on interest rates or the outlook of global economy can send shock waves through markets as investors move globally in or out of given equity, bonds or currency markets. The decisions taken by a single large asset manager can potentially trigger fund flows with significant system-wide repercussions. Understandably, the Financial Stability Board has published a proposal on how to identify non-bank non-insurer global systemically important financial institutions. After the large banks and the large insurers, the large funds require surveillance.[20]

In recent years, the market-making activities of banks have fallen, and they blame this on the tightening of regulation. Reduced market-making activities by institutions possessing the requisite experience and financial muscle mean that 'more investors are now following benchmarks'. The IMF has expressed repeated concerns over possible 'excess leverage in the derivatives positions of a number of investment funds':[21]

> With lower liquidity, less market making, and more benchmarking, asset prices are more likely to be driven by common shocks, particularly at higher frequencies, than by their respective idiosyncratic fundamentals. Both the decline in market liquidity and the increasing use of derivatives are associated with higher asset price correlations over the past five years. This is particularly evident during periods of stress, when flow liquidity reverses and volatility increases.[22]

All this is compounded by ever more extensive use of dealing technology:

> Treasury bonds and Treasury futures trade almost exclusively on electronic platforms, which allow algorithmic and high-frequency traders to capture an expanding market share. High-frequency trading is estimated to account for at least 50 percent of cash market volumes and 60 to

---

20   The proposal is made in cooperation with the International Organization of Securities Commissions and is available on the Financial Stability Board's website.
21   IMF 2015b, p. 23.
22   IMF 2015a, p. 35.

70 percent of futures trading. Even traditional market makers have increasingly adopted algorithmic trading strategies. Market participants report that liquidity provision has become more dependent on programmed reaction functions and less on client based relationships. In a more anonymous, short term, profit-oriented trading environment, fewer participants make their pools of liquidity available in risky conditions to help stabilize the market.[23]

The growth of electronic trading platforms should have, in principle, reduced search costs. But the implications of the associated advance of automated trades (algorithmic trading) are unclear. They are potentially adverse if such trading is mainly used to demand immediate liquidity or the algorithms are poorly designed. Conceivably, they may have increased the probability and severity of large market dislocations.[24]

Herding by mutual funds[25] in and out of given markets is especially disruptive in the case of emerging economy markets. 'If funds exacerbate the volatility of capital flows in and out of emerging markets or increase the likelihood of contagion, significant consequences will be endured by the recipient economies'.[26]

## 4    The Potential for Financial Turmoil in Emerging Countries

This potential stems from investor behaviour both by US mutual funds, hedge funds and asset managers, and by emerging countries' governments and corporations. US funds have given a large place to emerging countries' bonds in their portfolios and the latter have borrowed heavily. In their search for investments tapping into channels where surplus value appropriation was still expanding, from 2010 they turned to emerging countries. Concomitantly easy liquidity conditions made monetary and fiscal policies even more lax than before, with the result that 'private and public balance sheets have become more leveraged and thus are more sensitive to changes in domestic and external conditions'.[27] Risk has been accentuated by the fall in commodity prices, notably oil, which

---

23    IMF 2015a, p. 33.
24    IMF 2015b, p. 56.
25    The term 'funds' does not just mean 'mutual funds', which is a term often applied to US money market mutual funds in the US, but includes hedge funds and can also include investment funds/asset managers.
26    IMF 2015a, p. 95.
27    IMF 2014, p. 22.

has affected already vulnerable countries. In the case of emerging countries, 'spillovers' take place through trade, financial and commodity price linkages. Financial linkages include cross-border bank lending, portfolio debt and portfolio equity exposures. The IMF lists financial contagion shocks (via equity, bond and money markets), corporate debt shocks (affecting bank soundness), and commodity shocks (affecting net commodity exporters).

The 'common-creditor contagion' of the 1990s,[28] designated as 'co-movement' and 'single common factor contagion', is back on a much, much larger scale in government bond markets. The IMF's 2015 'global asset market disruption scenario' sees financial contagion through portfolio outflows from emerging markets as a major transmission channel. In 2013, a clear example of how this could take place, and potential impact on Brazil, Argentina and Turkey most notably, was given by the mere mention that the Fed might start ending quantitative easing and raise its rates just a little. The shock started in May 2013. Global markets 'were plunged into turmoil' by the Fed's announcement of its plans to reduce its government bond purchases, one form of quantitative easing. US Treasury yields rose sharply, global rates and volatility increased, and emerging economies' financial markets and currencies came under strong pressure as investors fled back to the US.[29] For reasons discussed in earlier chapters, the world crisis did not hit these countries initially. Hence their bond but also their stock markets seemed to represent good opportunities to tap into surplus value produced there. Gross capital flows to emerging markets grew fivefold from the early 2000s onwards and the most volatile component, portfolio flows as opposed to FDI, became particularly important. As discussed in Chapter 7 on the holding of government debt, the form of portfolio investment in emerging markets has changed. Foreign investors purchase local-currency debt in domestic markets, playing a dominant role in some, as in São Paulo.[30] Emerging market bond yields are observed to co-move, especially during stress episodes under a dominant 'single common factor' highly correlated to the 10-year US Treasury rate. The relationship has become stronger since 2013, implying that the US rate plays a key role in the transmission channel. The sensitivity of each country's bond yield to the common factor depends in part on the share of foreign ownership in local government bond markets, but domestic fundamentals also have an influence. 'Macroeconomic

---

28    See above Chapter 9, section 2.1.
29    For an account of the 2013 crisis, see IMF 2014, pp. 22–3.
30    The capacity to shift from issuing hard currency external debt to local currency domestic debt is known as overcoming the 'original sin' of low trustworthiness associated with the second Mexican debt crisis and the crises of the weaker South-East Asian economies.

imbalances have increased...while the increased participation of foreign investors in domestic bond markets exposes some economies to an additional source of market volatility and pressure on capital flows'. In the case of poor macroeconomic indicators or of shocks in other economies that have an impact on asset prices, Turkey, Argentina, Brazil and some South-East Asian countries are in danger of seeing asset managers seek to hedge exposures by taking positions in more liquid markets. This is what occurred in January–February 2014 when several countries suffered a second bout of financial crisis, notably those where government debt had risen in tandem with private sector indebtedness.

Emerging market economies' corporate debt has risen significantly during the past decade. That of nonfinancial firms across major emerging market economies increased from about $4 trillion in 2004 to well over $18 trillion in 2014. The average emerging market corporate debt-to-GDP ratio has also grown by 26 percentage points in the same period, but with notable differences between countries.[31] The IMF touches on possible unsustainable levels of debt leverage by firms, recalling that many financial crises in emerging markets (Mexico and Thailand notably) were preceded by rapid leverage growth. It cites 'the striking leverage increase in the construction sector is most notable in China and in Latin America. This increase relates to concerns expressed in recent years about the connection between global financial conditions, capital flows, and real estate price developments in some emerging markets'.[32] 'Leverage has risen more in more cyclical sectors, and has grown most in construction...[it] has also been associated with, on average, rising foreign currency exposures'.[33]

The full range of negative effects on trade, finance, and commodity price and the linkages between them are at work in countries exporting commodities. They include the loss of critical government revenues (Venezuela, Nigeria and Algeria); strains in private debt repayment capacity for oil and gas corporations (Argentina, Brazil, South Africa and Nigeria); exposure of these countries to the rise in global exchange rate volatility; and for oil-producing countries to the unexpectedly rapid and sharp fall in the world oil prices.[34]

---

[31] IMF 2015b, p. 82.
[32] In conjunction with this, household debt in Brazil, Singapore, Thailand, and Turkey has risen more than 40 percent since 2008 (IMF 2015a, p. 97).
[33] IMF 2015b, p. 87.
[34] IMF 2015a, p. ix.

The intensity of financial transactions, the diversity of assets traded, the potential channels of financial contagion and the expressions of endemic global financial instability are impressive. The question they raise concerns their present relation to production and trade and their capacity to trigger a new crisis in the 'real economy', as it is called. A tentative explanation is given in the conclusion, to which we now turn.

# Conclusion

This book has sought to offer an interpretation of the present functioning of global capitalism, the meaning of the term financialisation and the course of the world economic crisis. I have done this with the help of two interrelated notions, finance capital and financial capital or finance *qua* finance, seeking to introduce a historical perspective where possible. While emphasising the extraordinary strength and the new patterns of global exploitation by TNCs, the pillars of surplus value production and predatory appropriation, I have sought to analyse the operations and spectacular growth of interest-bearing capital – capital as commodity – in its contemporary organisational and institutional forms. I have done this by approaching what I name financial accumulation through a recall of events stretching over 70 years. Financial accumulation has brought with it the formation of fictitious capital on a massive scale and in new forms. It has fortified in an unprecedented manner the pretension of interest-bearing to autonomy. Data have been taken from IMF, BIS, UNCTAD and OECD as well as from central banks reports. Analyses from some partly critical staff papers of these organisations have been of considerable help. I have tried to write the book so that the reader will find a historical perspective on the present situation, appropriate extracts from *Capital* and from the works of other great classical Marxists which may encourage her or him to do further reading, and an introduction to data from official sources other than national accounts.

### The Institutional Difficulties of Doing Marxist Economic Research

As I wrote I became even more aware of the pressure put on Marxist research in economics through teaching, publication and academic recruitment. Short of eliminating it completely from academia, this pressure confines Marxism applied to the economics of society basically to questions amenable to mainstream macroeconomic investigation. There is also the ageing of people actively engaged in Marxist economics, as seen in most of the issues discussed in Harvey's *Limits to Capital* taken both as a landmark and a benchmark. The number of university departments in the world where Marxist research issues are accepted for PhD research is very small and the number of those where Marxists are recruited on the staff is even fewer. This is linked of course to the overall political situation of the Left in a context where many countries are experiencing a shift to the right, but also due in many countries to a well-established strategy of eliminating Marxism from academia.[1] Callinicos's statement that 'Marx's *Capital* is back where it belongs, at the centre of debate about Marxism and its purchase on the contemporary world'[2] is unfortunately not the case for economics. In Europe, how many departments shelter, as SOAS has been doing, a group like Research on Money and Finance or, in North America, those in the Department of Political Science at York University? There are very few Marxist journals and it takes a very long time to get any work published.

My arguments on the need to discuss finance capital and *financial* capital as two interrelated yet distinct notions obviously call for debate. In some chapters I have pointed to some general notions calling for research, for instance the updating in the context of globalisation of Marx's theory of the industrial reserve army. The potential research agenda includes obviously monographic and sector-level investigations of large banks, transnational industrial and service corporations and large retailers of which there is a cruel lack.[3] The theory of global oligopoly requires considerable research and debate.[4] There are too few regional or national studies of the type and quality of those cited in Chapter 4 on the Gulf States and on South Africa. Such studies are particularly precious in that they are historical and political, breaking down the rigid disciplinary barriers between economics and political science. All new research on fictitious capital, notably on assets constituting fictitious capital several times removed, would make the theory progress.

---

1   The grouping of heterodox economists chaired by André Orléan has attempted to alert public opinion to the situation in France where 'the domination of mainstream economics has finished by marginalising heterodox economists, whether they be post-Keynesians, institutionalists, Marxists or whatever. The situation has now become critical: the very existence of a minimal level of intellectual pluralism in university teaching and research in economics is at risk. Of the 120 professors appointed between 2005 and 2011, only 6 were affiliated to minority schools of thought'. http://assoeconomiepolitique.org/petition-pluralism-now/.
2   Callinicos 2014.
3   The dearth of studies is a problem not just for Marxist analysis but also for heterodox economists more generally: 'Neoclassical economists whose perspective dominates economics have done a terrible job of the corporation. In adhering to the idea that in an advanced economy the corporation can be construed as a "market imperfection", the well-trained neoclassical economist reveals his or her ignorance about the operation and performance of the modern business corporation and the modern economy to which it is central' (Lazonick 2016).
4   The ideal result would be to attain a result similar to Sweezy's (1946, pp. 285–6) summary of the general effects of monopoly.

## Persistent Very Low Global Growth Coupled with Endemic Financial Instability

Coming back to the book's central themes and their relation to the long course of the world economic crisis, I was worried that my analysis might be invalidated by on-going developments. It took me some time to set out my understanding of the changes in the credit system brought about by securitisation and shadow banking, and so of the precise processes of credit withdrawal and financial contagion which took place in 2007 and 2008; also to develop my present understanding of financialisation and to go beyond a mere further variation on my previous writing.[5] I could have been caught up by events, by changes in the world economic situation attenuating the divergence between the rates of growth of GDP and investment and that of claims on surplus value, by legislative measures reducing the size of assets traded in financial markets, or again by a new severe financial crisis with impacts on production and trade analogous to those of 2008. This has not been the case. The divergence has persisted if not increased as world GDP growth has crawled along while competition between funds has created an ever more fictitious buoyancy of financial markets. However, despite this, no new serious financial crisis, let alone one threatening the entire financial system, has occurred. The only moment of potential important crisis has been that in 2010–12 of the European banking system in the face of possible sovereign default (Greece) or a collapse of a part of a banking system based on real estate (Spain). At the price of a second recession in Europe and a falling back of the continent vis-à-vis other parts of the global economy, it was resolved in favour of creditors on account of the prevailing economic and political relations of power between capital and labour.

The IMF and BIS reports examined in Chapter 10 identify a number of factors leading to recurrent endemic financial instability. The BIS March Quarterly Review has further sharpened the analysis. Repeated announcements have been made of the possibility of a crisis provoking a new world recession. But the triggering of a major collapse in production and trade by a financial shock requires a deep intermeshing of credit and money and of production in the combined form of overproduction and a financial bubble. In 2008, the financial crisis triggered the US Great Recession because of over-accumulation and overproduction and a total dependency on credit of entire sectors and industries (real estate and construction and automobile). This is why the withdrawal of credit in an over-leveraged financial sector provoked the final phase in the

---

[5] Compare my definition in the introduction, along with my chapter, in the book edited by Riccardo Bellofiore and Giovanna Vertova (Bellofiore and Vertova 2014).

collapse of the housing boom and brought the automobile corporations to their knees, triggering recession in the US and within weeks in the world economy. Today as a result of the concerted rescue policies by the G20 in 2008–9, the situation is rather different. A global low growth regime has set in without any end in sight. A localised financial crisis can simply deepen it a little in the same way that the unforeseen fall in the price of oil has had an overall negative effect on world GDP growth. This regime includes a self-reproducing process of insufficient investment opportunities due to the state of the rate of profit and the unfavourable conditions for the realisation of what surplus value is produced. Only corporations with global reach and oligopoly power have to some extent restored their profit level. But they have no urgent incentive to invest, since their oligopolistic power allows them to manage to their advantage the underlying situation of 'controlled excess capacity' and to grow through an unabated process of further concentration and global restructuring through mergers and acquisitions.[6] Economic and political power relations are extremely strongly weighted in favour of capital, one of the consequences being the extremely high inequalities in wealth. These are now increasingly deplored in World Bank and OECD reports but are not going to change. Today, concern over the future of world growth is still marginal in the ranks of the ruling classes. When small circles attempt to draw attention in January 2016 to the dangers ahead and claim that they 'must prepare for a future of exponentially disruptive change',[7] they and their governments turn their heads away. Their twofold interrelated day-to-day agenda remains more than ever on the one hand the payment of government and household debt on time, allowing a regular flow of interest, and on the other hand the aggravation of the conditions of workers *largo sensu* through the reform of labour and social security legislation.

The roots of the combined buoyancy and instability of financial markets lie in the plethora of capital in the form of money capital centralised in banks, mutual funds and hedge funds and in the hoards managed by the financial departments of TNCs[8] and in the difficulties of making profits in financial markets in a 'crawling' world economy, to use Roberts's expression. Valorisation through the holding and trading of fictitious capital is becoming more and

---

6  These have increased significantly, reaching their pre-2008 level in 2014 (UNCTAD 2015a) and set to exceed it in 2015 ('Global M&A Set for Record in 2015 as Companies Pursue Mega Deals', http://www.bloomberg.com/news/articles/2015-07-29/).
7  See the 2016 Davos preparatory report at http://reports.weforum.org/global-risks-2016/.
8  An IMF working paper gives detailed information on the 'financial wealth' of corporations, with a special look at Japanese firms (Hashimoto and Kinoshita 2016).

more difficult. Assets more and more distant from the processes of surplus value production and appropriation are engineered by financial innovators and traded. In financial markets, each bank or fund manager seeks to gain a minute fraction of surplus value at the others' expense, moving continually from one type of asset to another. Financial profits are harder and harder to earn. Sharp competition takes place around interest-like commissions and fees, notably in merger and acquisition deals. The outcomes are the unabated intensity and diversity of asset trading along with numerous expressions of endemic global financial instability.

In the advanced capitalist countries the zero-bound interest rates weigh on bank profits and accentuate the difficulties of banks still holding non-performing loans or having made insufficiently considered risky investments in given markets. The current situation of European banks was discussed in this respect at the end of Chapter 8. Zero-bound interest will also weigh on financial-market retirement systems and the benefits they will provide and so affect effective demand. Elsewhere regional impacts may be stronger, as with the consequences of corporate (both public and private) and household debt in large emerging countries (Brazil, Turkey, Argentina) where there is considerable scope for contagion within domestic financial sectors and for domestic recessions to take place with important falls in production and employment. But outside the region, all this will do is consolidate the existing very slow global growth regime. The same goes for the marked slowdown of Chinese growth. The government has some leeway to limit the housing and shadow banking crisis, but the period during which high Chinese growth rates boosted the world economy is over. In the US, some credit markets are liable to experience shocks, but again all this will do is weigh on the US rate of growth and so on that of world GDP. Events in stock exchanges matter mainly for specific categories of investors. Their sharp fall in 2008 followed that of mortgage-backed assets, while income concentration has singularly reduced the impact of the 'wealth effect'. Ups and downs in stock markets express the nervousness of investors and their difficulties in managing their portfolios. They help financial journalists in writing papers, but are not good thermometers of economic activity.

### How Could Slow Growth be Brought to an End and a New Long Upswing Start?

In Chapter 1, I argued that the initial impulse of the long phase which came to an end in 2008 was the massive destruction of capital during the Great

Depression and the Second World War. It reflected my position on long waves. While downward phases are determined by factors endogenous to the process of capitalist accumulation leading to the fall in the rate of profit and over-accumulation, upturns are largely triggered by 'exogenous factors' – moments of massive expansion of markets, major technological breakthroughs and, in the twentieth century, a world war.

Given that neither of the two sole countries capable of waging a world war is at present preparing their population for the eventuality of the solution which ended the Great Depression of the 1930s, from where could a new surge in capitalist accumulation arise? The complete commodification, and not simply the privatisation, of public services, has been put forward by Huws as a possibility. It is one of the British ruling class's cherished projects and represents the 'expropriation of the results of past struggles by workers for the redistribution of surplus value in the form of universal public services'[9] (this is the most telling definition given by a Marxist scholar, even if it overlooks the fact that the working class benefitted in Britain, as in France and other countries, from the imperial status of its bourgeoisie). Other bourgeoisies are seeking to follow the same road. The social consequences are devastating and the rate of exploitation is increased. But it cannot be the basis for the 'next wave of accumulation'.[10] Another candidate for this role is the growth of the 'middle classes' in the big emerging economies and the expansion of their purchasing power. Besides the fact that China's growth rate began to stall in 2014, this mechanism cannot launch a new long wave of accumulation. Nor will further 'accumulation by dispossession', in particular in countries where the peasantry is still important.

Then there is the question as to whether the major technological changes associated with ICTs are capable of driving accumulation over several decades. For accumulation to be re-launched, the technological changes involved must be capable of opening whole new industries and, besides their effect on productivity, of creating their own demand. Only new technologies with extremely large investment and employment effects are capable of driving a new long wave of accumulation, associated with expansion through new markets. In the course of an intense debate, a neo-Schumpeterian approach was developed in the 1980s, with Christopher Freeman and Carlota Perez as central figures. This debate has been reopened. The role of ICTs in radically reshaping the organisation of work and everyday life is indubitable. The major issue is whether they possess investment and employment effects capable of driving a new long

---

9   Huws 2012, p. 64.
10  Huws 2012, p. 88.

wave of accumulation. Their strong overall labour-saving impacts, coupled with their effect of increasing the value of constant capital invested, suggest the contrary, notably if a Fourth Industrial Revolution, a quantum jump of the technologies which emerged in the Third, is in the offing as discussed below. In 2007, Carlota Perez[11] saw a huge potential for growth from ICTs, and she has not changed her position since. In work breaking with orthodox growth theory, Richard Gordon adopts Schumpeter's distinction between major inventions amounting to industrial revolutions and the 'subsequent incremental improvements which ultimately tap the full potential of the initial invention'.[12] Developing arguments first made in 2000,[13] Gordon argues that following the first two industrial revolutions (that of the late eighteenth and first half of the nineteenth century and that of the shorter industrial revolution starting in the late nineteenth century), the incremental innovation follow-up process lasted at least 100 years.[14] A central point is the 'once and for all' character of the major previous technological changes: 'Taking the inventions and their follow-up improvements together, many of these processes could happen only once. Notable examples are speed of travel, temperature of interior space, and urbanization itself'. The third IT-based industrial revolution has not had such effects. It 'began around 1960 and reached its climax in the dot.com era of the late 1990s, but its main impact on productivity has withered away in the past eight years'. New innovations since 2000 have centred on communication and data-processing technologies. These do not fundamentally change the standard of living in the US or other industrialised countries.[15] What they offer capital and state in the form of Big Data is an unprecedented capacity for social and political control. In the words of a US political scientist, 'we have a collective historical memory that technological progress brings a big and predictable stream of revenue growth across most of the economy. When it comes to the Web, those assumptions are turning out to be wrong or misleading'.[16] The OECD has tried to be reassuring: 'The main source of the productivity slowdown is not so much a slowing of innovation by the most globally advanced firms, but rather a

---

11  Perez 2007.
12  Gordon 2012. This point was made by Perroux in his major study of Schumpeter.
13  Gordon 2000.
14  Gordon 2012.
15  Gordon gives electric light, motor cars, or indoor plumbing as examples.
16  Cowen 2011. He uses the expression 'technological plateau' and points to the 'low-hanging fruit' which made rapid growth easy, including the cultivation of much previously unused land; the application and spread of what he views, much like Gordon, as 'once and for all' technological breakthroughs, notably transport, electricity, mass communications, refrigeration, sanitation and finally mass education.

slowing of the pace at which innovations spread out throughout the economy, a breakdown of the diffusion machine'.[17] The Kaldor-Verdoorn laws concerning the cumulative relations between growth and productivity certainly require revisiting, but they retain necessarily some degree of pertinence. BIS does not share the optimism of the authors of the OECD report. It sees 'adverse selection' at play and suggests that 'credit booms sap productivity growth as they gather pace, largely by allocating resources to the wrong sectors'. The concern of the authors of the Davos 2016 preparatory report on the 'Fourth Industrial Revolution' is again different. In the offing they see the 'transformation of entire systems of production, distribution and consumption as opposed to a product or an industry',[18] with huge effects on employment. Their assessment will perhaps be qualified or attenuated by further work, but no one can neglect the trend.[19] In the last paragraph of his review of Gordon's new book, Roberts sums up his own pros and cons:

> there may be life in capitalism globally yet even if it is in 'down mode' right now. Or maybe the potential labour force will not be 'properly exploited' by the capitalist mode of production and Gordon is right. The world rate of profit (not just the rate of profit in the mature G7 economies) stopped rising in the late 1990s and has not recovered to the level of the golden age for capitalism in the 1960s, despite the massive potential global labour force. It seems that the countervailing factors of foreign investment in the emerging world, combined with new technology, have not been sufficient to push up the world rate of profit in the last decade or so, so far. The downward phase of the global capitalist cycle is still in play.[20]

Capitalism comes out quite well of this analysis, its 'expiry date' still to come. But as I argue below, once the consequences of climate change and natural

---

17  OECD 2015, p. 12.
18  'Concern is growing about the effects of digital disintermediation, advanced robotics and the sharing economy on productivity growth, job creation and purchasing power. It is clear that the millennial generation will experience greater technological change over the next decade than the past 50 years, leaving no aspect of global society undisturbed. Scientific and technological breakthroughs – from artificial intelligence to precision medicine – are poised to transform our human identity'. http://reports.weforum.org/global-risks-2016/.
19  A carefully researched study estimates that 47 percent of US jobs are 'at risk' of being automated in the next 20 years (Frey and Osborne 2013).
20  Roberts 2016.

264                                                                                                              CONCLUSION

resource depletion come into the picture, the problem is not the future of capitalism but that of civilised society.

### Non-ecological Approaches to Capitalism's Possible 'Intrinsic Absolute Limits'

In his introduction to the Penguin Edition of Volume 3 of *Capital*, which I have never seen anyone quote and have only read quite recently, Mandel makes a number of theoretical developments on the 'destiny of capitalism'.[21] As opposed to Sweezy, Mandel discusses Grossman's theory of capitalist breakdown or collapse respectfully and seriously. It leads him into a discussion of the consequences of what he names 'robotism'. The new technologies were still in their infancy when this was written but for Mandel they already had portentous potential consequences. Given the forecasts discussed above it is important that they be read and discussed:

> [T]he extension of automation beyond a given ceiling leads, inevitably, first to a reduction in the total volume of value produced, then to a reduction in the total volume of surplus-value produced. This unleashes a fourfold combined 'collapse crisis': a huge crisis of decline in the rate of profit; a huge crisis of realization (the increase in the productivity of labour implied by robotism expands the mass of use-values produced in an even higher ratio than it reduces real wages, and a growing proportion of these use-values becomes unsaleable); a huge social crisis; and a huge crisis of 'reconversion' [in other words, of capitalism's capacity to adapt] through devalorisation – the *specific forms* of capital destruction threatening not only the survival of human civilisation but even the physical survival of mankind or of life on our planet.[22]

And a bit later on, so as to be understood, Mandel writes:

> it is evident that such a trend towards upgrading labour in productive sectors with the highest technological development must, of necessity, be accompanied by its very negation: a rise in mass unemployment, in the extent of marginalized sectors of the population, in the number of those who 'drop out' and of all those whom the 'final' development of

---

21  Mandel 1981, p. 78.
22  Mandel 1981, p. 87.

CONCLUSION

> capitalist technology expels from the process of production. This means only that the growing challenges to capitalist relations of production inside the factory are accompanied by growing challenges to all basic bourgeois relations and values in society as a whole, and these too constitute an important and periodically explosive element of the tendency of capitalism to final collapse.

And he then adds:

> not necessarily of collapse in favour of a higher form of social organization or civilization. Precisely as a function of capitalism's very degeneration, phenomena of cultural decay, of retrogression in the fields of ideology and respect for human rights, multiply alongside the uninterrupted succession of multiform crises with which that degeneration will face us (has already faced us). Barbarism, as one possible result of the collapse of the system, is a much more concrete and precise perspective today than it was in the twenties and thirties. Even the horrors of Auschwitz and Hiroshima will appear mild compared to the horrors with which a continuous decay of the system will confront mankind. Under these circumstances, the struggle for a socialist outcome takes on the significance of a struggle for the very survival of human civilization and the human race.[23]

He tempers this truly catastrophic perspective with a message of hope adapted from the problematic of *The Transitional Program*:

> The proletariat, as Marx has shown, unites all the objective prerequisites for successfully conducting that struggle; today, that remains truer than ever. And it has at least the potential for acquiring the subjective prerequisites too, for a victory of world socialism. Whether that potential will actually be realized will depend, in the last analysis, upon the conscious efforts of organized revolutionary Marxists, integrating themselves with the spontaneous periodic striving of the proletariat to reorganize society along socialist lines, and leading it to precise goals: the conquest of state power and radical social revolution. I see no more reason to be pessimistic today as to the outcome of that endeavour than Marx was at the time he wrote *Capital*.[24]

---

23   Mandel 1981, p. 89.
24   Mandel 1981, pp. 89–90.

That radical social revolution is the solution is true more than ever but climatic and ecological crises unforeseeable by Marx, as well as the political legacy of the twentieth century, do lead one to be pessimistic. As I said above, I only became acquainted with this text very recently. Previously my early reading of capitalist development[25] had made me receptive to thinking by philosophers from Central Europe. The first was Mészáros, with the following proposition from his 1995 book:

> Every system of social metabolic reproduction has its intrinsic absolute limits which cannot be transcended without changing the prevailing mode of control into a qualitatively different one. When such limits are reached in the course of historical development it becomes imperative to transform the system's structural parameters which normally circumscribe the overall margin of the reproductive practices feasible under the circumstances.[26]

This is followed by the further proposition that in the case of capitalism:

> as the margin for displacing the system's contradictions becomes ever narrower and its pretenses to the unchangeable status of *causa sui* palpably absurd notwithstanding the once unimaginable destructive power at the disposal of its personifications. For through the exercise of such power capital can destroy humankind in general – as indeed it seems to be bent on doing (and with it to be sure its own system of control) – but not selectively its historical antagonist [the working class].[27]

The other author who has encouraged me to explore the notion of the absolute limits of capitalist production is the German philosopher Robert Kurz, who has not been much translated into English. The last book he wrote[28] a little before he died, at a moment when it was becoming clear that the world economic and financial crisis was not going to be resolved quickly, contains an invitation to go deeper into Marx's notion of capital's 'immanent barriers' (which I discuss above in Chapter 1) and to explore the idea that there could come a point in history when these barriers might become absolute. Like Mandel, be it in a

---

25  Chesnais 1967. This article earned me a reputation of catastrophism.
26  Mészáros 1995, p. 142. Mészáros's political positions, in particular in support of Chavez's 'Socialism of the 21st Century', do not disqualify his theoretical work.
27  Mészáros 1995, p. 145.
28  Kurz 2011.

reading of Marx which has also raised much controversy,[29] Kurz points to the labour-saving and productivity-enhancing effects of ITC-related technologies and their effect in sharpening the contradictions of capitalist production.

> Given the level of contradiction which they reached we are confronted from now on with the task to reformulate the critique of the capitalist forms and in that of their abolition. This is simply the historical situation in which we are, and it would be futile to cry over the lost battles of the past. If capitalism comes up against its objectively absolute historical limits, it is nevertheless true that, for lack of a sufficient critical consciousness, the fight for emancipation can fail today also. The outcome would be then not a new spring of accumulation, but, as Marx said, the fall of all into barbarism.[30]

## The Advent of a New More Formidable Immanent Barrier and Its Implications

In the absence of factors capable of launching a new phase of sustained accumulation, the perspective is that of a situation in which the social and political consequences of slow growth and endemic financial instability, along with the political chaos they breed in certain regions today and potentially in others, will converge with the social and political impacts of climate change. The notion of barbarism, associated with the two World Wars and the Holocaust, and more recently with contemporary genocides, will then apply to them.

At the time of its formulation 'the second contradiction of capitalism'[31] was approached by O'Connor from the standpoint of the effects of the degradation and depletion of natural resources on costs, profits and accumulation. Similarly, Kovel argued that degradation and depletion would have an effect on profitability 'either directly, by so fouling the natural ground of production that

---

29  Notably on his interpretation in earlier work of the theory of value and the notion of abstract labour. This is quite marginal to the 2011 book on the crisis. See his presentation of the book in French (http://www.palim-psao.fr/article-theorie-de-marx-crise-et-depassement-du-capitalisme-a-propos-de-la-situation-de-la-critique-social-108491159.html), and the résumé of the principal arguments in a French journal (https://lectures.revues.org/7102).

30  http://www.palim-psao.fr/article-theorie-de-marx-crise-et-depassement-du-capitalisme-a-propos-de-la-situation-de-la-critique-social-108491159.html.

31  O'Connor 1998.

it breaks down, or indirectly through the reinternalization of the costs that had been expelled into the environment'.[32] Approaching the issue through the theory of accumulation and profitability must give way to something infinitely more serious, namely the effects on the entire structure of society, and this in a truly global world. Warnings about the dimensions of the dangers of climate change date back to the late 1980s and led to the setting up by the United Nations of the Intergovernmental Panel on Climate Change (IPCC). Global warming has been measured more and more precisely and its consequences documented by the IPCC's successive reports (1990, 1995, 2001, 2007 and 2014). They have not been heeded. Climate change 'scepticism' financed by oil lobbies has given way to lip-service recognition by governments and costly conferences with little or no effects. In linking the ecological question to the fall of our society into barbarism precedence must be attributed again to Mészáros in 2001:

> Marx was to some extent already aware of the 'ecological problem,' i.e. the problems of ecology under the rule of capital and the dangers implicit in it for human survival. In fact he was the first to conceptualize it. He talked about pollution and he insisted that the logic of capital – which must pursue profit, in accordance with the dynamic of self-expansion and capital accumulation – cannot have any consideration for human values and even for human survival. [...] What you cannot find in Marx, of course, is an account of the utmost gravity of the situation facing us. For us the threat to human survival is a matter of *immediacy*.[33]

By threat to human survival is of course meant a threat to civilisation as we have understood it up to now. Humans will survive, but if capitalism is not overthrown, they will live, at world level, in a society of the type Jack London described in his great dystopian novel *The Iron Heel*. Until revolutionary change takes place we are trapped by the relations and contradictions specific to the capitalist mode of production. A mode of production characterised by 'the unceasing movement of profit-making, the boundless drive for enrichment'[34] cannot heed a message which calls for an end to growth as it is traditionally understood and a negotiated and planned use of remaining resources. There are convincing reasons for arguing, as does Jason Moore, that the Capitalocene defined as 'the historical era shaped by relations privileging the endless accu-

---

32  Kovel 2002, pp. 39–40.
33  Mészáros 2001, p. 99.
34  Marx 1976, Vol. I, p. 254.

mulation of capital'[35] is a more correct term for an ecological successor era to the Holocene than the Anthropocene despite the fact that the latter has received widespread recognition and will be almost impossible to replace. Also for defending the position that the gradual modification of the relation between capital and the biospheric and biophysical conditions that permitted the emergence of human societies during the Holocene goes back to the 'long sixteenth century' and the time of merchant capital. It was then that the forms of military and political power resorted to by European nations to establish the exploitation of men and of resources began. Basic 'benchmarks' of capitalist activity came with industrial capital. Notably 'that of a growth at an average rate of around 2.25 percent since 1750 or so ... anything less than three percent becoming problematic', with the need 'for capital to find a path to a minimum compound three percent growth forever'.[36]

The accumulation of capital has taken the form of the development of specific industries. The combined global economic and ecological crisis of capitalism is simultaneously that of social relations of production and a given mode of material production, consumption, use of energy and materials or, again, the entire material base on which accumulation has taken place, notably over the last 60 years, and the industries associated with it – energy, automobile, road infrastructures and construction leading to energy-intense urban and semi-urban models – and in agricultural production the extensive use of agrochemicals.[37] The prolongation of this mode under capitalism implies ever more destructive forms of mining, oil drilling (Artic, deep-sea pre-salt), agricultural production (highly intensive use of chemicals and expansion of farmed land through deforestation) and oceanic resources. They represent 'capital's effort to reverse the productivity slowdown through a series of last-ditch scrambles for the last crumbs of cheap nature remaining'.[38] The agent of this destruction is the contemporary figure of the 'capitalist, i.e. as capital personified and endowed with consciousness and a will',[39] namely the large industrial and mining corporation and those who own and control it.[40]

It has now become clear that global warming and ecological depletion must be defined as 'immanent barriers' to capital in the full sense, and not,

---

35   Moore 2014.
36   Harvey 2010.
37   I have discussed this in Chesnais 2010 and Chesnais 2014.
38   Moore 2014, p. 37.
39   Marx 1976, p. 254.
40   As I end this book, news comes of the possibly greatest ecological crisis provoked under capitalism by the Brazilian mining corporation Vale on the river Doce.

as still in O'Connor's work, as an exterior, 'second contradiction'. In his book (which I received just upon finishing this conclusion), Moore writes that 'the limits to growth faced by capital are real enough: they are "limits" co-produced through capitalism. The world-ecological limit of capital is capital itself'.[41] This co-production dates back to the period of merchant capital and in the most recent period it has been shaped by globalisation and financialisation. This barrier is one which cannot, as set out in Volume III of *Capital*, Chapter 15, be temporarily resolved through 'the periodic devaluation of existing capital' or 'overcome by means that set up the barriers afresh and on a more powerful scale'.[42] The barrier is there to stay. Foster has taken the notion of capital's absolute limit or barrier and developed it in relation with the environment, giving a close commentary on the relevant texts by Marx. He sees the 'approaching ecological precipice'[43] as being ever closer. Resource depletion is irreversible or reversible only in a time span that could take centuries. The pace of global warming is out of control, for the time being at least, so deeply is the present carbon-intensive energy regime imbricated with the modes of producing and living forged by capitalism. In the 'best scenario' (one without qualitative feedback processes), the issue is raised as one of 'adaptation', and so determined by the class and rich and poor country divides which will decide who in the world is harmed most.[44] Five years ago, *The Economist* published a well-documented synthesis announcing that the 'fight to limit global warming to easily tolerated levels is over'.[45] The four major international conferences that have been held since have basically been cynical expensive communication operations aimed at deceiving the uninformed whose number is beginning to dwindle.

As emphasised by Mandel above, the fact that capitalism has reached its absolute limits does not mean that it will give way to a new mode of production.[46]

---

41   Moore 2015, p. 295.
42   Marx 1981, Vol. III, p. 358.
43   Foster 2013, p. 1.
44   Stengers's essay on Hurricane Katrina (Stengers 2008) allowed me to discuss this dimension (Chesnais 2009).
45   'Adapting to climate change. Global action is not going to stop climate change. The world needs to look harder at how to live with it', *The Economist*, 25 November 2010. 'Though they are unwilling to say it in public, the sheer improbability of such success has led many climate scientists, campaigners and policymakers to conclude that, in the words of Bob Watson, once the head of the IPCC and now the chief scientist at Britain's Department for Environment, Food and Rural Affairs, "Two degrees is a wishful dream"'.
46   The optimistic view is that of Amin with his theory of a century or even centuries long transition to socialism (Amin 2016).

The elites and the governments they control are more than ever attentive to the preservation and reproduction of the capitalist order. So its progressive subsidence along with the foreseeable, but also the unforeseeable, effects of climate change will be accompanied by wars and by ideological and cultural regression, both that provoked by the financialisation of everyday life, commodification and global uniformity and that taking the form of religious fundamentalism and fanaticism. Mortality on account of local wars, diseases and sanitary and nutritional conditions due to great poverty continue to be counted in the tens if not the hundreds of millions.[47] As the impacts of climate change increase in given parts of the world (the Ganges Delta, much of Africa, the South Pacific Islands), this will endanger the very conditions of social reproduction of the oppressed.[48] They will necessarily fight back or seek to survive as best they can. The outcome will be, as we are already starting to see, violent conflicts over water resources, civil wars prolonged by foreign intervention in the world's poorest countries, enormous refugee movements caused by war and climate change.[49] Those that dominate and oppress the world order see this as a threat to their 'national security'. In a recent report, the US Department of Defense writes that global climate change will have wide-ranging implications for US national security interests because it will aggravate 'poverty, social tensions, environmental degradation, ineffectual leadership, and weak political institutions that threaten domestic stability in a number of countries'.[50] Moore writes that 'the shift towards financialization, and the deepening capitalization in the sphere of reproduction, has been a powerful way of postponing the inevitable blowback. It has allowed capitalism to survive. But for how much longer?'[51] Should the question not be worded differently: can 'we' get rid of or overthrow capitalism so as to establish a totally different 'human society-in-nature relationship'? And if we can't, will civilised society survive? Because a mode of production in the process of collapse will take everything down with it.

And then there is the question of the identity of the 'we'. As Aldo Casas has recently argued at the 20th anniversary of the journal *Herriamienta*,

---

[47] Jason Moore has synthesised historical data showing that the transition from feudalism to merchant capitalism from the late medieval period to the seventeenth century was economic and social but also ecological in its manifestations, stretching from recurrent famine, the Black Death, and soil exhaustion to peasant revolts and the escalation of warfare (Moore 2002). On famine, disease and war in West Africa, see Méillassoux 1997.

[48] This point was already central in Chesnais and Serfati 2003.

[49] Dyer 2010.

[50] http://www.defense.gov/pubs/150724-Congressional-Report-on-National-Implications-of-Climate-Change.pdf.

[51] Moore 2015, p. 305.

the 'collective revolutionary social subject' has turned out to be much more 'complex, polymorph or multi-varied' than the one found in the *Communist Manifesto*, because 'the system of exploitation and oppression represented by capital' has this characteristic.[52] But clearly the 'we' must also be defined as including all those engaged in radical ecological struggles.

This is not an encouraging way to end a book, but in the words of both Gramsci and Orwell, 'telling the truth is a revolutionary act'. The younger generations of today and those that will follow them are and will increasingly be faced with extraordinarily difficult problems. Major battles in some countries, but also in all others a countless number of self-organised struggles at the local level, demonstrate their determination to face up to them. Seen from the viewpoint of the fight for social emancipation, their immediate perspective is the one summed up in the word spoken by Marx during the last recorded conversation we have, precisely a conversation with a young American journalist: 'struggle'.[53] The uprisings in different parts of the world and, as importantly, the innumerable local struggles in almost every country, many of which are simultaneously economic and ecological, show that this is understood. The immense challenge is that of centralising this latent revolutionary energy across the world through a renewed internationalism and in political forms which do not repeat those with the disastrous results of the last century.

---

52 See his speech at http://www.herramienta.com.ar/content/encuentro-de-reflexion-y-debate-20-anos-de-herramienta. It also includes lucid remarks about the need for a capacity for critique and auto-critique of the new grass-root social movements, and not just of traditional working-class parties, avant-garde organisations and trade unions.

53 'Going down to the depth of language, and rising to the height of emphasis, during an interspace of silence, I interrogated the revolutionist and philosopher in these fateful words, "What is?" And it seemed as though his mind were inverted for a moment while he looked upon the roaring sea in front and the restless multitude upon the beach. "What is?" I had inquired, to which, in deep and solemn tone, he replied: "Struggle!" At first it seemed as though I had heard the echo of despair; but, peradventure, it was the law of life' (John Swinton, 'A conversation with Marx', *The Sun*, New York, 6 September 1880. I am indebted to Pierre Dardot and Christian Laval who end their book on Marx in this same way: see Dardot and Laval 2012).

# References

Adrian, Tobias and Adam Ashcraft 2012, 'Shadow Banking Regulation', *Federal Reserve Bank of New York Staff Reports*, 559, April.
Adrian, Tobias and Hyun Song Shin 2009, 'The Shadow Banking System: Implications for Financial Regulation', *Federal Reserve Bank of New York Staff Reports*, 382, July.
——— 2010, 'The changing nature of financial intermediation and the financial crisis of 2007–9', *Federal Reserve Bank of New York Staff Reports*, 439.
Aglietta Michel 2006, 'The Future of Capitalism', in *The Hardship of Nations: Exploring the Paths of Modern Capitalism*, edited by Coriat Benjamin, Pascal Petit and Geneviève Schméder, Cheltenham: Edward Elgar.
Aglietta, Michel and Laurent Berrebi 2007, *Désordres dans le capitalisme mondial*, Paris: Odile Jacob.
Aglietta, Michel, Anton Brender and Virginie Coudert 1990, *Globalisation financière: L'aventure obligée*, Paris: Economica.
Aglietta, Michel and Sandra Rigot 2009, *Crise et rénovation de la finance*, Paris: Odile Jacob.
Aglietta, Michel, Sabrina Khanniche and Sandra Rigot 2010, *Les Hedge Funds: Entrepreneurs ou requins de la finance?*, Paris: Perrin.
Amato, Massimo and Luca Fontana 2012, *The End of Finance*, Cambridge: Polity Press.
Amin, Samir 1974, *Accumulation on a World Scale*: A Critique of the Theory of Underdevelopment, New York: Monthly Review Press.
——— 2010, *The Law of Worldwide Value*, New York: Monthly Review Press.
——— 2013, 'China 2013', *Monthly Review*, 64, 10 (March).
——— 2016, *Russia and the Long Transition from Capitalism to Socialism*, New York: Monthly Review Press.
Andersson, Rebecka and Jennie Wang 2011, 'The internationalization process of Chinese MNCs: A study of the motive for Chinese firms to enter developed countries', School of Business, Economics and Law, University of Gothenburg, available at: <https://gupea.ub.gu.se/bitstream/2077/26634/1/gupea_2077_26634_1.pdf>.
Andreff, Wladimir 1996, *Les Multinationales globales*, Paris: La Découverte.
——— (ed.) 2013, *La mondialisation, stade suprême du capitalisme: En hommage à Charles-Albert Michalet*, Paris: Presses Universitaires de Paris-Ouest-Nanterre.
——— 2016, 'Outward Foreign Direct Investment from BRICS countries: Comparing strategies of Brazilian, Russian, Indian and Chinese multinational companies', *European Journal of Comparative Economics* (forthcoming special issue on the BRICS).
Appelbaum Eileen and Rosemary Batt 2012, 'A Primer on Private Equity at Work Management, Employment, and Sustainability', *Center for Economic and Policy Research*, Washington DC, February.

Arbulu, Pedro 1998, 'La bourse de Paris au XIX$^e$ siècle: l'exemple d'un marché émergent devenu efficient', *Revue d'économie financière*, 49: 213–249.

Arestis, Philip and Murray Glickman 1999, 'Financial crisis in South-East Asia: Dispelling Illusion the Mynskyan Way', UEL, Department of Economics, Working Paper, 22, December, available at: <http://fr.scribd.com/doc/212298430/Arestis-y-Glickman-1999-Financial-Crisis-in-South-East-Asia#scribd>.

Ashman, Sam, Ben Fine and Susan Newman 2011, 'The Crisis in South Africa: Neoliberalism, Financialization and Uneven and Combined Development', *Socialist Register*, 47: 174–195.

Avdjiev, Stefan, Anastasia Kartasheva and Bilyana Bogdanova 2013, 'CoCos: A primer', *BIS Quarterly Review*, September.

Baba, Naohiko, Robert N. McCauley and Srichander Ramaswamy 2009, 'US dollar money market funds and non-US banks', *BIS Quarterly Review*, March.

Bank for International Settlements (BIS) 2007, 'Foreign exchange and derivatives market activity in 2007', *Triennial Central Bank Survey*, Basel, December.

——— 2010, 'Foreign exchange and derivatives market activity in 2010', *Triennial Central Bank Survey*, Basel, December.

——— 2011a, 'Principles for the supervision of financial conglomerates', available at: <www.bis.org/publ/joint27.pdf>.

——— 2011b, 'Global systemically important banks: Assessment methodology and the additional loss absorbency requirement', available at: http://www.bis.org/publ/bcbs207.htm.

——— 2013, 'OTC interest rate derivatives turnover in April 2013: preliminary global results', available at: http://www.bis.org/publ/rpfx13ir.pdf.

——— 2014a, '84th Annual Report', 2013–14, Basel, June.

——— 2014b, 'Triennial Central Bank Survey Foreign exchange turnover in April 2013: preliminary global results', available at: http://www.bis.org/publ/rpfxf13fxt.pdf.

——— 2015, 'OTC derivatives statistics at end 2014', available at: http://www.bis.org/publ/otc_hy1504.pdf.

Baran, Paul and Paul Sweezy 1996, *Monopoly Capital*, New York: Monthly Review Press.

Barbour, Violet 1966, *Capitalism in Amsterdam in the 17th Century*, 2nd edition, Ann Arbor, MI: Ann Arbor Paperbacks.

Barker, William 2007, 'The Global Foreign Exchange Market: Growth and Transformation', *Bank of Canada Review*, Autumn.

Baronian, Laurent 2013, *Marx and Living Labour*, London: Routledge.

Baronian, Laurent and Matari Pierre 2011, 'From the Orchestra Conductor to the Agent of the Shareholder', forthcoming (paper presented at the 2011 Historical Materialism Conference).

Beblawi, Hazem 1990, 'The Rentier State in the Arab World', in *The Arab State*, edited by Giorgio Luciani, London: Routledge.

Bellofiore, Riccardo 1998, 'Comment on de Brunhoff and Meacci', in *Marxian Economics, A Reappraisal: Essays on Volume III of Capital*, London: Macmillan Press, available at: <http://digamo.free.fr/bellof98.pdf>.

―――― 2014, 'The Great Recession and the contradictions of contemporary capitalism', in *The Great Recession and the Contradictions of Contemporary Capitalism*, edited by Riccardo Bellofiore and Giovanna Vertova, Cheltenham: Edward Edgar.

Berg, Nathalie and Bryan Roberts 2012, *Walmart: Key Insights and Practical Lessons from the World's Largest Retailer*, London: Kogan Page.

Berle, Adolph and Gardiner Means 1967, *The Modern Corporation and Private Property*, 2nd edition, New York: Harcourt, Brace and World.

Bernanke, Bernard 2005, 'The Global Saving Glut and the U.S. Current Account Deficit', Sandridge Lecture, Virginia Association of Economists, Richmond, Virginia, March, available at: <http://www.federalreserve.gov/boarddocs/speeches/2005/200503102/default.htm>.

Bhatia, Ashok Vir and Tamim Bayoumi 2012, 'Leverage? What Leverage? A Deep Dive into the U.S. Flow of Funds in Search of Clues to the Global Crisis', International Monetary Fund Working Paper, 12/162, June.

Bihr, Alain 2006, *La préhistoire du capital: Le devenir-monde du capitalisme*, Volume 1, Lausanne: Éditions Page deux.

Blundell-Wignall, Adrian 2007, 'An Overview of Hedge Funds and Structured Products: Issues in Leverage and Risk', *OECD Financial Market Trends*, 92: 1.

―――― 2012, 'Solving the Financial and Sovereign Debt Crisis in Europe', *OECD Financial Market Trends*, Vol. 2010, Issue 2.

Blundell-Wignall, Adrian and Patrick Slovik 2011, 'A Market Perspective on the European Sovereign Debt and Banking Crisis', *OECD Journal: Financial Market Trends*, Vol. 2010, Issue 2: 1–28.

Blundell-Wignall, Adrian and Paul Atkinson 2012, 'Deleveraging, Traditional versus Capital Markets Banking and the Urgent Need to Separate and Recapitalise G-SIFI Banks', *OECD Journal: Financial Market Trends*, Vol. 2012, Issue 1: 7–44.

Bord, Vitaly M. and João A.C. Santos 2012, 'The Rise of the Originate-to-Distribute Model and the Role of Banks in Financial Intermediation', *Economic Policy Review*, 16, no. 2.

Borio, Claudio 2014, 'The international monetary and financial system: Its Achilles heel and what to do about', *BIS Working Papers*, no. 356.

Borio, Claudio and Piti Disyatat 2011, 'Global imbalances and the financial crisis: Link or no link?', *BIS Working Papers*, no. 346.

Bouvier, Jean 1961, *Le Crédit Lyonnais de 1863 à 1882, les années de formation d'une banque de dépôt*, Paris: SEVPEN.

―――― 1974, 'Les traits majeurs de l'imperialisme francais avant 1914', *Le Mouvement social*, 86.

Boyer, Robert 1987, *La théorie de la régulation: Une analyse critique*, Paris: La Découverte. Published in English by Columbia University Press, New York, 1990.

Boyer, Robert and Mickaël Clévenot 2011, 'Interview with Engelbert Stockhammer', *Revue de la régulation*, 10, no. 2.

Braverman, Harry 1974, *Labor and Monopoly Capital: The Degradation of Work in the Twentieth Century*, New York: Monthly Review Press.

Brenner, Robert 2002, *The Boom and the Bubble: The US in the Word Economy*, London: Verso.

Brock, James W. 2011, 'Economic concentration and economic power: John Flynn and a quarter-century of mergers', *The Antitrust Bulletin*, 56, no. 4.

Bryan, Dick and Michael Rafferty 2006, 'Money in Capitalism or Capitalist Money?', *Historical Materialism*, 14, no. 1: 75–95.

——— 2012, 'Why We Need to Understand Derivatives in Relation to Money: A Reply to Tony Norfield', *Historical Materialism*, 20, no. 3: 97–109.

Buch, Claudia, Catherine Koch and Michael Koetter 2011, 'Crises, rescues and policy transmissions through international banks', Deutsche Bundesbank Economic Discussion Papers, 15, available at: <http://www.bundesbank.de/Redaktion/EN/Stan dardartikel/Bundesbank/Research_Centre/research_data_micro_data_external_ position_publications.html>.

Cain, P.J. and A.G. Hopkins 1993, *British Imperialism: Innovation and Expansion, 1688–1914*, London and New York: Longman.

Callinicos, Alex 2014, *Deciphering Capital: Marx's Capital and its Destiny*, London: Bookmarks.

Carcanholo, Reinaldo A. and Paulo Nakatani 1999, 'O capital especulativo parasitário: uma precisão teórica sobre o capital financeiro, característico da globalização', *Ensaios FEE*, Porto Alegre, 20, no. 1: 284–304.

Carcanholo, Reinaldo and Mauricio Sabadini 2008, 'Capital Ficticio y Ganancias Ficticias', *Herriamenta*, 37, available at: <http://www.herramienta.com.ar/revista-herramienta-n-37/capital-ficticio-y-ganancias-ficticias>.

Carchedi, Guglielmo 2011, 'Behind and beyond the crisis', *International Socialist Journal*, 132.

Carchedi, Guglielmo and Michael Roberts 2013, 'The long roots of the present crisis', *World Review of Political Economy*, 4, no. 1, available at: <http://resistir.info/livros/carchedi_roberts_2013.pdf>.

Caron, François 1979, *An Economic History of Modern France*, New York: Columbia University Press.

Carroll, William 2008, 'The corporate elite and the transformation of finance capital: A view from Canada', *Sociological Review*, 56, no. 1: 44–63.

——— 2013, 'Whither the transnational capitalist class?', *Socialist Register 2014*, London: The Merlin Press.

REFERENCES 277

Carroll, William, Meindert Fennema and Eelke M. Heemskerk 2010, 'Constituting Corporate Europe: A Study of Elite Social Organization', *Antipode*, 42, no. 4: 811–843.

Cassiolato, José Eduardo, Marcelo Pessoa de Matos and Helena M.M. Lastres 2014, *Desenvolimiento e Mundializaçio: O Brazil e o Pensiamento de François Chesnais*, Rio de Janeiro: Ediçäo E-Papers.

Caves, Richard 1974, 'Industrial corporations: The industrial economics of foreign investment', *Economica*, August.

Censer, Jack Richard 2004, 'The Night the Old Regime Ended: August 4, 1789, and the French Revolution', *Journal of Social History*, 37, no. 4: 1113–1115.

Chandler, Alfred 1990, *Scale and Scope*, Cambridge, MA: Harvard University Press.

Chang, Ha-Joon, Hong-Jae Park and Chul Gyue Yoo 1998, 'Interpreting the Korean Crisis: Financial Liberalisation, Industrial Policy and Corporate Governance', *Cambridge Journal of Economics*, 22, no. 6: 735–746.

Chandrasekbar C.P. 2016, 'National Development Banks in a Comparative Perspective, in UNCTAD, Rethinking Development Strategies After The Financial Crisis, Genva.

Chesnais, François 1967, 'La contradiction entre les forces productives et les rapports sociaux de production et ses traits spécifiques dans le système capitaliste', (signed as Etienne Laurent) La Vérité, Paris.

——— 1981, 'Capital financier et groupes financiers: recherche sur l'origine des concepts et leur utilisation en France', in *Internationalisation des Banques et des Groupes Financiers*, under the direction of Charles-Albert Michalet, Paris: Éditions du CNRS.

——— 1993, 'The French National System of Innovation', in *National Systems of Innovation: A Comparative Analysis*, edited by Richard Nelson, Oxford: Oxford University Press.

——— 1994, *La mondialisation du capital*, Paris: Syros.

——— 1996, 'Mondialisation financière et vulnérabilité systémique', in *La mondialisation financière: Genèse, coût et enjeux*, edited by François Chesnais, Paris: Syros.

——— 1997, *La mondialisation du capital*, 2nd expanded edition, Paris: Syros.

——— 2000, 'Crises de la finance ou prémisses de crises économiques propres au régime d'accumulation actuel', in *Les pièges de la finance mondiale*, edited by François Chesnais and Dominique Plihon, Paris: La Découverte/Syros.

——— 2001, 'La théorie du régime d'accumulation financiarisé: contenu, portée et interrogations', *Forum de la régulation*, Paris, 11–12 Octobre.

——— 2004, 'La mondialisation de l'armée industrielle de réserve', *Carré Rouge*, 30.

——— 2006a, 'The special position of the United States in the finance-led regime: how exportable is the US venture capital industry?', in *The Hardship of Nations*, edited by Benjamin Coriat, Pascal Petit and Genevieve Schméder, Cheltenham: Edward Elgar.

——— 2006b, 'La prééminence de la finance au sein du « capital en général », le capital fictif et le mouvement contemporain de mondialisation du capital', in Séminaire d'Etudes Marxistes, *La finance capitaliste*, Actuel Marx Confrontation, Paris: Presses Universitaires de France.

———— 2007, 'Notes sur la portée et le cheminement de la crise financière', Congrès Marx International V, Nanterre, October, revised on 01 November 2007 and published in *La Brèche-Carré Rouge*, 1, November.

———— 2009, '« Socialisme ou barbarie »: les nouvelles dimensions d'une alternative', *Contretemps*, available at: <http://contretemps.eu>.

———— 2010, 'Ecologie, lutte sociale et construction d'un projet révolutionnaire dans les conditions du XXI° siècle', in *Pistes pour un anticapitalisme vert*, edited by Vincent Gay, Paris: Syllepse.

———— 2011, *Les dettes illégitimes: Quand les banques font main basse sur les politiques publiques*, Paris: Éditions Raison d'Agir.

———— 2014, 'Uma interpretação sobre a situação econômica mundial seguida por considerações sobre a crise do meio ambiente vista do ponto de vista da "sociedade mundial"', in *Políticas estratégicas de inovação e mudança estrutural – volume 1: sustentabilidade socioambiental em um contexto de crise*, edited by José E. Cassiolato, Maria Gabriela Podcameni and Maria Clara C. Soares, Rio de Janeiro: E-papers.

Chesnais, Francois and Laurent Baronian 2013, 'La política monetaria y financiera de los Chicago boys y la crisis financiera de 1982', *Actuel Marx Intervenciones, Edición chilena*, 15, no. 2: 99–112.

Chesnais, François and Jean-Pierre Divés 2002, *Que se vayan todos: Le peuple argentin se soulève*, Paris: Éditions Nautilus.

Chesnais, François and Dominique Plihon (eds.) 2000, *Les pièges de la finance mondiale*, Paris: La Découverte/Syros.

Chesnais, François and Catherine Sauviat 2003, 'The financing of innovation-related investment in the contemporary global finance-dominated accumulation regime', paper presented in Rio de Janeiro in 2000 and published in *Systems of Innovation and Development, Evidence from Brazil*, edited by Helena M.M. Lastres, José E. Cassiolato and Maria Lucia Maciel, Cheltenham: Edward Elgar.

Chesnais, François and Claude Serfati 1992, *L'armement en France: Genèse, ampleur et coût d'une industrie*, Paris: Nathan.

———— 2003, 'Les conditions physiques de la reproduction sociale', *Capital contre nature*, under the direction of J-M Harribey and Michael Löwy, Actuel Marx Confrontation, Paris: Presses Universitaires de France.

Choonara, Joseph 2009, 'Marxist Accounts of the Present Crisis', *International Socialist Journal*, June, Issue 123, available at: http://isj.org.uk/marxist-accounts-of-the-current-crisis/.

———— 2011, 'Once more (with feeling) on Marxist accounts of the crisis', *International Socialist Journal*, October, Issue 132, available at: http://isj.org.uk/once-more-with-feeling-on-marxist-accounts-of-the-crisis/.

Claessens, Stijn, Zoltan Pozsar, Lev Ratnovski and Manmohan Singh 2012, 'Shadow Banking: Economics and Policy', IMF Staff Discussion Note, SDN, 12, 12, 4 December.

Clegg, Jeremy and Hinrich Voss 2012, 'Chinese Direct Investment in the European Union', *Europe China Research and Advice Network*, available at: <www.chathamhouse.org/sites/files/chathamhouse/public/Research/Asia/0912ecran_cleggvoss.pdf>.

Coase, Ronald 1937, 'The Nature of the Firm', *Economica*, 4.

Cogan, Philip 2009, *The Money Machine: How the City Works*, 6th revised and updated edition, London: Penguin.

Contractor, Farok J., Vikas Kumar, Sumit K. Kundu and Torben Pedersen 2010, 'Reconceptualizing the Firm in a World of Outsourcing and Offshoring: The Organizational and Geographical Relocation of High-Value Company Functions', *Journal of Management Studies*, 47, no. 8.

Coriat, Benjamin 2006, 'Moves Towards Finance-led Capitalism: The French Case', in *The Hardship of Nations: Exploring the Paths of Modern Capitalism*, edited by Benjamin Coriat, Pascal Petit and Geneviève Schméder, Cheltenham: Edward Elgar.

Coriat, Benjamin, Pascal Petit and Geneviève Schméder 2006, *The Hardship of Nations: Exploring the Paths of Modern Capitalism*, Cheltenham: Edward Elgar.

Cosio-Pascal, Enrique 2008, 'The Emerging of a Multilateral Forum for Debt Restructuring: The Paris Club', *UNCTAD Discussion Papers*, 192, November.

Council of Economic Advisers 2016, Benefits of Competition and Indicators of Market Power, Issue Brief, Washington DC, April 27 <www.whitehouse.gov/sites/default/files/page/files/20160414ceacompetition issue_brief.pdf>.

Covitz, Daniel, Nellie Lang and Gustavo Sanchez 2009, 'The Evolution of a Financial Crisis: Panic in the Asset-Backed Commercial Paper Market', *Finance and Economic Discussion Papers*, 36, Washington DC: Federal Reserve Board, available at: <http://www.federalreserve.gov/pubs/feds/2009/200936/200936pap.pdf>.

Cowen, Tyler 2011, *The Great Stagnation: How America Ate All the Low-Hanging Fruit of Modern History, Got Sick, and Will (Eventually) Feel Better*, New York: Dutton.

Dardot, Pierre and Christian Laval 2012, *Marx, prénom Karl*, Paris: Gallimard.

De Brunhoff, Suzanne 1967, *Marx on Money*, London: Pluto Press.

―――― 1987, 'Fictitious Capital', in *The New Palgrave Dictionary of Economics*, edited by John Eatwell, Murray Milgate and Peter Newman, Basingstoke: Palgrave.

―――― 1998, 'Money, Interest and Finance in Marx's Capital', in *Marxian Economics, A Reappraisal: Essays on Volume III of Capital*, edited by Riccardo Bellofiore, London: Macmillan Press.

―――― 2004, 'Marx's Contribution to the Search for a Theory of Money', in *Marx's Theory of Money: Modern Appraisals*, edited by Fred Moseley, London: Palgrave

Macmillan. Online December 2008, available at: <http://ioakimoglou.netfirms.com/resources/Lesxi-Kataskopwn/Marx-on-Money.pdf>.

―――― 1973, *La Politique monétaire: une essai d'interprétation marxiste*, Paris: Presses Universitaires de France.

Dedrick, Kenneth, Jason Kraemer and Greg Linden 2008, *Who Profits from Innovation in Global Value Chains? A study of the iPod and notebook PCs*, Alfred Sloane Foundation Industry Studies, available at: <http://web.mit.edu/iso8/pdf/Dedrick_Kraemer_Linden.pdf>.

DeLong, Bradford D. 1991, 'Did J.P. Morgan's Men Add Value? An Economist's Perspective on Financial Capitalism', in *Inside the Business Enterprise: Historical Perspectives on the Use of Information*, edited by Peter Temin, Chicago, IL: University of Chicago Press, available at: <http://www.nber.org/books/temi91-1>.

DeLong, Bradford D. and Richard S. Grossman 1993, '"Excess Volatility" on the London Stock Market, 1970–1990', available at: <http://citeseerx.ist.psu.edu/viewdoc/download?doi=10.1.1.184.9069&rep=rep1&type=pdf>.

Dertouzos, Michael, Robert Solow and Richard Lester 1989, *Made in America: Regaining the Productive Edge*, Cambridge, MA: MIT Press.

D'Hulster, Katia 2009, 'The Leverage Ratio: A New Binding Limit on Banks', *World Bank, Financial and Private Sector Development Vice-Presidency*, note no. 11, December, available at: http://www.worldbank.org/financialcrisis/pdf/levrage-ratio-web.pdf.

Doctor, Mahrukh 2010, 'Brazil's Rise and the Role of Big Business', *Bologna Journal of International Affairs*, 13, Spring, available at: http://bcjournal.org/volume-13/brazils-rise-and-the-role-of-big-business.html.

Domhoff, William G. 1967, *Who Rules America: Power, Politics and Social Change*. New York: McGraw Hill, with seven subsequent re-editions.

―――― 2013, 'Interlocking Directorates in the Corporate Community', available at: http://www2.ucsc.edu/whorulesamerica/power/corporate_community.html.

Dos Santos, Paulo L. 2009, 'On the Content of Banking in Contemporary Capitalism', *Historical Materialism*, 17, no. 2: 83–118.

Duménil, Gérard and Dominique Lévy 1999, *Le Triangle Infernal: Crise, mondialisation, financiarisation*, Actuel Marx Confrontation, Paris: Presses Universitaires de France.

―――― 2004, Neoliberal Income Trends: Wealth, Class and Ownership in the USA, *New Left Review*, N°30, November–December.

―――― 2011a, *The Crisis of Neoliberalism*, Cambridge, MA: Harvard University Press.

―――― 2011b, 'The Crisis of the Early 21st Century: A Critical Review of Alternative Interpretations', available at: http://www.jourdan.ens.fr/levy/dle2011e.pdf.

Dunning, John 1993, *Multinational Enterprises and the Global Economy*, Wokingham: Addison-Wesley Publishing Company.

―――― 1998, 'The New Style Multinationals – Circa the Late 1980s and Early 1990s', in *Explaining International Production*, edited by John Dunning, London: Unwin Hyman.

Durand, Cédric 2014, *Le capital fictif: Comment la finance s'approprie notre avenir*, Paris: Les Prairies ordinaires.

Durand, Cédric and Philippe Leger 2014, 'Over-accumulation, Rising Costs and "Unproductive" Labor: The Relevance of the Classic Stationary State Issue for Developed Countries', *Review of Radical Political Economics*, 46, no. 1, 35–53.

Dyer, Gwynne 2010, *Climate Wars: The Fight for Survival as the World Overheats*, Melbourne, Scribe Publishers.

Eaglan, Mackenzie and Julia Pollack 2012, 'US Military Technology Supremacy Under Threat', American Enterprise Institute, November, available at: http://www.aei.org/files/2012/11/26/-us-military-technological-supremacy-under-threat_172916742245.pdf.

Elhefnawy, Nader 2012, 'Review of The New Industrial State', available at: http://naderelhefnawy.blogspot.fr/2013/02/2012-in-review-notable-posts.html.

Eichengreen, Barry J. 1982, 'The Proximate Determinants of Domestic Investment in Victorian Britain', *Journal Economic History*, 42, no. 1: 87–95.

―――― 1995, *Golden Fetters: The Gold Standard and the Great Depression, 1919–1939*, New York: Oxford University Press.

―――― 2005, 'Global Imbalances and the Lessons of Bretton Woods', available at: http://www.nber.org/papers/w10497.

Elwell, Craig K. 2011, 'Brief History of the Gold Standard in the United States', Congressional Research Service, 23 June, available at: http://fas.org/sgp/crs/misc/R41887.pdf.

Embassy of the Argentine Republic 2012, *Argentina's 2001 Debt Default: Myths and Realities*, Washington DC, April.

Epstein, Gerald A. (ed.) 2005, *Financialization and the World Economy*, London: Edward Elgar.

Epstein, Gerald A. and Arjun Jayadev 2005, 'The Rise of Rentier Incomes in OECD Countries: Financialization, Central Bank Policy and Labor Solidarity', in *Financialization and the World Economy*, edited by Gerald A. Epstein, London: Edward Elgar.

Ernst, Dieter 2008, 'Can Chinese IT Firms Develop Innovative Capabilities Within Global Knowledge Networks?', in *Greater China's Quest for Innovation*, edited by Marguerite G. Hancock, Henry S. Rowen and William F. Miller, Stanford, CA: Shorenstein Asia Pacific Research Center.

―――― 2009, 'A New Geography of Knowledge in the Electronic Industries? Asia's Role in Global Innovation Networks', *East-West Center*, Policy Study, 54, available at: http://www.eastwestcenter.org/publications/new-geography-knowledge-electronics-industry-asias-role-global-innovation-networks.

Esteves, Rui Pedro 2011, 'The *Belle Epoque* of International Finance: French Capital Exports, 1880–1914', Oxford University Department of Economics Discussion Paper

Series, 534, February, available at: http://www.economics.ox.ac.uk/materials/working_papers/paper534.pdf.

ETC Group 2013, 'Putting the Cartel before the Horse … and Farm, Seeds, Soil, Peasants, etc. Who Will Control Agricultural Inputs, 2013?', *Communiqué*, September, 111, available at: http://www.etcgroup.org/sites/www.etcgroup.org/files/CartelBeforeHorse11Sep2013.pdf.

European Commission 2010, 'The Financial Conglomerates Directive', Brussels, available at: http://ec.europa.eu/internal_market/financial-conglomerates/supervision.

European Parliament Socialist Group (PSE/EP) 2006, *Hedge Funds and Private Equity: A Critical Analysis*, Strasbourg.

European Systemic Risk Board 2014, 'Is Europe Overbanked?', Report of the Advisory Scientific Committee, 4, June, available at: http://www.esrb.europa.eu/pub/pdf/asc/Reports_ASC_4_1406.pdf?4fa1ede5965b4df5613605d6bab04a6b.

Farhi, Maryse and Marcos Antonio Macedo Cintra 2009, 'The financial crisis and the global shadow banking system', Crise du capitalisme financier, *Revue de la régulation: Capitalisme, institutions, pouvoirs*, 1st Semester, Spring.

Fattorelli, Maria Lucia and Rodrigo Ávila 2013, *Os numeros da dívida*, Auditoria Cidadã da Dívida, available at: http://www.divida-auditoriacidada.org.br.

Faulkner, Harold U. 1960, *American Economic History*, 8th edition, New York: Harper and Row.

Financial Stability Board 2011, 'Shadow Banking: Strengthening Oversight and Regulation', Recommendations of the Financial Stability Board, 27 October.

Fine, Ben and Laurence Harris 1977, 'Surveying the Foundations', *Socialist Register*, 14: 106–120.

Fitzsimmons, Michael P. 2003, *The Night the Old Regime Ended: August 4, 1789, and the French Revolution*, University Park, PA: Pennsylvania State University Press.

Flynn, John J. 1988, 'The Reagan Administration's Antitrust Policy, "Original Intent" and the Legislative History of the Sherman Act', *The Antitrust Bulletin*, 33, 259.

Fohlin, Caroline 2005, 'The History of Corporate Ownership and Control in Germany', in *A History of Corporate Governance around the World: Family Business Groups to Professional Managers*, edited by Randall K. Morck, Chicago, IL: University of Chicago Press, available at: http://www.nber.org/chapters/c10271.pdf.

Foster, John Bellamy 2000, *Marx's Ecology: Materialism and Nature*, New York: Monthly Review Press.

―――― 2008, 'Marx's *Grundrisse* and the Ecological Contradictions of Capitalism', in *Karl Marx's Grundrisse: Foundations of the Critique of Political Economy 150 Years Later*, edited by Marcello Musto, New York: Routledge.

―――― 2010, 'The Financialization of Accumulation', *Monthly Review*, 62, 5 (October).

―――― 2012, 'The Planetary Emergency', *Monthly Review*, 64, 7 (December).

REFERENCES 283

———— 2013, 'The Epochal Crisis – The Combined Capitalist Economic and Planetary Ecological Crises', *Monthly Review*, 65, 5 (October).
Foster, John Bellamy and Fred Magdoff 2009, *The Great Financial Crisis: Causes and Consequences*, New York: Monthly Review Press.
Foster, John Bellamy and Hannah Holleman 2010, 'The Financial Power Elite', *Monthly Review*, 62, 1 (May).
Freeman, Richard 1995, 'Control by the Food Cartel Companies: Profiles and Histories', *Executive Intelligence Review*, December, available at: http://www.larouchepub.com/other/1995/2249_cartel_companies.html.
———— 2008, 'The New Global Labor Market', available at: http://www.irp.wisc.edu/publications/focus/pdfs/foc261.pdf.
Frey, Carl B. and Michael A. Osborne 2013, 'The Future of Employment: How Susceptible Are Jobs to Computerisation?', available at: http://www.oxfordmartin.ox.ac.uk/downloads/academic/The_Future_of_Employment.pdf.
Fridenson, Patrick 1972, *Histoire des usines Renault, tome 1: naissance de la grande entreprise 1888–1939*, Paris: Seuil.
Friedman, Eli 2012, 'China in Revolt', available at: https://www.jacobinmag.com/2012/08/china-in-revolt/.
Furtado, Celso 1970, *Obstacles to Development in Latin America*, New York: Anchor Books-Doubleday.
———— 1999, *Global Capitalism*, translated by Jorge Navarrete, Mexico: Fondo de Cultura Economica.
Galbraith, John Kenneth 1967, *The New Industrial State*, Princeton, NJ: Princeton University Press.
Garbarivicius, Tomas and Franck Dierick 2005, 'Hedge Funds and Their Implications for Financial Stability', European Central Bank Occasional Papers, no. 34, August.
Garside, William and John Greaves 1996, 'The Bank of England and Industrial Intervention in Interwar Britain', *Financial History Review*, 3, no. 1, April.
Gaulard, Mylene 2009, 'Les limites de la croissance chinoise', *Revue Tiers Monde*, 200, December.
Geier, John 2012, 'Capitalism's Long Crisis', *International Socialist Journal*, 88.
Gereffi, Gary 1994, 'The Organisation of Buyer-driven Global Commodity Chains: How US Retailers Shape Overseas Production', in *Commodity Chains and Global Capitalism*, edited by Gary Gereffi and Miguel Korzeniewicz, Westport, CT: Greenwood Press.
———— 2001, 'Beyond the Producer-driven/Buyer-driven Dichotomy: The Evolution of Global Value Chains in the Internet Era', *IDS Bulletin*, 32, no. 3.
Gill, Louis 1996, *Fondements et limites du capitalisme*, Montreal: Les Editions du Boréal.
———— 2011, *La crise financière et monétaire mondiale*, Québec: Collection Mobilisations, M-Editeur.

Glyn, Andrew 2006, *Capitalism Unleashed*, Oxford: Oxford University Press.

Glyn, Andrew and Robert Sutcliffe 1972, *British Capitalism, Workers and the Profit Squeeze*, London: Penguin Books.

Goldner, Loren 2013, 'Fictitious Capital and Contracted Social Reproduction Today, China and Permanent Revolution', available at: http://www.metamute.org/editorial/articles/fictitious-capital-and-contracted-social-reproduction-today-china-and-permanent-revolution.

Gonjo, Yasuo 1993, *Banque coloniale ou Banque d'affaires – La Banque de l'Indochine sous la III$^e$ République*, Paris: Comité pour l'histoire économique et financière de la France / IGPDE.

Gopalan, Sasidaran and Ramkishen S. Rajan 2010, 'India's FDI Flows: Trying to Make Sense of the Numbers', UN Economic and Social Commission for Asia and the Pacific, *Artnet Newslettre*, 5.

Gordon, John Steele 2008, 'A Short Banking History of the United States Why Our System is Prone to Panic', *Wall Street Journal*, 10 October.

Gordon, Robert J. 2000, 'Interpreting the "One big wave" in US Long-term Productivity Growth', *National Bureau of Economic Research*, Working Paper 7752, Washington DC, available at: http://www.nber.org/papers/w7752.pdf.

——— 2012, 'Is US Growth Over? Faltering Innovation Confronts the Six Headwinds', NBER Working Paper 18315, available at: http://www.nber.org/papers/w18315.

——— 2016, 'The Rise and Fall of American Growth: The US Standard of Living Since the Civil War', Princeton, NJ: Princeton University Press.

Gorton, Gary and Andrew Metrick 2010, *Regulating the Shadow Banking System*, available at: http://www.brookings.edu/~/media/projects/bpea/fall%202010/2010b_bpea_gorton.pdf.

Gowan, Peter 1999, *The Global Gamble: Washington's Faustian Bid for World Dominance*, London and New York: Verso.

Greenlaw, David, Jan Hatzius, Anil K. Kashyap and Hyun Song Shin 2008, 'Leveraged Losses: Lessons from the Mortgage Market Meltdown', *US Monetary Policy Forum Report*, 2.

Griffith-Jones, Stephany 1998, *Global Capital Flows: Should They Be Regulated?*, London: St. Martin's Press.

Grossman, Henryk 1992 [1929], *The Law of Accumulation and Breakdown of the Capitalist System*, London: Pluto Press.

Guillén, Arturo 2013, 'Financialization and Financial Profit', paper presented at the Fourth Annual Conference on 'Political Economy Activism and Alternative Economic Strategies', IIPPE, The Hague, 9–11 July, available at: http://gesd.free.fr/guillen13.pdf.

Gupta, Arun 2013, 'The Wal-Mart Working Class', *Socialist Register 2014*, London: Merlin Press.

Guttmann, Robert 1994, *How Credit-Money Shapes the Economy: The United States in a Global System*, New York: M.E. Sharpe, Amonk.

Hanieh, Adam 2012, 'Finance, Oil and the Arab Uprisings: The Global Crisis and the Gulf States', *Socialist Register*, 48: 176–199.

Hanlon, John 2006 '"Illegitimate Debt": When Creditors Should be Liable for Improper Loans', in *Sovereign Debt at the Crossroads: Challenges and Proposals for Resolving the Third World Debt Crisis*, edited by Chris Jochnick and Fraser A. Preston, Oxford: Oxford University Press.

Harman, Chris 2010, 'Not All Marxism is Dogmatism: A Reply to Michel Husson', *International Socialism*, 125.

Hart-Landsberg, Martin, Seongjin Jeong and Richard Westra 2007, 'Introduction', in *Marxist Perspectives on South Korea in the Global Economy*, Farnham: Ashgate, available at: http://www.ashgate.com/isbn/9780754648161.

Harvey, David 1999 [1982], *Limits to Capital*, 2nd edition, London: Verso.

―――― 2003, *The New Imperialism*, Oxford: Oxford University Press.

―――― 2010, *The Enigma of Capital and the Crisis this Time*, Atlanta, GA: American Sociological Association Meetings, 16 August.

―――― 2012, 'The Urban Roots of Financial Crises', in *The Crisis and the Left*, edited by Leo Panitch, Greg Albo and Vivek Chibber, London: Socialist Register.

―――― 2013, *A Companion to Marx's Capital*, Volume 2, London: Verso.

Hashimoto, Yuko and Noriaki Kinoshita 2016, 'The Financial Wealth of Corporations: A First Look at Sectoral Balance Sheet Data', IMF Working Paper WP/16/11.

Heinrich, Michael 2013, 'Crisis Theory, the Law of the Tendency of the Profit Rate to Fall, and Marx's Studies in the 1870s', *Monthly Review*, 64, 11.

Helleiner, Eric 1994, *States and the Reemergence of Global Finance: From Bretton Woods to the 1990s*, Ithaca, NY: Cornell University Press.

Henry, Clement 2004, 'Algeria's Agonies: Oil Rent Effects in a Bunker State', available at: http://chenry.webhost.utexas.edu/public_html/Algeria_Agonies.pdf.

Henwood, Doug 1997, *Wall Street*, London: Verso.

Hernandez, Manuel A. and Maximo Torero 2011, 'Fertilizer Market Situation: Market Structure, Consumption and Trade Patterns, and Pricing Behavior', IFPRI Discussion Paper 01058, available at: http://www.ifpri.org/sites/default/files/publications/ifpridp01058.pdf.

Higginbottom, Andy 2011, 'Gold Mining in South Africa Reconsidered: New Mode of Exploitation, Theories of Imperialism and Capital', *Economies et Sociétés*, 45, 2.

Hilferding, Rudolf 1910, *Finance Capital*, available at: https://www.marxists.org/archive/hilferding/1910/finkap/.

Ho-Fung, Hun 2012, 'Sinomania: Global Crisis, China's Crisis', in *The Crisis and the Left*, edited by Leo Panitch, Greg Albo and Vivek Chibber, London: Socialist Register.

Horta, Loro 2013, 'China's Southern Europe Spending Spree', *The Diplomat*, East Asia Economy, 20 September, available at: http://thediplomat.com/2013/09/20/chinas-southern-european-spending-spree/.

Howse, Robert 2007, 'The Concept of Odious Debt in International Public Law', UNCTAD Discussion Paper 185, July.

Hudson, Michael 2011, *Europe's Transition from Social Democracy to Oligarchy*, available at: http://michael-hudson.com/2011/06/how-financial-oligarchy-replaces-democracy/.

Husson, Michel 2008, *Un pur capitalisme*, Lausanne: Editions Page 2.

——— 2009, 'Le marxisme n'est pas un dogmatisme', 28 June, available at: http://www.alencontre.com.

——— 2010, 'La hausse tendancielle du taux de profit', January, available at: http://hussonet.free.fr/tprof9.pdf.

——— 2013, 'La théorie des ondes longues et la crise du capitalisme contemporain', December, available at: http://hussonet.free.fr/mandelmh13.pdf.

Huws, Ursula 2012, 'Crisis as Capitalist Opportunity: The New Accumulation through Public Service Commodification', in *The Crisis and the Left*, edited by Leo Panitch, Greg Albo and Vivek Chibber, London: Socialist Register.

——— 2014, *Labor in the Digital Economy: The Cybertariat Comes of Age*, New York, Monthly Review Press.

Hymer, Stephen 1972a, 'The Multinational Firm and the Law of Uneven Development', in *Economics and World Order from the 1970s to the 1990s*, edited by Jagdish Bhawgati, New York: Free Press.

——— 1972b, 'The Internationalisation of Capital', *Journal of Economic Issues*, 6, no. 1.

Institute for International Finance 2009, *Reform in the Financial Services Industry: Strengthening Practices for a More Stable System Risk*, Washington DC, December.

IMF 2014, *Global Financial Stability Report*, Washington DC, April.

——— 2015a, *Global Financial Stability Report*, Washington DC, April.

——— 2015b, *Global Financial Stability Report*, Washington DC, October.

INSEE 2012, *Insee Première*, 1399, March, available at: http://www.insee.fr/fr/ffc/ipweb/ip1399/ip1399.pdf.

Ivanova, Maria N. 2011, 'Money, Housing and World Market: The Dialectic of Globalised Production', *Cambridge Journal of Economics*, 35, no. 5: 853–871.

——— 2013, 'The Dollar as World Money', *Science & Society*, 77, no. 1: 44–71.

Jackson, James K. 2013, 'Foreign Ownership of U.S. Financial Assets: Implications of a Withdrawal', *Congressional Research Service*, 8 April.

Jeffers, Esther and Dominique Plihon 2013, 'Le shadow banking system et la crise financière', *La documentation française*. Cahiers français, no. 375, June.

Johnson, Simon 2009, 'The Quiet Coup', *Atlantic Monthly*, May.

Kalecki, Michael 1943, *Studies in Economic Dynamics*, London: Allen and Unwin.

Kaltenbrunner, Annina, Susan Newman and Juan Pablo Painceira 2012, 'Financialisation of Natural Resources: A Marxist Approach', paper presented at the 9th International Conference Developments in Economic Theory and Policy, Bilbao, June.

Kennedy, William P. 1982, 'Economic Growth and Structural Change in the United Kingdom, 1870–1914', *Journal of Economic History*, 42, no. 1: 105–114.

Keynes, John Maynard 1920, *The Economic Consequences of the Peace*, New York: Harcourt, Brace, and Howe.

――― 1925, *The Economic Consequences of Mr. Churchill*, London: Leonard and Virginia Woolf.

――― 1936, *The General Theory of Employment, Interest and Money*, London: MacMillan.

King, Michael R. and Dagfinn Rime 2010, 'The $4 trillion Question: What Explains FX Growth Since the 2007 Survey?', *BIS Quarterly Review*, December.

Kliman, Andrew 2012, *The Failure of Capitalist Production: Underlying Causes of the Great Recession*, London: Pluto Press.

Kliman, Andrew and Williams, Shanon D. 2014, 'Why "financialisation" hasn't depressed US productive investment', *Cambridge Journal of Economics*, accessed at http://cje.oxfordjournals.org/content/early/2014/09/05/cje.beu033.

Konings Martijn 2010, 'Beyond the Re-regulation Agenda', in *The Great Credit Crash*, edited by M. Konings, London: Verso.

Kovel, Joel 2002, *The Enemy of Nature*, London: Zed Press.

Kregel, J.A. 1998, 'Derivatives and Global Capital Flows: Applications to Asia', *Cambridge Journal of Economics*, 22, no. 6: 677–692.

Krippner, Greta 2004, 'What is Financialization?', mimeo, Department of Sociology, UCLA, cited in Epstein 2005.

――― 2005, 'The Financialization of the American Economy', *Socio-Economic Review*, 3, no. 2: 173–208.

――― 2011, *Capitalizing on Crisis*, Cambridge, MA: Harvard University Press.

Kurz, Robert 2011, *Vies et mort du capitalisme. Chroniques de la crise*, Paris: Lignes.

Labrinidis, George 2014a, 'The Forms of World Money', Research on Money and Finance Discussion Paper 45, May.

――― 2014b, 'International Reserves in the Era of Quasi-world Money', Research on Money and Finance Discussion Paper 46, October.

Lacoste, Yves 1957, 'L'industrie du ciment', *Annales de Géographie*, 66, no. 357.

Lapavitsas, Costas 1997, 'Two Approaches to the Theory of Interest-Bearing Capital', *Journal of international Political Economy*, 2, no. 1: 85–106.

――― 2009, 'Financialisation, or the Search for Profits in the Sphere of Circulation', *Ekonomiaz*, 72, no. 3.

――― 2010, 'Financialisation and Capitalist Accumulation: Structural Accounts of the Crisis of 2007–2009', available at: http://se.ruc.edu.cn/upload/20101105/5516956.pdf.

—— 2011, 'Theorizing Financialization', *Work, Employment and Society*, 25, no. 4: 611–626.

—— (ed.) 2012, *Financialisation in Crisis*, Leiden: Brill.

—— 2013, *Profiting Without Production: How Finance Exploits Us All*, London: Verso.

Lazonick, William 1991, *Business Organization and the Myth of the Market Economy*, Cambridge: Cambridge University Press.

—— 2012, 'The Financialization of the U.S. Corporation: What Has Been Lost, and How It Can Be Regained', *The Academic-Industry Research Network*, University of Massachusetts Lowell.

—— 2014, 'Profits without Prosperity', *Harvard Business Review*, September, available at: https://hbr.org/2014/09/profits-without-prosperity/ar/1.

Lazonick, William and Mary O'Sullivan 2000, 'Maximizing Shareholder Value: A New Ideology for Corporate Governance', *Economy and Society*, 29, no. 1: 13–35.

Levy-Leboyer, Maurice 1977, 'La balance des paiements et l'exportation des capitaux francais', in *La position internationale de la France, aspects economiques et financiers, XIX$^e$ et XX$^e$ siecles*, edited by Maurice Levy-Leboyer, Paris: Editions Ecole des Hautes Etudes en Sciences Sociales.

Lenin, Vladimir I. 1917, *Imperialism, the Highest Stage of Capitalism*, available at: https://www.marxists.org/archive/lenin/works/1916/imp-hsc/.

Levina, Irene G. 2012, 'The Sources of Financial Profit: A Theoretical and Empirical Investigation of the Transformation of Banking in the US', *Dissertations*, paper 616, available at: http://scholarworks.umass.edu/cgi/viewcontent.cgi?article=1617&context=open_access_dissertations.

Lewis, Michael 2011, *The Big Short: Inside the Doomsday Machine*, London: Penguin.

Lewis, W. Arthur 1978, *Growth and Fluctuations*, London: Allen and Unwin.

Lichtenstein, Nelson (ed.) 2006, *Wal-Mart: The Face of Twenty-First Century Capitalism*, New York: The New Press.

Lietaer, Bernard 1997, 'Global Currency Speculation and its Implications', International Forum on Globalization, *IFG News*, 2, available at: http://www.twnside.org.sg/title/nar-cn.htm.

Liikanen Report 2012, 'Report of the European Commission's High-level Expert Group on Bank Structural Reform', Brussels.

Lin, Justin and Volker Treichel, 'The Unexpected Global Financial Crisis: Researching its Root Cause', Policy Research Working Paper 5937, World Bank, Washington DC.

Lordon, Frédéric 2000, *Fonds de pension, piège à cons? – Mirage de la démocratie actionnariale*, Paris: Raisons d'Agir.

Luxemburg, Rosa 1913, *The Accumulation of Capital*, available at: https://www.marxists.org/archive/luxemburg/1913/accumulation-capital/.

Magdoff, Harry and Paul Sweezy 1972, *The Dynamics of US Capitalism*, New York: Monthly Review Press.

## REFERENCES

——— 1987, *Stagflation and the Financial Explosion*, New York: Monthly Review Press.

Magdoff, Fred, John Bellamy Foster and Frederick Buttel (eds.) 2000, *Hungry for Profit: The Agribusiness Threat to Farmers, Food and the Environment*, New York: Monthly Review Press.

Mandel, Ernst 1962, *Traité d'économie marxiste*, Paris: Julliard.

——— 1970, *Europe vs. America: Contradictions of Imperialism*, New York: Monthly Review Press.

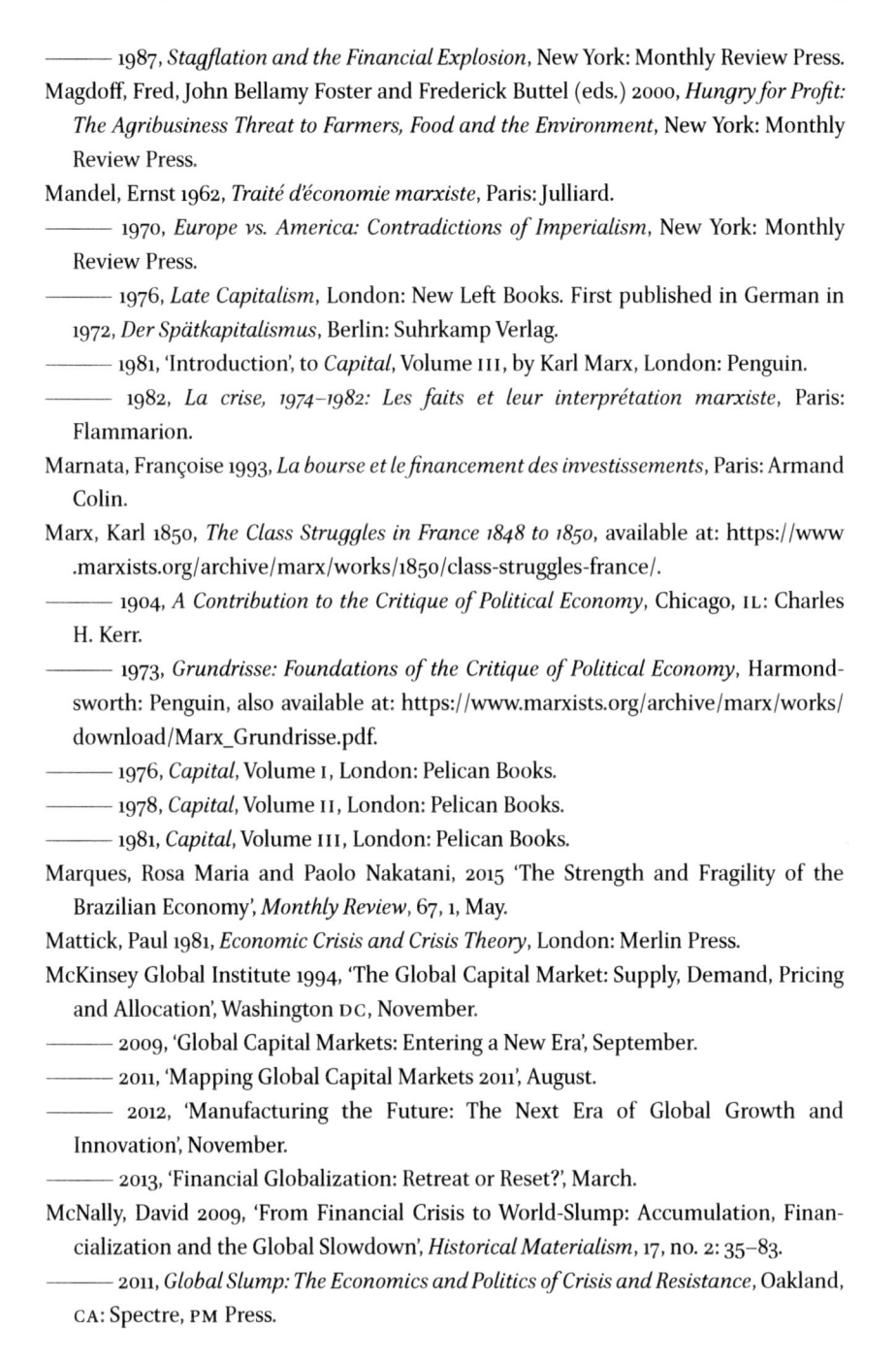

——— 1976, *Late Capitalism*, London: New Left Books. First published in German in 1972, *Der Spätkapitalismus*, Berlin: Suhrkamp Verlag.

——— 1981, 'Introduction', to *Capital*, Volume III, by Karl Marx, London: Penguin.

——— 1982, *La crise, 1974–1982: Les faits et leur interprétation marxiste*, Paris: Flammarion.

Marnata, Françoise 1993, *La bourse et le financement des investissements*, Paris: Armand Colin.

Marx, Karl 1850, *The Class Struggles in France 1848 to 1850*, available at: https://www.marxists.org/archive/marx/works/1850/class-struggles-france/.

——— 1904, *A Contribution to the Critique of Political Economy*, Chicago, IL: Charles H. Kerr.

——— 1973, *Grundrisse: Foundations of the Critique of Political Economy*, Harmondsworth: Penguin, also available at: https://www.marxists.org/archive/marx/works/download/Marx_Grundrisse.pdf.

——— 1976, *Capital*, Volume I, London: Pelican Books.

——— 1978, *Capital*, Volume II, London: Pelican Books.

——— 1981, *Capital*, Volume III, London: Pelican Books.

Marques, Rosa Maria and Paolo Nakatani, 2015 'The Strength and Fragility of the Brazilian Economy', *Monthly Review*, 67, 1, May.

Mattick, Paul 1981, *Economic Crisis and Crisis Theory*, London: Merlin Press.

McKinsey Global Institute 1994, 'The Global Capital Market: Supply, Demand, Pricing and Allocation', Washington DC, November.

——— 2009, 'Global Capital Markets: Entering a New Era', September.

——— 2011, 'Mapping Global Capital Markets 2011', August.

——— 2012, 'Manufacturing the Future: The Next Era of Global Growth and Innovation', November.

——— 2013, 'Financial Globalization: Retreat or Reset?', March.

McNally, David 2009, 'From Financial Crisis to World-Slump: Accumulation, Financialization and the Global Slowdown', *Historical Materialism*, 17, no. 2: 35–83.

——— 2011, *Global Slump: The Economics and Politics of Crisis and Resistance*, Oakland, CA: Spectre, PM Press.

―――― 2012, 'Explaining the Crisis or Heresy Hunting? A Response to Joseph Choonara', *International Socialist Journal*, March, 134, available at: http://isj.org.uk/explaining-the-crisis-or-heresy-hunting-a-response-to-joseph-choonara/.

―――― 2014, 'Blood of the Common Wealth', *Historical Materialism*, 22, no. 2: 3–32.

Mehrling, Perry 2001, *The New Lombard Street: How the Fed Became the Dealer of Last Resort*, Princeton, NJ: Princeton University Press.

Méillassoux, Claude 1997, *L'économie de la vie*, Lausanne: Editions Page 2.

Melman, Seymour 1983, *Profits Without Production*, New York: Alfred A. Knopf.

Mérieux, A. and C. Marchand 1996, *Les marchés financiers américains*, Paris: La Revue d'Economie Financière (collection La Bibliothèque).

Merler, Sylvia and Jean Pisani-Ferry 2012, 'Une relation risquée: l'interdépendance entre dette bancaire et dette souveraine et la stabilité financière dans la zone euro', *Banque de France, Revue de la Stabilité Financière*, 16 April.

Mészáros, István 1995, *Beyond Capital*, New York: Monthly Review Press.

―――― 2001, *Socialism or Barbarism*, New York: Monthly Review Press.

Michalet, Charles-Albert 1985, *Le capitalisme mondial*, 2nd edition, Paris: Presses Universitaires de France.

Milberg, William and Deborah Winkler 2009, 'Globalization, Offshoring and Economic Insecurity in Industrialized Countries', DESA Working Paper 87 (ST/ESA/2009/DWP/87), November.

―――― 2012, *Trade Crisis and Recovery: Restructuring of Global Value Chains*, Policy Research Working Paper 5294, The World Bank, May.

Minqi, Li 2008, *The Rise of China and the Demise of the Capitalist World-Economy*, London: Pluto Press.

Minqui, Li, Feng Xino and Andong Zu 2007, 'Long Waves, Institutional Changes and Historical Trends: A Study of the Long Term Movement of the Profit in the Capitalist World Economy', *Journal of World-Systems Research*, 13, no. 1: 33–54.

Minsky, Hyman 1986, *Stabilizing an Unstable Economy*, New Haven, CT: Yale University Press.

―――― 1992, 'The Financial Instability Hypothesis', Working Paper 74, Levy Economics Institute of Bard College.

Mishra, Ram Kumar 2009, 'State Owned Enterprises in India: Reviewing the Evidence', Occasional Paper, OECD *Working Group on Privatisation and Corporate Governance of State Owned Enterprises*, OCDE, Paris.

Mitchell, Stacy 2015, 'One in Four Local Banks Has Vanished Since 2008. Why We Should Treat It as a National Crisis', *Institute for Local Self-Reliance*, available at: http://ilsr.org/vanishing-community-banks-national-crisis/.

Moore, Jason W. 2002, 'The Crisis of Feudalism: An Environmental History', available at: http://www.jasonwmoore.com/uploads/Moore__Crisis_of_Feudalism__An_Environmental_History__O_E__2002_.pdf.

——— 2014a, 'The Capitalocene, Part I: On the Nature & Origins of Our Ecological Crisis', available at: http://www.jasonwmoore.com/Essays.html.

——— 2014b, 'The Capitalocene, Part II: Abstract Social Nature and the Limits to Capital', available at: http://www.jasonwmoore.com/uploads/The_Capitalocene__Part_II__June_2014.pdf.

——— 2015, *Capitalism in the Web of Life*, London and New York: Verso.

Morgan, Dan 1979, *Merchants of Grain*, New York: Viking.

Morin, François 1974, *La structure financière du capitalisme français*, Paris: Calmann Lévy.

——— 2011, *Un monde sans Wall Street?*, Paris: Editions du Seuil.

——— 2015, *L'hydre mondiale: L'oligopole bancaire*, Montréal: Lux éditeur.

Mukhopadhyaya, Jayanta Nath, Malabika Roy and Ajitava Raychaudhuri 2008, *An Analytical Study of the Changing Structure of the Cement Industry of India*, available at: http://www.iimidr.ac.in/iimi/images/IMJ/Volume4_Issue1/An%20Analytical%20Study%20of%20the%20Changing.pdf.

Musto, Marcello 2008, 'History, Production and Method in the 1857 "Introduction"', in *Karl Marx's Grundrisse: Foundations of the Critique of Political Economy 150 Years Later*, edited by Marcello Musto, London and New York: Routledge.

Nashashibi, Karim 2002, 'Fiscal Revenues in South Mediterranean Arab Countries: Vulnerabilities and Growth Potential', IMF Working Paper, WP/02/67.

Nelson, Prado Alves Pinto 1998, 'Finance Capital Revisited', in *Marxian Economics, A Reappraisal: Essays on Volume III of Capital*, London: Macmillan Press.

Newton, Scott 2010, 'The Sterling Devaluation of 1967, the International Economy and Post-War Social Democracy', *English Historical Review*, 75, 515: 912–945.

Norfield, Tony 2012, 'Derivatives and Capitalist Markets: The Speculative Heart of Capital', *Historical Materialism*, 20, no. 1: 103–132.

——— 2013, 'Derivatives, Money, Finance and Imperialism: A Response to Bryan and Rafferty', *Historical Materialism*, 21, no. 2: 149–168.

——— 2014, 'Capitalist Production Good, Capitalist Finance Bad', available at: http://www.economicsofimperialism.blogspot.co.uk/2014/01/capitalist-production-good-capitalist.html.

——— 2016, *The City: London and the Global Power of Finance*, London: Verso.

O'Connor, James 1998, *Natural Causes: Essays in Ecological Marxism*, New York: Guilford Press.

OECD 2008, 'Pharmaceutical Pricing Policies in a Global Market', Paris.

——— 2011, 'Trade Policy Papers', no. 114.

——— 2012, 'Financial Contagion in the Era of Globalised Banking', *OECD Economics Department Policy Notes*, 14 June.

——— 2015, *The Future of Productivity*, Paris.

Oman, Charles 1984, *New Forms of Investment in Developing Countries*, OECD Development Center, Paris.

——— (ed.) 1989, *New Forms of Investment in Developing Countries: Mining, Petrochemicals, Automobiles, Textiles, Food*, OECD Development Center, Paris.

Omarova, Saule T. 2013, 'Large U.S. Banking Organizations' Activities in Physical Commodity and Energy Markets: Legal and Policy Considerations', 23 July, available at: http://www.banking.senate.gov/public/index.cfm?FuseAction=Hearings.Testimony&Hearing_ID=cca72cb5-a8fd-427a-978a-a51140a75cb0&Witness_ID=310565d9-de2c-40af-b2b0-8f3b5870c04a.

Onetti, Alberto and Alessia Pisoni 2009, 'Ownership and Control in Germany: Do Cross-shareholdings Reflect Bank Control on Large Corporations', *Corporate Ownership & Control*, 6, no. 4, available at: http://www.virtusinterpress.org/IMG/pdf/Paper18.pdf.

Orléan, André 1999, *Le Pouvoir de la finance*, Paris: Odile Jacob.

O'Sullivan, Mary 2015, Introduction to *Dividends of Development: Fits and Starts in the History of US Securities Markets, 1865–1919*, Oxford: Oxford University Press, available at: https://www.unige.ch/sciences-societe/inhec/files/9014/4414/1301/Ch_0_Introduction_06_10_15.pdf.

Paley, Thomas I. 2010, 'The Limits of Minsky's Financial Instability Hypothesis as an Explanation of the Crisis', *Monthly Review*, 61, no. 11.

Palloix, Christian 1975, *L'internationalisation du capital: Eléments critiques*, Paris: Maspero.

Palmade, Guy 1961, *Capitalisme et capitalistes français au XIX° siècle*, Paris: Armand Colin.

Panitch, Leo and Sam Gindin 2011, 'The Crisis This Time', in *The Crisis This Time*, edited by Leo Panitch, Greg Albo and Vivek Chibber, London: Socialist Register.

——— 2012, *The Making of Global Capitalism: The Political Economy of American Empire*, London: Verso.

Panizza, Ugo 2008, *Domestic and External Public Debt in Developing Countries*, UNCTAD Discussion papers, 188, March.

Panizza, Ugo, Federico Sturzenegger and Jeromin Zettelmeyer 2012, 'International Government Debt', UNCTAD Discussion papers, 199, June.

Paulani, Leda Maria 2010a, 'The Autonomization of Truly Social Forms in Marx's Theory: Comments on Money in Contemporary Capitalism', Sixth International Marx Congress, Nanterre.

——— 2010b, 'Brazil in the Crisis of the Finance-led Accumulation Regime', *Review of Radical Political Economics*, 42, no. 3: 363–372.

——— 2015a, 'Modernity and Capitalist Progress in the Periphery: The Brazilian case', *European Journal of Social Theory*, available at: http://est.sagepub.com/content/early/2015/09/07/1368431015600018.full.pdf+html.

―――― 2015b, 'O processo de inserçao da economia brasiliera no capitalismo financeirizado e o papel do Estado', DIEESE, Sao Paulo.

―――― 2015c, 'Política e Classes Sociais no Capitalismo Neoliberal: o que a Economia tem a dizer?', in *Relatório final de pesquisa do projeto temático FAPESP Política e Classes Sociais no Capitalismo Neoliberal no Brasil*, by Armando Boito.

Payer, Cheryl 1974, *The Debt Trap: The IMF and the Third World*, New York: Monthly Review Press.

Peetz, Dietmar and Heribert Genreith 2011, 'Institute for Applied Risk Management, The Financial Sector and the Real Economy', *Real-world Economics Review*, 57, September.

Perez, Carlota 2007, 'Great Surges of Development and Alternative Forms of Globalization', available at: http://www.carlotaperez.org/papers/GreatSurges_and_Globalization.pdf.

Perroux, François 1965, *La Pensée économique de Joseph Schumpeter: Les dynamiques du capitalisme*, Geneva: Librairie Droz.

Petrovic, Misha and Gary Hamilton 2006, 'Making Global Markets: Wal-Mart and its Suppliers', in *Wal-Mart: The Face of Twenty-First Century Capitalism*, edited by N. Lichtenstein, New York: The New Press.

Piketty, Thomas and Emmanuel Saez 2006, 'The Evolution of Top Incomes: A Historical and International Perspective', *American Economic Review: Papers and Proceedings*, 96, no. 2: 200–205.

Pisano, Gary and Willy Shih 2009, 'Restoring American Competitiveness', *Harvard Business Review*, July–August.

Plessis, Alain 1982, *La Banque de France et ses deux cents actionnaires sous le Second Empire*, Geneva: Droz.

Plihon, Dominique and Esther Jeffers 2013, in 'La finance mise au pas?', *La Documentation françaises*, Cahiers français n°375.

Pollard, Sydney 1985, 'Capital Exports 1870–1914: Harmful or Beneficial', *The Economic History Review*, 38, no. 4: 489–514.

Pollin, Robert 1996, 'Contemporary Economic Stagnation in World Historical Perspective', *New Left Review*, 219(September/October): 109–118.

Porter, Michael E. 1992, 'Capital Disadvantage: America's Failing Capital Investment System', *Harvard Business Review*, 70, no. 5: 65–82.

Quinn, Bill 2000, *How Wal-Mart is Destroying America and the World*, Berkeley, CA: Ten Speed Press.

Revue d'Economie industrielle 1989, 'Les groupes industriels et financiers', no. 47.

Riesser, J. 1911, *The German Great Banks and their Concentration in Connection with the Economic Development of Germany*, Washington DC: Government Printing Office.

Roberts, Michael 2014a, 'Tendencies, Triggers and Tulips', 14–16 February, available at: https://thenextrecession.files.wordpress.com/2014/02/presentation-to-the-third-seminar-of-the-fi-on-the-economic-crisis.pdf.

―――― 2014b, 'Is Capital Past Its Use-By Date?', 6 March, available at: https://thenextrecession.wordpress.com/2014/03/06/is-capitalism-past-its-use-by-date/.

―――― 2016, 'Richard J Gordon and the Rise and Fall of American Capitalism', 14 March, available at: https://thenextrecession.wordpress.com/2016/02/14/richard-j-gordon-and-the-rse-and-fall-of-american-capitalism/.

Robinson, Joan 1956, *The Accumulation of Capital*, London: Macmillan.

Rogoff, Keneth 1991, *Third World Debt*, available at: http://www.econlib.org/library/Enc1/ThirdWorldDebt.html.

Romer, Christina D. 1992, 'What Ended the Great Depression?', *The Journal of Economic History*, 52, no. 4: 757–784.

Rosen, Richard J. 2010, 'The Impact of the Originate-to-Distribute Model on Banks Before and During the Financial Crisis', *Federal Reserve Bank of Chicago*, Working Paper no. 2010-20, November.

Roy, William G. 1997, *Socializing Capital: The Rise of the Large Industrial Corporation in America*, Princeton, NJ: Princeton University Press.

Ruane, Kathleen Ann and Michael V. Seitzinger 2010, 'Hedge Funds: Legal History and the Dodd-Frank Act', *Congressional Research Service*, 16 July.

Russo Daniela 2010, 'OTC Derivatives: Financial Instability Challenges and Responses from Authorities', *Banque de France Financial Stability Review*, no. 14.

Sabadini, Mauricio de S. 2008, *Le capital fictif et ses effets sur la macroéconomie et sur le monde du travail au Brésil*, unpublished PhD thesis, Université Paris 1 – Panthéon Sorbonne, Centre d'Économie de la Sorbonne (CES), November, available at: http://tel.archives-ouvertes.fr/tel-00354467/en/.

Sabadini, Mauricio de S. and Márcio Lupatini 2014, 'Globalizaçio and Financializaçio in François Chesnais', in Cassiolato et al.

Séminaire d'Etudes Marxistes 2006, *La finance capitaliste*, Actuel Marx Confrontation, Paris: Presses Universitaires de France.

Shields Dennis A., 2010, 'Consolidation and Concentration in the U.S. Dairy Industry', Congressional Research Service, Washington DC, April. http://nationalaglawcenter.org/wp-content/uploads/assets/crs/R41224.pdf.

Schenk, Catherine R. 2009, 'The Retirement of Sterling as a Reserve Currency after 1945: Lessons for the US Dollar?', available at: http://www.cirje.e.u.tokyo.ac.jp/research/workshops/history/history_paper2009/history1109.pdf.

Scherer, Frederick M. 1970, *Industrial Market Structure and Economic Performance*, Chicago, IL: Rand McNally College Publishing Company.

Shiller, Robert J. 2005, *Irrational Exuberance*, Princeton, NJ, Princeton University Press.

Schumpeter, Joseph 1939, *Business Cycles: A Theoretical, Historical and Statistical Analysis of the Capitalist Process*, New York: McGraw-Hill Book Company.

——— 1976 [1943], *Capitalism, Socialism and Democracy*, London: Allen and Unwin.

Scott, Robert E. 2007, 'Costly Trade with China: Millions of Jobs Displaced', *Economic Policy Brief*, Washington DC.

Serfati, Claude 1996, 'Le rôle actif des groups à dominantes industriels dans la financiarisation de l'économie', in *La Mondialisation financière: Genèse, coût et enjeux*, edited by François Chesnais, Paris: Collection Alternatives économiques, Editions Syros.

——— 2008, 'Financial Dimensions of Transnational Corporations, Global Value Chains and Technological Innovation', *Journal of Innovation Economics*, 2, no. 2: 35–61.

——— 2013, 'The New Configuration of the Capitalist Class', *Socialist Register 2014*, London: The Merlin Press.

——— 2015, 'Imperialism in Context: The Case of France', *Historical Materialism*, 23, no. 2: 52–93.

Servan-Sheiber, Jean-Jacques 1968, *Le Défi américain*, Paris: Editions Dénoël.

Smith, John 2010, *Imperialism and the Globalisation of Production*, unpublished PhD thesis, University of Sheffield, available at: http://www.mediafire.com/?5r339mnn4zmubq7.

——— 2011, 'Imperialism and the Law of Value', *Global Discourse*, 2, no. 1, available at: https://global-discourse.com/contents.

Smith, Murray and Johan Butovsky 2012, 'Profitability and the Roots of Global Crisis', *Historical Materialism*, 20, no. 4: 39–74.

Socialist Group of the European Parliament (PSE/EP) 2006, *Hedge Funds and Private Equity, A Critical Analysis*, Strasburg and Brussels.

Steindl, Frank G. 2007, 'What Ended the Great Depression? It was not World War II', *The Independent Review*, 12, no. 2: 179–197.

Stengers, Isabelle 2008, *Au temps des catastrophes: Résister à la barbarie qui vient*, Paris: La Découverte.

Stockhammer, Engelbert 2004, 'Financialisation and the Slowdown of Accumulation', *Cambridge Journal of Economics*, 28, no. 5: 719–741.

——— 2008, 'Some Stylized Facts on the Finance-Dominated Accumulation Regime', *Competition and Change*, 12, no. 2: 184–202.

Stoskopf, Nicolas 2002, *Les patrons du Second Empire: Banquiers et financiers parisiens*, Paris: Picard-Cenomane.

Stulz René M. 2009, 'Financial Derivatives: Lessons from the Subprime Crisis', *The Milken Institute Review*, First Quarter: 58–70.

Suret-Canal, Jean 1962, *Afrique Noire occidentale et central: L'Ere coloniale, 1900–1945*, Volume 2, Paris: Editions Sociales.

Sweezy, Paul 1946, *The Theory of Capitalist Development*, London: Dennis Dobson.

Teixeira Rodrigo Alves and Tomas Nielsen Rotta 2012, 'Dimensions of Capital Autonomization Valueless Knowledge – Commodities and Financialization: Productive and Financial', *Review of Radical Political Economics*, 44: 448–467.

Toussaint, Eric 2014, *Bancocratie*, Brussels, Editions Aden. (English edition in 2015, *Bankocracy*, Resistance Books and IIRE).

Trotsky, Leon 1906, *Results and Prospects*, available at: https://www.marxists.org/archive/trotsky/1931/tpr/rp-index.htm.

—— 1931, German and French Introductions to *The Permanent Revolution*, available at: https://www.marxists.org/archive/trotsky/1931/tpr/pr-index.htm.

—— 1934–5, *Whither France?*, available at: https://www.marxists.org/archive/trotsky/1936/whitherfrance/.

—— 1973 [1932], 'Answers to Questions by the New York Times (February 15, 1932)', *Writings of Leon Trotsky*, New York: Pathfinder Press.

UNCTAD 2004, 'World Investment Report 2004', Geneva, June.

—— 2011, 'World Investment Report 2011', Geneva, June.

—— 2013a, 'World Investment Report 2013', Geneva, June.

—— 2013b, 'Trade and Development Report 2013', Geneva, September.

—— 2014a, 'World Investment Report 2014', Geneva, June.

—— 2014b, 'Trade and Development Report 2014', Geneva, September.

—— 2015a, 'World Investment Report 2014', Geneva, June.

—— 2015b, 'Trade and Development Report 2014', Geneva, September.

US Government Accountability Office (GAO) 2009, *Hedge Funds, Overview of Regulatory Oversight, Counterparty Risks, and Investment Challenges*, 7 May.

US Government Printing Office 2011, *The Financial Crisis Inquiry Report*, The Financial Crisis Inquiry Commission, 25 February, available at: http://www.gpo.gov/fdsys/pkg/GPO-FCIC/pdf/GPO-FCIC.pdf.

Vasudevan, Ramaa 2009, 'From the Gold Standard to the Floating Dollar Standard: An Appraisal in the Light of Marx's Theory of Money', *Review of Radical Political Economics*, 41, no. 4: 471–491.

Veblen Thorstein 1923a, *The Engineers and the Price System*, New York: B.W. Huebsch.

—— 1923b, *Absentee Ownership and American Business in Recent Times*, New Brunswick, NJ: Transaction Publishers.

# Glossary of Financial Terms

**Asset-Backed Security (ABS):** Financial security backed by a loan or a lease against assets other than real estate. An ABS is essentially the same thing as a mortgage-backed security (MBS), except that the securities backing it are assets such as automobile loans and leases, credit card debt, royalties, etc.

**Bond:** Along with equity bonds are the oldest debt securities or assets and today the principal financial instrument used by investors. The issuer (a government, a local public authority or a corporation) owes bond-holders a debt and, depending on the terms of the bond, is obliged to pay them interest and to repay the principal at a determined date. Interest is payable at fixed intervals. Government bonds (also named sovereign bonds) are classified in three main categories: bills, debt securities maturing in less than one year; notes, debt securities maturing in one to 10 years; and bonds, debt securities maturing in more than 10 years. Both corporate and government bonds are issued in primary markets held by underwriting groups (investment banks and in Europe of large universal banks) and are negotiable in secondary markets.

**Brokerage:** The financial function of mediating between sellers and buyers of securities. For its services, a broking firm, today generally a department or affiliate of an investment bank or in Europe of a universal bank, charges fees. When a broking firm buys or sells securities for itself and not a client, it is said to be undertaking principal or *proprietary* trade.

**Capital gain:** A gain made by an investor in an asset market through successful speculation. When its current price exceeds the price at which it was bought the investor may choose to realise the gain by trading the asset, or keep the gains unrealised by holding on to the asset, typically in the hope of further price-increases. Capital gains are one component of financial profits.

**Collateralised Debt Obligation (CDO):** A structured financial product that pools together cash flow-generating assets and repackages this asset pool into tranches that can be sold to investors. A collateralised debt obligation (CDO) is so-called because the pooled assets – such as mortgages, bonds and loans – are essentially debt obligations that serve as collateral for the CDO. Protection against default depends on a prioritised ranking. Holders of more senior tranches of the CDO are paid first, followed by holders of mezzanine-tranches, and finally equity-tranches. As a result, the senior tranches of a CDO generally have a higher credit rating and offer lower coupon rates than the junior tranches, which offer higher coupon rates to compensate for their higher default risk.

**Collateralised Debt Obligation Squared:** This is identical to a CDO except for the assets securing the obligation. Unlike the CDO, which is backed by a pool of bonds, loans and other credit instruments, CDO-squared arrangements are backed by CDO tranches. CDO-squared allows banks to resell the credit risk that they have taken in CDOs. They are 'CDOs once removed'.

**Credit Default Swap (CDS):** A contract between two parties in which the buyer makes regular payments to the seller in exchange for a payoff in the event that an underlying credit instrument (such as a loan) defaults. The buyer of the CDS makes a series of payments (the CDS 'fee' or 'spread') to the seller and, in exchange, receives a payoff if the loan defaults. In essence, it is a form of insurance against default on debt. A CDS is said to be 'naked' when the holder is not required to own the insured asset. It means that an investor can take out insurance on bonds without actually owning them. It is speculation taken to its highest degree. Practised on a large scale it exerts very strong pressure on the underlying loan as with Greek debt in 2011.

**Derivative:** A financial asset whose value directly derives from the value of underlying entities such as a currency, a commodity (oil), an index, or an interest rate. Derivatives have no intrinsic value. They were created to hedge against risk. The two main initial forms were futures (see below) and options and the first main underlying assets were commodities and currencies. Derivative transactions now include a variety of financial contracts, including CDOs.

**Equity:** An ownership-claim on a corporation and along with bonds the oldest form of asset or security. Holders of corporate equity own a share of the corporation and are entitled to proportional shares of dividend payments made by the corporation to equity holders. Equity, also named shares, is traded in stock markets.

**Equity Buyback:** Capital-market operation through which a corporation buys back some of its own shares from shareholders, leaving fewer shares outstanding.

**Financial Intermediation:** Activity whereby economic agents with funds who want to lend and those who want to borrow are brought together. In the case of banks, the theory or view of financial intermediation denies or relegates to a secondary role the money creation function through the granting of credit. With regards to specialised non-bank financial corporations, the view claims that they offer lenders and borrowers the benefits of maturity and risk transformation.

**Futures Contract:** A standardised, exchange-traded contract to buy or sell a specified quantity of a particular commodity or asset at a certain future date. Examples include oil futures, through which trading parties agree to buy or sell oil for delivery at future dates. Most trading in futures does not involve parties seeking to obtain or sell the actual commodity or asset in the future. They involve parties either seeking to speculate on particular price movements between the present and the contract's maturity, or to build a particular risk-profile for their asset-portfolio.

**Hedge Fund:** Generally a privately owned investment fund, administered by professional investment managers and open to a limited range of investors. Hedge funds are unregulated as opposed to banks, pension funds and mutual funds. They engage in the most highly speculative operations and charge high levels of fixed and 'performance' fees. They are very selective and open only to wealthy and institutional investors. Some hedge funds are affiliates of pension funds and all large banks have hedge-fund-like affiliates.

**Investment Bank:** A very old financial institution, now reduced to a few US and Swiss corporations, that provides non-financial corporations and governments with the range of services necessary to raise funds in capital markets. Investment-banking functions include underwriting the issue of corporate securities, brokerage services and various forms of corporate advisory services, notably M&As. In the lead-up to the 2008 financial crisis investment banks also raised funds directly in capital markets and loaned them to hedge funds as well as undertaking proprietary trading. Investment banks may often own large primary resources.

**Institutional investors:** Financial organisations that centralise large amounts of savings for investment. They include pension funds, mutual funds and insurance companies offering life insurance, which in some countries represent a major form of savings. They invest on behalf of their clients, who have claims on the funds managed by the institutional investor.

**Leverage:** The use of borrowed money in the pursuit of an investment. Leverage is used in attempts to augment profitability. A high debt/equity ratio indicates that a corporation has been aggressive in financing its operations with debt. This will result in volatile earnings from loans or proprietary trading and if the leverage ratio is very high, it will increase the chances of a default or bankruptcy.

**Liquidity:** A market for a bond, equity or a commodity is said to be liquid to the extent that there are sufficient buyers and sellers making it easy it to perform a transaction in a particular security or instrument (in Keynesian parlance, to exercise their 'liquidity preference'). A liquid security, such as a share in a large listed company or a government bond, is easy to price and can be bought or sold without significant price impact. With an illiquid instrument, trying to buy or sell may change the price, if it is even possible to transact.

**London Interbank Offered Rate (LIBOR):** A set of daily reference interest rates, at which banks are making unsecured loans to each other in the London interbank money market.

**Mortgage-Backed Security (MBS):** A debt security where payments to holders originate in the repayment of mortgage.

**Mutual fund:** A collective investment scheme where the savings of many small individual investors are pooled and invested into corporate securities, short-term debt or government bonds. Investors become shareholders of the fund, and have a proportional claim on the value of its investments. Mutual funds are widely used by wage-earners in many countries as a complementary or principal means for building retirement savings.

**Money market funds (MMFs):** specialised financial corporations which collect funds from institutional and wholesale investors and lend them to banks. A banking system intermediated through MMFs is more unstable than one in which large investors interact directly with banks. Since MMFs can be subject to run-like redemptions from their investors, they may react to them by running the banks in which they have deposited, amplifying the impact of the initial redemptions.

**Over-the-counter trading (OTC):** The trading of financial assets that takes place directly between two parties without use of a trading exchange that regulates, standardises, polices and lists prices for transactions. Also referred to as the 'third market', OTC allows institutional investors and high-risk bank affiliates to trade blocks of securities directly, rather than through an exchange, and anonymity to buyers and escaping regulation.

**Pension fund:** A collective investment scheme set up by private and public employers into which employers and scheme members pay contributions in order to build up a lump sum to provide an income in retirement. There are two main types of pension scheme – defined contribution pension schemes and defined benefit pension schemes. Defined benefit pension schemes guarantee an income in retirement based on tenure at an employer and the wage earned. In a defined contribution scheme benefits depend on contributions from individual scheme member, with additions from their employer in most cases, but also on stock market returns. In the US the most widely used defined contribution scheme is the so-called 401 (K) regulated saving plan.

**Retail banking:** Banking that involves the provision of services directly to individuals as opposed to corporations or other businesses. This includes commercial banking services such as individual savings, current or savings accounts. It may also include the provision of services more closely associated with investment banking, such as investment funds, retirement funds or related funds supplied to individual clients.

**Shadow banking system:** the set of financial relations between banks and non-bank financial corporations outside the regular banking system developed as a result of off-balance operations, securitisation and OTC transactions. The shadow banking system is considered since the 2008 crisis to create systemic risk through maturity/liquidity transformation, leverage and flawed credit risk transfer.

**Special Investment Vehicle (SIVs) or Special Purpose Vehicle (SPVs):** A legally autonomous financial entity, typically a subsidiary of another corporation, whose operations are limited to the acquisition and issuance of certain assets. SPVs have been used widely by banks to facilitate the creation and issuance of mortgage-backed CDOs. They allowed banks to devolve risks associated with CDOs away from their own balance-sheets, reducing the need to set aside capital reserves against possible losses associated with those instruments.

GLOSSARY OF FINANCIAL TERMS 301

**Securitisation:** Extension of the term security from the 1970s onwards to designate the transfer of cash-flow generating assets, notably mortgage loans, by the initiator of a debt obligation. First used as off-balance instruments by banks and in the US government sponsored mortgage corporations, securitisation developed into a complex process of pooling and repackaging of cash-flow generating assets to other investors. This included notably the pooling of differently secure mortgage-backed securities (MBSs), notably 'subprime' borrowers not meeting 'prime' or top level mortgage-underwriting guidelines, into CDOs. But securitisation can involve a variety of vehicles and underlying assets.

**Treasury Bills (T-Bills):** Short-term government debt issued by the US Department of Treasury, prized for its total liquidity.

**Universal bank:** Term used mainly for large European banks engaged both in retail and in investment banking. They have successfully resisted proposals for their split-up made in the wake of the financial crisis.

# Topic Index

accumulation   1–5, 8–9, 11–12, 14–15, 17–32, 34–47, 49–53, 68–72, 88–90, 123–24, 173–74, 185–86, 261, 267–69, 288–90
   hoards   38
   hoarding   15, 43, 61, 69, 186, 187
   means of production   4, 88–89
   money capital   5, 15, 46, 51, 68–71, 121, 245
Anti-trust   5, 96, 127, 144
Argentina   55, 101, 115, 143, 149, 188, 195–97, 253–54, 260, 281
Australia   52, 59, 99, 134, 152–53, 213
autonomisation   7, 16

Bank for International Settlements (BIS)   1, 21, 62, 109, 175, 178–80, 183–184, 216–17, 241, 243, 244–50, 258, 263, 274
banking   8–9, 20–21, 74, 91–92, 100, 110–11, 177–79, 198–211, 213–21, 223–24, 232–42, 250, 258, 292, 299–301
   originate-to-distribute banking model   209–10
   proprietary trading   74, 208, 223, 299
   retail banking   208, 218, 238, 300
banks   5–9, 18–21, 44–50, 59–61, 63–78, 91–96, 108–14, 176–81, 191–95, 198–211, 213–23, 230–44, 246–48, 250–51, 297–301
   commercial   8, 20, 46–47, 59, 65, 70, 74, 200–204, 207–8, 210, 214–15, 221–22, 233, 235, 238
   conglomerates   73–74, 95, 109–10, 191, 202, 207, 215, 220, 274
   investment   20, 46–47, 49–50, 84–85, 98, 101–2, 200–205, 207–10, 214–15, 218, 220–23, 226–27, 230–31, 243–44, 297–301
   universal   20, 95, 199, 204, 206–9, 214, 216, 243, 297, 301
barbarism   265, 267–68, 290
boards of directors   93–95, 102, 106
   interlocking boards   93, 102, 106
bonds   55–56, 61–66, 81–83, 101, 103, 178–79, 189–90, 194, 196–98, 202–3, 210–11, 236–37, 242–43, 251–52, 297–99

   asset-backed   202, 211
   corporate   62, 200, 223, 297–99
   government   56, 62–63, 65, 81–83, 101, 103, 175, 189, 194, 198, 236–37, 242, 245, 297, 299
   high-yield high-risk   103
   junk   103, 236
   mortgage-backed   15, 202, 211, 297
Brady bonds   65
Brazil   55, 64–65, 73, 143, 149–51, 153–54, 168, 170, 172, 188, 190–92, 253–54, 260, 277–78, 280
Britain   25–26, 59, 91, 98–100, 125, 193, 261, 270, 281, 283
British Empire   47, 99

Canada   43, 99, 125, 135, 146, 152–53, 179, 213, 274, 276
capital   1–38, 40–49, 51–58, 61–95, 101–15, 119–25, 127–31, 133–43, 147–53, 173–77, 185–90, 256–62, 268–70, 274–82, 289–94
   commodities trading   109
   industrial   5–6, 8, 11–13, 16–17, 42–43, 45, 52, 67–72, 83–85, 90–91, 93–95, 98–99, 102–3, 113, 134–36
   interest-bearing   7–8, 44–45, 51, 53, 64, 67–71, 73, 75, 77–83, 85–89, 91, 109, 134–35, 174–75, 256
   merchant   5, 7–8, 67, 113–15, 123, 269–70
   money-dealing   68
   retail   114, 117, 180
capital-as-function   78, 93, 102, 104
capital-as-property   78, 93, 102, 104
capitalist crises   3, 22
capitalist production   21, 23–24, 27–28, 32, 34–35, 68, 71, 80, 88–89, 93, 134, 174, 266–67, 287, 291
centralisation of capital   72, 148
China   1, 3, 10–12, 22, 28–29, 33–34, 38–41, 43–44, 61, 116, 146–54, 171–72, 175, 283–84, 286
climate change   24, 43, 263, 267–68, 270–71
Club of Paris   55, 64, 66

# TOPIC INDEX

commodities   32–33, 35–36, 58–59, 87, 89, 91, 109–12, 114–17, 123, 128–29, 169, 171, 182–83, 185–87, 296
   commodities boom   128, 175
   commodities derivatives   183
   commodities traders   115, 117
concentration of capital   67, 88–89, 133, 142, 151
concentration ratios   144–45
corporate control   104
corporate governance   12, 17, 93, 97, 102–3, 277, 282, 288, 290
corporate ownership   95, 282, 292
corporations   5–6, 8–9, 13–14, 45–46, 73–77, 93–97, 103–17, 119–22, 124–26, 130–34, 142–49, 154, 198–202, 216–18, 298–301
   financial   5–6, 8–9, 13–14, 73–74, 76–77, 105–6, 108–17, 125–26, 183–84, 198–99, 220, 222–23, 241–42, 245–46, 298–300
   non-financial   5, 67, 76, 93, 105–6, 108–9, 112, 148, 156, 158, 183, 190, 198–99, 245, 249
credit default   181, 183–84, 239, 244, 298
credit system   2, 16, 19, 22, 69–70, 72, 85, 89, 136, 198–200, 258

debt   36–38, 41, 51, 53–58, 61–66, 70–73, 173–74, 188–99, 230–31, 235–37, 239–50, 253–54, 285–86, 292–94, 297–99
   developing country   56, 66
   government   9, 15, 37–38, 53–54, 56, 61–62, 65, 70–71, 188–95, 236–37, 245, 248, 253–54, 297, 301
   household   38, 41, 77, 79, 185, 198–99, 212, 254, 259–60
derivatives   15, 111, 126, 128–29, 181–88, 217–19, 222–23, 225–26, 228–29, 231, 241–42, 251, 274, 291, 294–95
   theory   185–86, 249
dividends   6, 9, 14, 17, 68, 79, 81, 91, 104, 113, 125, 174, 178, 186, 190
Dodd-Frank Act   130, 224

ecological depletion   269
Ecuador   55, 188, 192–94
emerging countries   2, 21, 39, 116, 143, 145, 148, 151, 234, 247, 249, 252–53, 260

Eurodollar market   47, 133
European banks   20, 74, 76, 174, 206, 208, 216–17, 219–20, 234, 238–41, 243, 260, 301
European Central Bank (ECB)   73, 177, 204, 206, 224, 236–41, 242–43, 237
European Commission   107, 109, 242, 282, 288
European Round Table (ERT)   107
Eurozone   9, 20–21, 54, 61, 152–53, 174, 177–78, 199, 205, 220, 236–38, 241, 243–44, 247–48, 250
exports   32–33, 39–40, 45, 61, 101, 136, 140, 144, 148, 152, 155, 167–68, 189, 195, 282
   capital   33, 61, 101, 136, 152, 282, 293
   goods and services   144

Fed   64, 110–11, 128, 132, 190, 194, 199–200, 202, 209, 212, 233, 235–36, 238, 246–47, 253
   interest policy   212
Federal Reserve System   110
fetishism   9, 16, 18, 86, 88, 212
   money fetishism   16, 18, 86, 88
   number fetishism   88
fictitious capital   16–18, 20–22, 25, 35–37, 68, 72, 81–82, 84–86, 179, 182–83, 185–86, 212, 245, 256–57, 259
   derivatives   18, 173, 182–83, 185–86, 249
finance capital   5–6, 8, 44–46, 91, 93–95, 97, 99, 101, 103, 107–9, 113–15, 117, 123, 135–36, 256–57
   definition   5, 69
   power bloc   8
financial accumulation   9, 11, 15, 26, 43–45, 47, 50, 56, 68, 71, 173–74, 177, 179, 186, 256
financial assets   14–15, 36–37, 62, 173, 175, 177, 179, 181, 183, 185, 187–89, 191, 193, 195, 197
   deposits   37, 74, 173
   equity securities   37, 173
   government debt securities   37
financial capital   5–9, 17, 65–67, 73, 80, 88, 106, 109, 256–57
financial crises   6, 15, 44, 47, 62–63, 85, 200, 206, 220, 232, 254, 285

financial globalisation   8, 11–15, 19, 37, 46,
    62–64, 71, 173–74, 188, 218, 220, 232
  indicators   37, 174
  theory   12, 14
  transactions   46, 173
financialisation   1–2, 12–16, 18–20, 55, 57,
    78–79, 103–5, 113–14, 155, 158, 198–99,
    201, 203, 270–71, 287–88
financial profits   6, 49, 68, 73–75, 77, 114, 142,
    178, 198, 245, 260, 297
  banking profits   74, 114
financial speculation   21, 50, 219, 237
  exchange rates   50
  stock market   220
foreign exchange   14–15, 29, 47–50, 63, 65, 74,
    98, 112, 141, 178–81, 190, 218–19, 228, 230,
    274
  clearing houses   50
  exchange transactions   50, 181
  foreign exchange market (Forex)   49
foreign loans   51, 190
France   13–15, 18, 99–102, 115, 118, 121, 125,
    142–44, 205–7, 238–39, 257, 276–78,
    280, 288–90, 293–96
funds   8–9, 17–20, 56–57, 105, 109, 150,
    178–80, 196–202, 211, 214–15, 219–35,
    241–42, 247–52, 273–75, 298–300
  hedge   8–9, 18, 20, 105, 179–80, 194,
    196–97, 214–15, 219–31, 233, 241–42,
    247–52, 282–83, 294–96, 298–99
  mutual   18–19, 69, 74, 189–90, 199–202,
    211, 214, 219, 226, 233, 245, 247, 249–52,
    259, 298–99
  pension   18–19, 56–57, 103, 105, 109, 125,
    132, 179, 199–202, 214, 225–26, 228, 245,
    248, 298–99
  sovereign wealth   123, 148, 150, 174–75

Germany   52, 54, 59, 92, 94–95, 98–99, 118,
    125, 134, 146, 168–69, 205–6, 238–39,
    292, 294
Glass-Steagall Act   20, 110, 200, 202–3
global commodity chains   161
global economic and financial crisis   222
globalisation   2, 8, 10–15, 24–25, 27–28, 37,
    41–42, 44–47, 49–51, 61–65, 71–72, 137,
    158, 173–75, 187–89

financial   8, 11–15, 19, 22, 44–47, 61–65,
    71–72, 173–75, 177, 179, 183, 187–91, 199,
    220, 232
  industrial corporations   13–14, 45
global value chains (GVCs)   159, 165
global warming   268–70
Greece   54, 152, 188, 223, 236, 241–43, 258

IMF   1, 3, 40, 54, 64–66, 73, 152, 181, 189,
    194–95, 215–16, 243, 245–54, 256,
    285–86
imperialism   9, 12, 32, 43, 53, 101, 125, 134,
    138, 172, 276, 285–86, 288–89, 291,
    295
India   11–12, 25, 40–41, 99, 146–47, 149, 151,
    153, 156, 162, 169, 171–72, 284, 290–91
industrial reserve army   11, 32–33, 41–43, 174,
    257
  globalisation   44, 174, 257
  theory   43, 257
institutional investors   56, 211, 222, 225–26,
    229, 244, 251, 299–300
insurance companies   9, 56, 69, 95, 108,
    125–26, 132, 179, 200, 207, 216–17, 226,
    299
integration   5, 63, 65, 92, 94–95, 102, 139, 237,
    241
  horizontal   94, 139
  vertical   92, 94, 139
interest rate   49, 65–66, 177, 181, 183,
    190–91, 194, 213, 219, 235, 237, 247,
    274, 298
internationalisation of productive capital
    13, 133, 135, 137–39, 141, 143, 145, 147, 149,
    151, 153, 155, 157
international production   138, 140, 158, 163,
    165, 167, 281
  non-equity modes   158, 163, 165
international reserve currency   48
  dollar   48
  pound sterling   48
investor 'risk appetite'   246
ITC   201, 267

Japan   10–11, 25, 28, 40, 48, 50, 60, 125, 175,
    180, 246
July Monarchy   73, 100

TOPIC INDEX

labour time   42, 69, 166, 170–71
law of value   11, 158, 169, 295
  global   169, 295
London Metal Exchange   128–29

Maastricht Treaty   177, 204–5, 236
market-based retirement schemes   56, 58, 69
mergers   5, 94–95, 107, 109, 115, 142–43, 145, 203, 207, 229, 237, 245, 250, 259
mergers and acquisitions (M&As)   5, 142
Mexico   43, 53–55, 63–64, 101, 119, 143, 147, 149, 168, 233, 254, 283
money trust   8, 95–96
monopoly   6, 12, 91, 103, 114–15, 117, 121–22, 133, 138, 140–42, 144, 146, 166, 274, 276
monopsony   16, 93, 115, 117, 119–20, 161
multinational enterprises (MNEs)   13, 137

NAFTA   28, 65

OECD   13, 28, 39, 49, 53, 137, 145, 149, 159, 181, 209, 229, 238, 241–43, 256, 259, 262–63
offshore finance   155
  offshore financial centres   155
offshoring   38, 114, 158–59, 163–64, 170, 279, 290
oligopoly   16, 122, 126, 133, 142, 144, 146–49, 166, 178, 191, 213, 217–19, 257, 259
  domestic   133, 147, 218
  global   133, 142, 146–49, 166, 191, 217–18, 257, 259
  global banking   217–18
  theory   133, 257
outsourcing   42, 104, 114, 158, 163–65, 170–71, 279
over-accumulation   1–2, 11, 19–20, 22–23, 25–26, 36, 38–41, 52–53, 63, 258, 261
overexploitation   162, 169–70
overproduction   1–2, 11, 19–20, 22–23, 25–26, 29, 34, 36, 38, 63, 85, 258

petrodollars   51, 53
profit   1–4, 6–7, 17–18, 22–23, 29–35, 70, 74–75, 77–81, 87, 103–4, 120–22, 134–37, 174, 263–64, 284–86
  financial profit   15, 74, 77, 285, 288

natural resource-based monopoly profit   121
profit of enterprise   7, 79, 81, 87
unceasing movement of profit-making   268
Pound sterling   46, 48, 61

quantitative easing   21, 177, 245–48, 253

rate of exploitation   1, 12, 18, 23, 32–33, 41–42, 170, 261
rent   53, 69, 71, 76, 93, 121–22, 136–38, 149, 169–71, 174, 285
rentier capital   9, 45
rentier states   122
retirement schemes   56, 58, 69, 71
  market-based   56, 58, 69
Russia   40, 101, 146, 149, 153, 156, 273

securities   19–20, 37–38, 61, 69–70, 83, 173–76, 200–202, 209–12, 214, 221–25, 229–31, 245, 249–51, 297, 299–301
  mortgage-backed security (MBS)   297
securitisation   19–20, 22, 29, 63, 185, 199, 209–10, 212–14, 232–33, 235, 249, 258, 300–301
shadow banking   20, 199, 202, 209, 214–17, 221, 224, 232–35, 237–39, 258, 260, 273, 282, 284, 300
shareholders   8, 44, 67, 78–79, 84, 94, 96–97, 102–5, 140, 142, 147, 149, 158, 298–99
  share buy-backs   105
  shareholder activism   105
  shareholder value   103–4
South Africa   11, 18, 59, 99, 123–24, 153, 168, 192–93, 254, 257, 274, 286
surplus value   3–4, 6–7, 15–16, 28–30, 34, 51–52, 71–77, 79–81, 93, 113–15, 131–36, 158–59, 169–71, 245, 258–61
  creation   6, 16, 36, 67, 72, 75, 84, 208
  inter-capitalist division   93

taxation   47, 77, 82, 156, 191
tax havens   47, 55, 116, 152–53, 155–56
transnational corporations (TNCs)   137
trusts   8, 91–92, 95–96, 211

UNCTAD   3, 64–66, 118, 137, 143–45, 148, 150–52, 155–59, 161, 163, 165–67, 256, 277, 279, 292
   World Investment Reports   143, 148, 155
United Kingdom   168, 207, 287
Uruguay Round negotiations   54
US   19–23, 28–30, 33–36, 38–50, 53–58, 60–64, 95–100, 104–7, 115–16, 118–22, 141–45, 148–55, 173–76, 198–204, 211–15
   US Commodities Futures Trading Commission (CFTC)   110

US Senate Banking, Housing and Urban Affairs Committee   110

world market   2–3, 10–13, 24–25, 28, 39, 41–42, 45, 59, 93, 133, 142, 146, 169, 171, 286
world money   49, 58–60, 185–86, 286–87
   dollar   49, 60, 186, 286
   theory   58, 185, 287
WTO   3, 10, 25, 29, 39, 65, 139, 141, 158, 168

# Index of Names

Adrian, Tobias   216, 230–31, 273, 275
Aglietta, Michel   14, 20, 39, 198, 221–22, 231–32, 273
Andreff, Wladimir   13, 137, 151, 273
Appelbaum, Eileen   150–51, 273
Arbulu, Pedro   101, 274
Arestis, Philip   63, 274
Ashman, Sam   11, 18, 123–24, 274
Avdjiev, Stefan   244, 274

Baran, Paul   103, 137, 147, 274
Barbour, Violin   69, 274
Barker, William   180, 274
Baronian, Laurent   34, 54, 63, 78, 103, 274, 278
Batt, Rosemary   150–51, 273
Bayoumi, Tamim   211, 275
Beblawi, Hazem   122, 275
Bellofiore, Riccardo   16, 29, 84, 258, 275, 280
Berg, Nathalie   118–19, 161, 275
Berle, Adolph   97, 275
Bhatia, Ashok   211, 275
Bihr, Alain   29, 275
Blundell-Wignall, Adrian   181, 229, 238, 241–42
Borio, Claudio   175–77, 275
Bouvier, Jean   100–101, 275
Boyer, Robert   17, 276
Braverman, Harry   42, 276
Brenner, Robert   48, 276
Brock, James W.   144, 276
Bryan, Dick   185–88, 275–76, 291
Butovsky, Johan   18, 30–31, 33, 35, 295

Cain, P.J.   98–99, 276
Callinicos, Alex   22, 172, 257, 276
Carcanholo, Reinaldo   75, 276
Carchedi, Guglielmo   23, 33–34, 276
Caron, François   100, 276
Carroll, William   106–8, 276–77
Cassiolato, José Eduardo   277–78, 294
Caves, Richard   147, 277
Censer, Jack Richard   277
Chandler, Alfred   138, 277

Chesnais, François   10, 13–15, 20, 27, 43, 54, 56, 58, 63, 85, 100, 102, 145, 183, 195, 266, 269–71
Choonara, Joseph   27, 278, 290
Cintra, Macedo   215, 282
Claessens, Stijn   216, 279
Coase, Ronald   140, 279
Cogan, Philip   223, 279
Contractor, Farok   163–64, 279
Coriat, Benjamin   14, 273, 277, 279
Cosio-Pascal, Enrique   65
Covitz, Daniel   235, 279
Cowen, Tyler   262, 279

Dardot, Pierre   272, 279
De Brunhoff, Suzanne   58, 60, 68–69, 79, 84–85, 275, 279
Dedrick, Kenneth   280
DeLong, Bradford D.   98, 100, 280
D'Hulster, Katia   221, 280
Dierick, Franck   224–25, 283
Doctor, Mahrukh   153, 280
Domhoff, William G.   106, 280
Dos Santos, Paulo   74–75, 280
Duménil, Gerard   6, 14, 17, 26, 35–36, 54, 75, 125, 175, 213, 280
Dunning, John   13, 137–38, 140–41, 151, 158, 281
Durand, Cedric   18, 85, 281

Eichengreen, Barry J.   4, 60–61, 98, 281
Elhefnawy, Nader   103, 281
Elwell, Craig   60, 281
Engels, Friedrich   24, 27, 88, 91, 171
Epstein, Gerald   12–13, 78, 281, 287
Ernst, Dieter   166, 281, 289
Esteves, Rui Pedro   282

Farhi, Maryse   215, 282
Fattorelli, Maria Lucia   191, 282
Faulkner, Harold   96, 282
Fine, Ben   11, 18, 30, 117, 123–24, 159, 166, 274, 282
Fitzsimmons, Michael   282

## INDEX OF NAMES

Flynn, John   144, 276, 282
Fohlin, Caroline   95, 282
Foster, John Bellamy   6, 11, 15, 270, 283, 289
Freeman, Richard   41, 115, 261, 283
Frey, Carl B.   263, 283
Fridenson, Patrickson   101, 283
Friedman, Eli   28, 283
Furtado, Celso   13, 283

Galbraith, John Kenneth   102–3, 283
Garbarivicius, Tomas   224, 283
Garside, William   98, 283
Gaulard, Mylene   39, 283
Geier, John   34, 283
Gereffi, Gary   160–61, 283–84
Gill, Louis   29, 49, 81, 284
Gindin, Sam   2, 9, 11, 22, 28, 47–48, 292
Glickman, Murray   63, 274
Glyn, Andrew   27, 284
Goldner, Loren   18, 284
Gonjo, Yasuo   101, 284
Gopalan, Sasidaran   153, 284
Gordon, Robert   4, 33, 262–63, 284, 294
Gorton, Gary   212, 284
Gowan, Peter   11, 47, 201, 284
Greaves, John   98, 283
Greenlaw, David   220, 284
Griffith-Jones, Stephany   64
Grossman, Henryk   31–32, 100, 264, 280, 285
Guillén, Arturo   285
Gupta, Arun   120–21, 285
Guttmann, Robert   61, 81, 85, 200–202, 285

Hanieh, Adam   11, 123, 175, 285
Hanlon, John   55, 193, 285
Harman, Chris   29, 285
Hart-Landsberg, Martin   29, 63
Harvey, David   7–8, 18, 23, 30, 52–53, 68–69, 71–72, 80–81, 86, 114, 199–200, 256, 269, 285
Hashimoto, Yuk   259, 285
Heinrich, Michael   23, 205, 285
Helleiner, Eric   44, 285
Henry, Clement   101, 103, 122, 129, 282, 285
Henwood, Doug   199, 285
Hernandez, Manuel A.   147, 285
Higginbottom, Andy   286

Hilferding, Rudolf   5–8, 10, 12, 75, 91–92, 94, 102, 113, 117, 135–38, 183, 286
Ho-Fung, Hun   39
Hopkins, A.G.   98–99, 276
Howse, Robert   53, 193, 286
Hudson, Michael   286
Husson, Michel   29–30, 125, 285–86
Huws, Ursula   42, 261, 286
Hymer, Stephen   13, 137, 139–40, 286

Ivanova, Maria N.   18, 38, 49, 58, 61, 182, 286

Jackson, James K.   176, 287
Jeffers, Esther   20, 238, 287, 293
Jeong, Seongjin   285
Johnson, Simon   48–49, 287

Kalecki, Michael   287
Kaltenbrunner, Annina   117, 287
Kennedy, William P.   98, 287
Keynes, J.M.   9, 46, 59–60, 78, 175, 233, 287
King, Michael R.   59, 179–80, 287
Kinoshita, Noriaki   259, 285
Kliman, Andrew   17, 27, 30, 33, 35, 287
Konings, Martijn   9, 16, 88, 287
Kovel, Joel   267–68, 287
Kraemer, Jason   166, 280
Kregel, J.A.   63, 287
Krippner, Greta   12, 16–17, 112–13, 287
Kurz, Robert   266–67, 287

Labrinidis, George   59–60, 287
Lacoste, Yves   147, 287
Lapavitsas, Costas   2, 6, 14, 18, 51, 60, 67–68, 75–76, 78, 114, 185, 287
Laval, Christian   272, 279
Lazonick, William   17, 96, 104–5, 158, 257, 288
Lenin, V.I.   5–9, 12, 92, 101, 134, 138, 288
Levina, Irene G.   76, 213, 288
Lévy, Dominique   6, 14, 17, 26, 35–36, 54, 75, 175, 213, 280, 291
Lewis, Michael   99–100, 288
Lichtenstein, Nelson   288, 293
Lietaer, Bernard   50, 288
Liikanen Report   76, 206–8, 218, 237–39, 241–42, 288

## INDEX OF NAMES

Lin, Justin   223, 230, 288
Linden, Greg   166, 280
Lordon, Frédéric   56, 289
Luxemburg, Rosa   51–53, 77, 134–35, 289

Magdoff, Harry   11, 283, 289
Mandel, Ernest   14, 26, 107, 109, 264–66, 270, 289
Marnata, Françoise   289
Marques, Rosa Maria   192, 289
Marx, Karl   4–8, 10, 14–16, 23–25, 27, 30–34, 57–59, 67–74, 78–89, 91, 169–71, 265–70, 272, 278–80, 289
Mattick, Paul   24, 289
McKinsey Global Institute   36–38, 62–63, 154, 173, 189–90, 289
McNally, David   2, 10, 18, 27, 49, 58, 88, 222, 290, 294
Means, Gardiner   4–5, 23–24, 27, 32, 34, 51–52, 58, 60–61, 76–77, 79–81, 88–90, 97, 186–87, 231, 298–99
Mehrling, Perry   236, 290
Méillassoux, Claude   271, 290
Melman, Seymour   290
Merler, Sylvia   178, 290
Mészáros, István   266, 268, 290
Metrick, Andrew   212, 284
Michalet, Charles-Albert   11, 13, 137, 140, 273, 277, 290
Milberg, William   158, 164, 167, 290
Minqi, Li   11, 288, 290
Minsky, Hyman   85, 290, 292
Mishra, Ram Kumar   149, 290
Mitchell, Stacy   204, 290
Moore, Jason W.   5, 268–71, 291
Morgan, Dan   96–97, 111–12, 115–16, 128, 130, 179, 190, 199, 202–4, 218–19, 223, 227, 229, 233, 235
Morin, François   13, 112, 178, 218, 291
Musto, Marcello   7, 10, 283, 291

Nakatani, Paulo   75, 192, 276, 289
Nashashibi, Karim   122, 291
Nelson, Prado Alves Pinto   193, 277, 288, 291
Newman, Susan   11, 18, 123–24, 274, 279, 287
Norfield, Tony   11, 18, 33, 47, 59, 77, 99, 182–83, 185, 188, 213, 276, 291

O'Connor, James   267, 270, 291
Oman, Charles   165, 292
Omarova, Saule T.   110–11, 115, 128, 292
Onetti, Alberto   95, 292
Orléan, André   14, 257, 292
Osborne, Michael A.   263, 283
O'Sullivan, Mary   96–97, 104, 288, 292

Painceira, Juan Pablo   287
Paley, Thomas   292
Palloix, Christian   13, 137, 292
Palmade, Guy   100, 292
Panitch, Leo   2, 9, 11, 22, 28, 47–48, 285–86, 292
Panizza, Ugo   190, 195, 292
Paulani, Leda Maria   14, 20, 123, 150, 190, 192, 292
Payer, Cheryl   54, 293
Perez, Carlota   261–62, 293
Perroux, François   262, 293
Petrovic, Misha and Gary Hamilton   120, 293
Piketty, Thomas   174, 293
Pisani-Ferry, Jean   171, 178
Pisano, Gary and Willy Shih   104, 293
Pisoni, Alessia   95, 292
Plessis, Alain   100, 293
Plihon, Dominique   20, 238, 277–78, 287, 293
Pollard, Sydney   98–99, 293
Pollin, Robert   75, 293
Porter, Michael E.   95, 104, 147, 293
Pozsar, Zoltan   216, 279

Quinn, Bill   121, 293

Rafferty, Michael   185–88, 276, 291
Rajan, Ramkishen   153, 284
Riesser, J.   98, 294
Rime, Dagfinn   179–80, 230, 287
Roberts, Bryan   3, 18, 23, 34, 118–19, 156, 161, 259, 263, 275–76, 294
Rogoff, Kenneth   65, 294
Romer, Christina D.   25, 294
Rosen, Richard J.   210, 294
Rotta, Tomas Nielsen   16, 296
Roy, William G.   95, 291, 294
Ruane, Kathleen Ann   224, 294
Russo, Daniela   184, 294

Sabadini, Mauricio de S.   14, 75, 276, 294
Saez, Emmanuel   174, 293
Schenk, Catherine R.   48, 294
Scherer, Frederick M.   144, 294
Schumpeter, Joseph   84, 147, 262, 293, 295
Scott, Robert E.   38, 176, 291, 295
Seitzinger, Michael V.   224, 294
Serfati, Claude   14, 100, 106, 112–13, 271, 278, 295
Shiller, Robert E.   86, 246, 295
Smith, John   11–12, 18, 30–31, 33, 35, 42, 76, 78, 162, 164, 166, 170–72, 194, 295
Steindl, Frank G.   25, 295
Stengers, Isabelle   270, 295
Stockhammer, Engelbert   17, 79, 276, 295
Stoskopf, Nicolas   100, 295

Stulz, René M.   183, 295
Suret-Canal, Jean   101
Sweezy, Paul   5, 8, 17, 23, 31, 103, 137, 147, 257, 264, 274, 289, 296

Teixeira, Rodrigo Alves   16, 296
Toussaint, Eric   109–10, 219, 296
Treichel, Volker   223, 230, 288
Trotsky, Leon   2, 10, 102, 296

Vasudevan, Ramaa   58, 59, 296
Veblen, Thorstein   96, 296

Westra, Richard   285
Williams, Shanon D.   17, 287
Winkler, Deborah   158, 167, 290